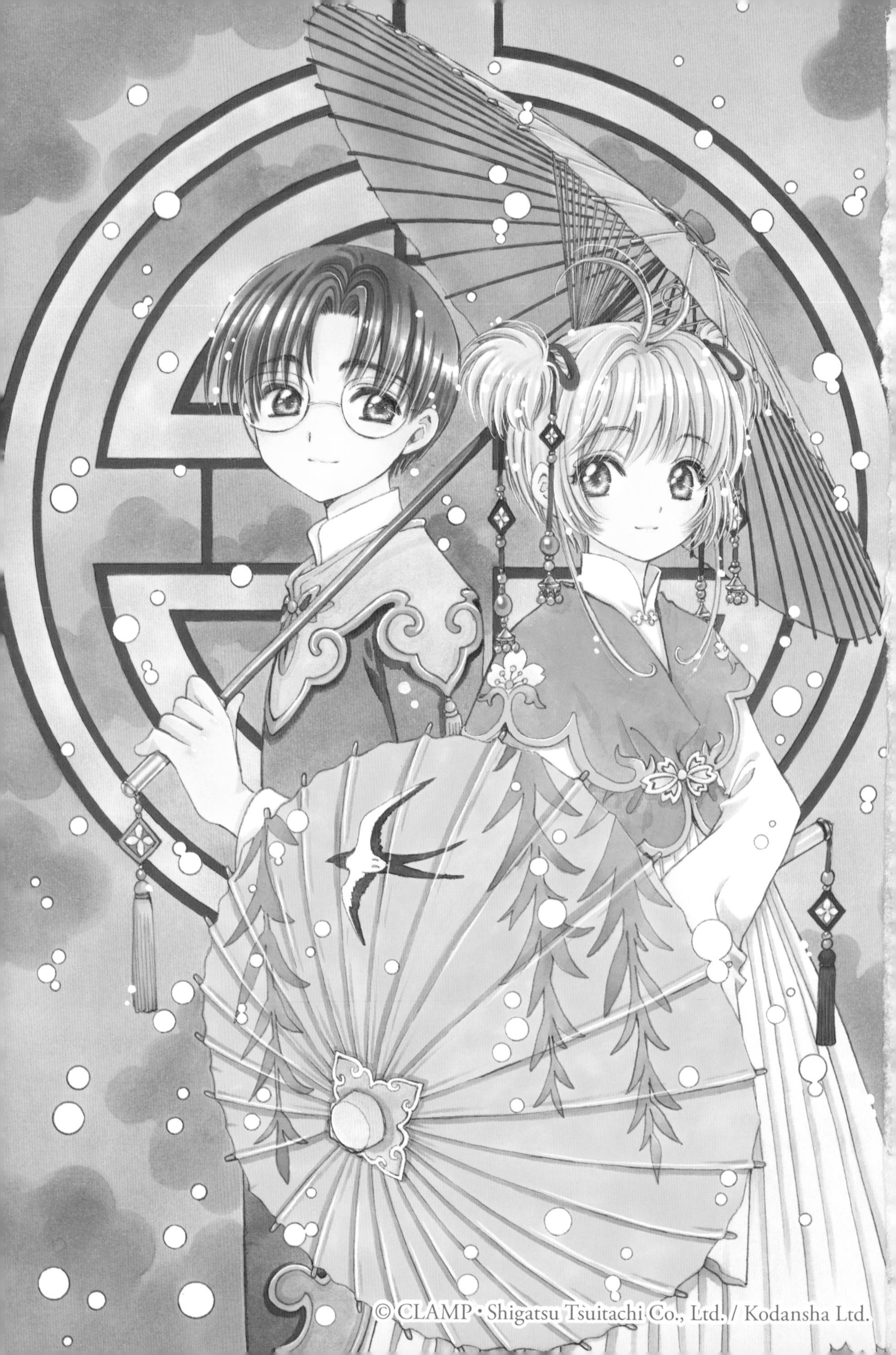

Collector's Edition

CARDCAPTOR SAKURA

Staff

Satsuki Igarashi

Nanase Ohkawa

Tsubaki Nekoi

Mokona

Planning

and presented by

CLAMP

I FEAR I MIGHT MAKE THINGS DIFFICULT FOR YOU SOON, YOUNG SAKURA...

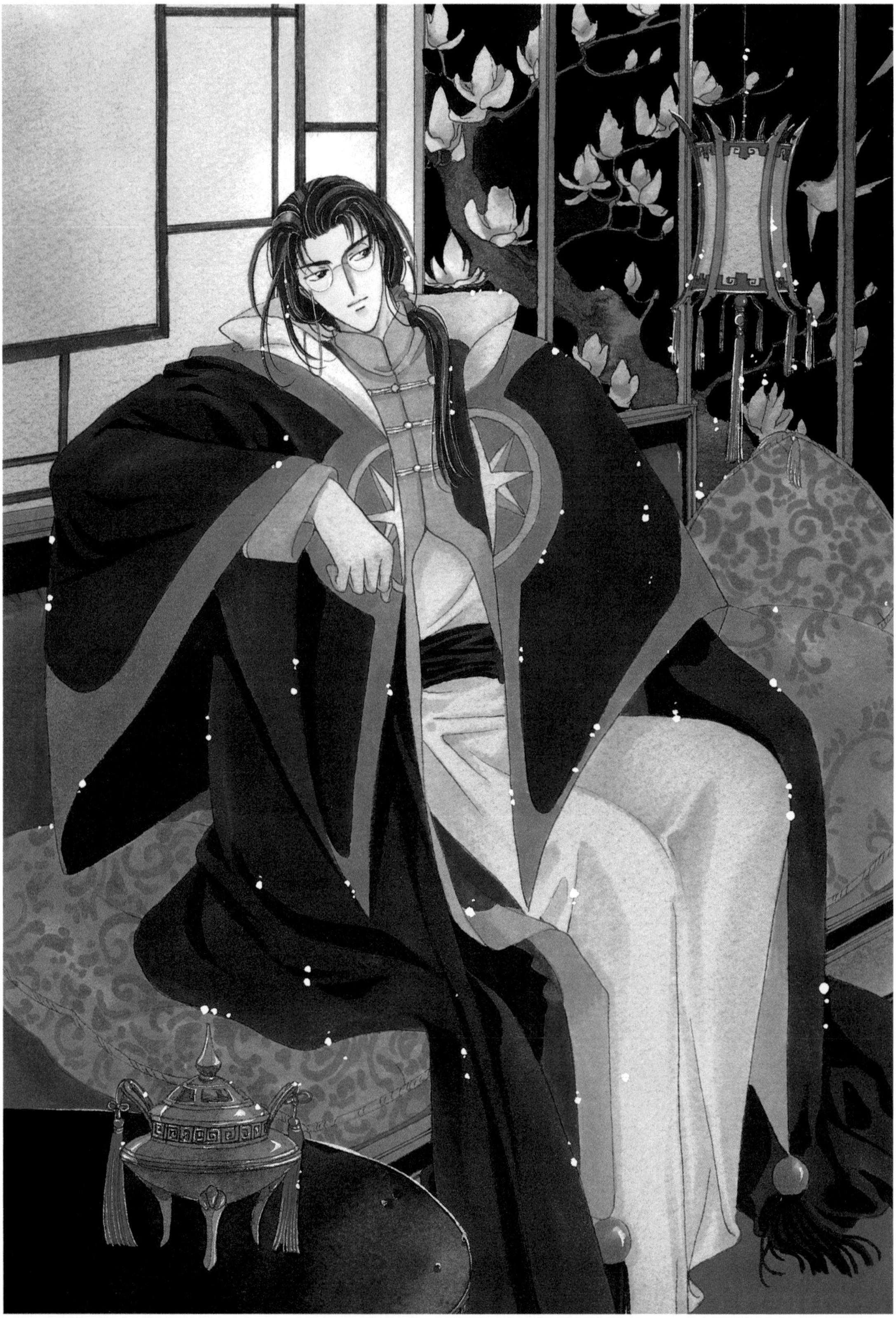

BUT AS YOU SAID YOURSELF, I'M SURE YOU'LL BE ALL RIGHT.

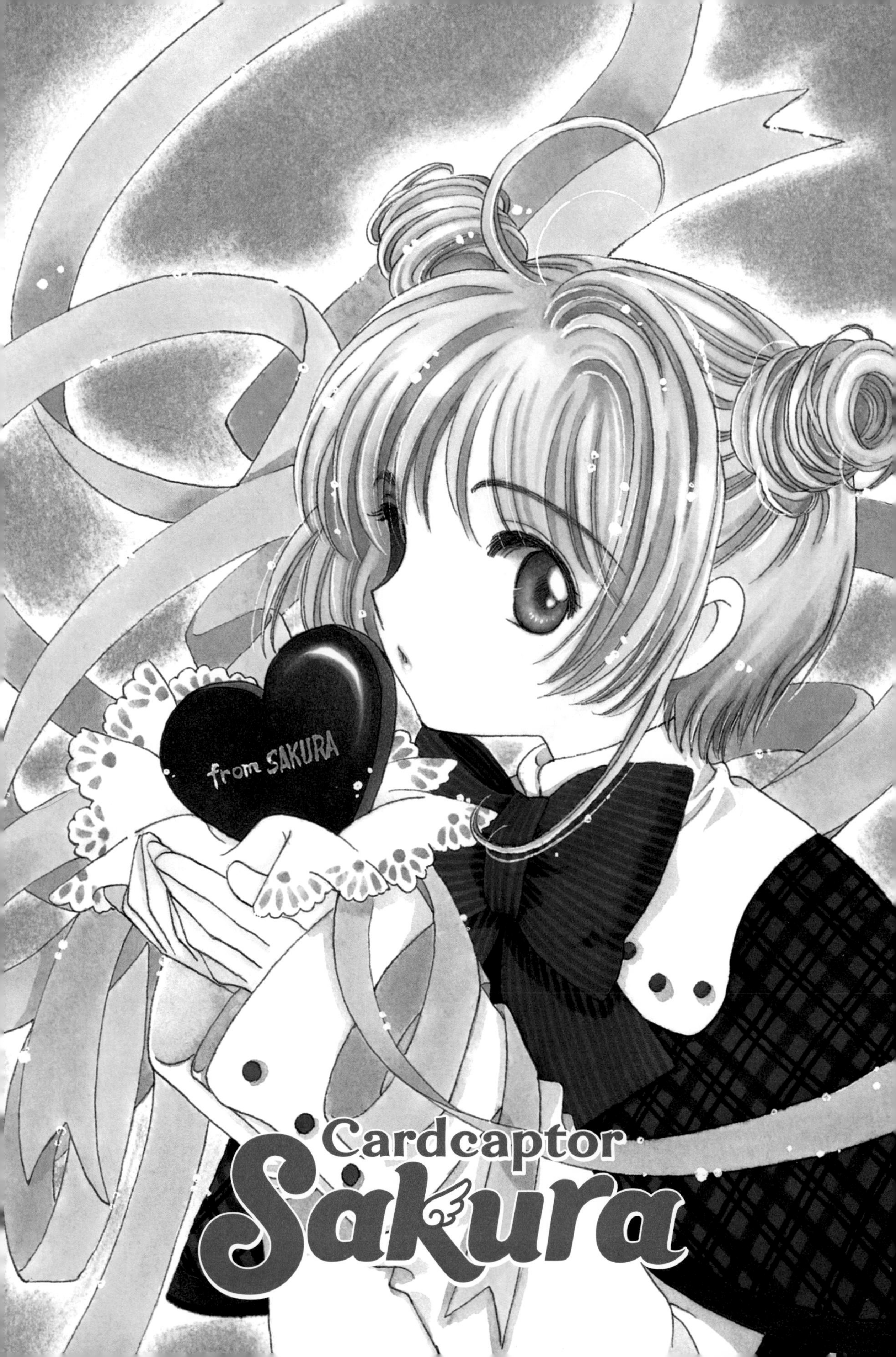
from SAKURA
Cardcaptor
Sakura

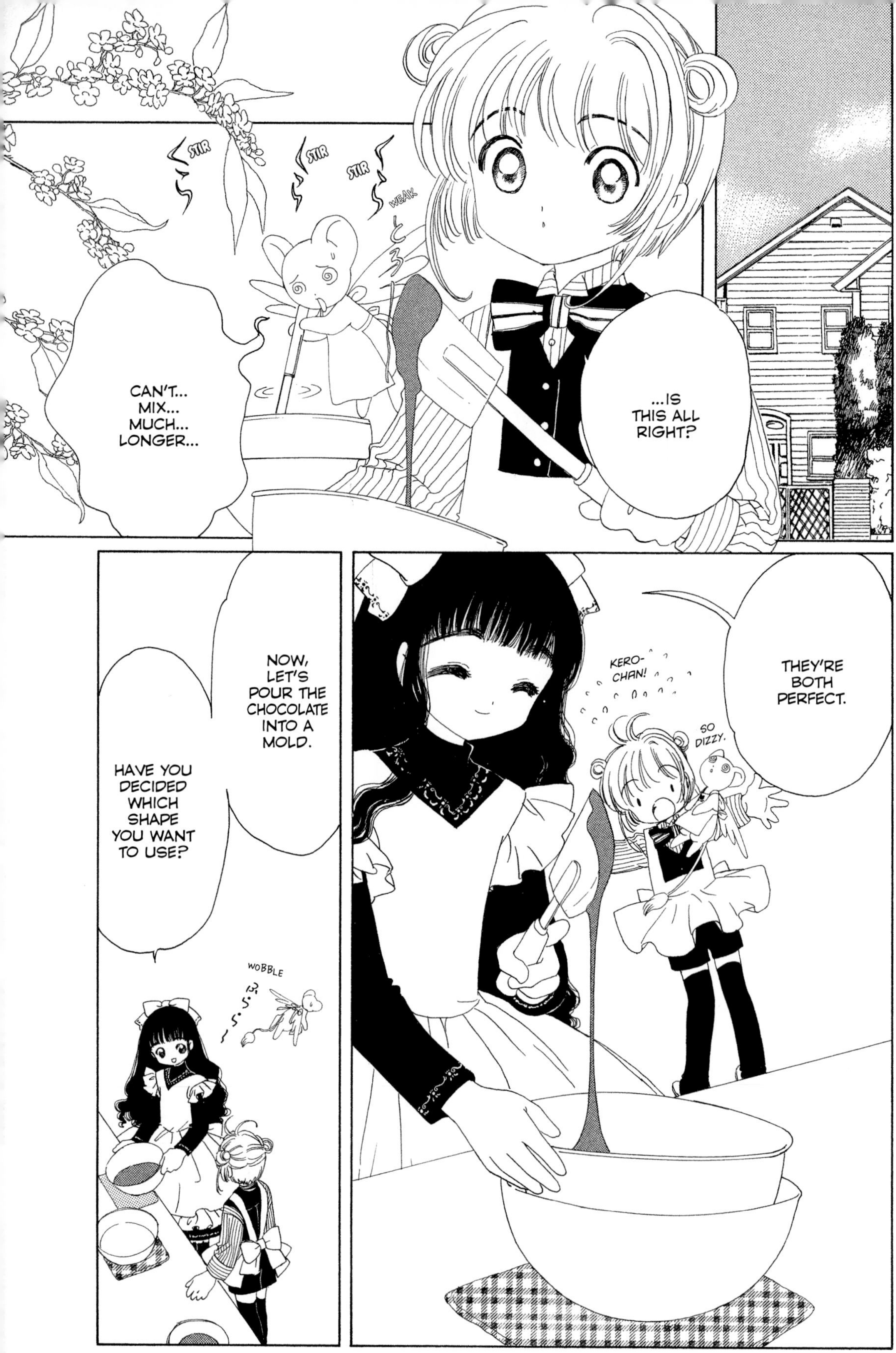
...IS THIS ALL RIGHT?
STIR
STIR
STIR
WEAK
CAN'T... MIX... MUCH... LONGER...
THEY'RE BOTH PERFECT.
KERO-CHAN!
SO DIZZY.
NOW, LET'S POUR THE CHOCOLATE INTO A MOLD.
HAVE YOU DECIDED WHICH SHAPE YOU WANT TO USE?
WOBBLE

THIS IS FOR THE OTHERS...

...AND THIS ONE IS FOR YUKITO-SAN.

OF COURSE! IT 'S FOR VALENTINE'S DAY.

PHEW

IT'S DONE!

CLAP CLAP

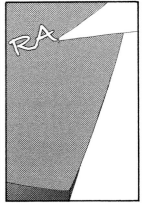

RA

6

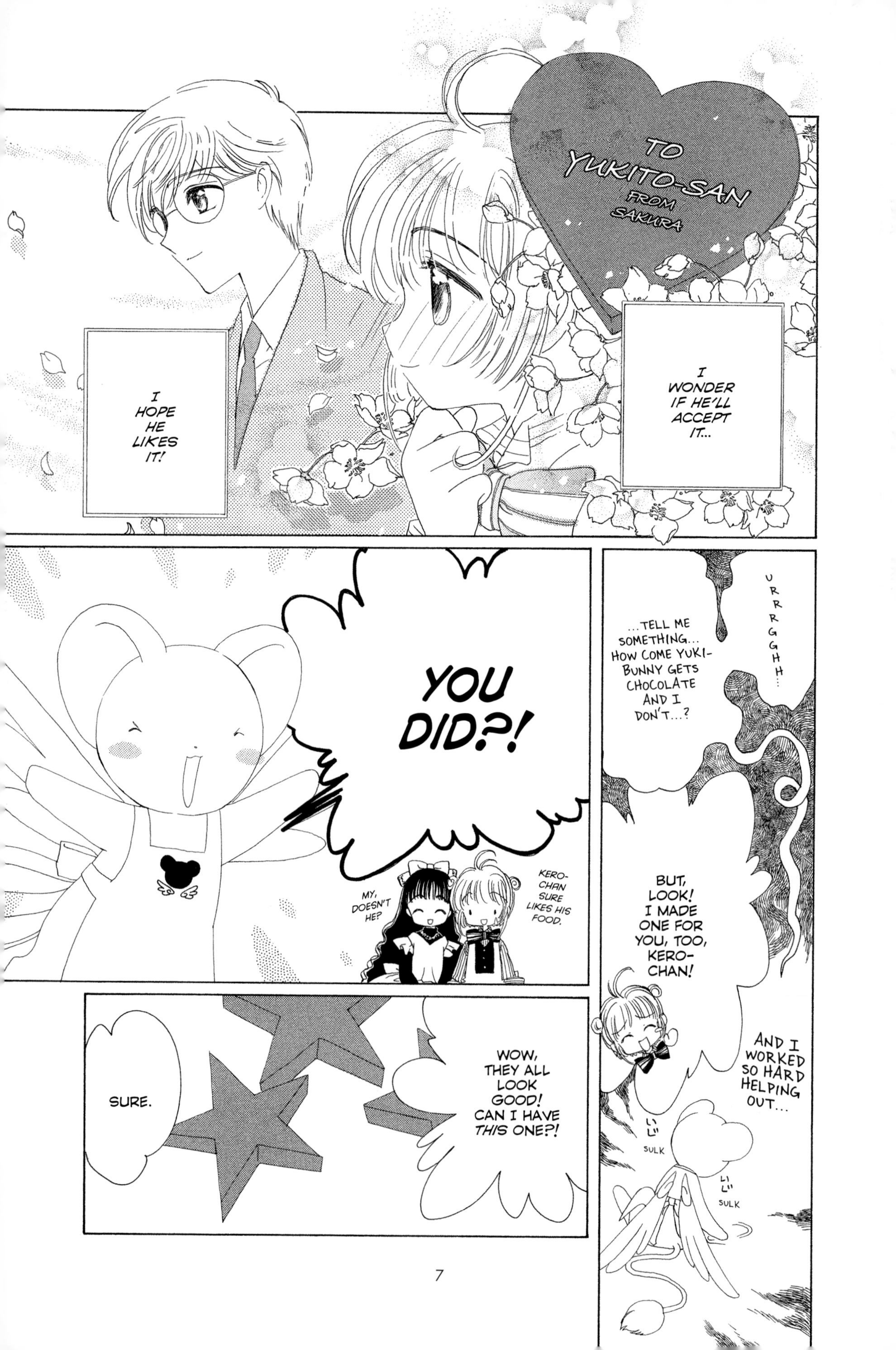
TO YUKITO-SAN FROM SAKURA
I WONDER IF HE'LL ACCEPT IT...
I HOPE HE LIKES IT!
URRRGGHH...
...TELL ME SOMETHING... HOW COME YUKI-BUNNY GETS CHOCOLATE AND I DON'T...?
BUT, LOOK! I MADE ONE FOR YOU, TOO, KERO-CHAN!
AND I WORKED SO HARD HELPING OUT...
いじ SULK
いじ SULK
YOU DID?!
KERO-CHAN SURE LIKES HIS FOOD.
MY, DOESN'T HE?
WOW, THEY ALL LOOK GOOD! CAN I HAVE *THIS* ONE?!
SURE.

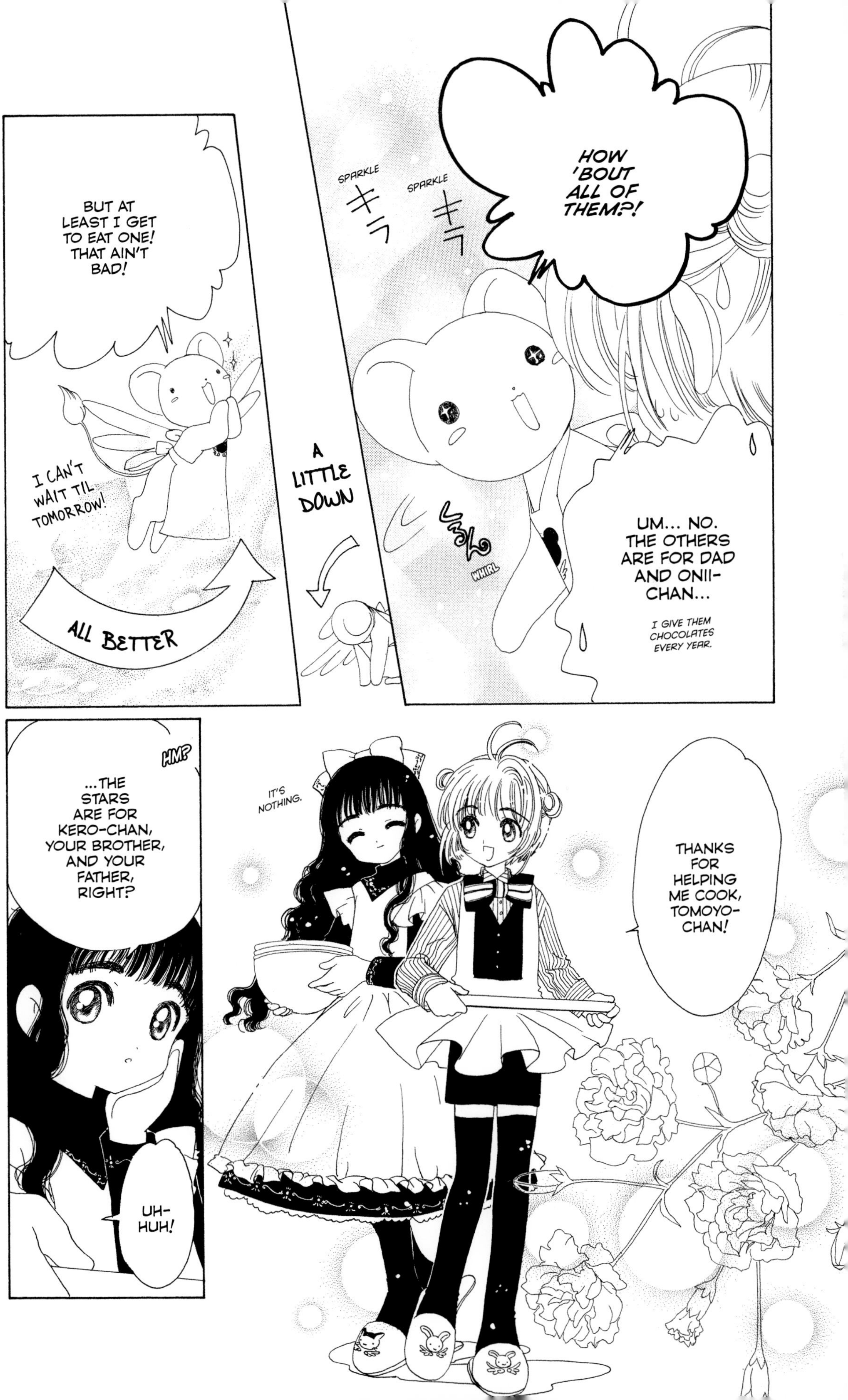
HOW 'BOUT ALL OF THEM?!
SPARKLE
キラ
SPARKLE
キラ
くるん
WHIRL
UM... NO. THE OTHERS ARE FOR DAD AND ONII-CHAN...
I GIVE THEM CHOCOLATES EVERY YEAR.
A LITTLE DOWN
BUT AT LEAST I GET TO EAT ONE! THAT AIN'T BAD!
I CAN'T WAIT TIL TOMORROW!
ALL BETTER
THANKS FOR HELPING ME COOK, TOMOYO-CHAN!
IT'S NOTHING.
HM?
...THE STARS ARE FOR KERO-CHAN, YOUR BROTHER, AND YOUR FATHER, RIGHT?
UH-HUH!

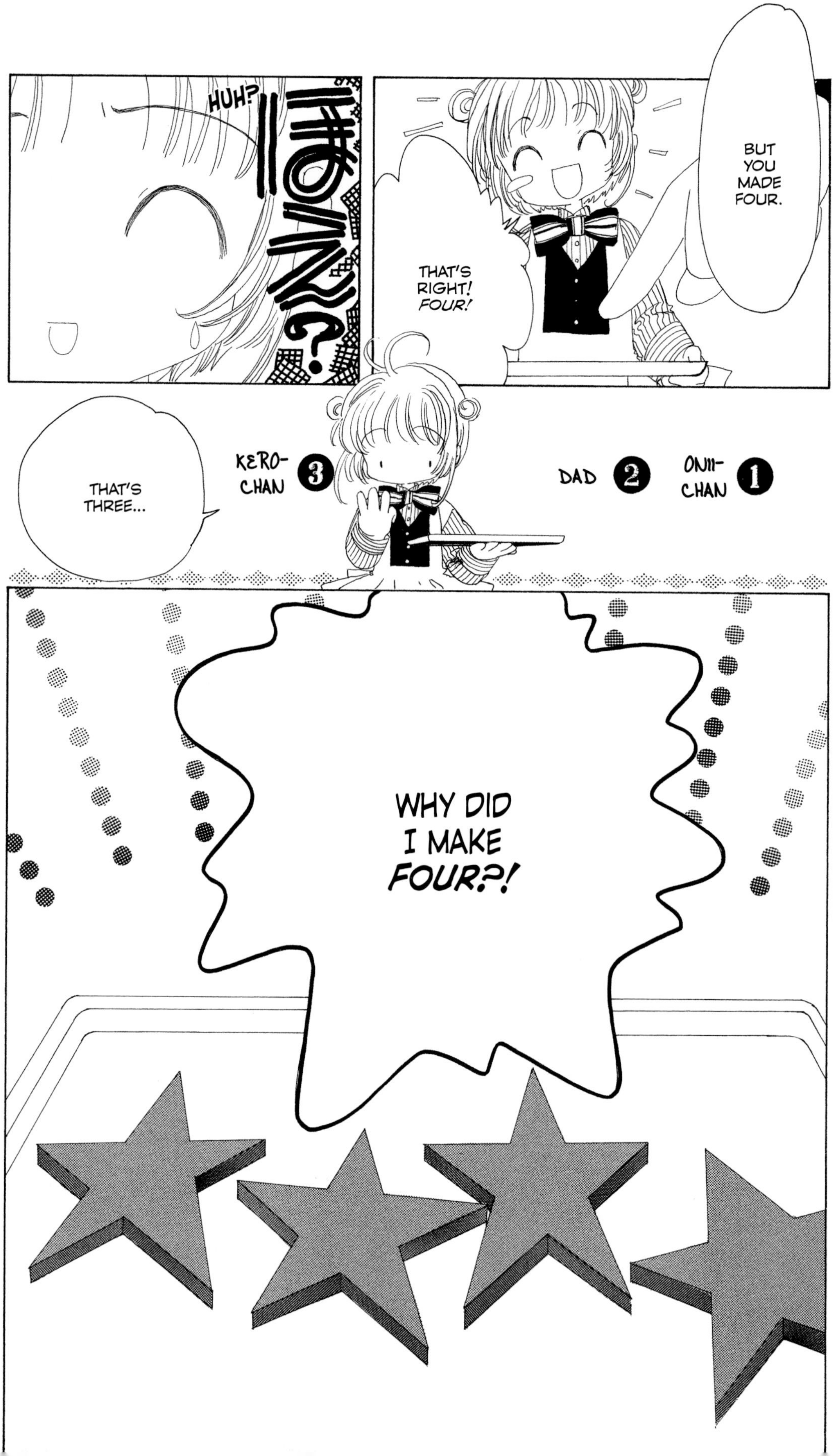

BUT YOU MADE FOUR.
THAT'S RIGHT! FOUR!
HUH?
ONII-CHAN 1
DAD 2
KERO-CHAN 3
THAT'S THREE...
WHY DID I MAKE FOUR?!

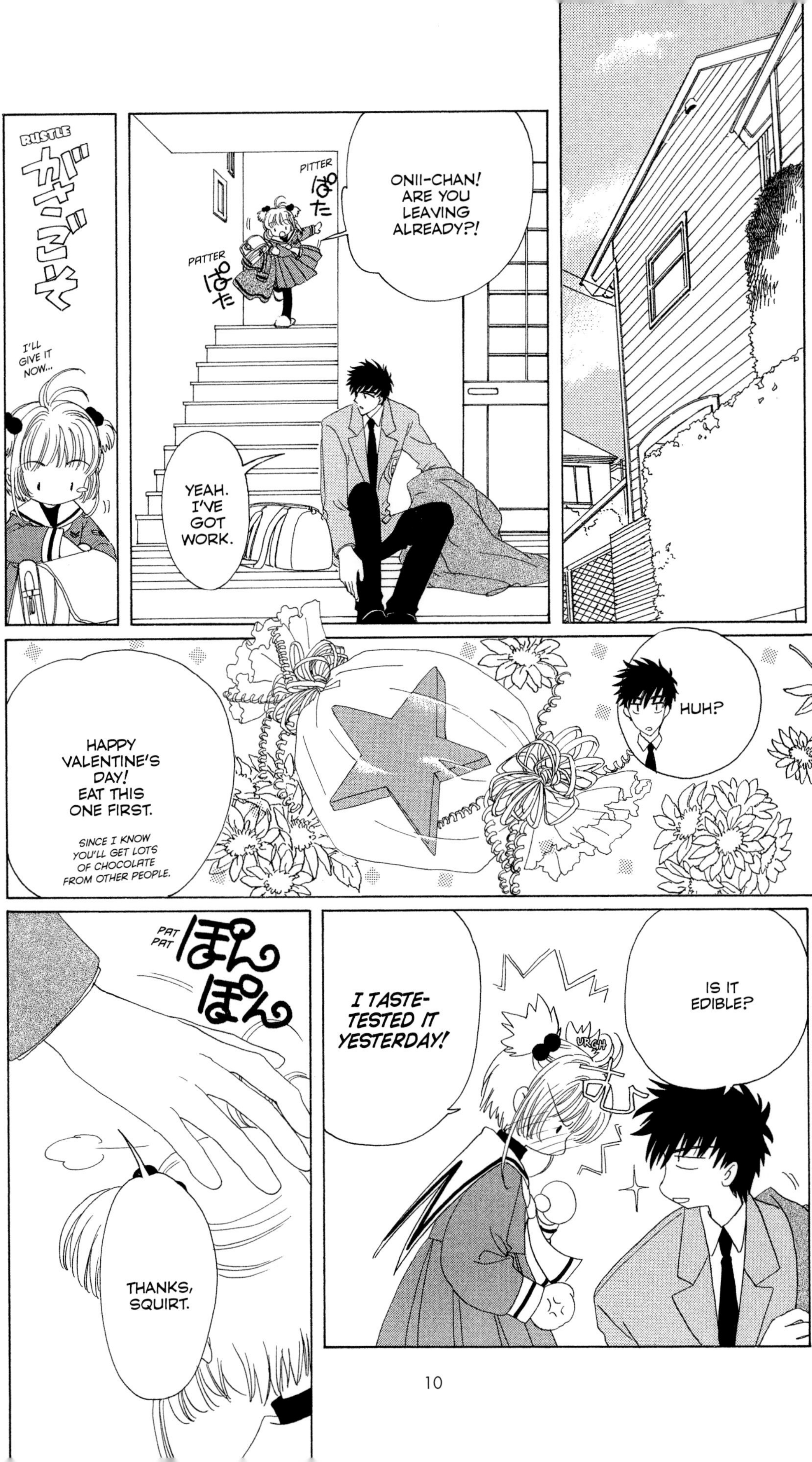
ONII-CHAN! ARE YOU LEAVING ALREADY?!
PITTER ぱた
PATTER ぱた
YEAH. I'VE GOT WORK.
RUSTLE がさごそ
I'LL GIVE IT NOW...
HUH?
HAPPY VALENTINE'S DAY! EAT THIS ONE FIRST.
SINCE I KNOW YOU'LL GET LOTS OF CHOCOLATE FROM OTHER PEOPLE.
IS IT EDIBLE?
URGH
I TASTE-TESTED IT YESTERDAY!
PAT PAT ぽんぽん
THANKS, SQUIRT.

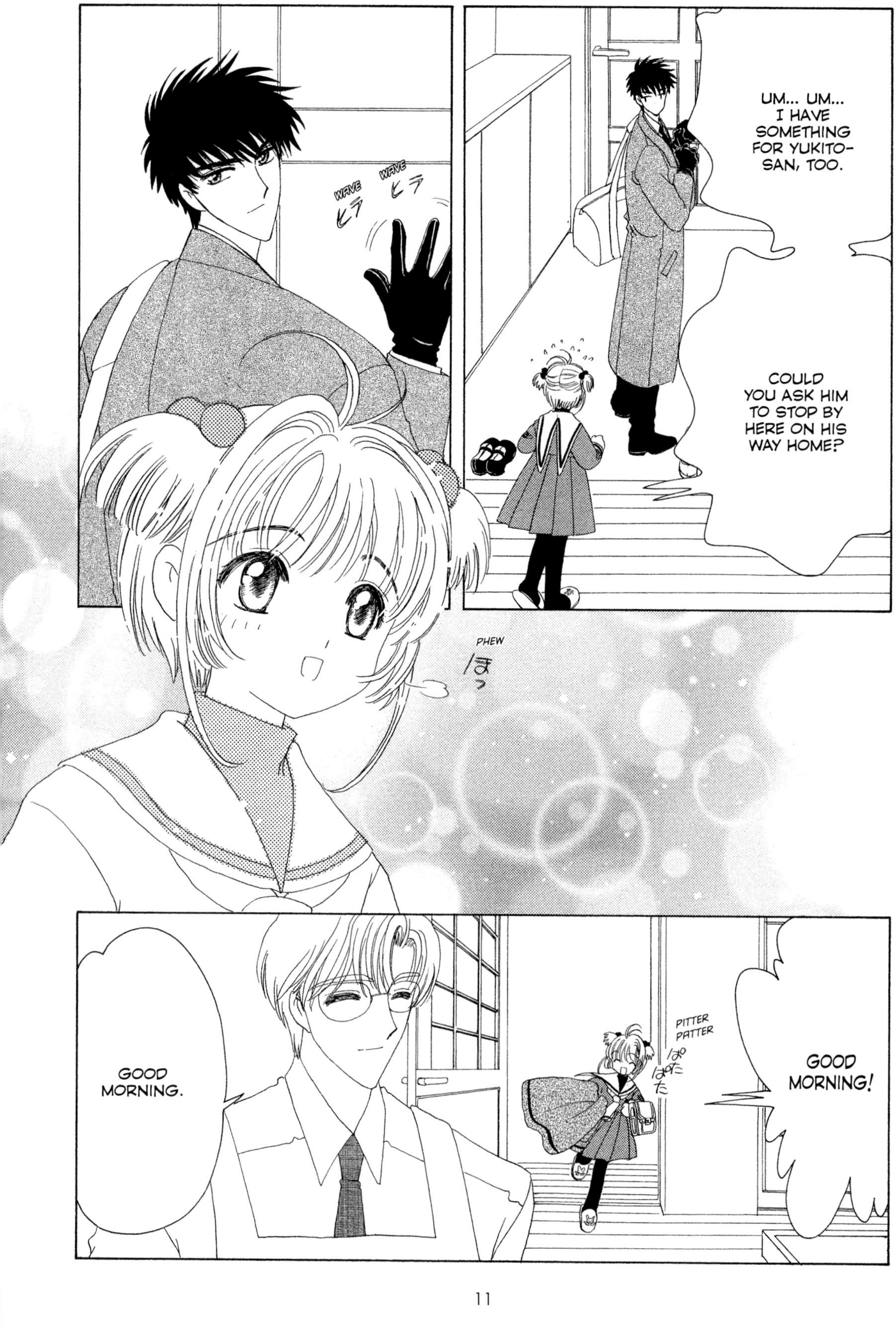

UM... UM... I HAVE SOMETHING FOR YUKITO-SAN, TOO.
COULD YOU ASK HIM TO STOP BY HERE ON HIS WAY HOME?
WAVE ヒラ
WAVE ヒラ
PHEW ほっ
GOOD MORNING!
PITTER PATTER ぱたぱた
GOOD MORNING.

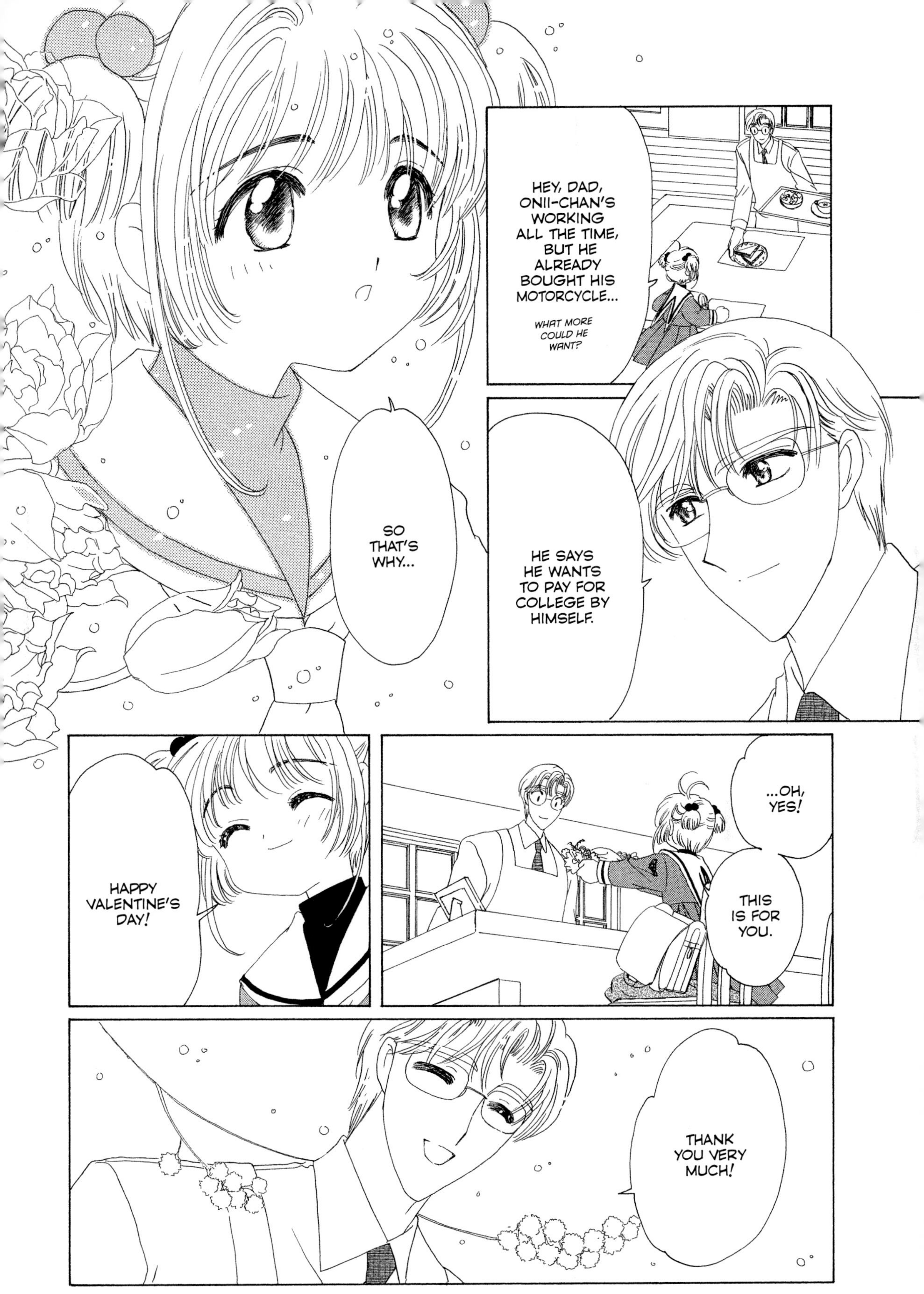
HEY, DAD, ONII-CHAN'S WORKING ALL THE TIME, BUT HE ALREADY BOUGHT HIS MOTORCYCLE...
WHAT MORE COULD HE WANT?
HE SAYS HE WANTS TO PAY FOR COLLEGE BY HIMSELF.
SO THAT'S WHY...
...OH, YES!
THIS IS FOR YOU.
HAPPY VALENTINE'S DAY!
THANK YOU VERY MUCH!

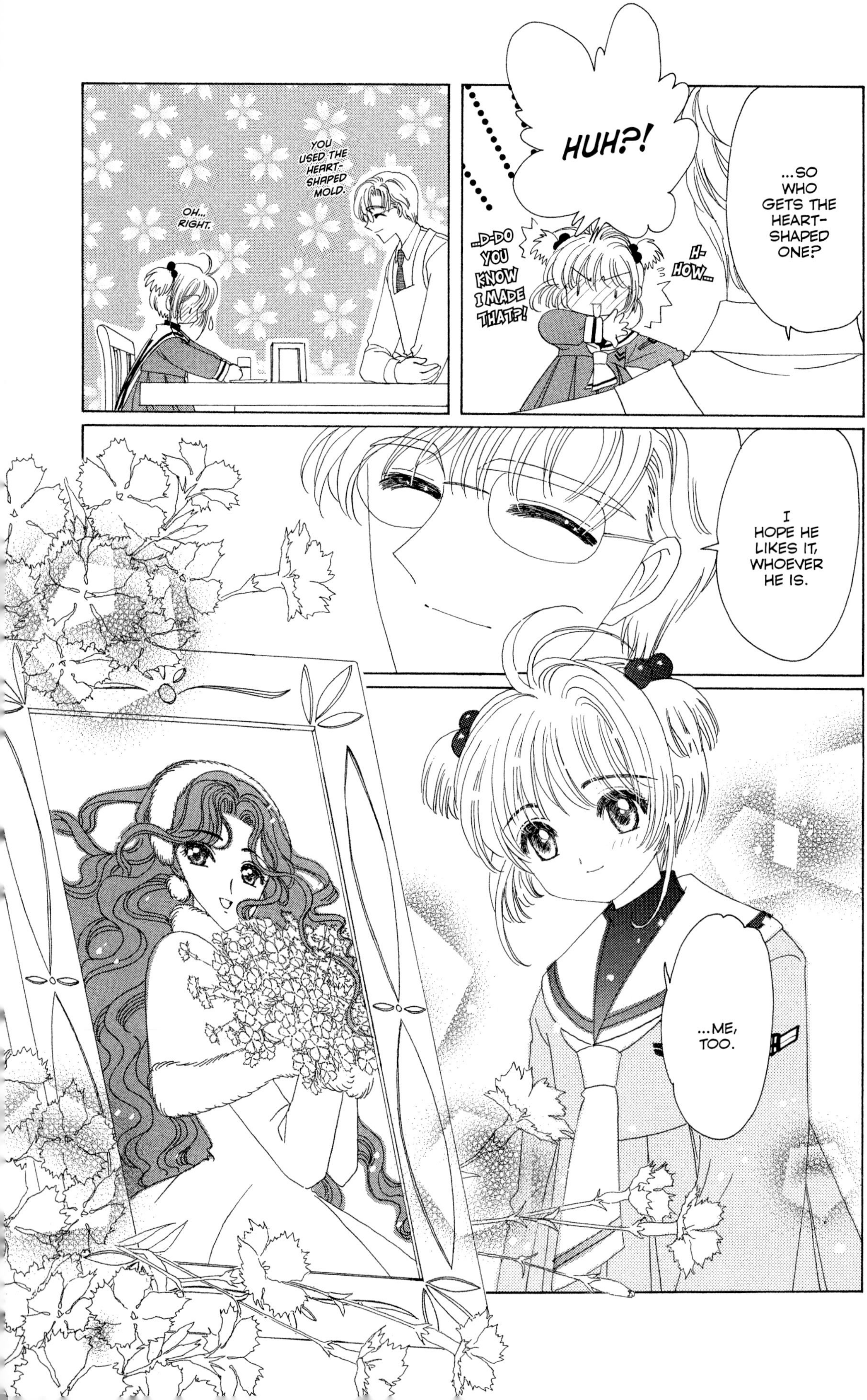
...SO WHO GETS THE HEART-SHAPED ONE?
HUH?!
H-HOW...
...D-DO YOU KNOW I MADE THAT?!
YOU USED THE HEART-SHAPED MOLD.
OH... RIGHT.
I HOPE HE LIKES IT, WHOEVER HE IS.
...ME, TOO.

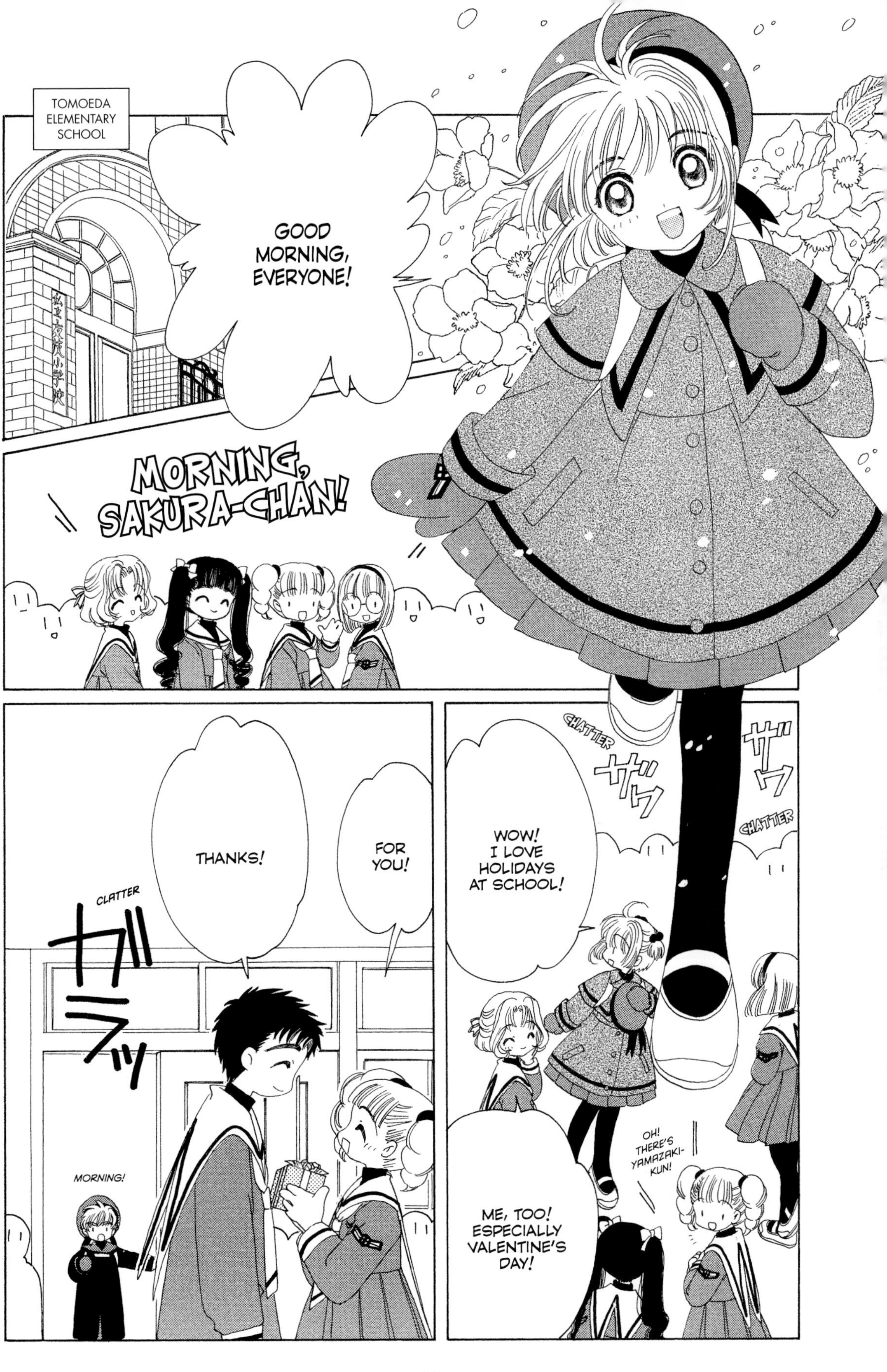
TOMOEDA ELEMENTARY SCHOOL
GOOD MORNING, EVERYONE!
MORNING, SAKURA-CHAN!
CHATTER
CHATTER
WOW! I LOVE HOLIDAYS AT SCHOOL!
ME, TOO! ESPECIALLY VALENTINE'S DAY!
OH! THERE'S YAMAZAKI-KUN!
CLATTER
FOR YOU!
THANKS!
MORNING!

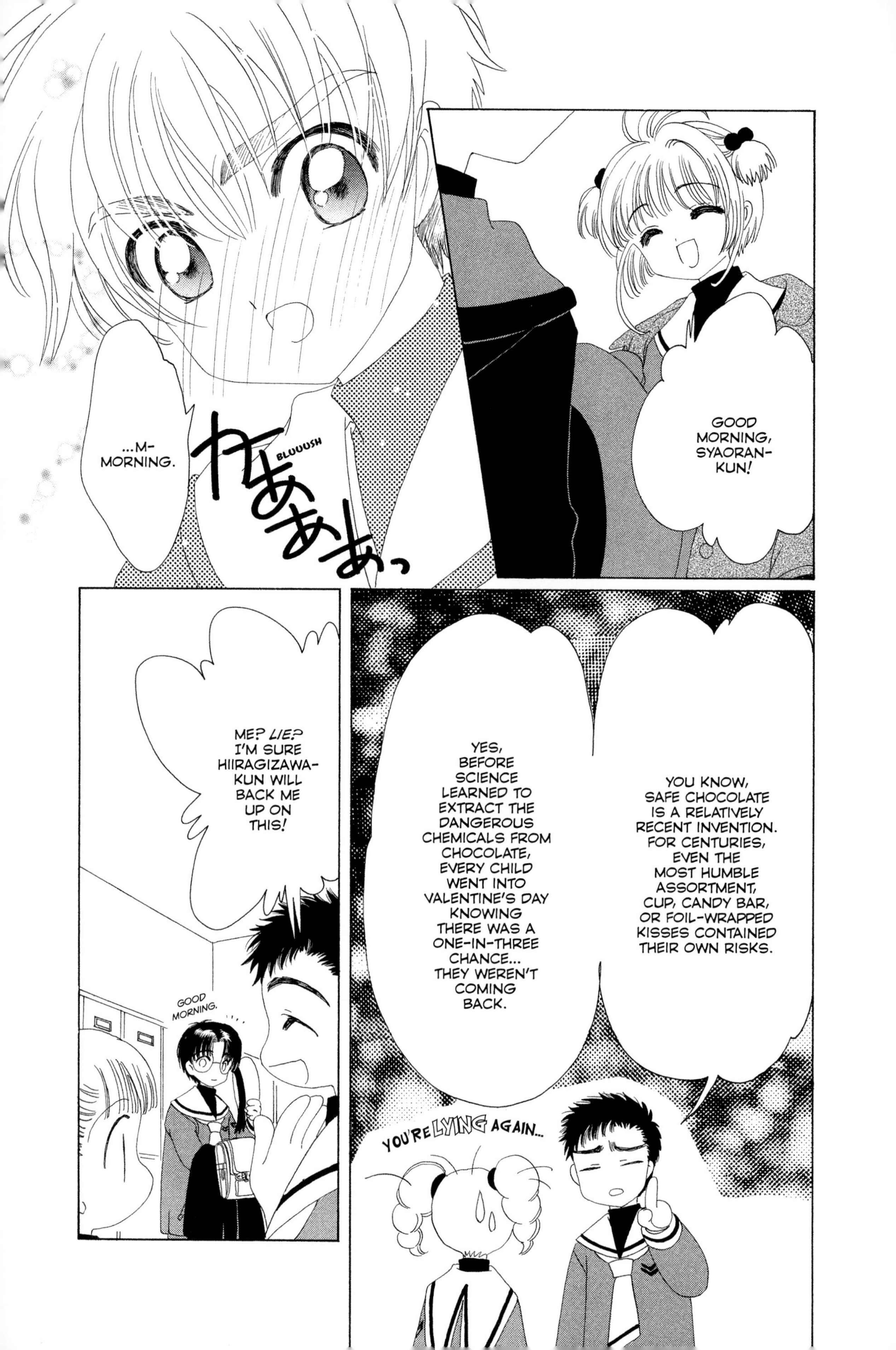
GOOD MORNING, SYAORAN-KUN!
...M-MORNING.
わあああっ
BLUUUSH
YOU KNOW, SAFE CHOCOLATE IS A RELATIVELY RECENT INVENTION. FOR CENTURIES, EVEN THE MOST HUMBLE ASSORTMENT, CUP, CANDY BAR, OR FOIL-WRAPPED KISSES CONTAINED THEIR OWN RISKS.
YES, BEFORE SCIENCE LEARNED TO EXTRACT THE DANGEROUS CHEMICALS FROM CHOCOLATE, EVERY CHILD WENT INTO VALENTINE'S DAY KNOWING THERE WAS A ONE-IN-THREE CHANCE... THEY WEREN'T COMING BACK.
YOU'RE LYING AGAIN...
ME? LIE? I'M SURE HIIRAGIZAWA-KUN WILL BACK ME UP ON THIS!
GOOD MORNING.

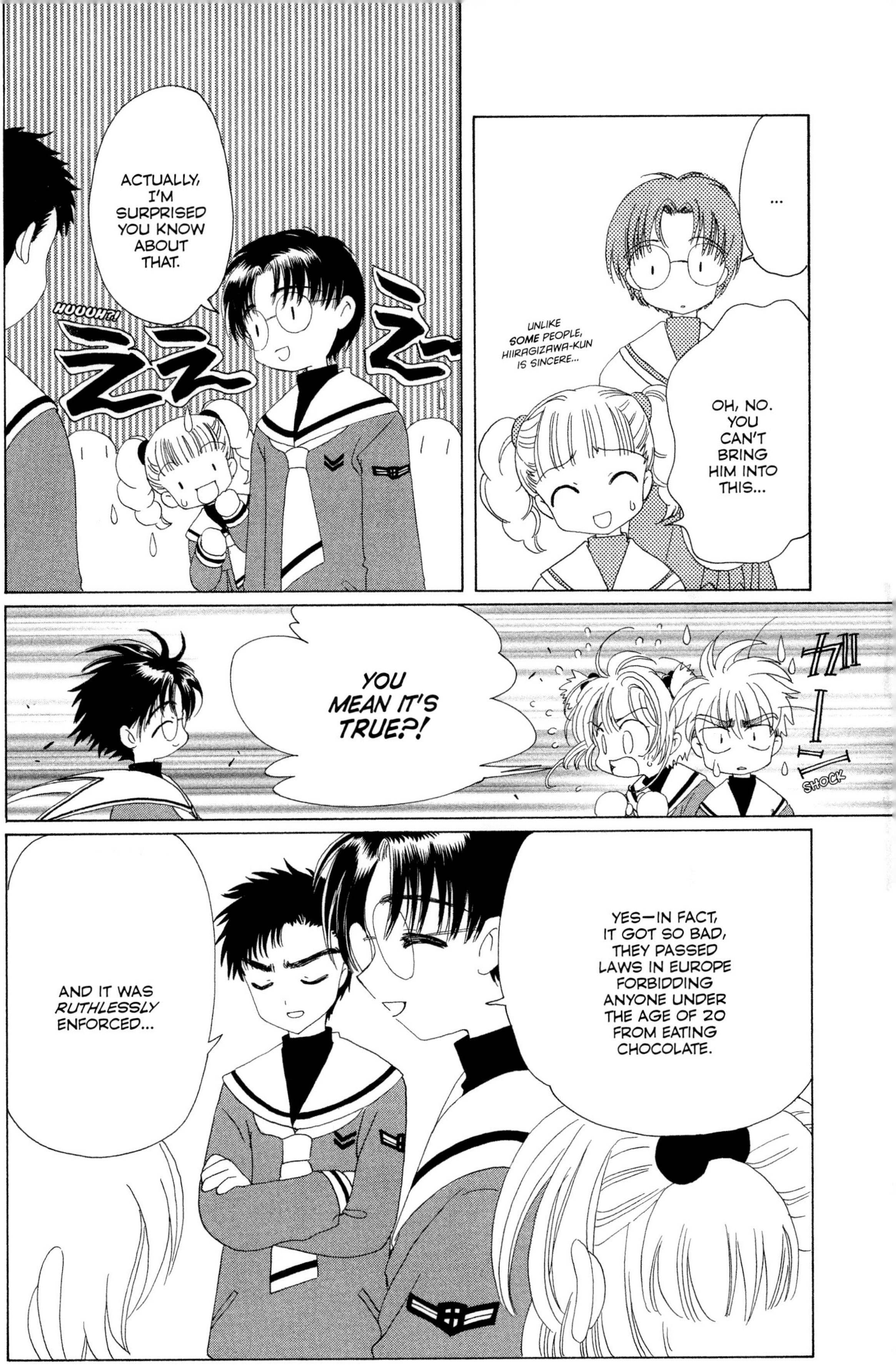
...
UNLIKE SOME PEOPLE, HIIRAGIZAWA-KUN IS SINCERE...
OH, NO. YOU CAN'T BRING HIM INTO THIS...
ACTUALLY, I'M SURPRISED YOU KNOW ABOUT THAT.
HUUUH?!
YOU MEAN IT'S TRUE?!
SHOCK
YES—IN FACT, IT GOT SO BAD, THEY PASSED LAWS IN EUROPE FORBIDDING ANYONE UNDER THE AGE OF 20 FROM EATING CHOCOLATE.
AND IT WAS RUTHLESSLY ENFORCED...

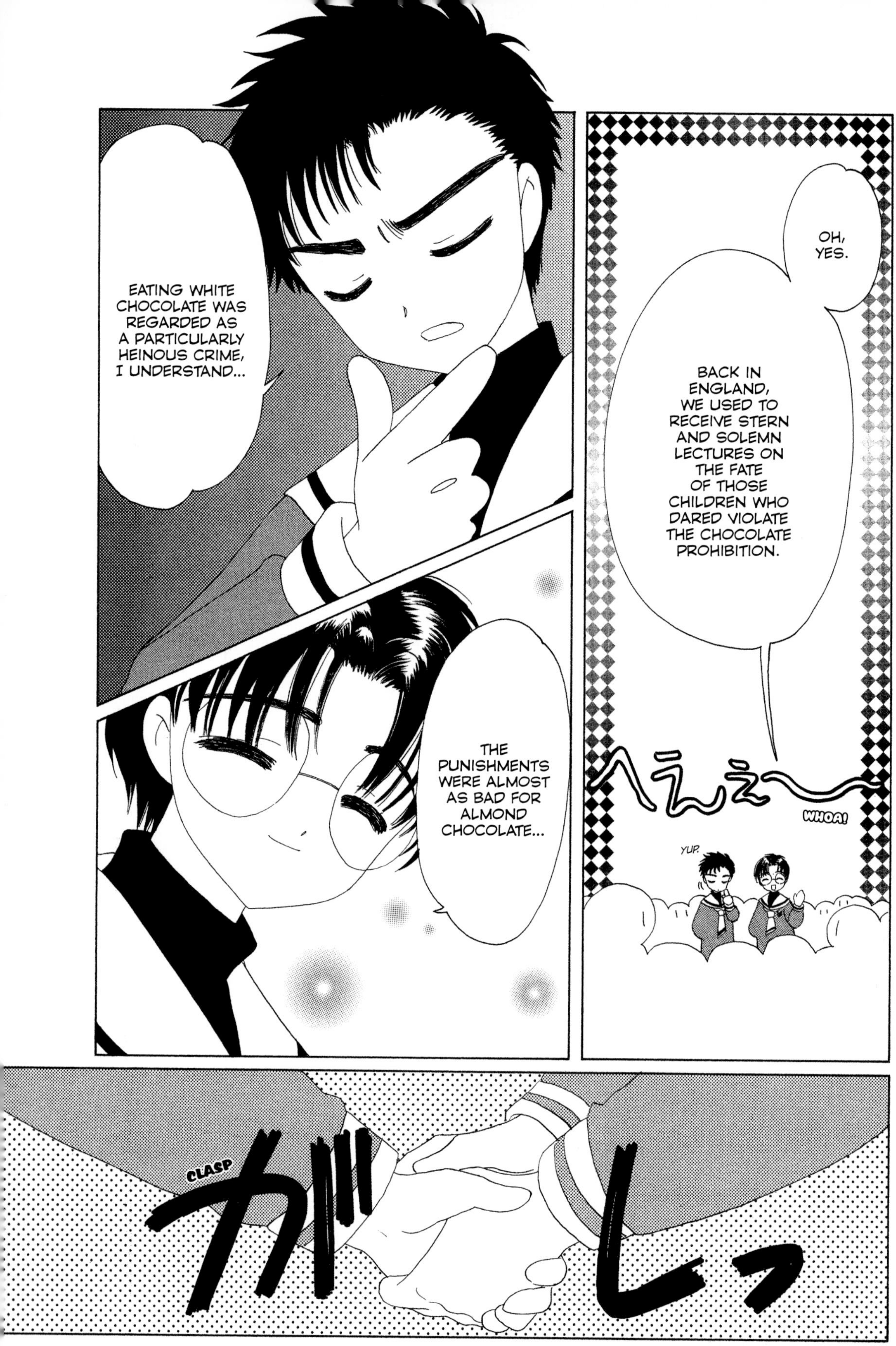
OH, YES.
BACK IN ENGLAND, WE USED TO RECEIVE STERN AND SOLEMN LECTURES ON THE FATE OF THOSE CHILDREN WHO DARED VIOLATE THE CHOCOLATE PROHIBITION.
へぇぇ〜〜
WHOA!
YUP.
EATING WHITE CHOCOLATE WAS REGARDED AS A PARTICULARLY HEINOUS CRIME, I UNDERSTAND...
THE PUNISHMENTS WERE ALMOST AS BAD FOR ALMOND CHOCOLATE...
ガシッ
CLASP

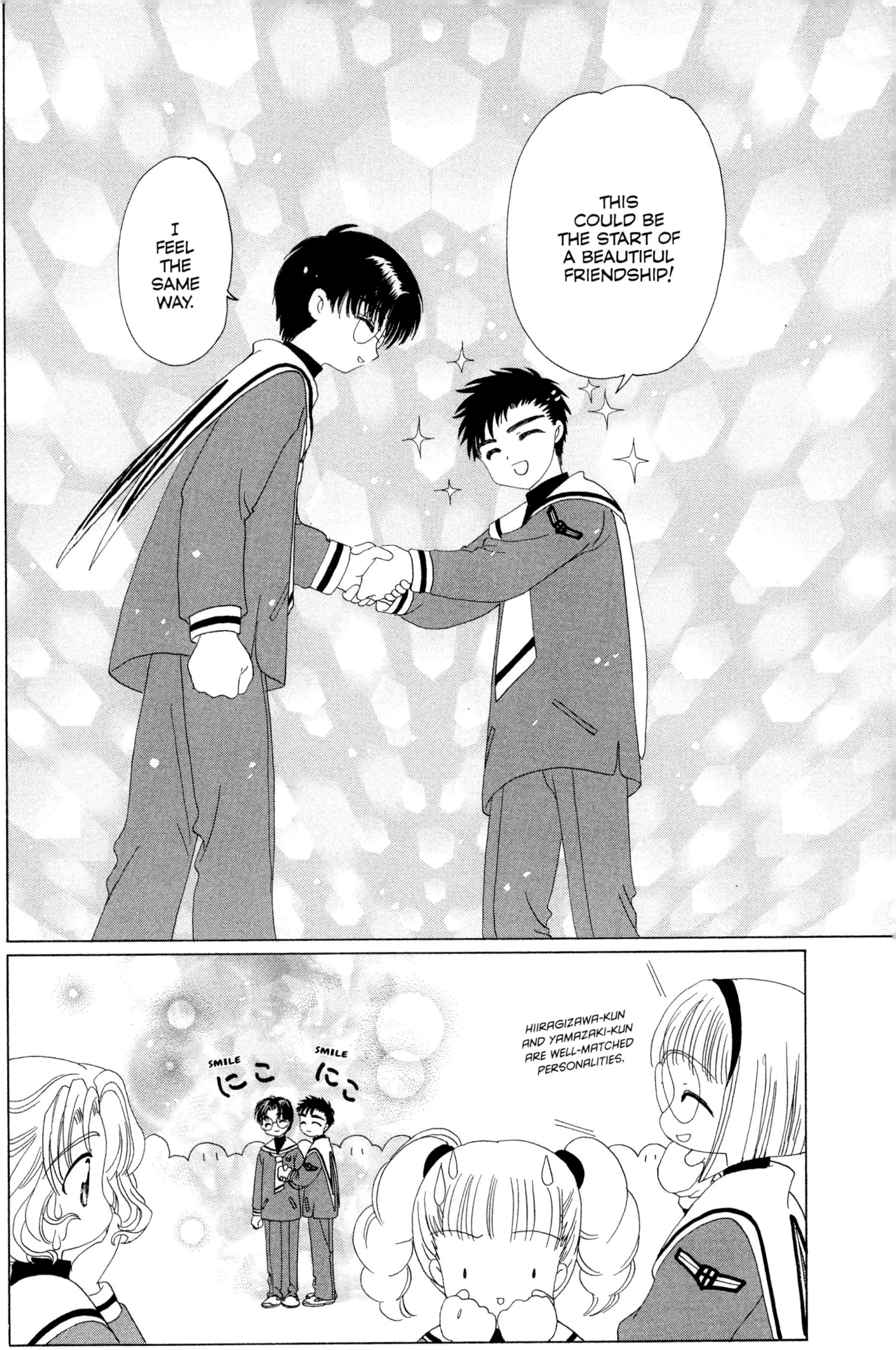
THIS COULD BE THE START OF A BEAUTIFUL FRIENDSHIP!
I FEEL THE SAME WAY.
HIIRAGIZAWA-KUN AND YAMAZAKI-KUN ARE WELL-MATCHED PERSONALITIES.
SMILE
にこ
SMILE
にこ

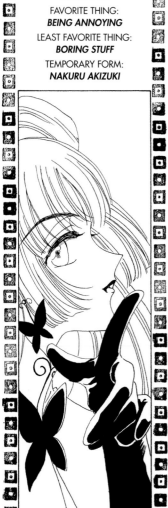

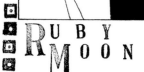

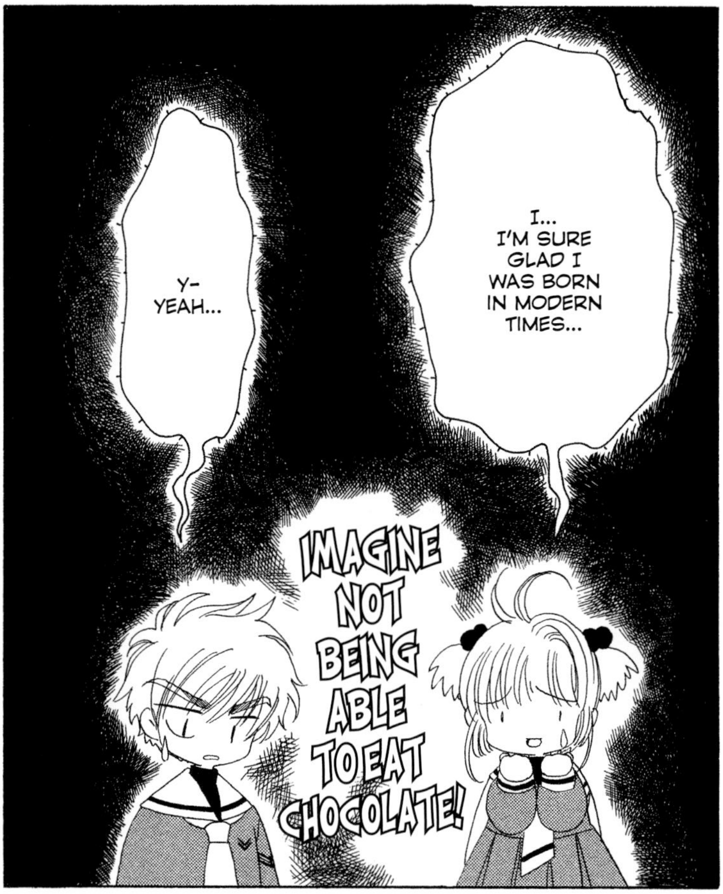
I... I'M SURE GLAD I WAS BORN IN MODERN TIMES...
Y-YEAH...
IMAGINE NOT BEING ABLE TO EAT CHOCOLATE!
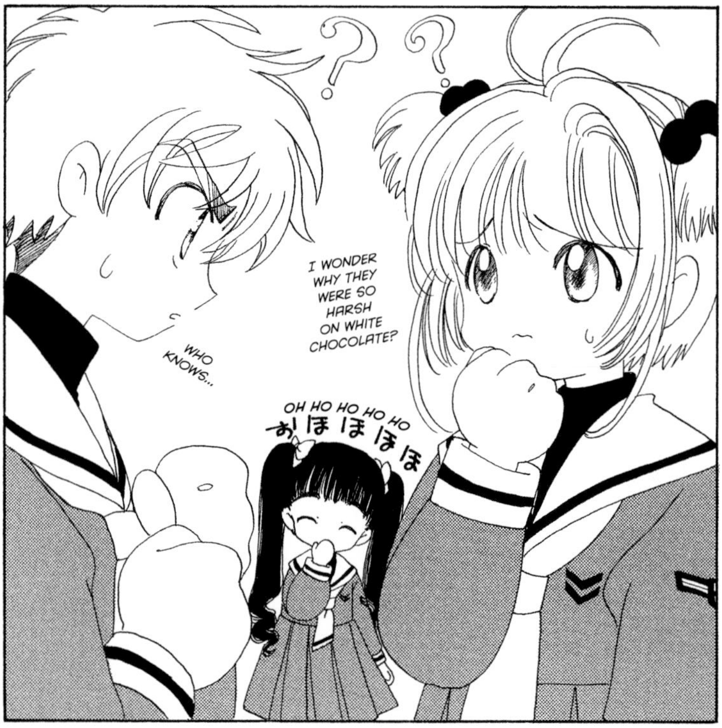
I WONDER WHY THEY WERE SO HARSH ON WHITE CHOCOLATE?
WHO KNOWS...
OH HO HO HO HO
おほほほほ

24

RUBY MOON

MASTER:
ERIOL HIIRAGIZAWA

BIRTHDATE:
SECRET (DIFFERENT FROM NAKURU'S)

SYMBOL:
MOON

ASPECT:
LIGHT

EYES:
DARK RED

HAIR:
RED

MAGIC:
WESTERN

FAVORITE FOOD:
DOESN'T EAT

FAVORITE THING:
BEING ANNOYING

LEAST FAVORITE THING:
BORING STUFF

TEMPORARY FORM:
NAKURU AKIZUKI

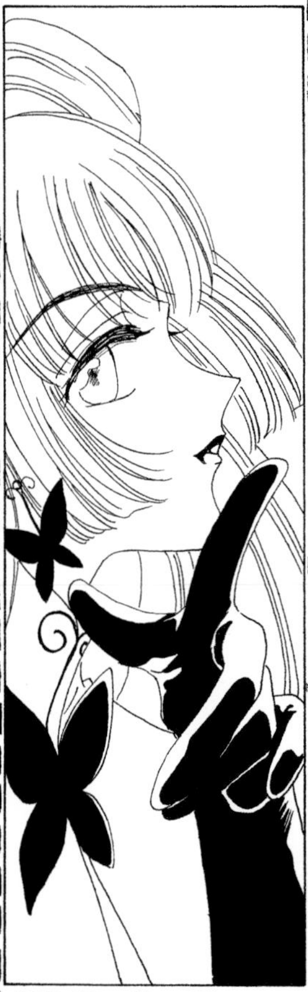

RUBY MOON

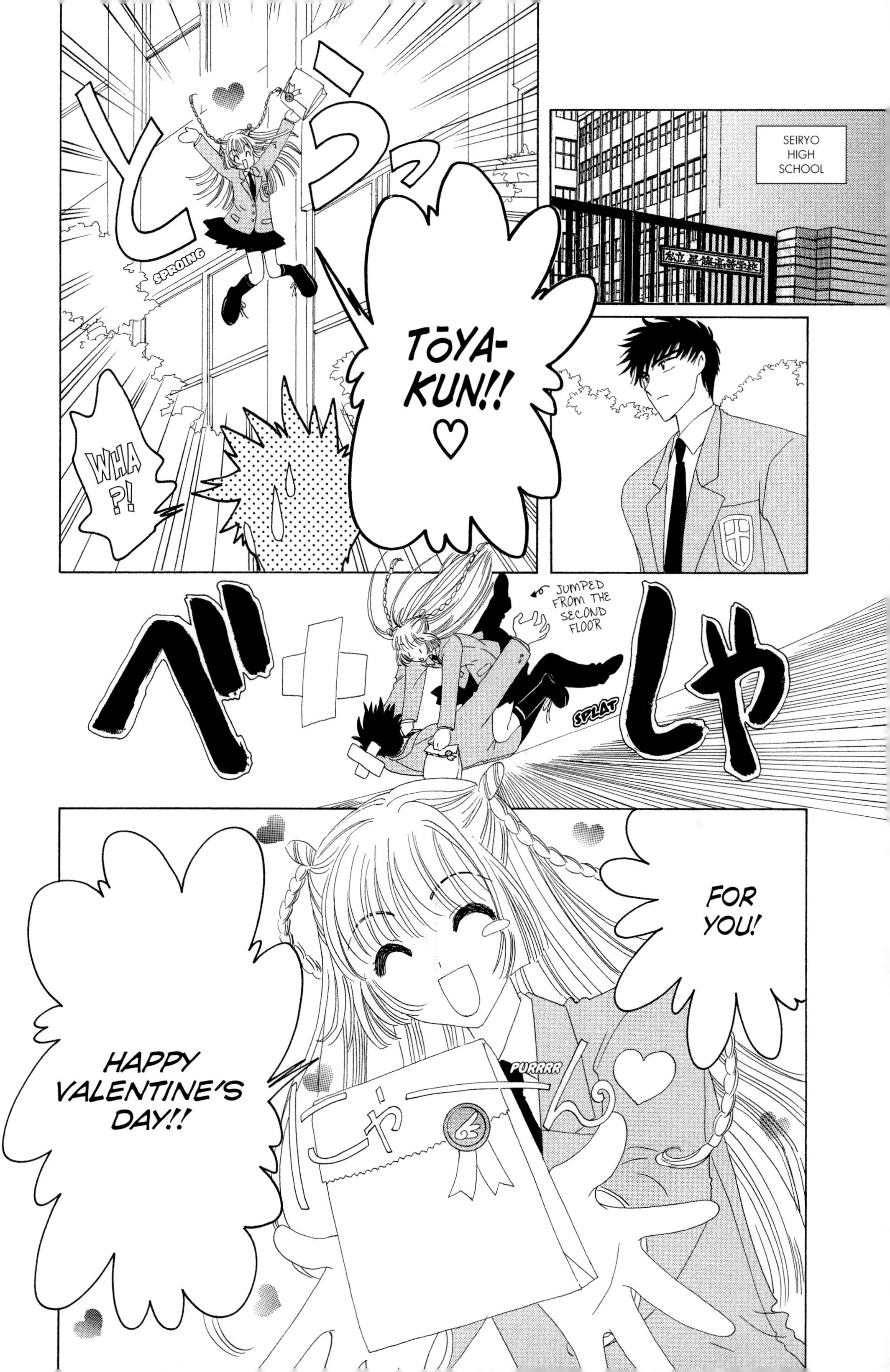

SEIRYO HIGH SCHOOL
TŌYA-KUN!! ♡
SPROING
WHA ?!
JUMPED FROM THE SECOND FLOOR
SPLAT
FOR YOU!
PURRRR
HAPPY VALENTINE'S DAY!!

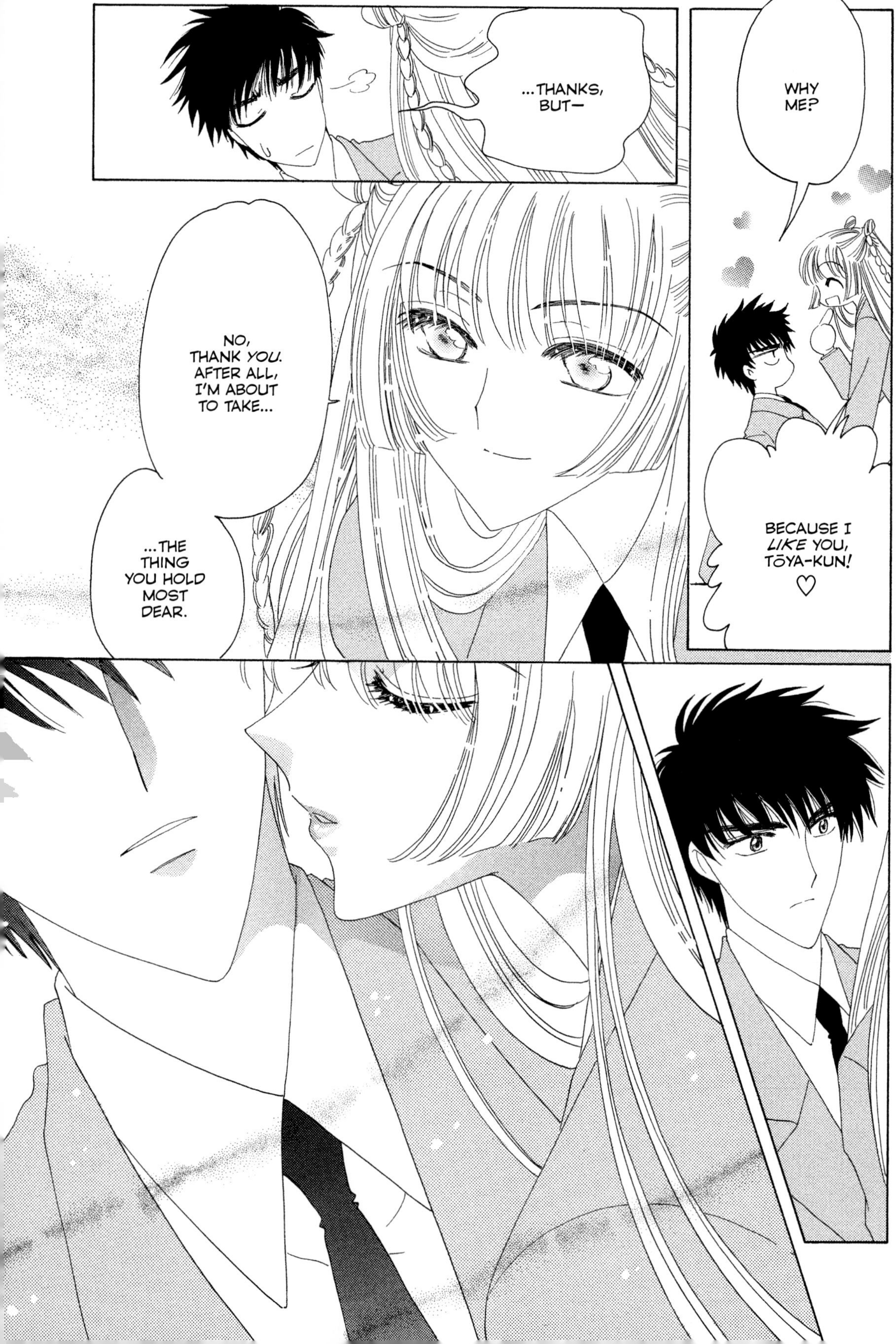
WHY ME?
BECAUSE I *LIKE* YOU, TŌYA-KUN! ♡
...THANKS, BUT—
NO, THANK *YOU*. AFTER ALL, I'M ABOUT TO TAKE...
...THE THING YOU HOLD MOST DEAR.

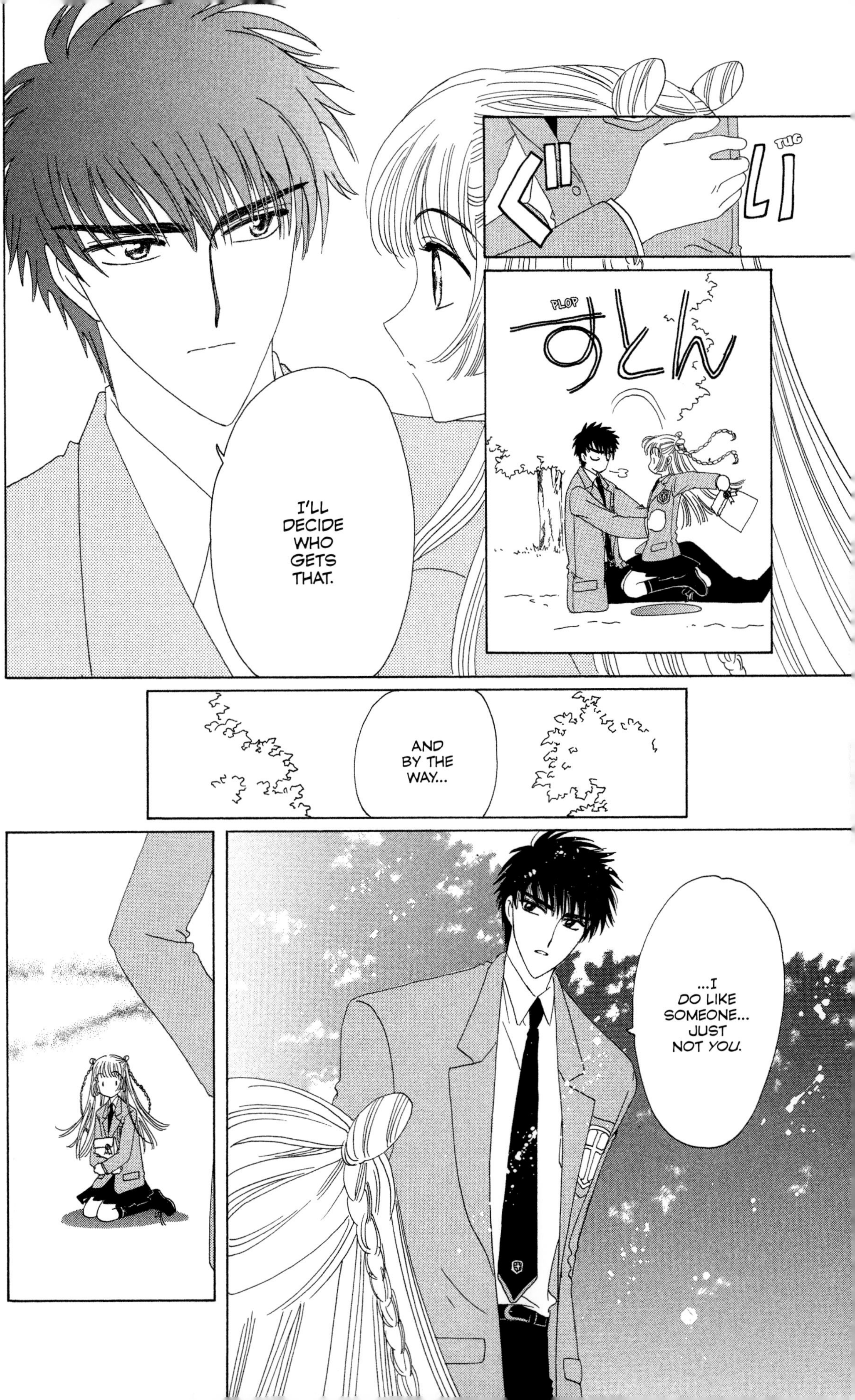
ぐい
TUG
すとん
PLOP
I'LL DECIDE WHO GETS THAT.
AND BY THE WAY...
...I *DO* LIKE SOMEONE... JUST NOT *YOU*.

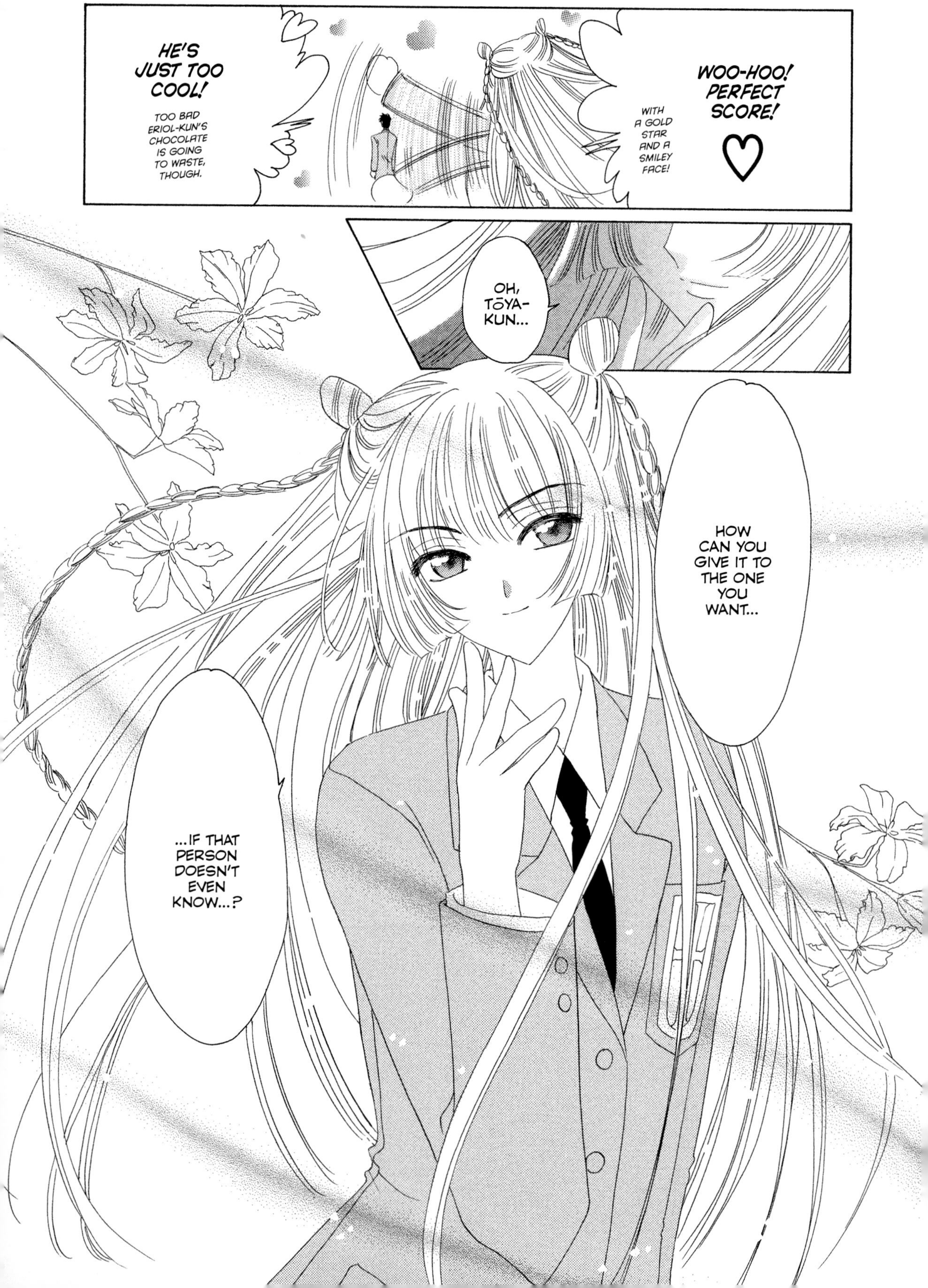
WOO-HOO! PERFECT SCORE! ♥
WITH A GOLD STAR AND A SMILEY FACE!
HE'S JUST TOO COOL!
TOO BAD ERIOL-KUN'S CHOCOLATE IS GOING TO WASTE, THOUGH.
OH, TŌYA-KUN...
HOW CAN YOU GIVE IT TO THE ONE YOU WANT...
...IF THAT PERSON DOESN'T EVEN KNOW...?

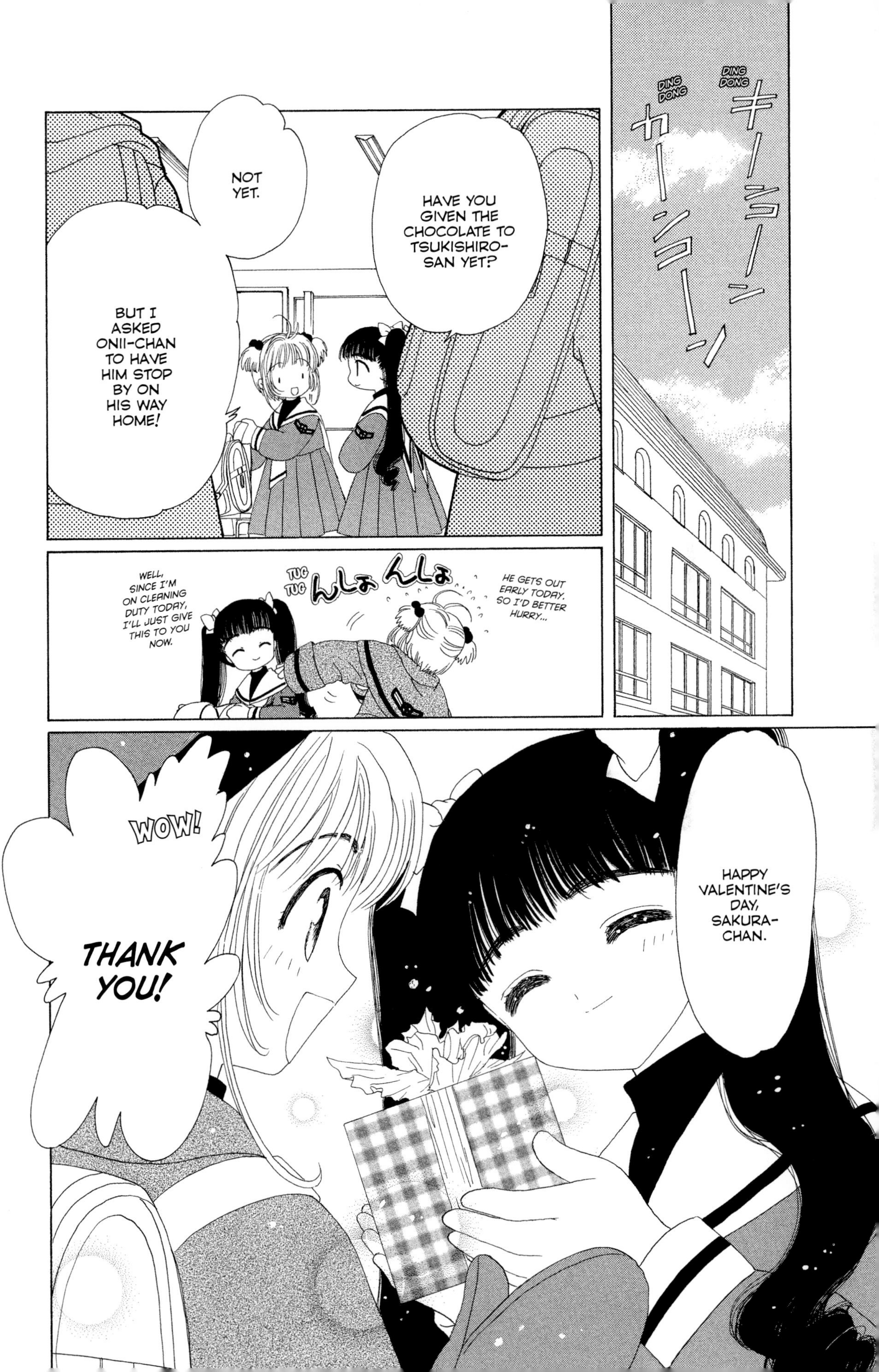
DING DONG
DING DONG
HAVE YOU GIVEN THE CHOCOLATE TO TSUKISHIRO-SAN YET?
NOT YET.
BUT I ASKED ONII-CHAN TO HAVE HIM STOP BY ON HIS WAY HOME!
HE GETS OUT EARLY TODAY. SO I'D BETTER HURRY...
TUG TUG
んしょ んしょ
WELL, SINCE I'M ON CLEANING DUTY TODAY, I'LL JUST GIVE THIS TO YOU NOW.
HAPPY VALENTINE'S DAY, SAKURA-CHAN.
WOW!
THANK YOU!

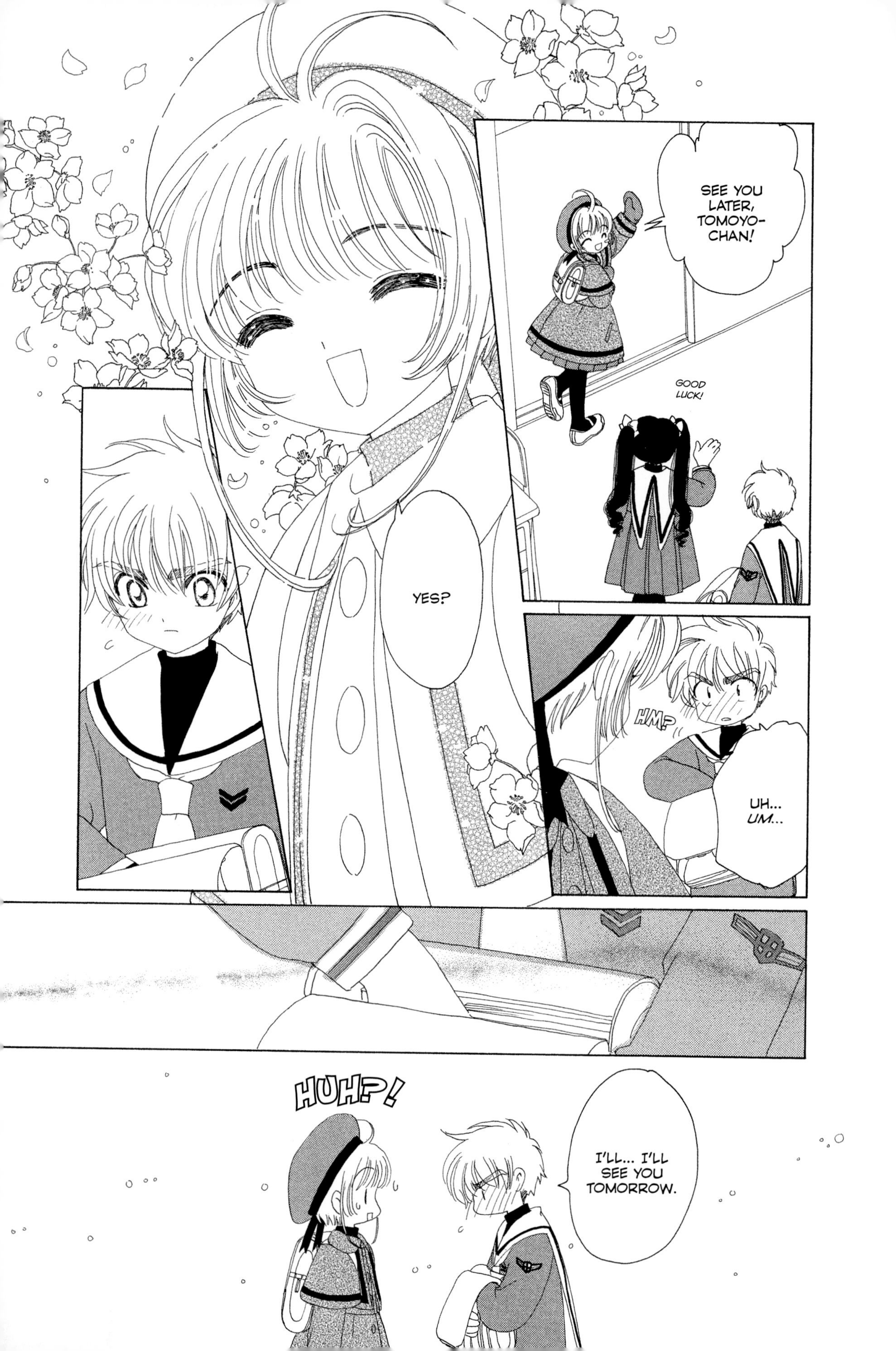
SEE YOU LATER, TOMOYO-CHAN!
GOOD LUCK!
HM?
UH... UM...
YES?
I'LL... I'LL SEE YOU TOMORROW.
HUH?!

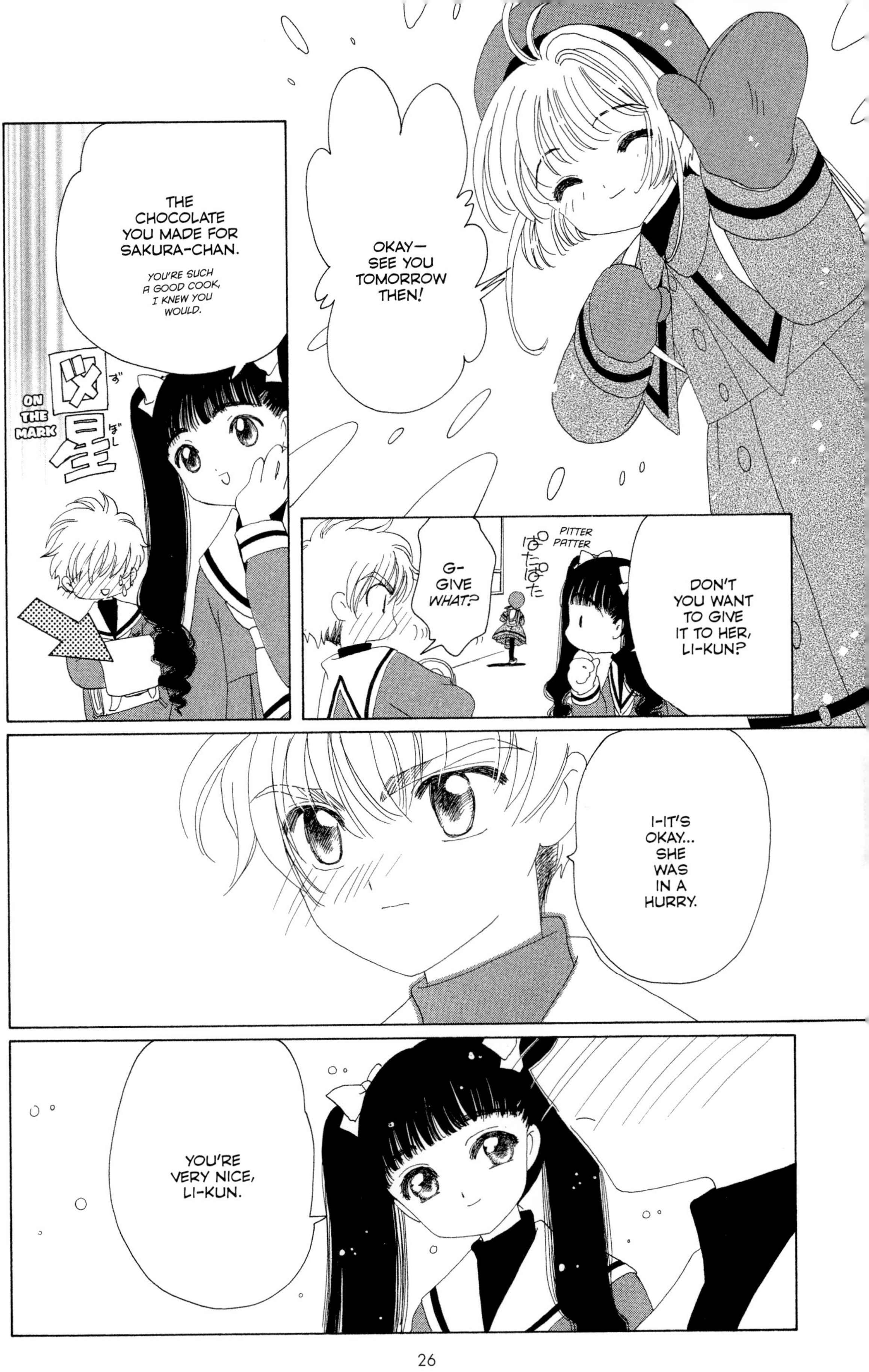
OKAY— SEE YOU TOMORROW THEN!
DON'T YOU WANT TO GIVE IT TO HER, LI-KUN?
PITTER PATTER
ぱたぱた
G- GIVE WHAT?
THE CHOCOLATE YOU MADE FOR SAKURA-CHAN.
YOU'RE SUCH A GOOD COOK, I KNEW YOU WOULD.
図星
ON THE MARK
I-IT'S OKAY... SHE WAS IN A HURRY.
YOU'RE VERY NICE, LI-KUN.

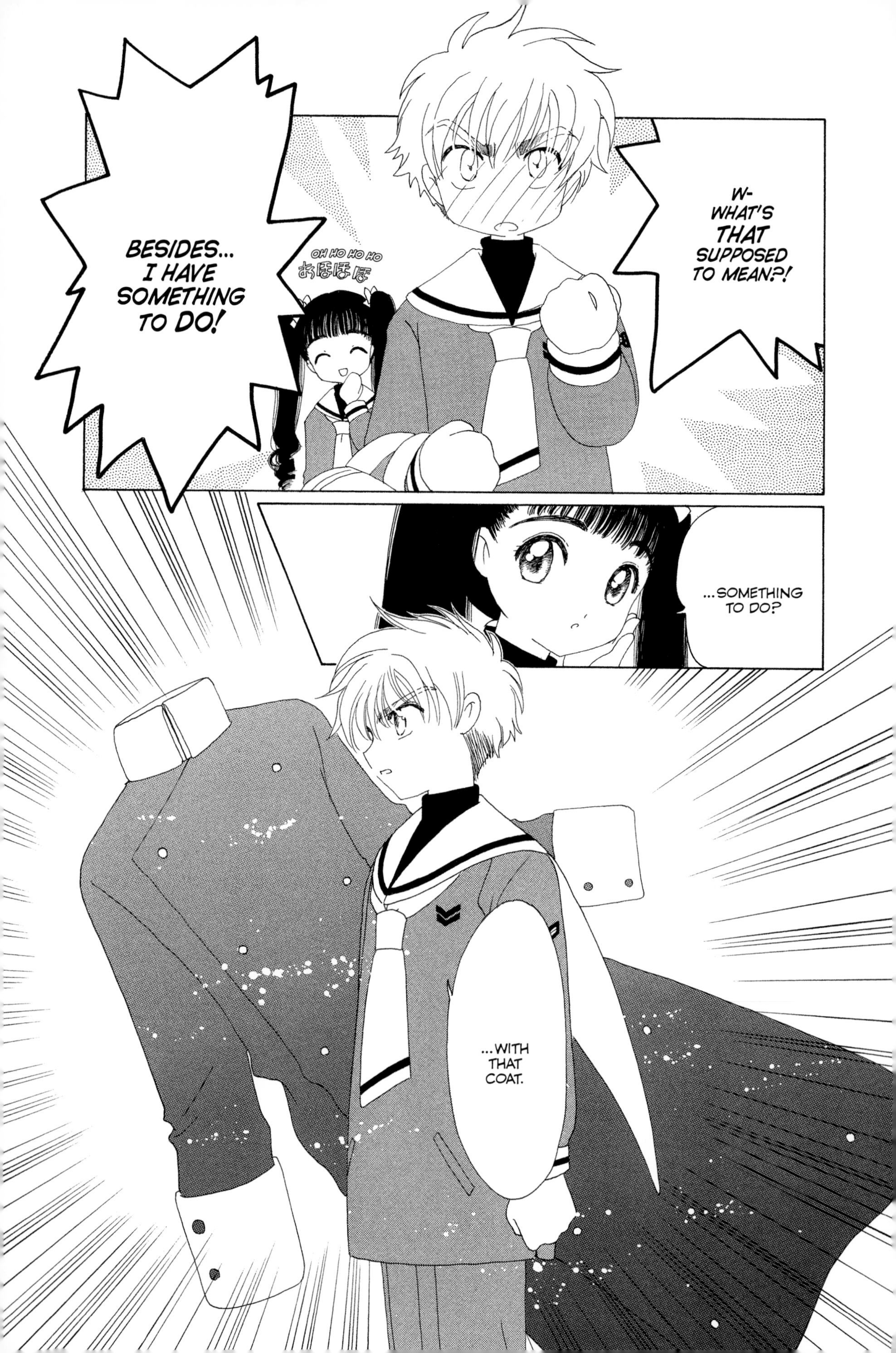
W-
WHAT'S
THAT
SUPPOSED
TO MEAN?!
OH HO HO HO
おほほほ
BESIDES...
I HAVE
SOMETHING
TO DO!
...SOMETHING
TO DO?
...WITH
THAT
COAT.

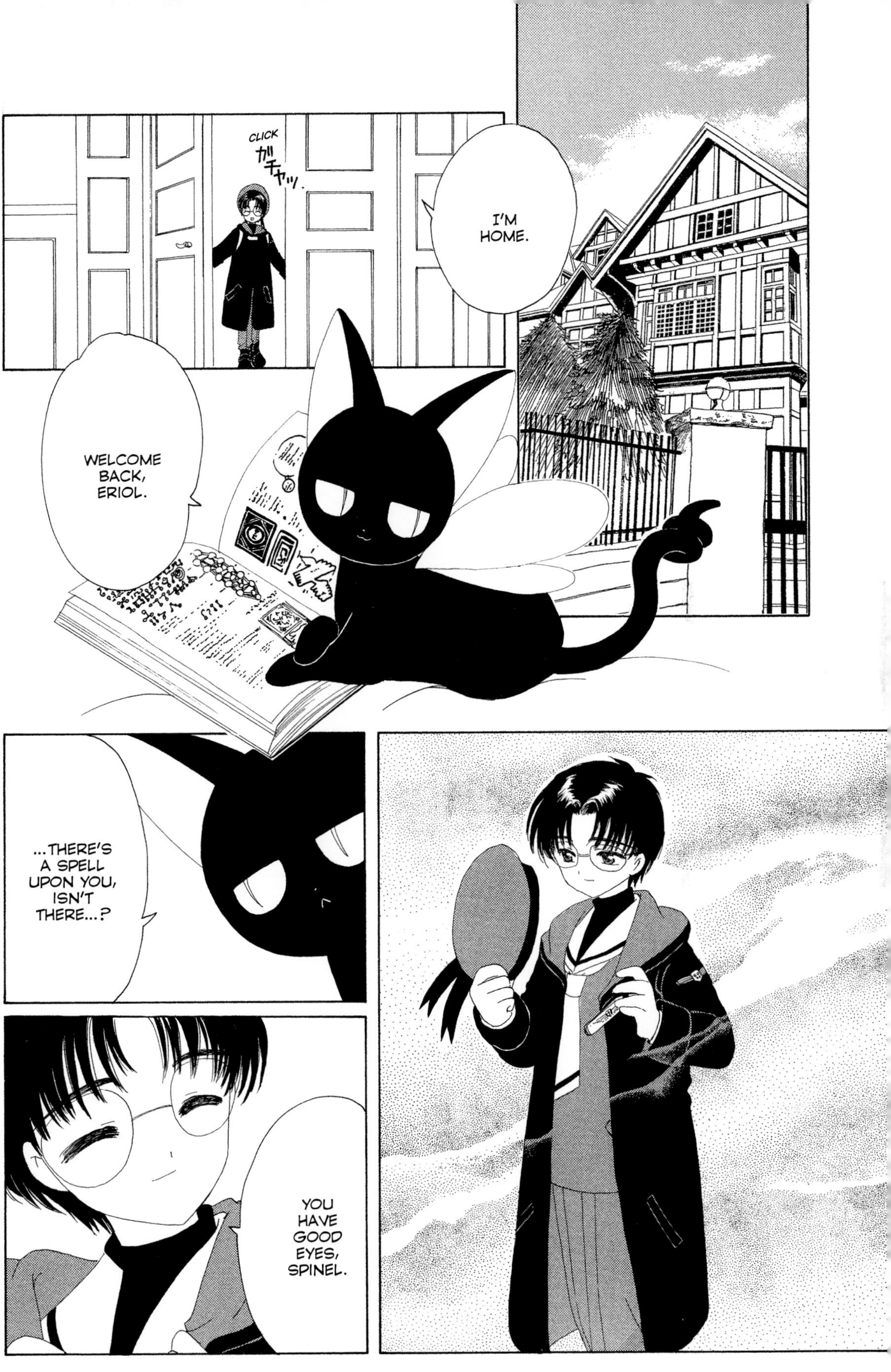
I'M HOME.
CLICK
ガチャッ.
WELCOME BACK, ERIOL.
...THERE'S A SPELL UPON YOU, ISN'T THERE...?
YOU HAVE GOOD EYES, SPINEL.

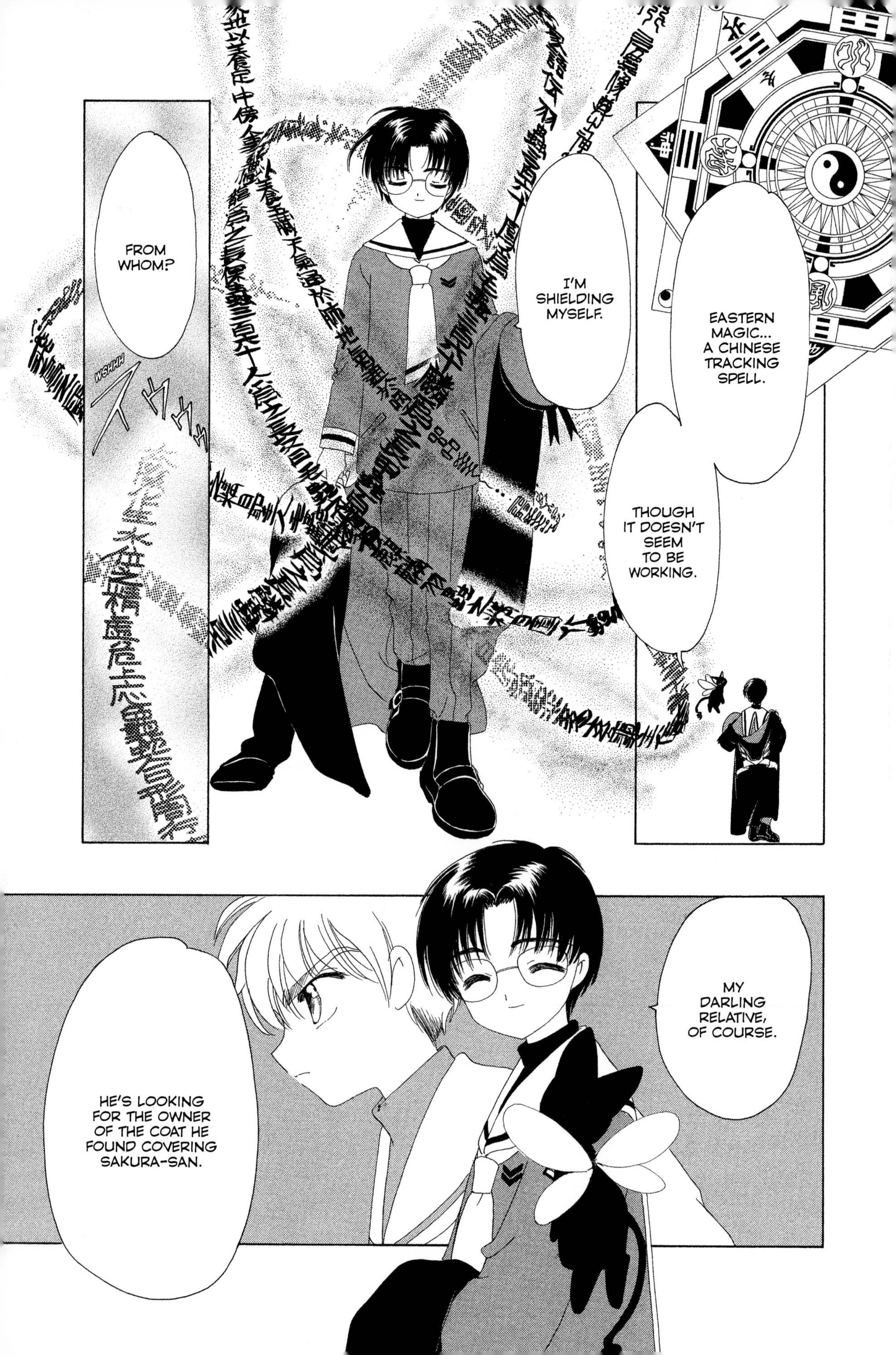
EASTERN MAGIC... A CHINESE TRACKING SPELL.
THOUGH IT DOESN'T SEEM TO BE WORKING.
I'M SHIELDING MYSELF.
FROM WHOM?
WSHHH
MY DARLING RELATIVE, OF COURSE.
HE'S LOOKING FOR THE OWNER OF THE COAT HE FOUND COVERING SAKURA-SAN.

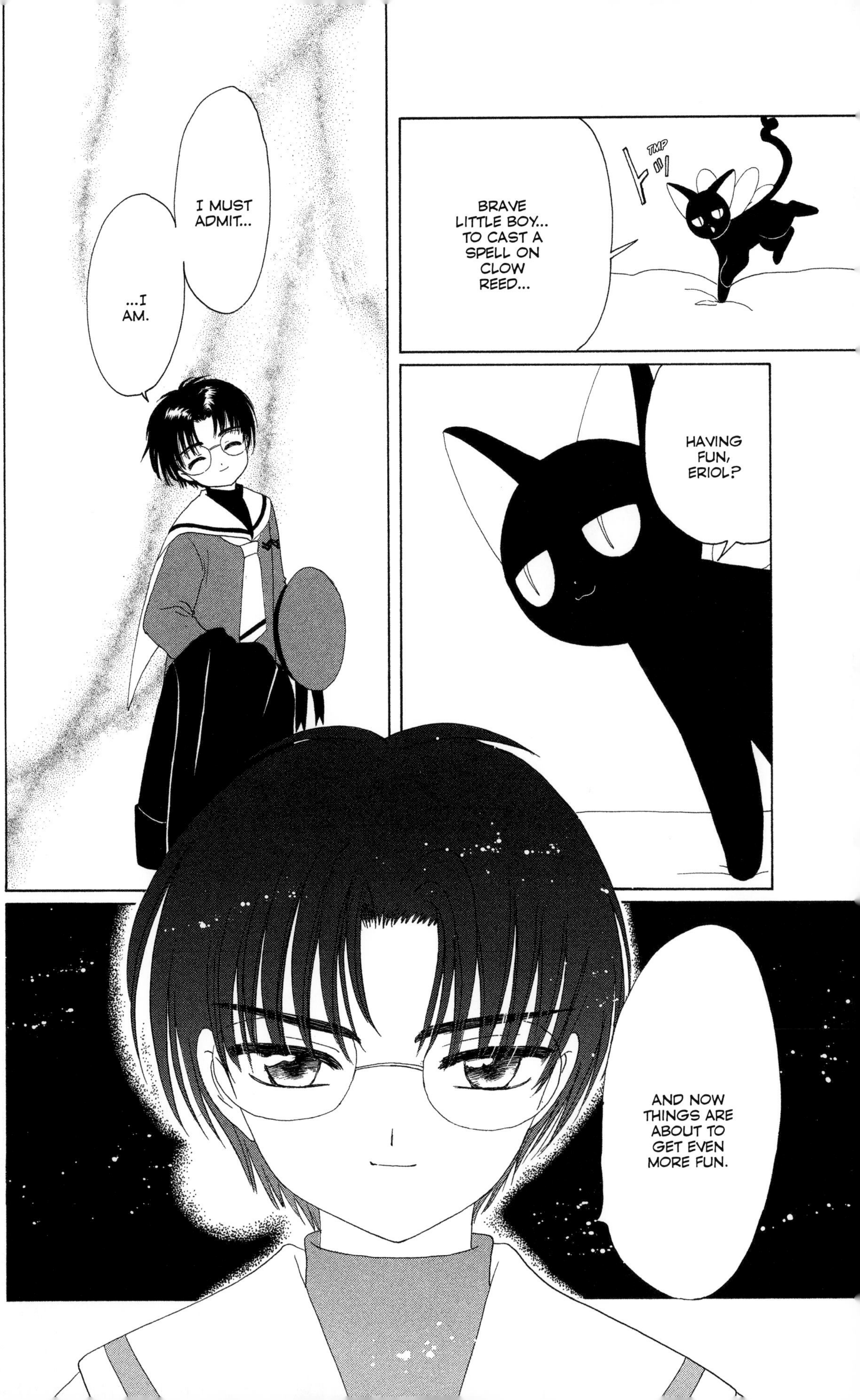
TMP
BRAVE LITTLE BOY... TO CAST A SPELL ON CLOW REED...
HAVING FUN, ERIOL?
I MUST ADMIT...
...I AM.
AND NOW THINGS ARE ABOUT TO GET EVEN MORE FUN.

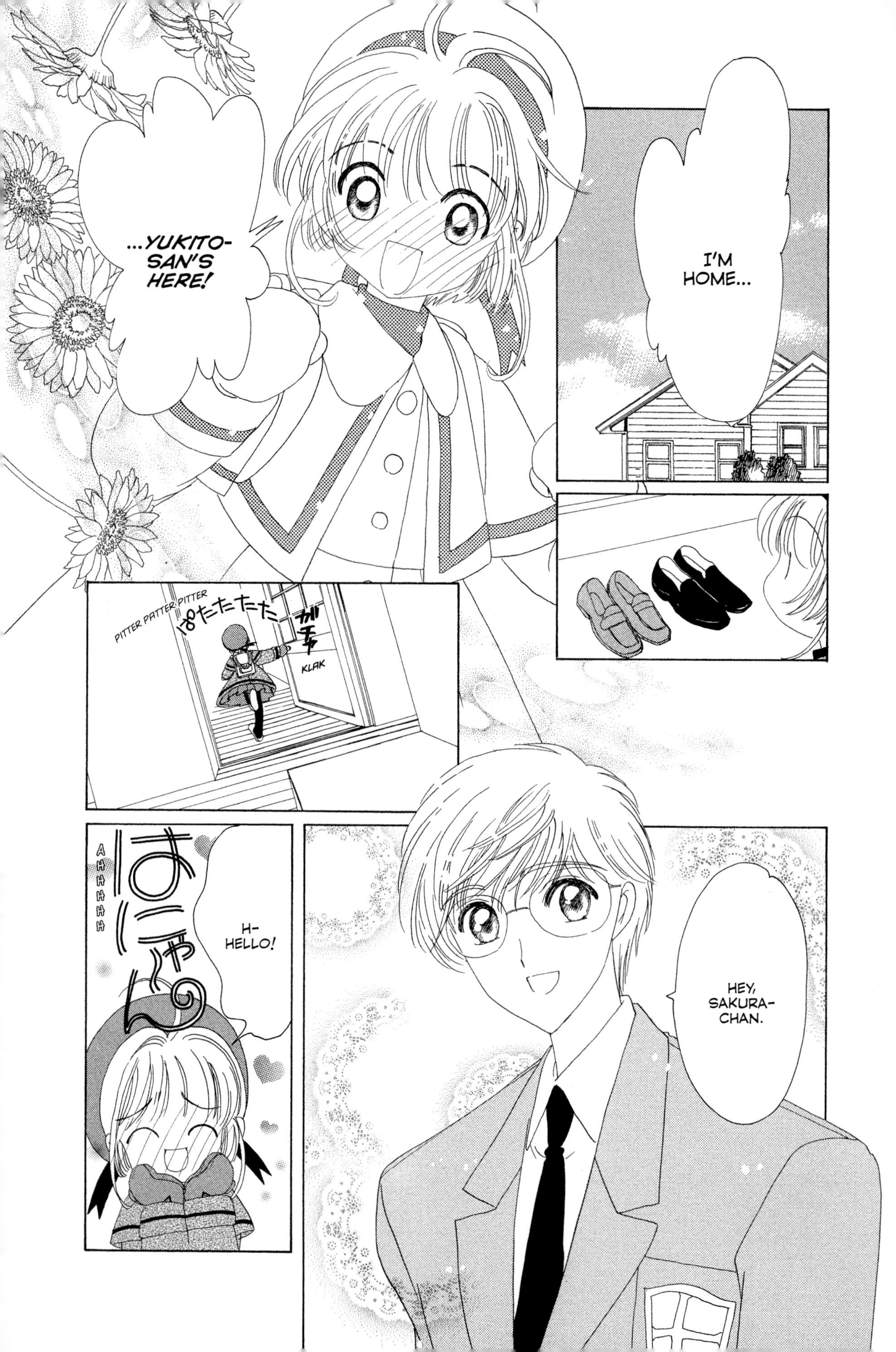
I'M HOME...
...YUKITO-SAN'S HERE!
PITTER PATTER PITTER
ぱたたたた
ガチャ
KLAK
HEY, SAKURA-CHAN.
H-HELLO!
はにゃ〜ん
AHHHHHH

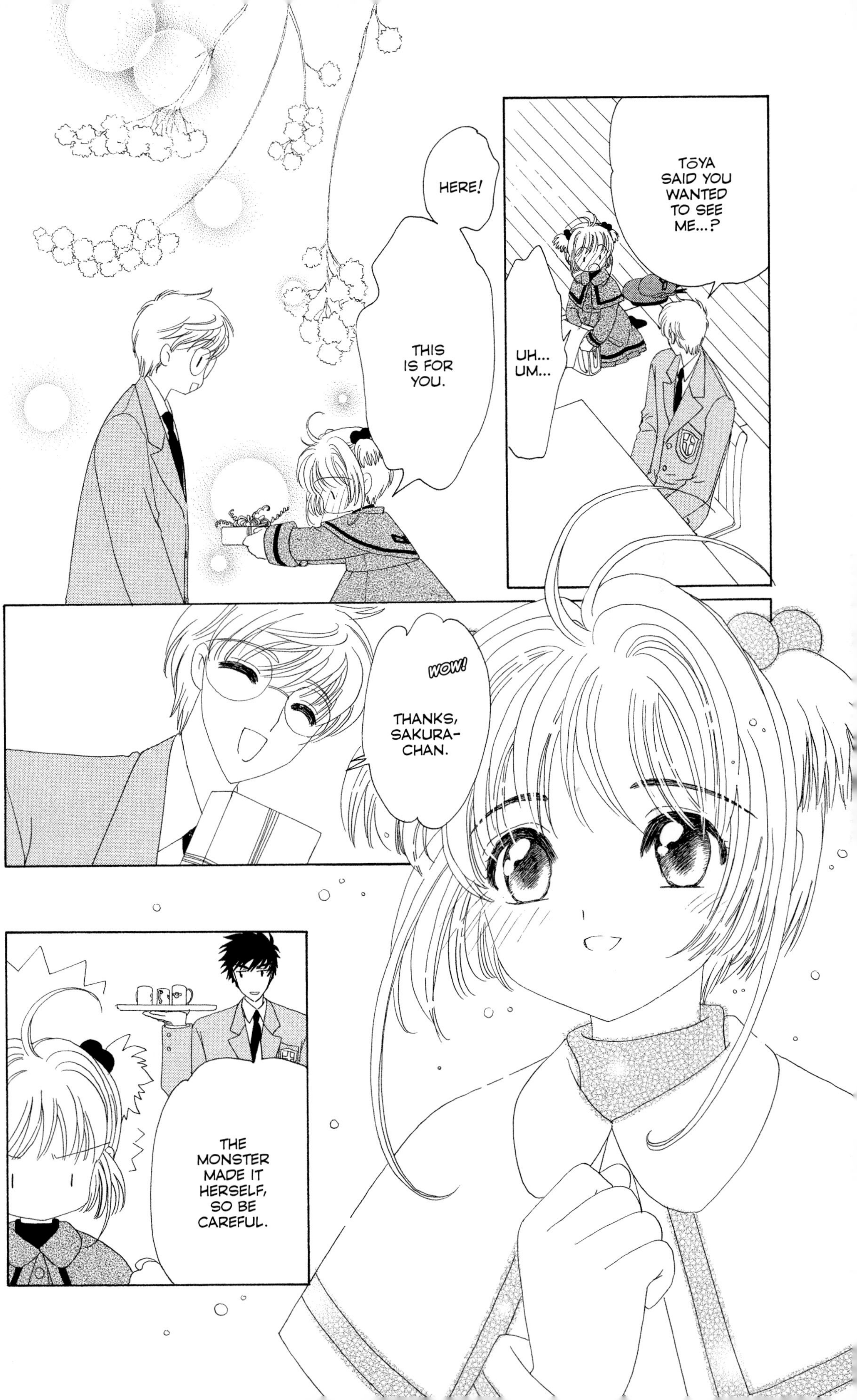
TŌYA SAID YOU WANTED TO SEE ME...?
UH... UM...
HERE!
THIS IS FOR YOU.
WOW!
THANKS, SAKURA-CHAN.
THE MONSTER MADE IT HERSELF, SO BE CAREFUL.

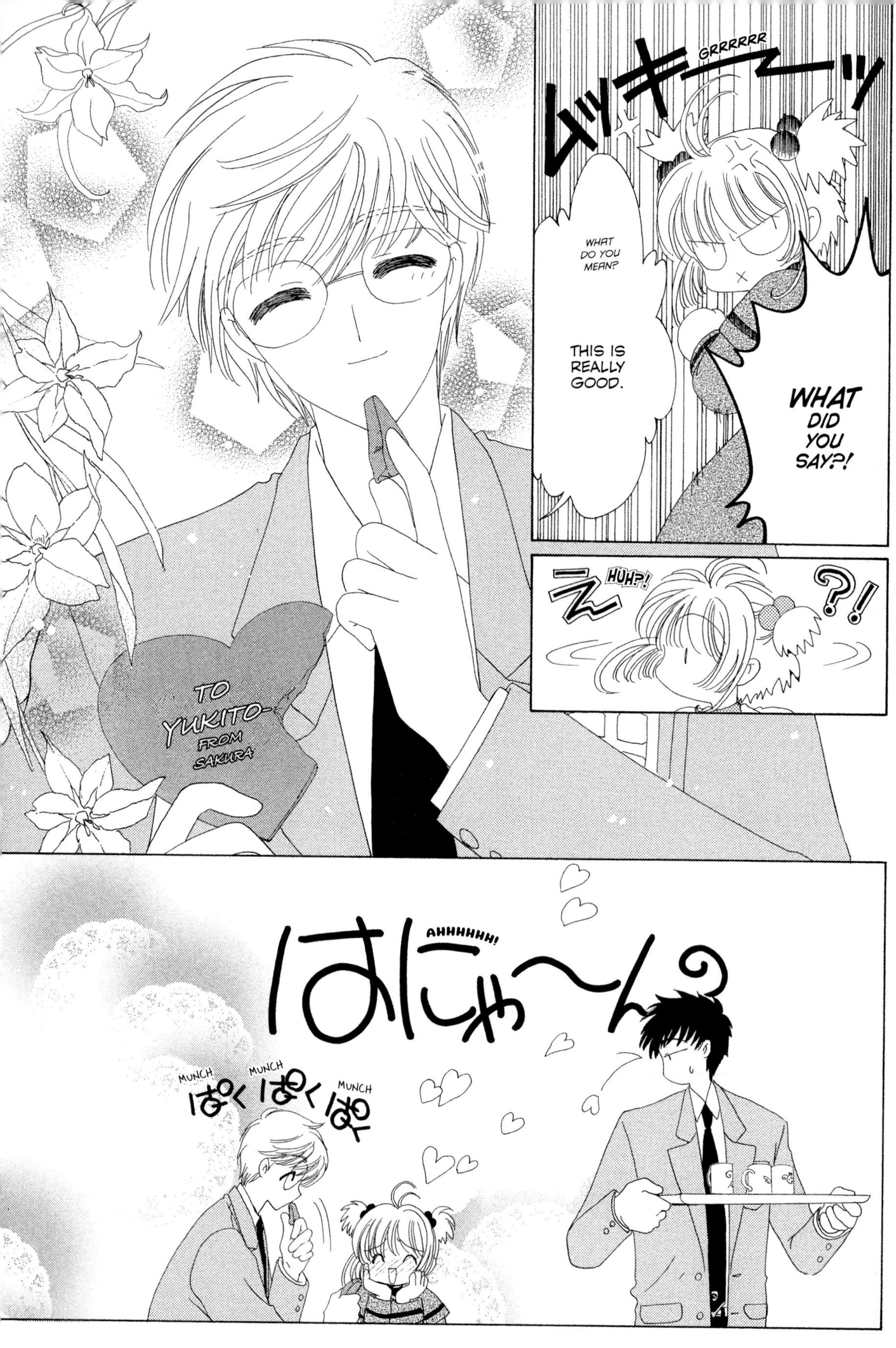
GRRRRR
WHAT DID YOU SAY?!
WHAT DO YOU MEAN?
THIS IS REALLY GOOD.
HUH?!
?!
TO YUKITO- FROM SAKURA
AHHHHHHH!
MUNCH MUNCH MUNCH

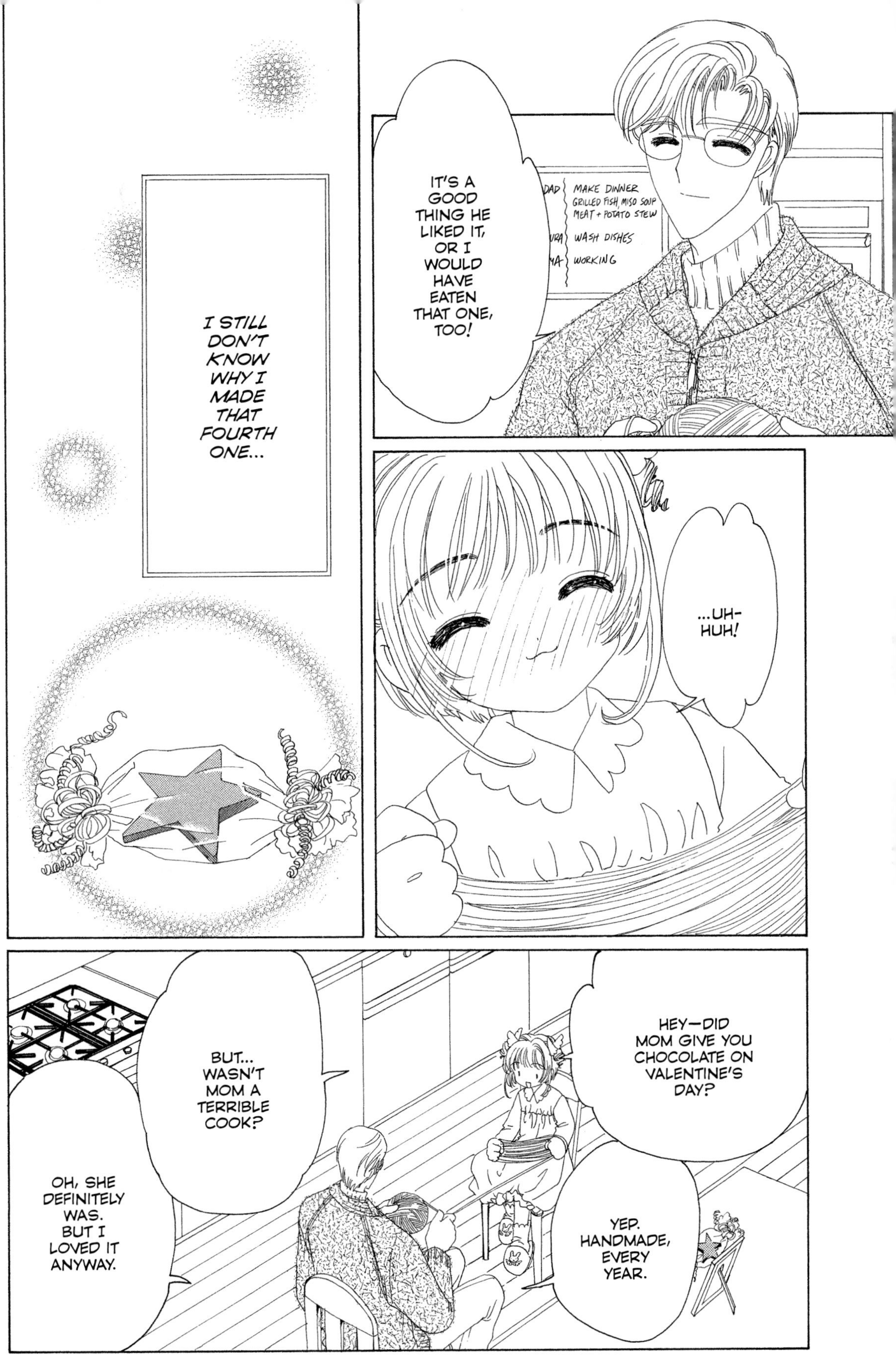
IT'S A GOOD THING HE LIKED IT, OR I WOULD HAVE EATEN THAT ONE, TOO!
DAD
MAKE DINNER
GRILLED FISH, MISO SOUP
MEAT + POTATO STEW
WASH DISHES
WORKING
...UH-HUH!
I STILL DON'T KNOW WHY I MADE THAT FOURTH ONE...
HEY—DID MOM GIVE YOU CHOCOLATE ON VALENTINE'S DAY?
YEP. HANDMADE, EVERY YEAR.
BUT... WASN'T MOM A TERRIBLE COOK?
OH, SHE DEFINITELY WAS. BUT I LOVED IT ANYWAY.

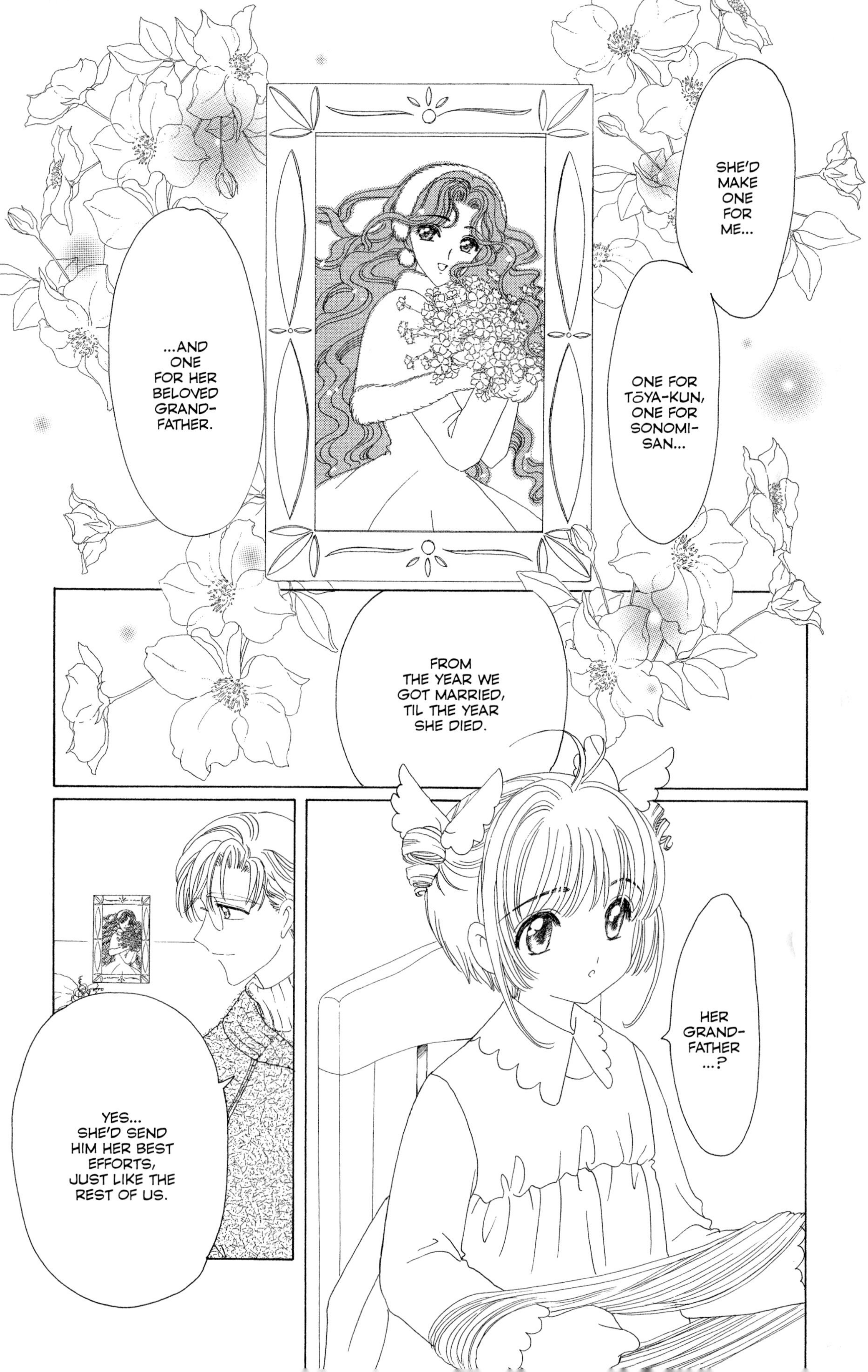
SHE'D MAKE ONE FOR ME...
ONE FOR TŌYA-KUN, ONE FOR SONOMI-SAN...
...AND ONE FOR HER BELOVED GRAND-FATHER.
FROM THE YEAR WE GOT MARRIED, TIL THE YEAR SHE DIED.
HER GRAND-FATHER ...?
YES... SHE'D SEND HIM HER BEST EFFORTS, JUST LIKE THE REST OF US.

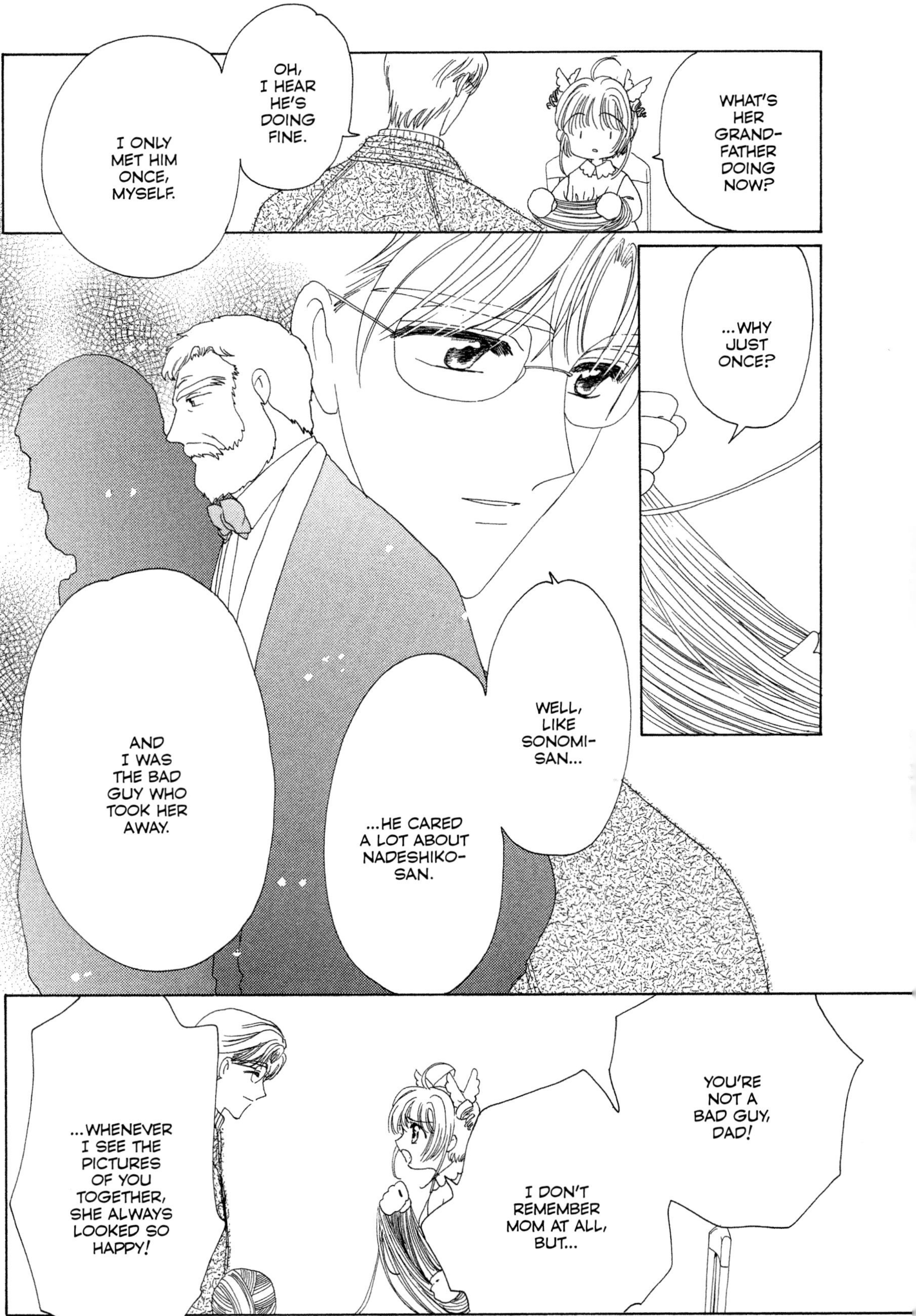

WHAT'S HER GRAND-FATHER DOING NOW?
OH, I HEAR HE'S DOING FINE.
I ONLY MET HIM ONCE, MYSELF.
...WHY JUST ONCE?
WELL, LIKE SONOMI-SAN...
...HE CARED A LOT ABOUT NADESHIKO-SAN.
AND I WAS THE BAD GUY WHO TOOK HER AWAY.
YOU'RE NOT A BAD GUY, DAD!
I DON'T REMEMBER MOM AT ALL, BUT...
...WHENEVER I SEE THE PICTURES OF YOU TOGETHER, SHE ALWAYS LOOKED SO HAPPY!

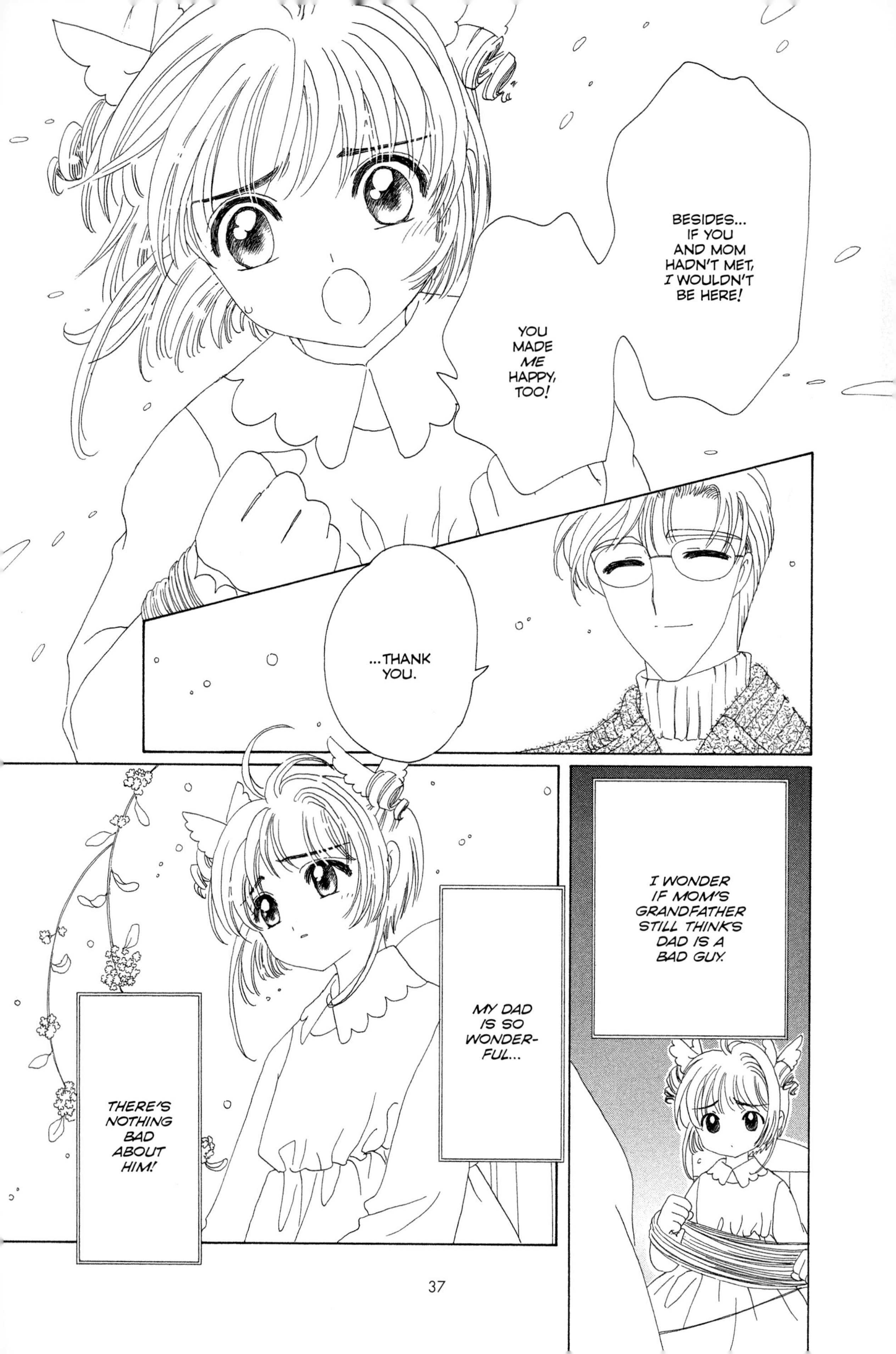
BESIDES... IF YOU AND MOM HADN'T MET, I WOULDN'T BE HERE!
YOU MADE ME HAPPY, TOO!
...THANK YOU.
I WONDER IF MOM'S GRANDFATHER STILL THINKS DAD IS A BAD GUY.
MY DAD IS SO WONDER-FUL...
THERE'S NOTHING BAD ABOUT HIM!

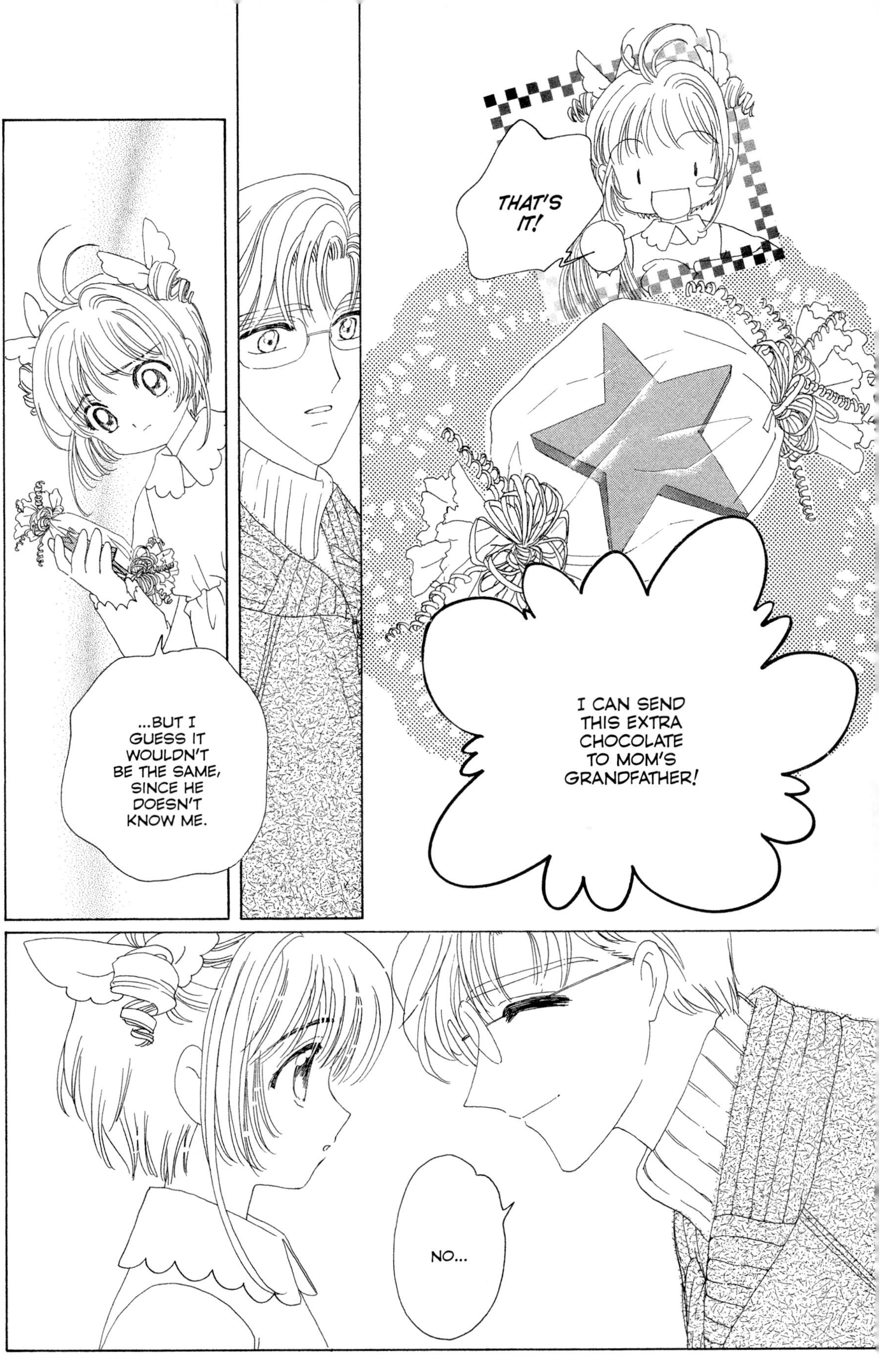
THAT'S IT!
I CAN SEND THIS EXTRA CHOCOLATE TO MOM'S GRANDFATHER!
...BUT I GUESS IT WOULDN'T BE THE SAME, SINCE HE DOESN'T KNOW ME.
NO...

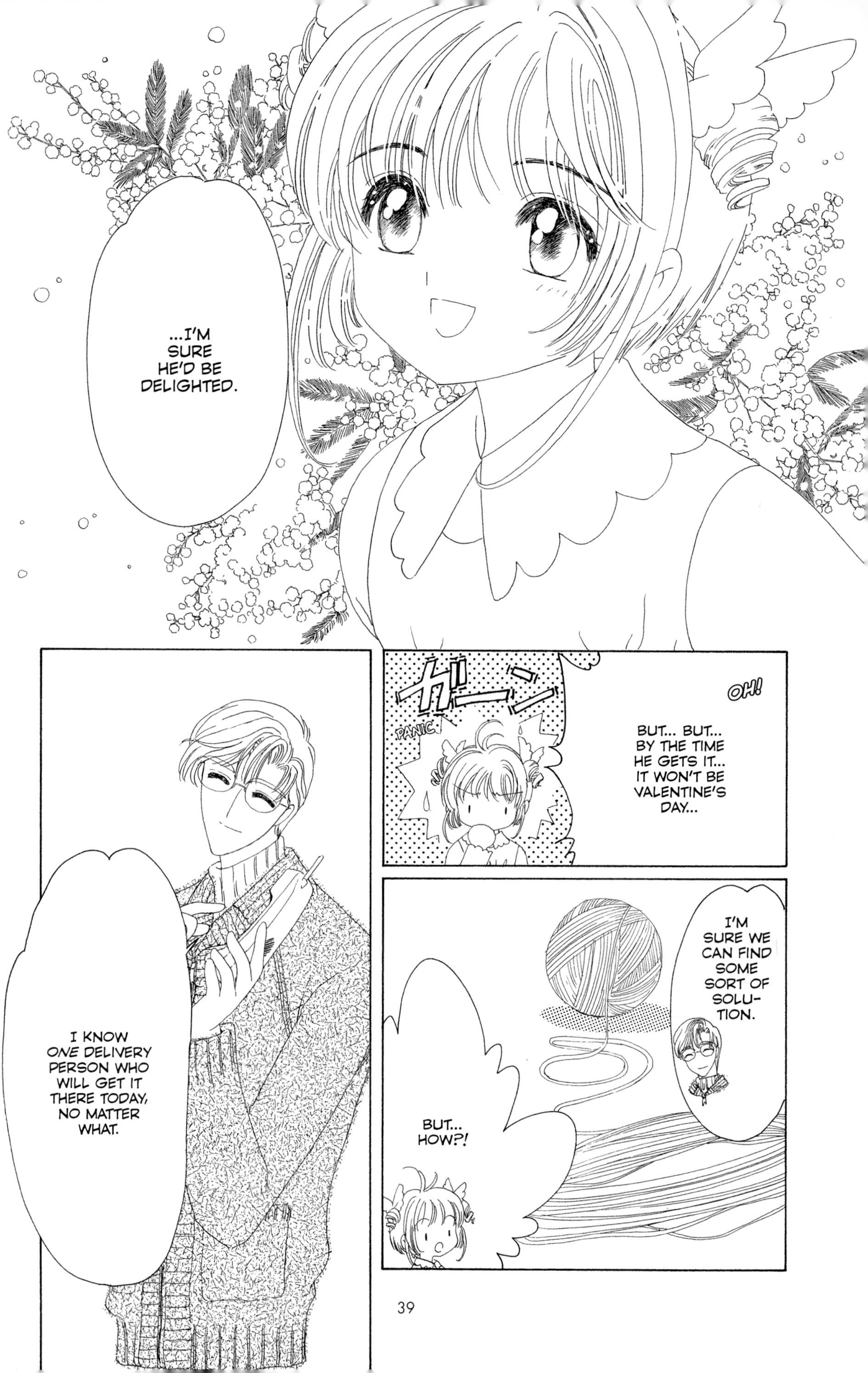
...I'M SURE HE'D BE DELIGHTED.
OH!
BUT... BUT... BY THE TIME HE GETS IT... IT WON'T BE VALENTINE'S DAY...
PANIC
I'M SURE WE CAN FIND SOME SORT OF SOLU-TION.
BUT... HOW?!
I KNOW *ONE* DELIVERY PERSON WHO WILL GET IT THERE TODAY, NO MATTER WHAT.

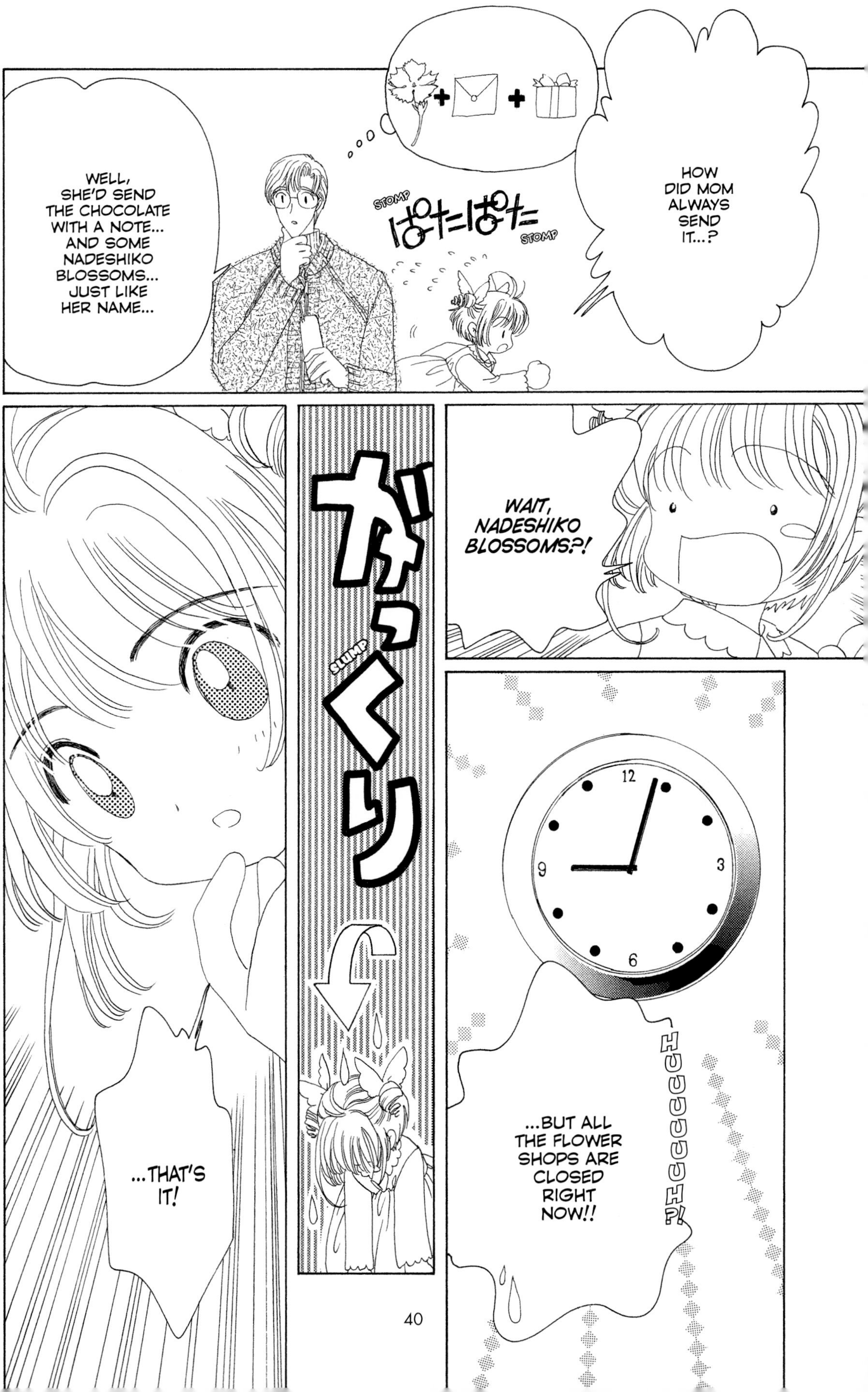
HOW DID MOM ALWAYS SEND IT...?
STOMP
ぱたぱた
STOMP
WELL, SHE'D SEND THE CHOCOLATE WITH A NOTE... AND SOME NADESHIKO BLOSSOMS... JUST LIKE HER NAME...
WAIT, NADESHIKO BLOSSOMS?!
...BUT ALL THE FLOWER SHOPS ARE CLOSED RIGHT NOW!!
HCCCCCCH?!
がっくり
SLUMP
...THAT'S IT!

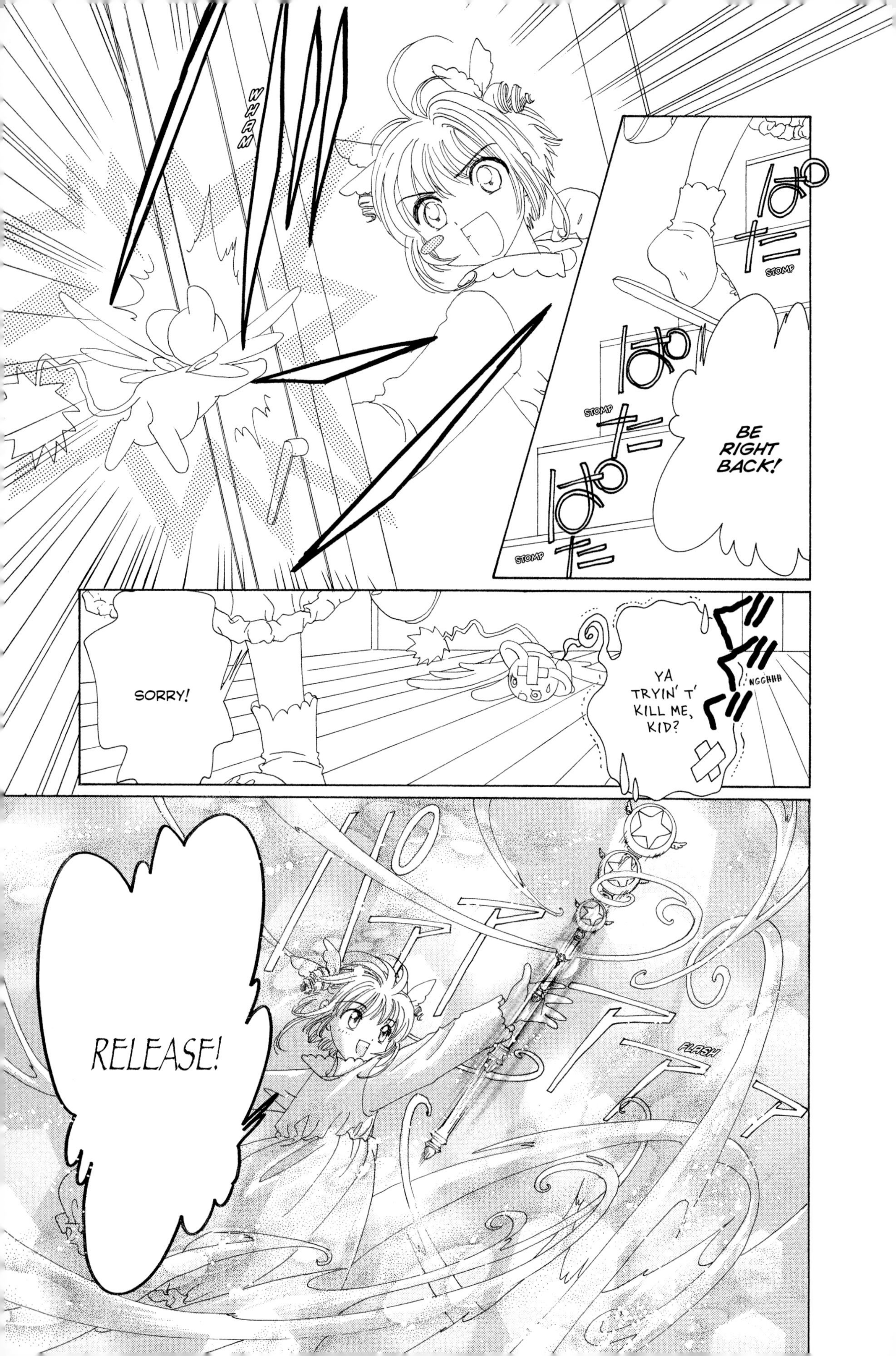
STOMP
STOMP
STOMP
BE RIGHT BACK!
WHRM
NGGHHH
YA TRYIN' T' KILL ME, KID?
SORRY!
FLASH
RELEASE!

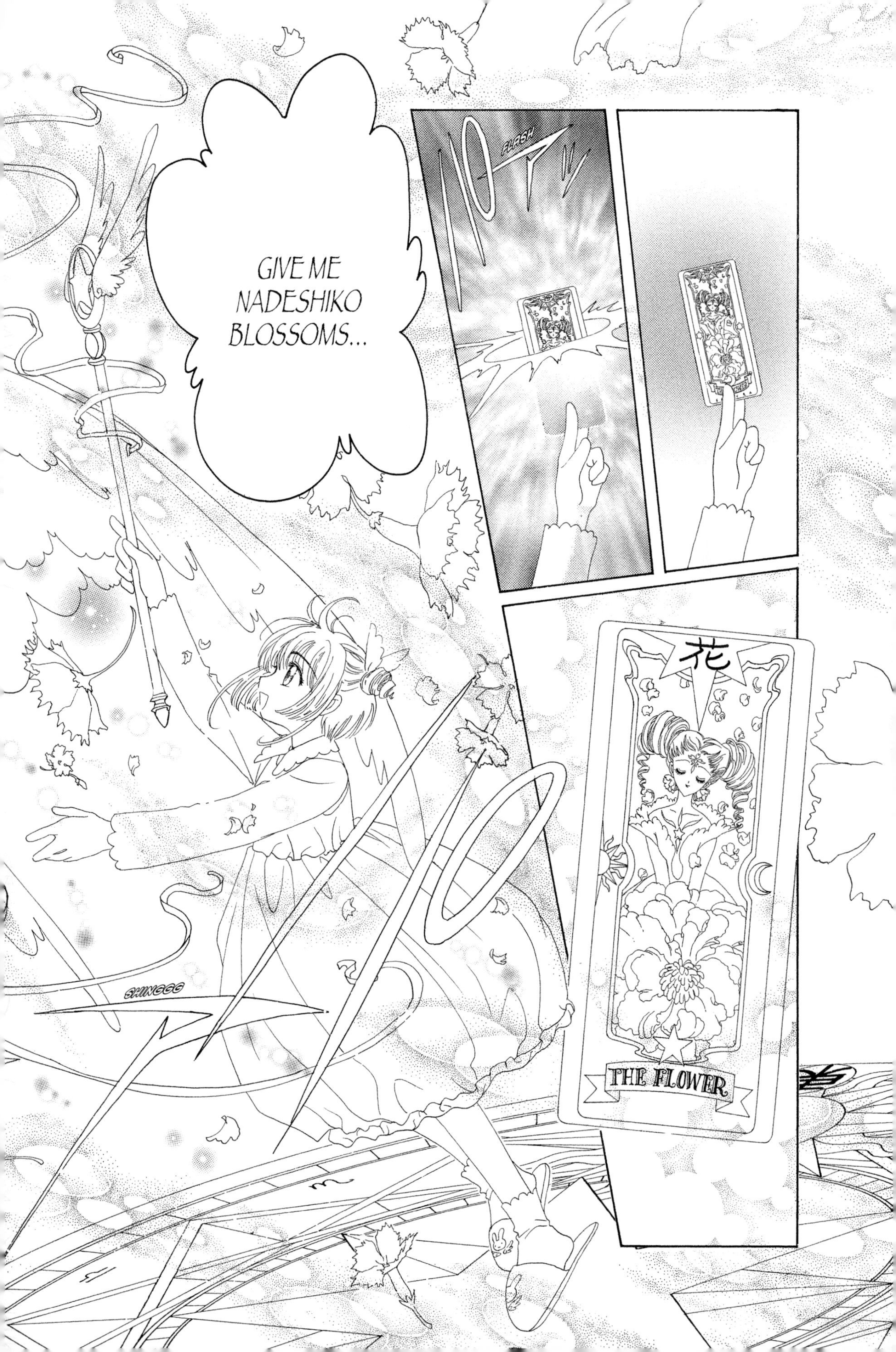
FLASH
花
THE FLOWER
GIVE ME NADESHIKO BLOSSOMS...
SHINGGG

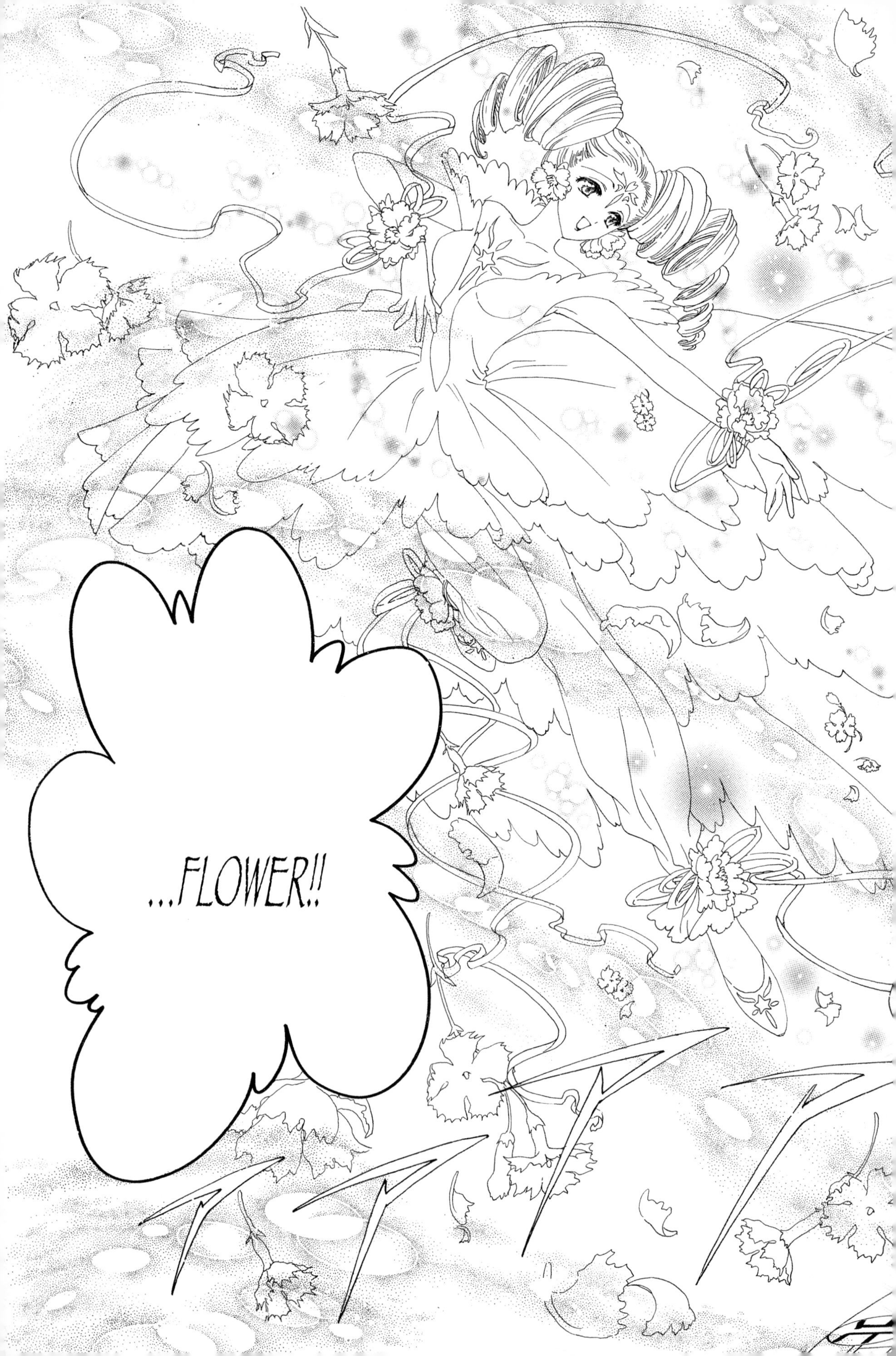
...FLOWER!!

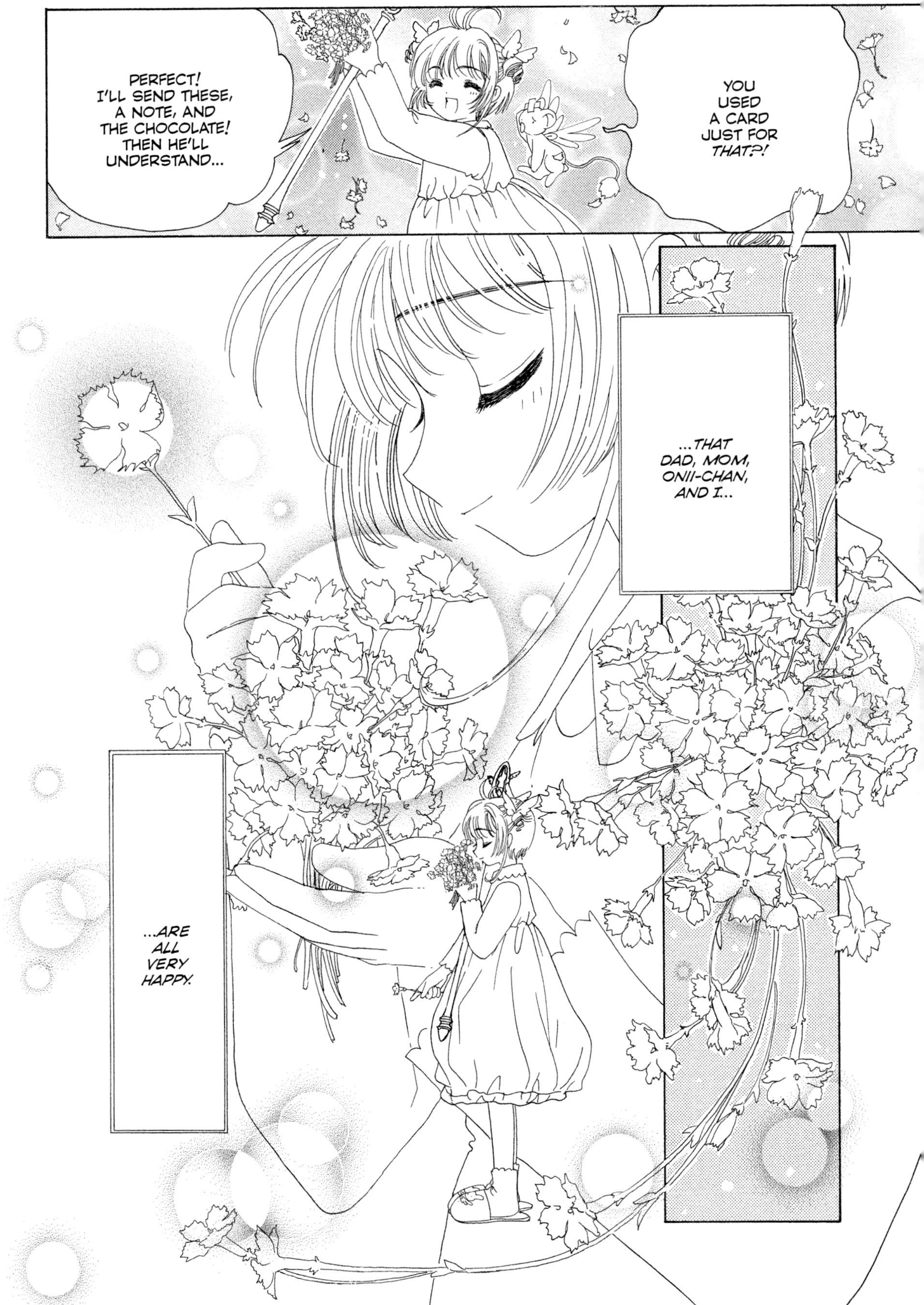
YOU USED A CARD JUST FOR THAT?!
PERFECT! I'LL SEND THESE, A NOTE, AND THE CHOCOLATE! THEN HE'LL UNDERSTAND...
...THAT DAD, MOM, ONII-CHAN, AND I...
...ARE ALL VERY HAPPY.

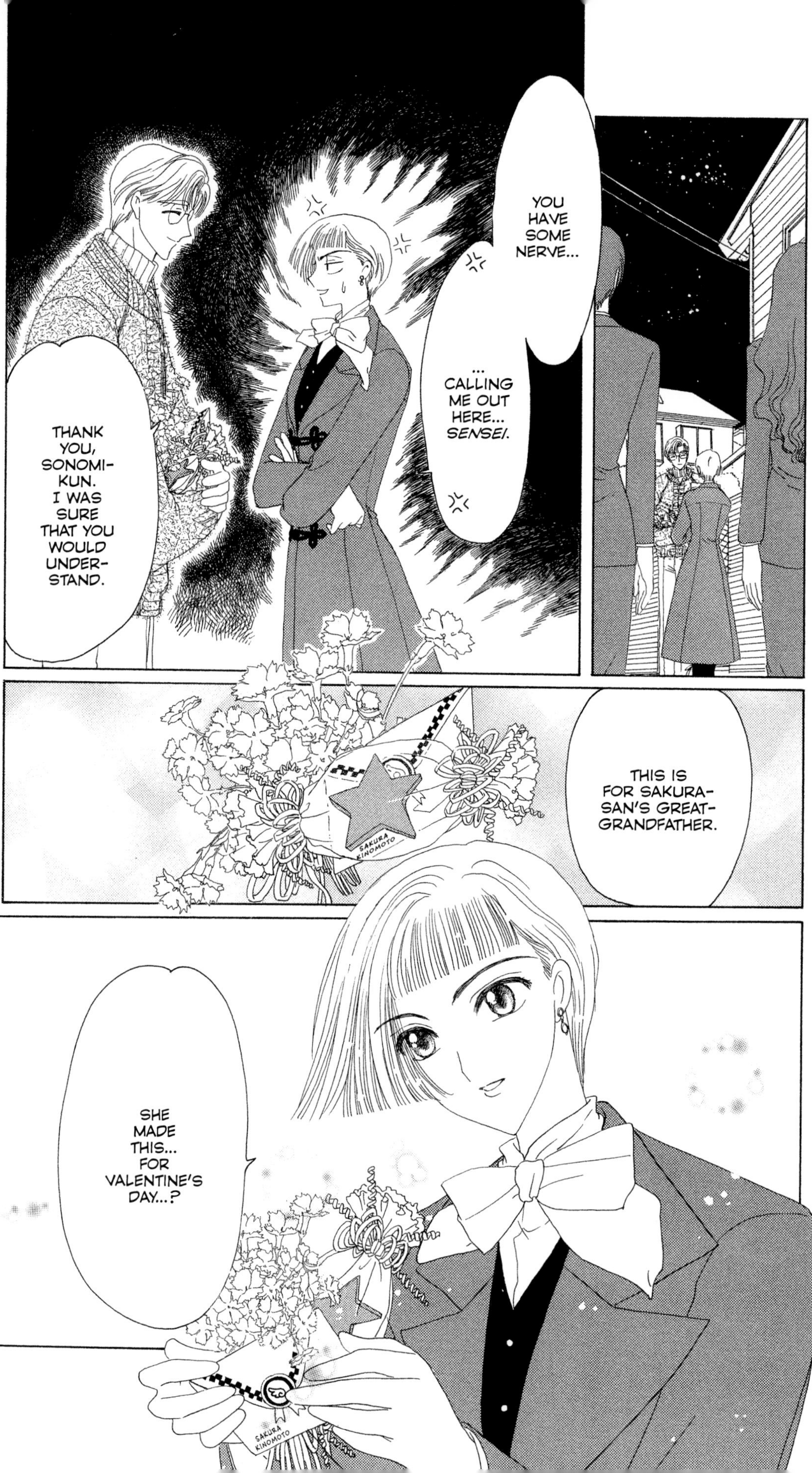
YOU HAVE SOME NERVE...
... CALLING ME OUT HERE... *SENSEI*.
THANK YOU, SONOMI-KUN. I WAS SURE THAT YOU WOULD UNDER-STAND.
THIS IS FOR SAKURA-SAN'S GREAT-GRANDFATHER.
SAKURA KINOMOTO
SHE MADE THIS... FOR VALENTINE'S DAY...?
SAKURA KINOMOTO

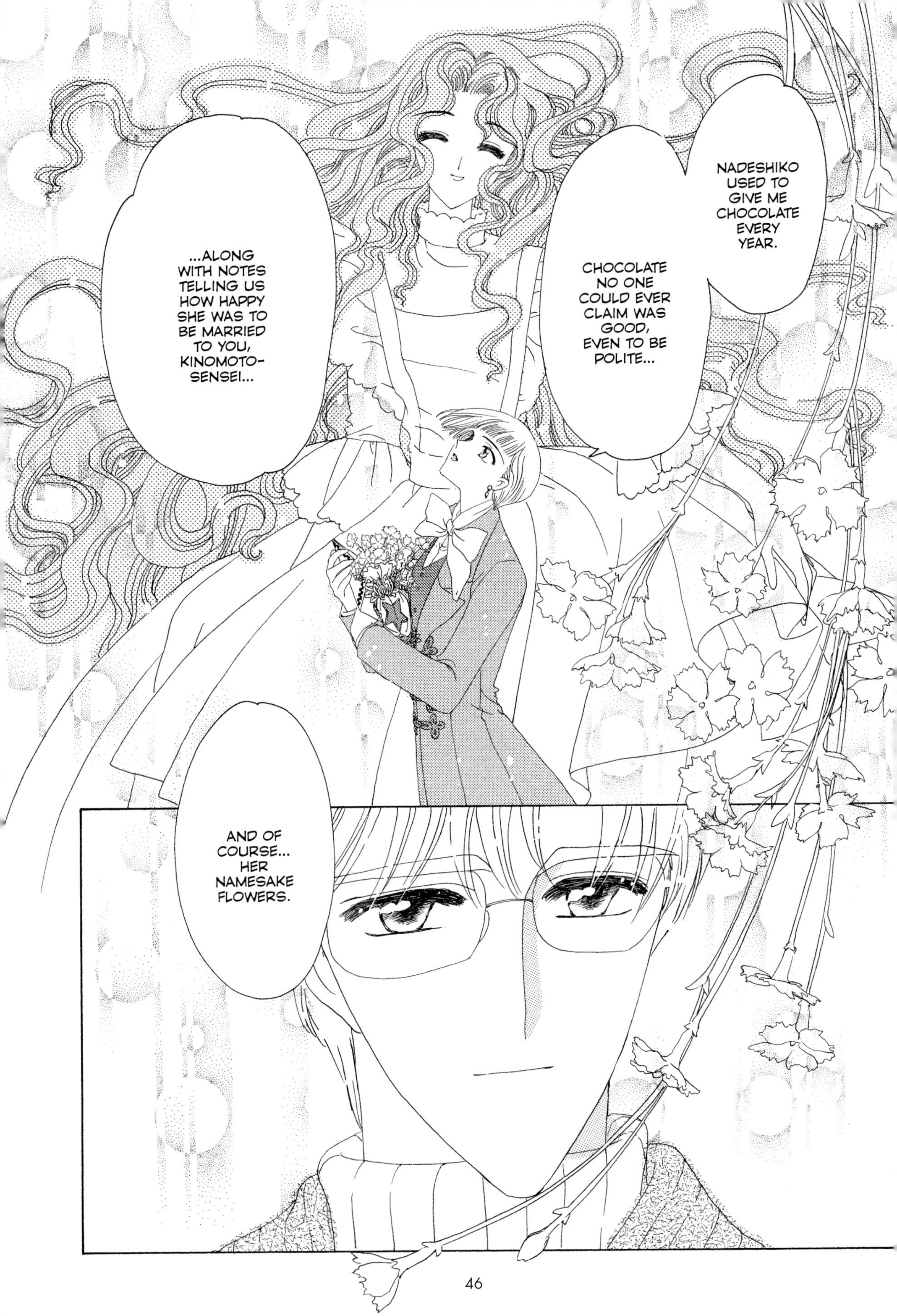
NADESHIKO USED TO GIVE ME CHOCOLATE EVERY YEAR.
CHOCOLATE NO ONE COULD EVER CLAIM WAS GOOD, EVEN TO BE POLITE...
...ALONG WITH NOTES TELLING US HOW HAPPY SHE WAS TO BE MARRIED TO YOU, KINOMOTO-SENSEI...
AND OF COURSE... HER NAMESAKE FLOWERS.

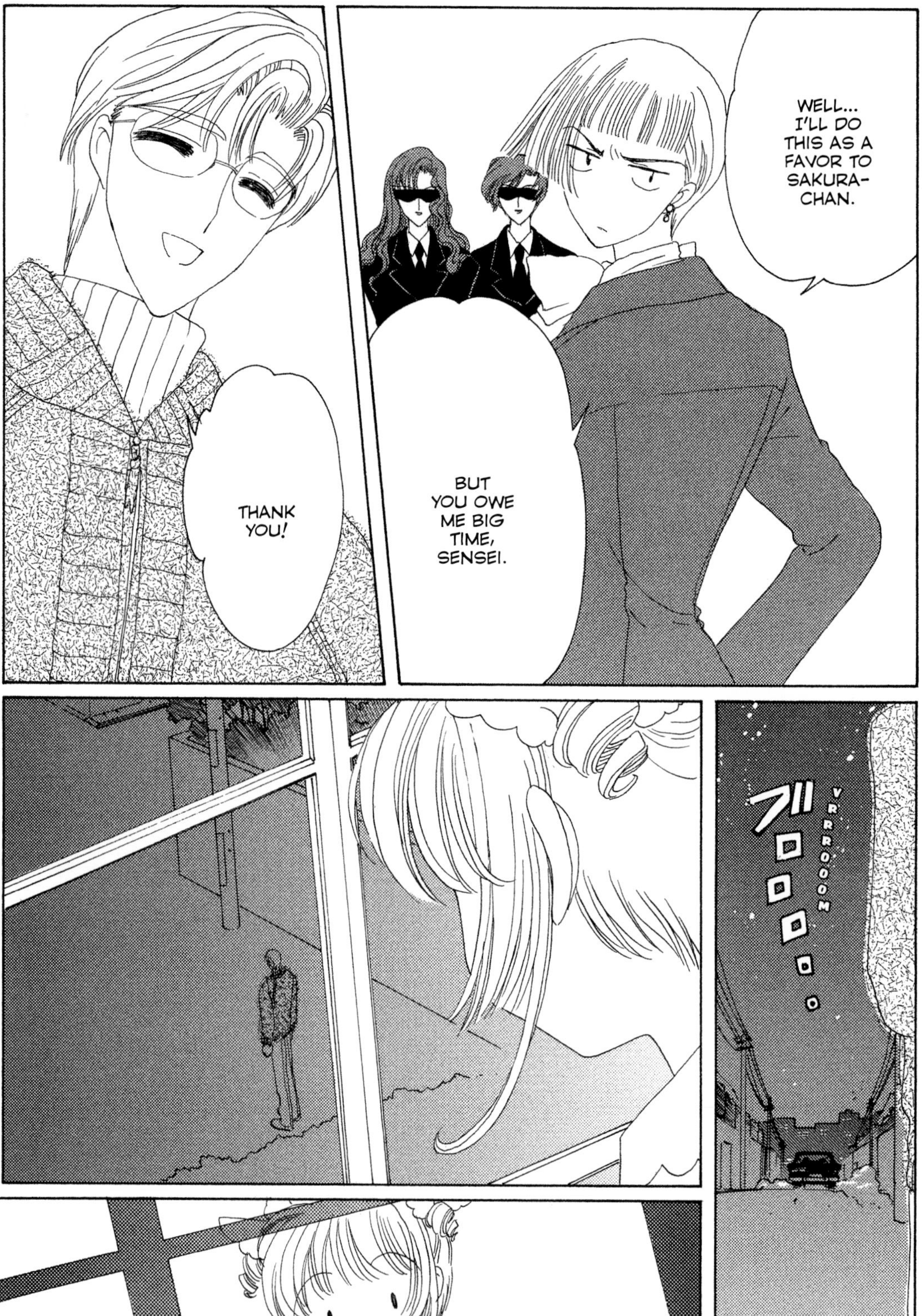
WELL... I'LL DO THIS AS A FAVOR TO SAKURA-CHAN.
BUT YOU OWE ME BIG TIME, SENSEI.
THANK YOU!
VRRROOOM

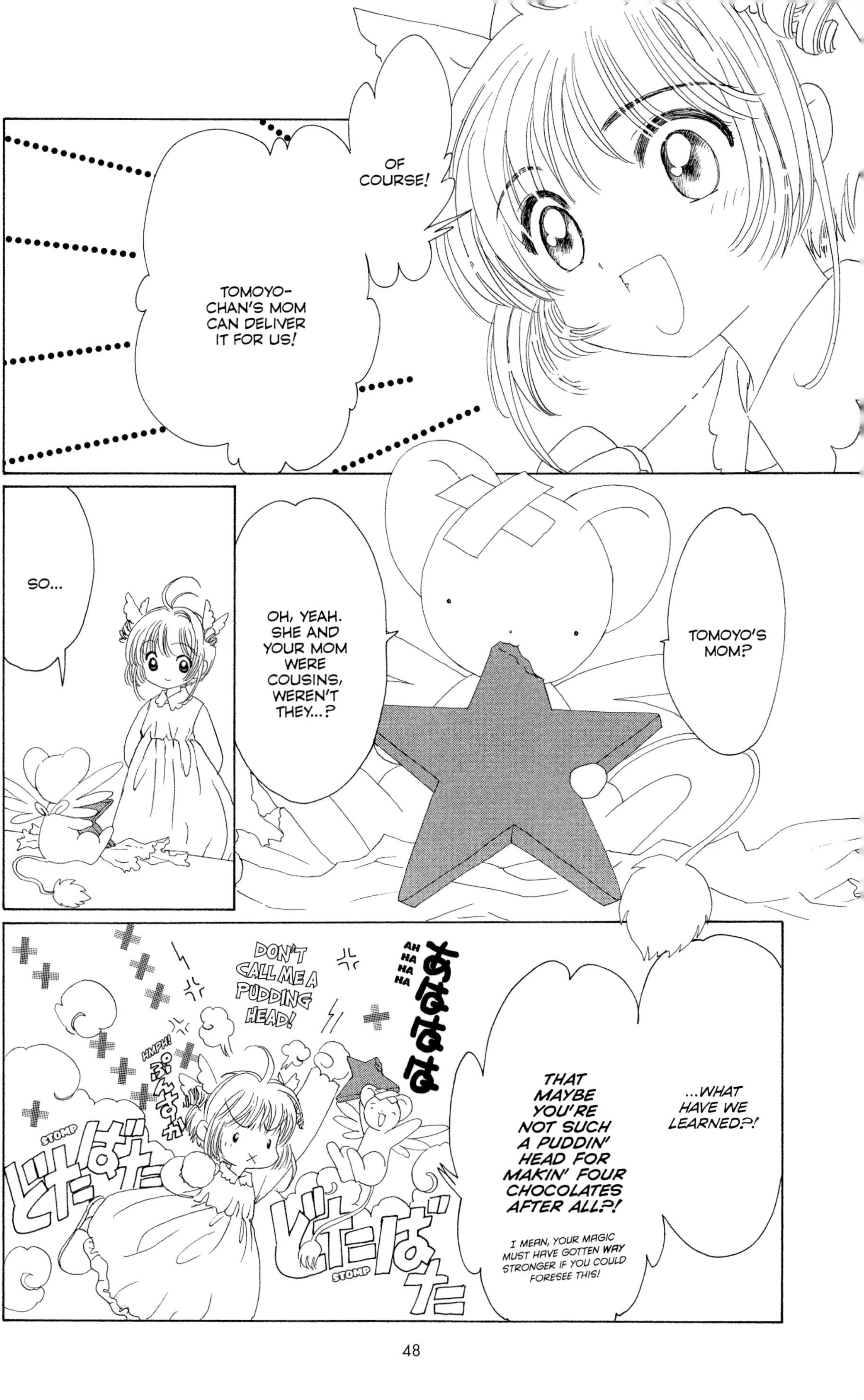
OF COURSE!
TOMOYO-CHAN'S MOM CAN DELIVER IT FOR US!
TOMOYO'S MOM?
OH, YEAH. SHE AND YOUR MOM WERE COUSINS, WEREN'T THEY...?
SO...
...WHAT HAVE WE LEARNED?!
THAT MAYBE YOU'RE NOT SUCH A PUDDIN' HEAD FOR MAKIN' FOUR CHOCOLATES AFTER ALL?!
I MEAN, YOUR MAGIC MUST HAVE GOTTEN WAY STRONGER IF YOU COULD FORESEE THIS!
あははは
AH HA HA HA
DON'T CALL ME A PUDDING HEAD!
ぷんすか
HMPH!
どたばた
STOMP
どたばた
STOMP

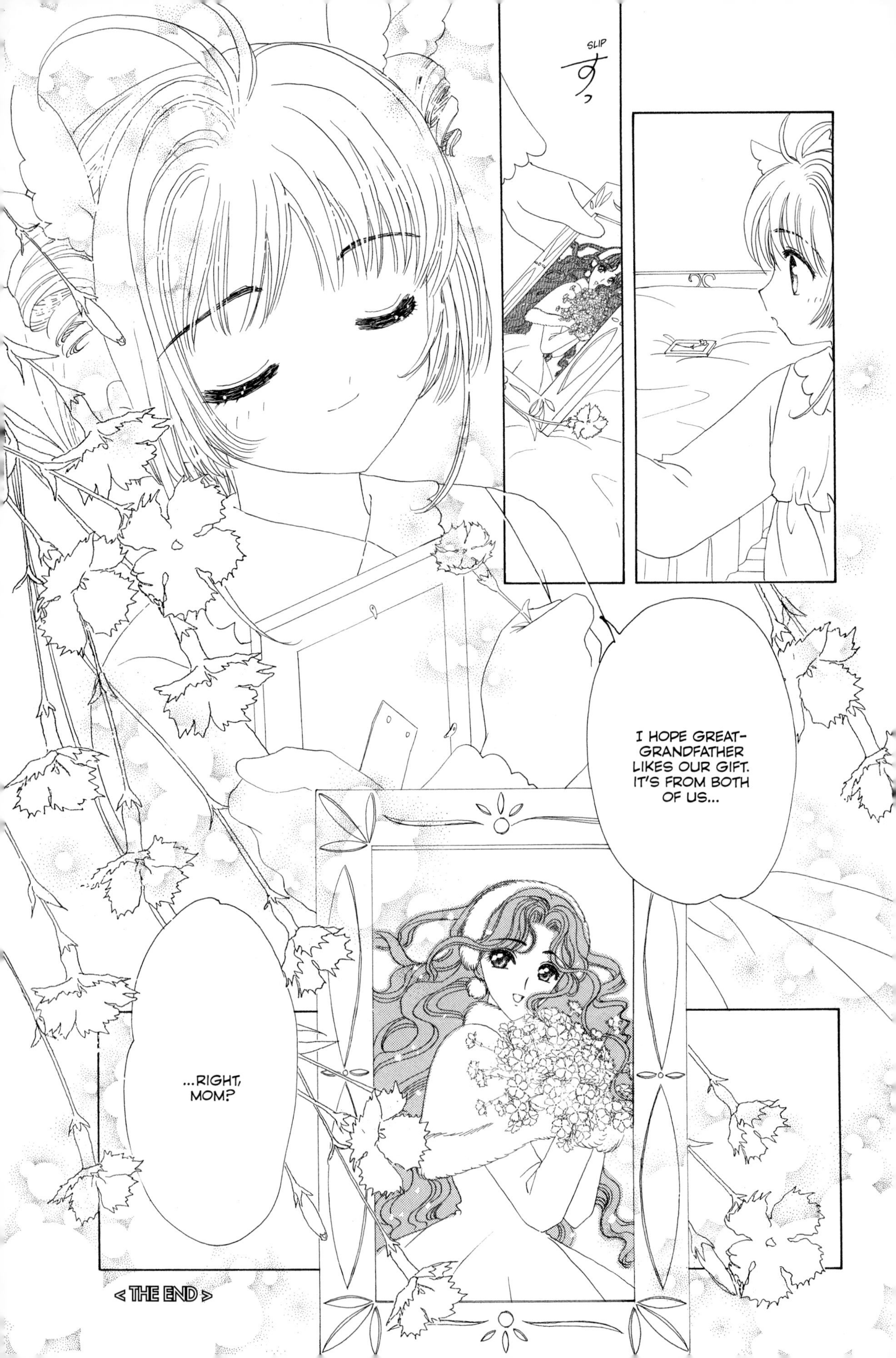
SLIP
すっ
I HOPE GREAT-GRANDFATHER LIKES OUR GIFT. IT'S FROM BOTH OF US...
...RIGHT, MOM?
< THE END >

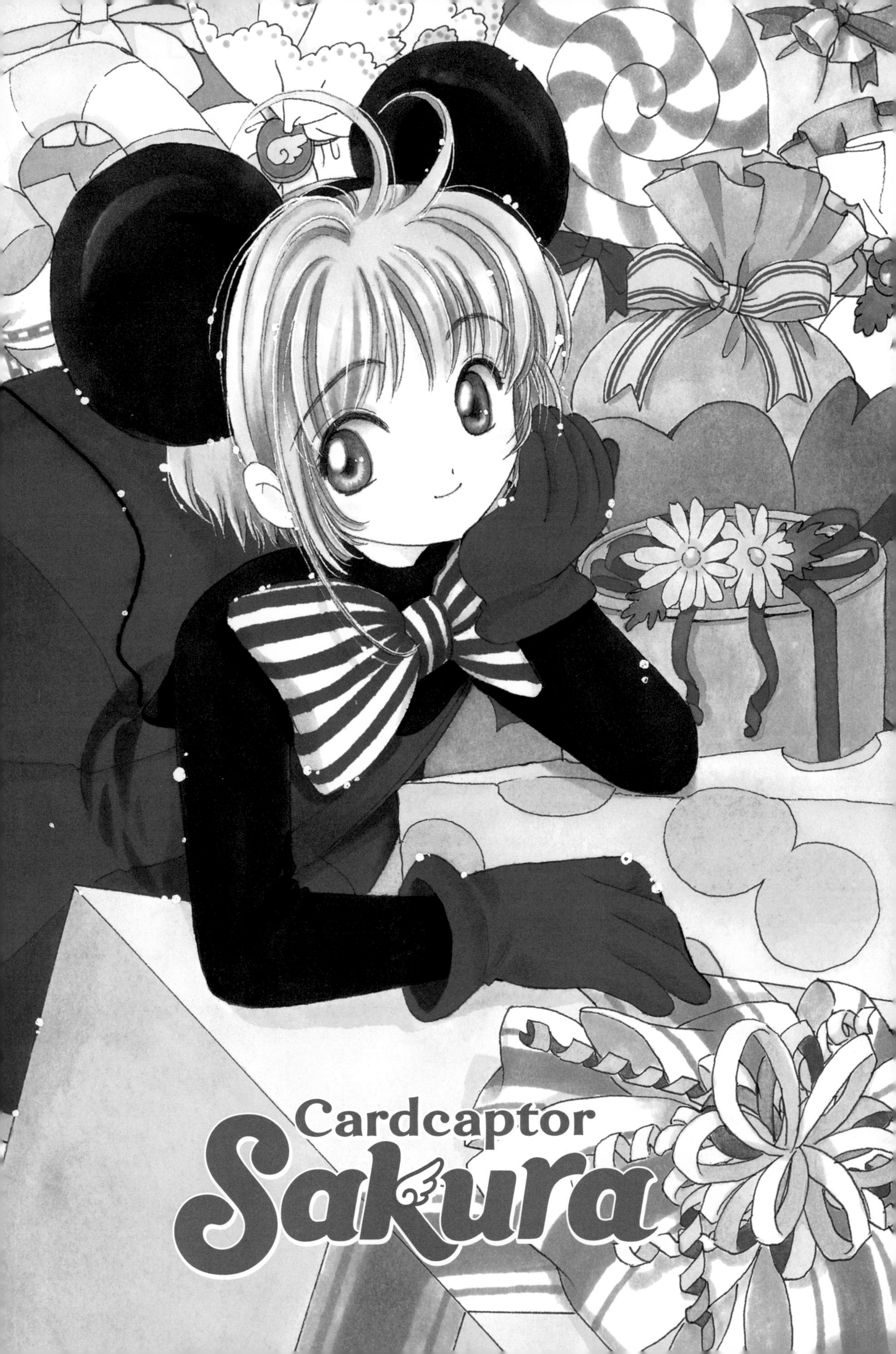
Cardcaptor
Sakura

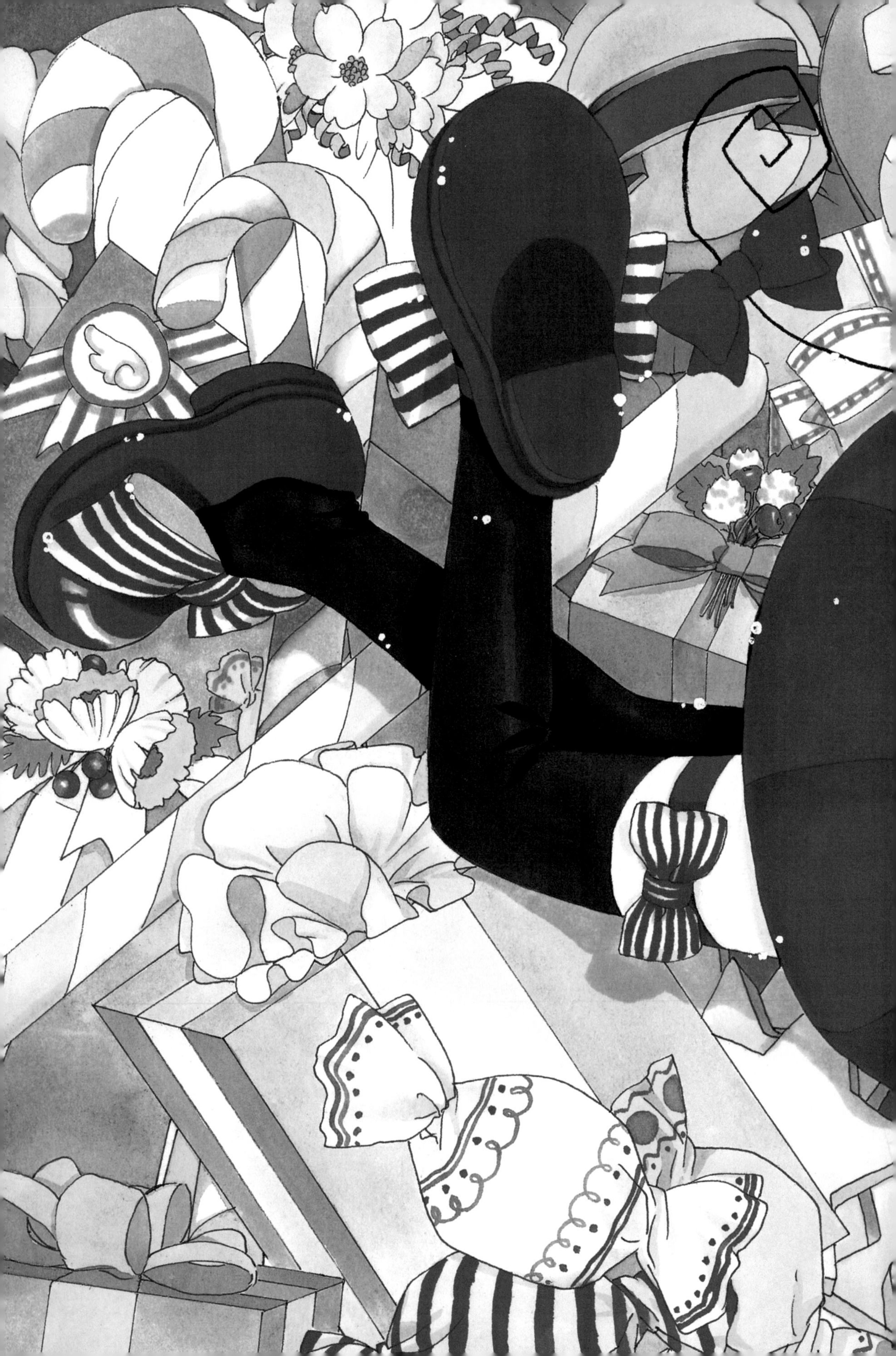

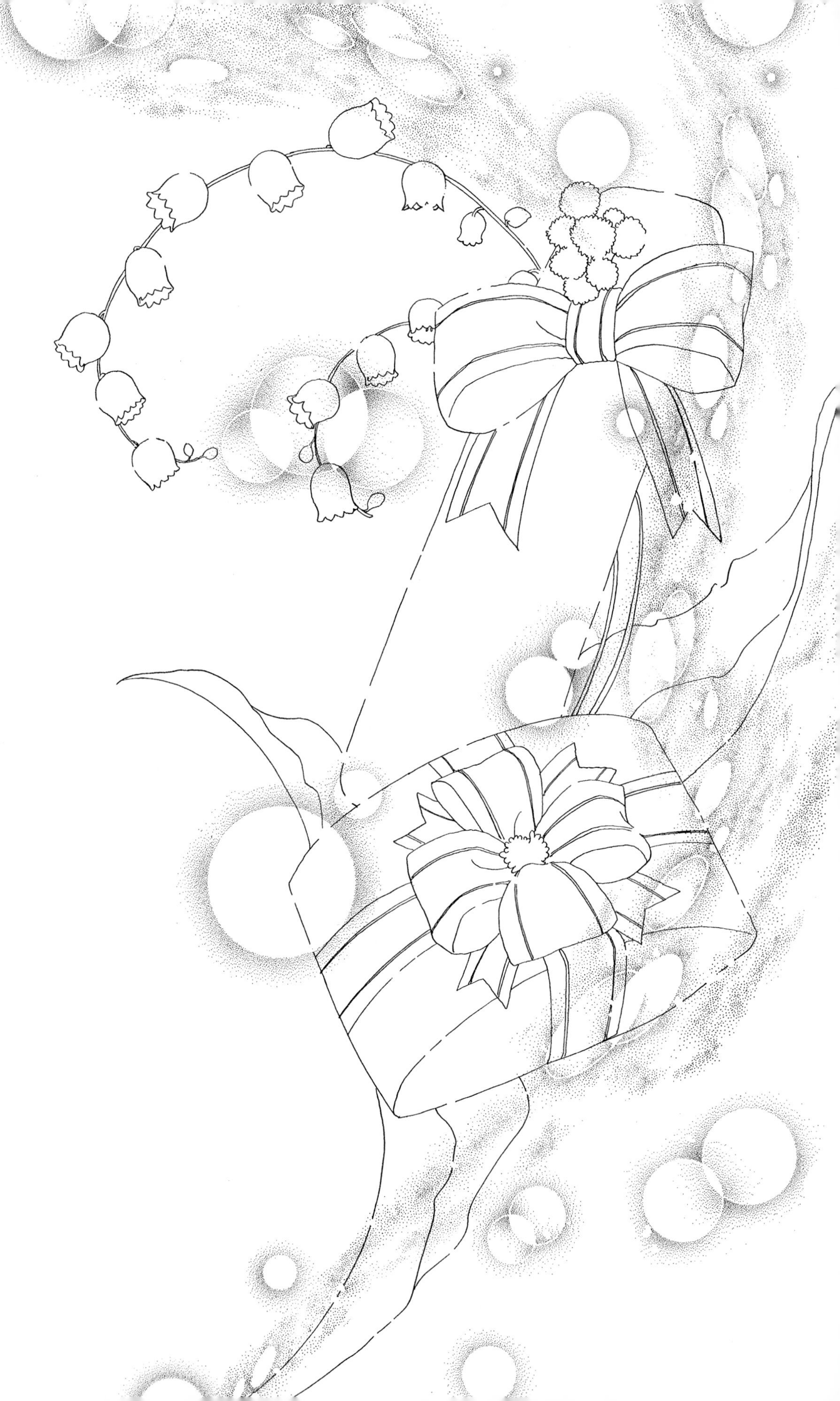

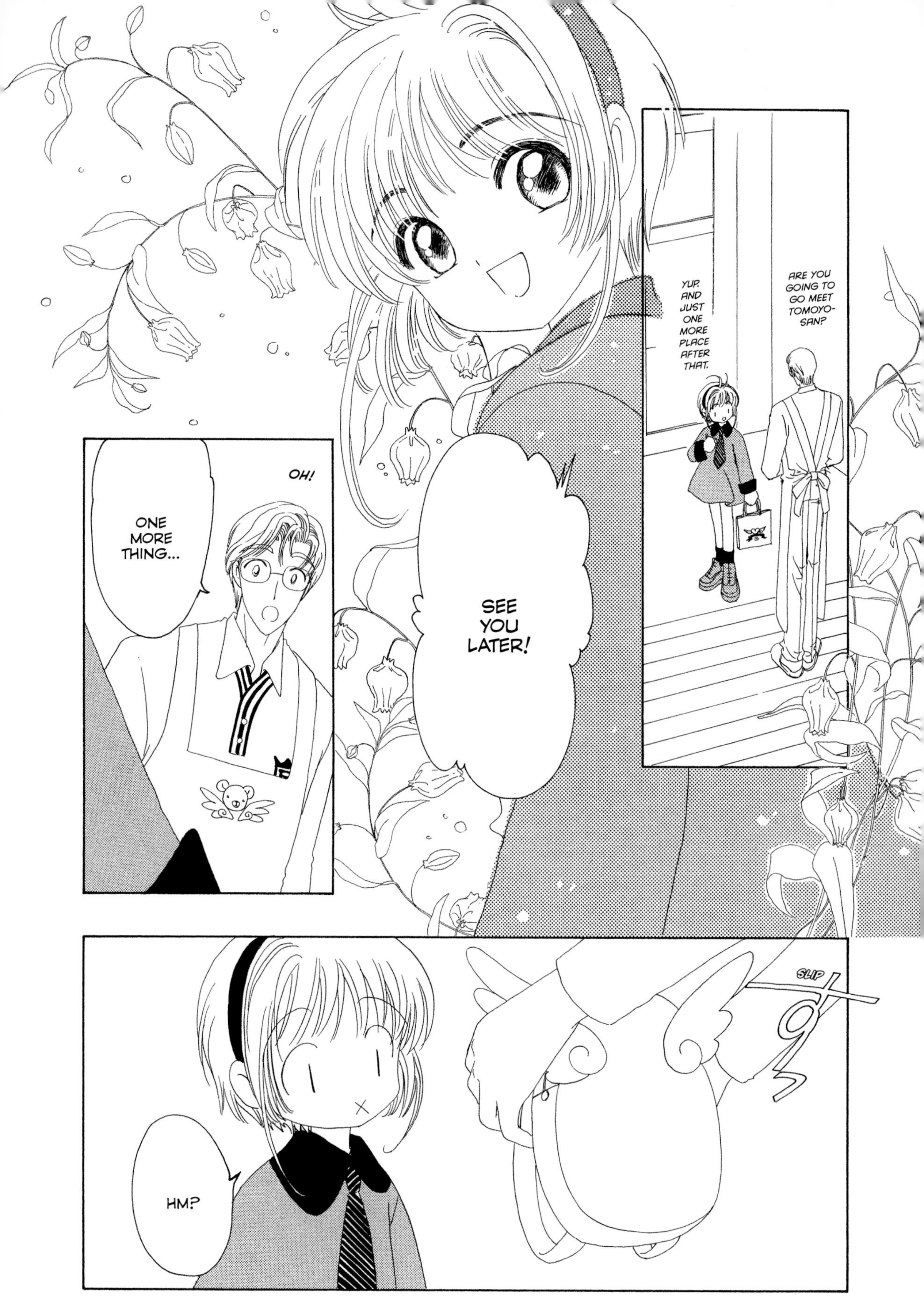
ARE YOU GOING TO MEET TOMOYO-SAN?
YUP. AND JUST ONE MORE PLACE AFTER THAT.
SEE YOU LATER!
OH!
ONE MORE THING...
SLIP
HM?

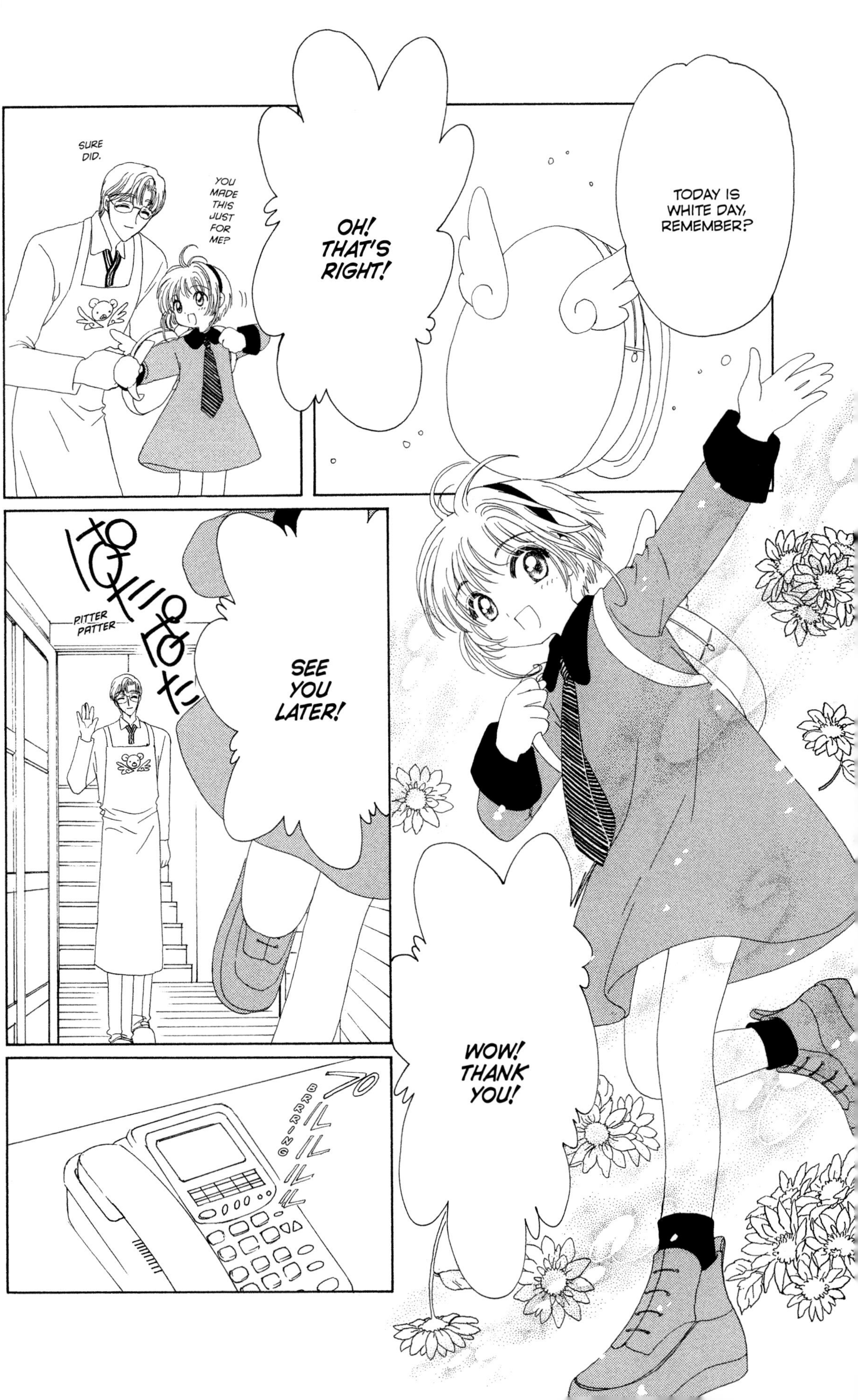
TODAY IS WHITE DAY, REMEMBER?
OH! THAT'S RIGHT!
YOU MADE THIS JUST FOR ME?
SURE DID.
WOW! THANK YOU!
SEE YOU LATER!
PITTER PATTER
BRRRING

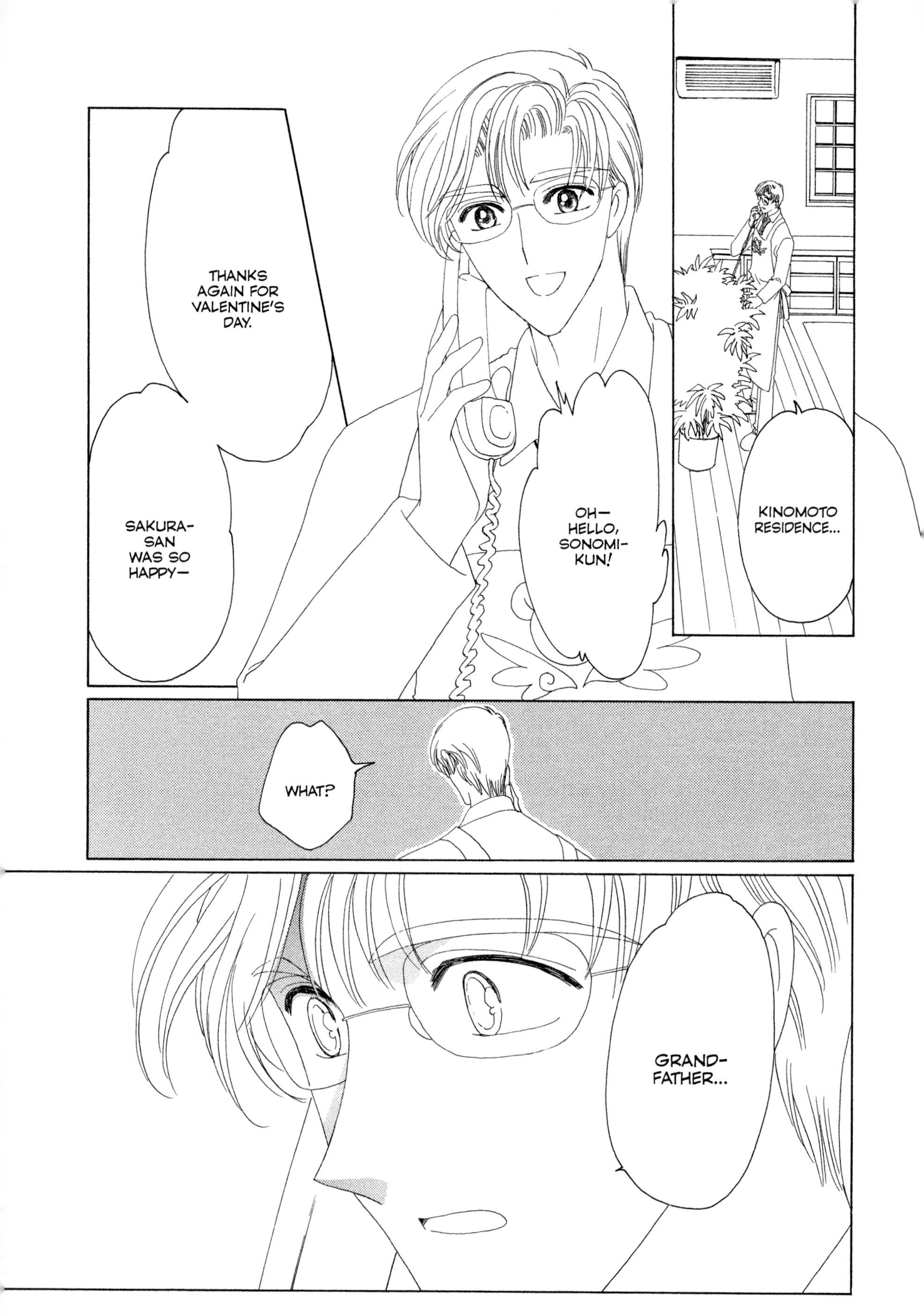
KINOMOTO RESIDENCE...
OH— HELLO, SONOMI-KUN!
THANKS AGAIN FOR VALENTINE'S DAY.
SAKURA-SAN WAS SO HAPPY—
WHAT?
GRAND-FATHER...

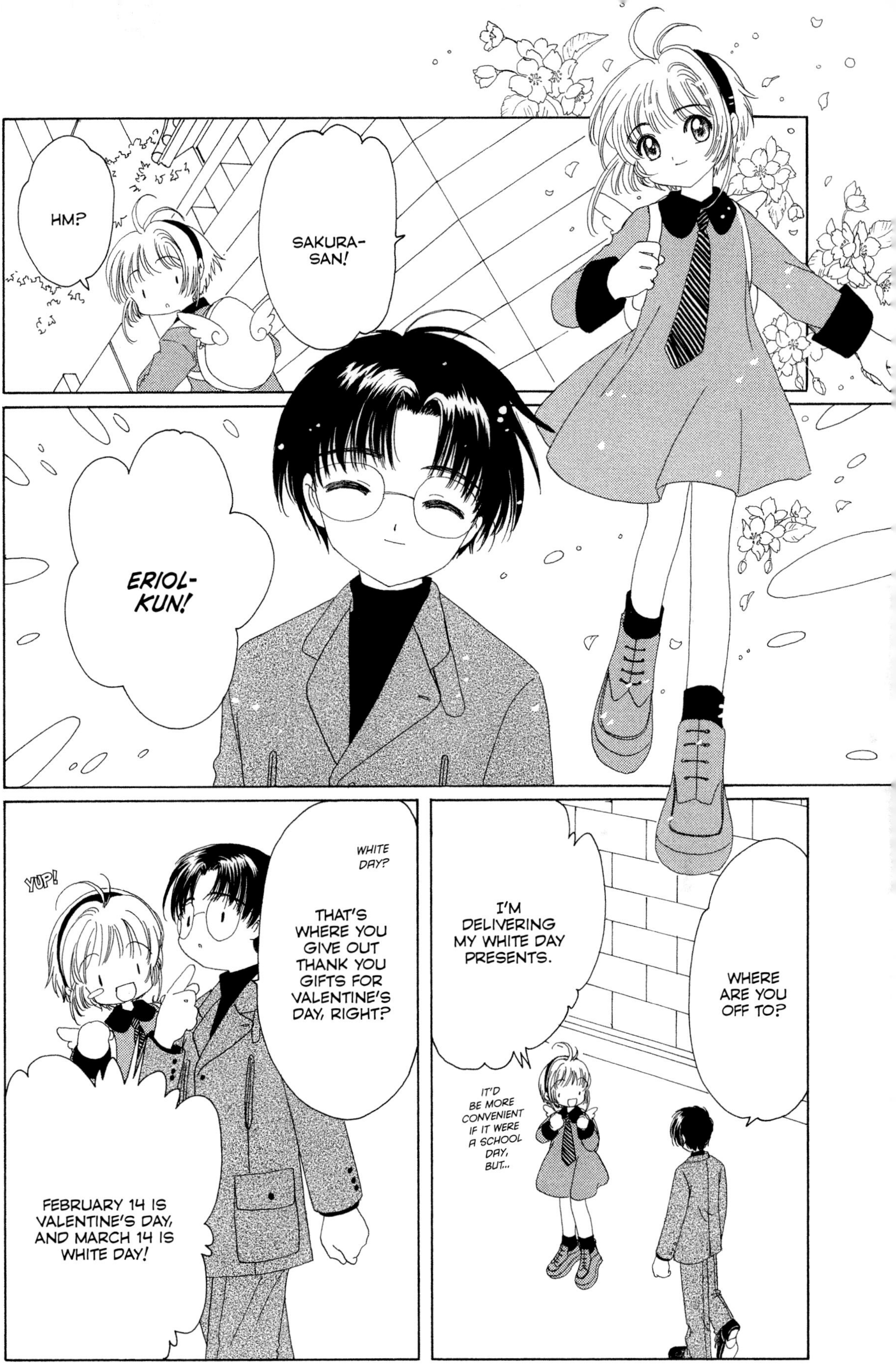
SAKURA-SAN!
HM?
ERIOL-KUN!
WHERE ARE YOU OFF TO?
I'M DELIVERING MY WHITE DAY PRESENTS.
IT'D BE MORE CONVENIENT IF IT WERE A SCHOOL DAY, BUT...
WHITE DAY?
THAT'S WHERE YOU GIVE OUT THANK YOU GIFTS FOR VALENTINE'S DAY, RIGHT?
YUP!
FEBRUARY 14 IS VALENTINE'S DAY, AND MARCH 14 IS WHITE DAY!

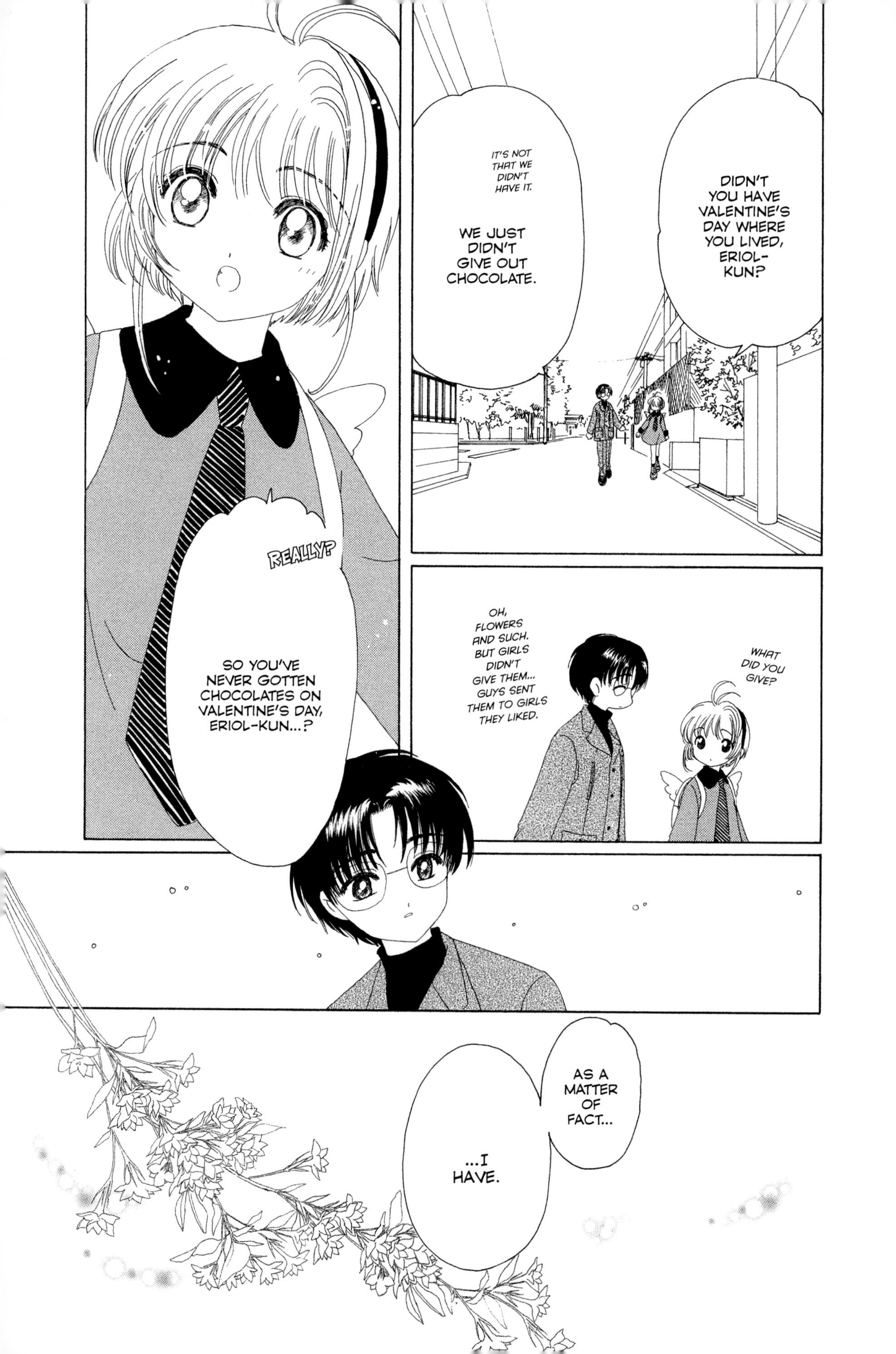
DIDN'T YOU HAVE VALENTINE'S DAY WHERE YOU LIVED, ERIOL-KUN?
IT'S NOT THAT WE DIDN'T HAVE IT.
WE JUST DIDN'T GIVE OUT CHOCOLATE.
WHAT DID YOU GIVE?
OH, FLOWERS AND SUCH. BUT GIRLS DIDN'T GIVE THEM... GUYS SENT THEM TO GIRLS THEY LIKED.
REALLY?
SO YOU'VE NEVER GOTTEN CHOCOLATES ON VALENTINE'S DAY, ERIOL-KUN...?
AS A MATTER OF FACT...
...I HAVE.

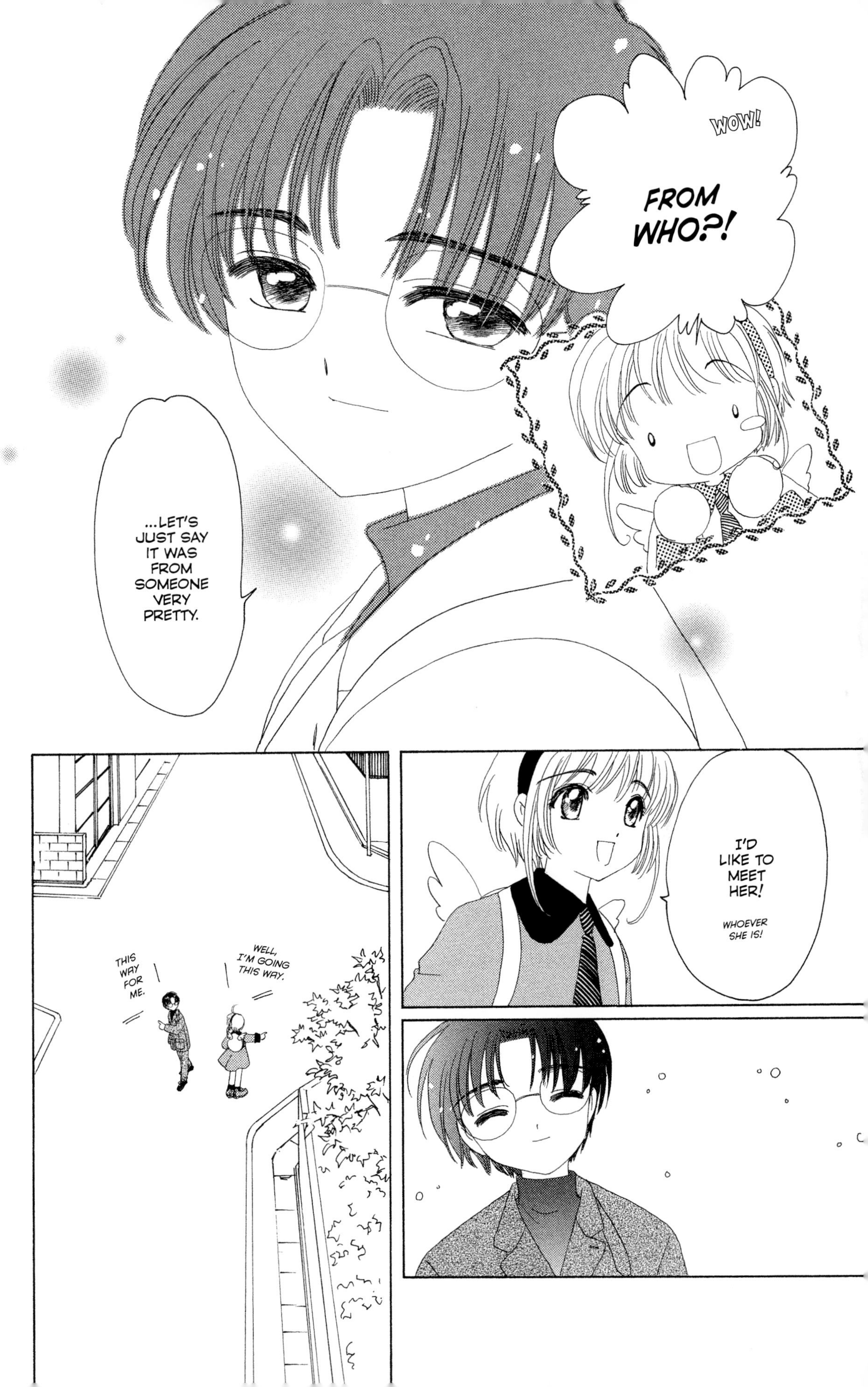

WOW!
FROM WHO?!
...LET'S JUST SAY IT WAS FROM SOMEONE VERY PRETTY.
I'D LIKE TO MEET HER!
WHOEVER SHE IS!
WELL, I'M GOING THIS WAY.
THIS WAY FOR ME.

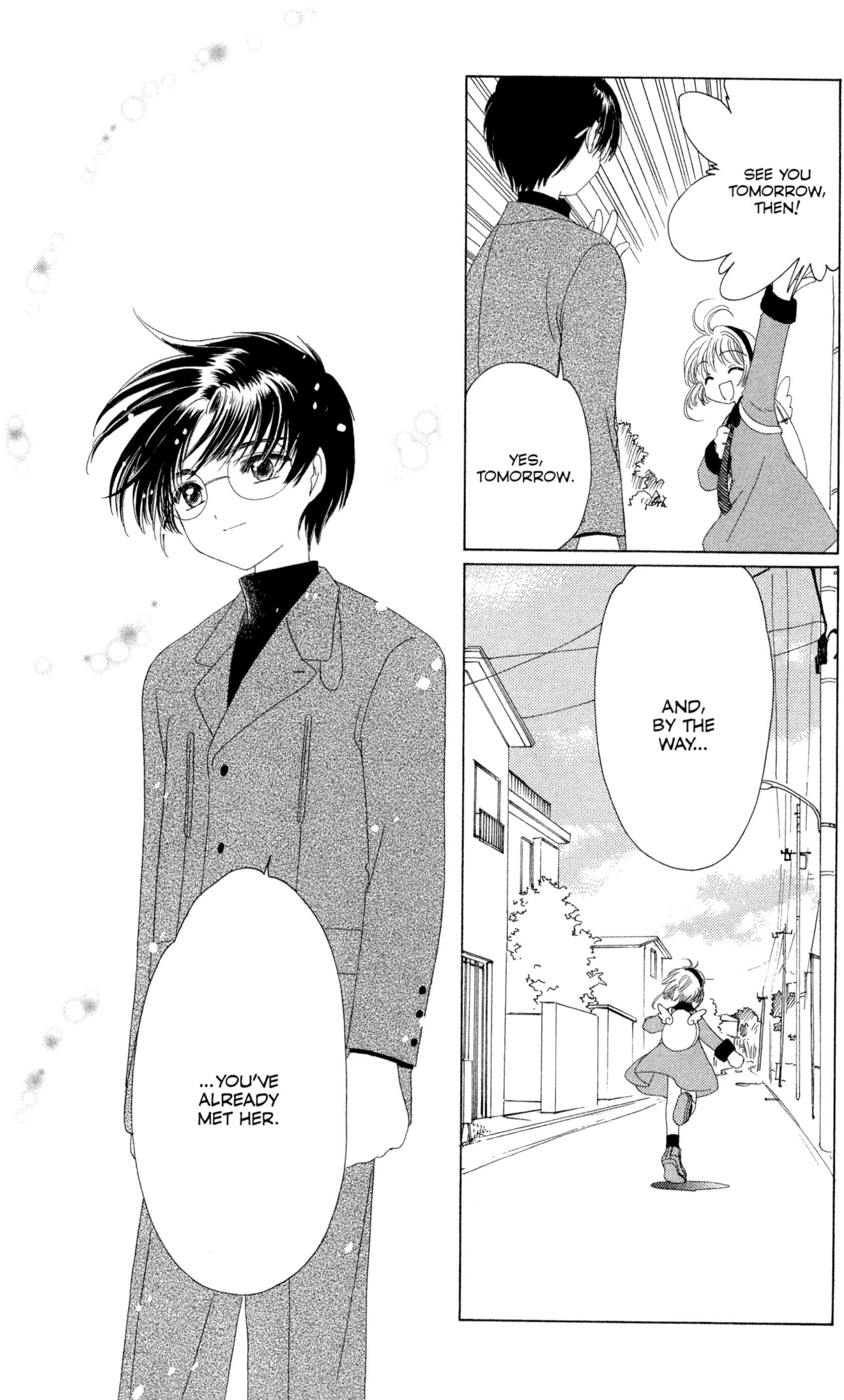
SEE YOU TOMORROW, THEN!
YES, TOMORROW.
AND, BY THE WAY...
...YOU'VE ALREADY MET HER.

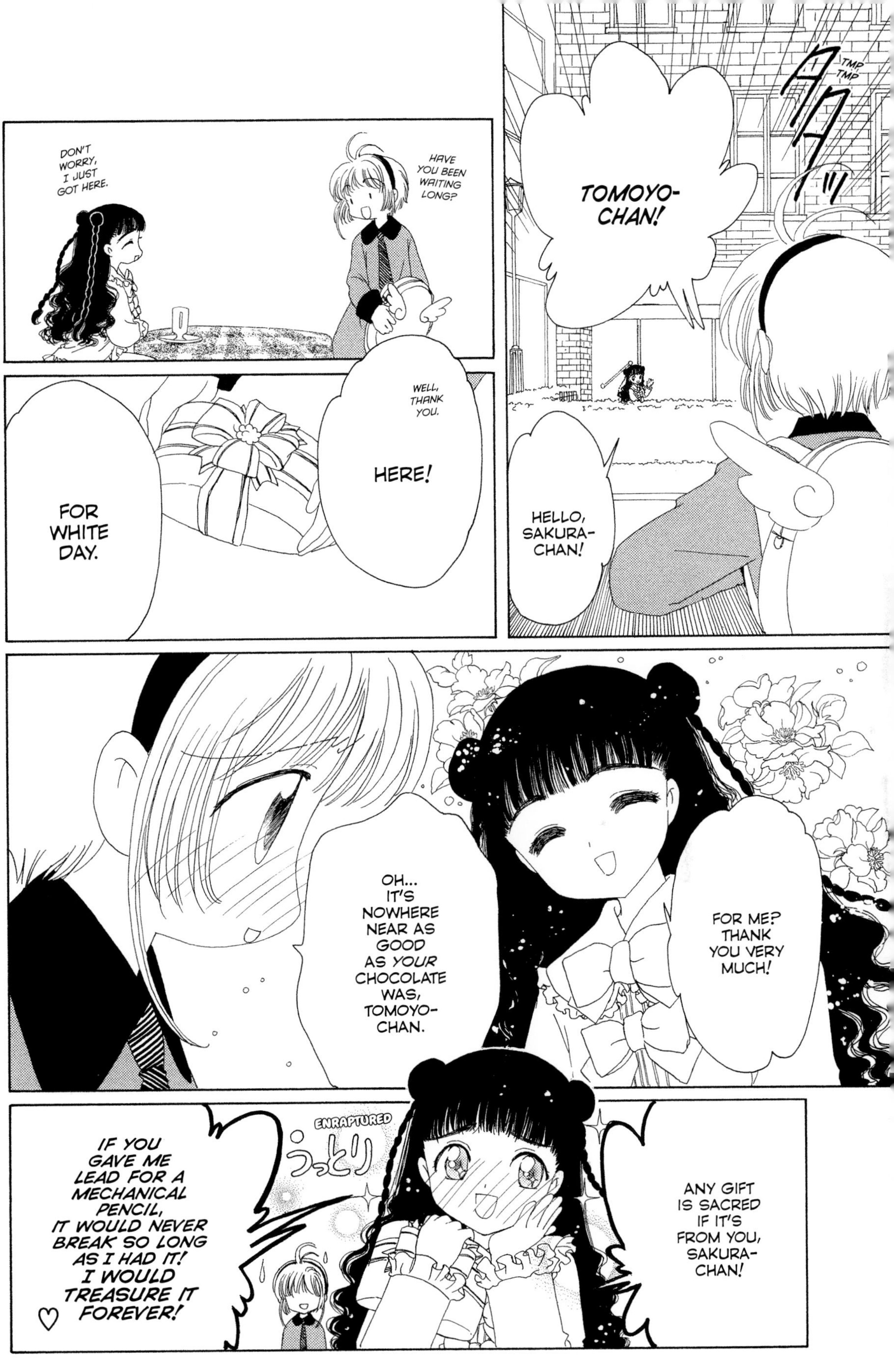
TMP TMP
タタッ
TOMOYO-CHAN!
HELLO, SAKURA-CHAN!
HAVE YOU BEEN WAITING LONG?
DON'T WORRY, I JUST GOT HERE.
WELL, THANK YOU.
HERE!
FOR WHITE DAY.
FOR ME? THANK YOU VERY MUCH!
OH... IT'S NOWHERE NEAR AS GOOD AS *YOUR* CHOCOLATE WAS, TOMOYO-CHAN.
ANY GIFT IS SACRED IF IT'S FROM YOU, SAKURA-CHAN!
ENRAPTURED
うっとり
IF YOU GAVE ME LEAD FOR A MECHANICAL PENCIL, IT WOULD NEVER BREAK SO LONG AS I HAD IT! I WOULD TREASURE IT FOREVER! ♡

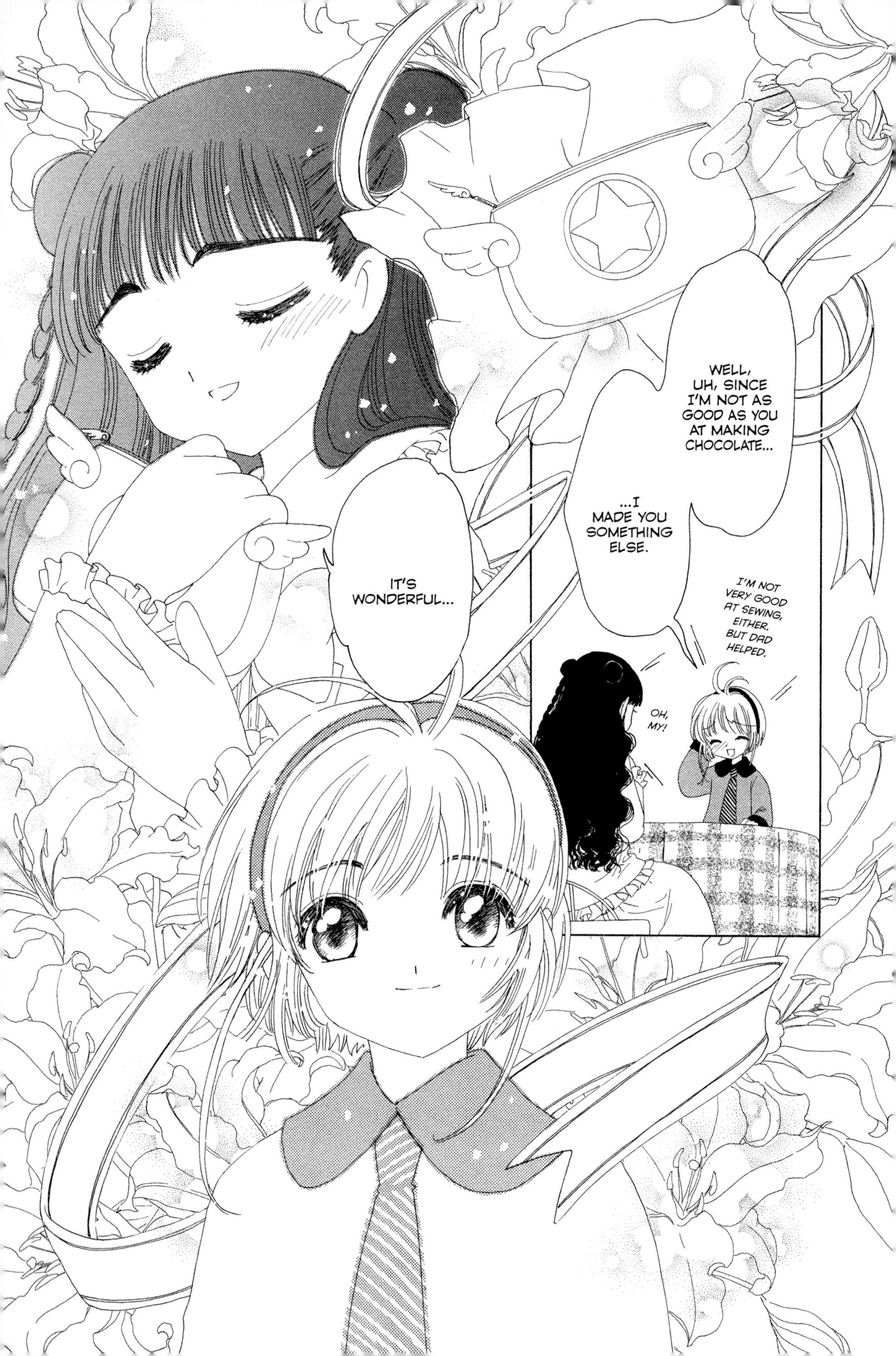
WELL, UH, SINCE I'M NOT AS GOOD AS YOU AT MAKING CHOCOLATE...
...I MADE YOU SOMETHING ELSE.
I'M NOT VERY GOOD AT SEWING, EITHER. BUT DAD HELPED.
OH, MY!
IT'S WONDERFUL...

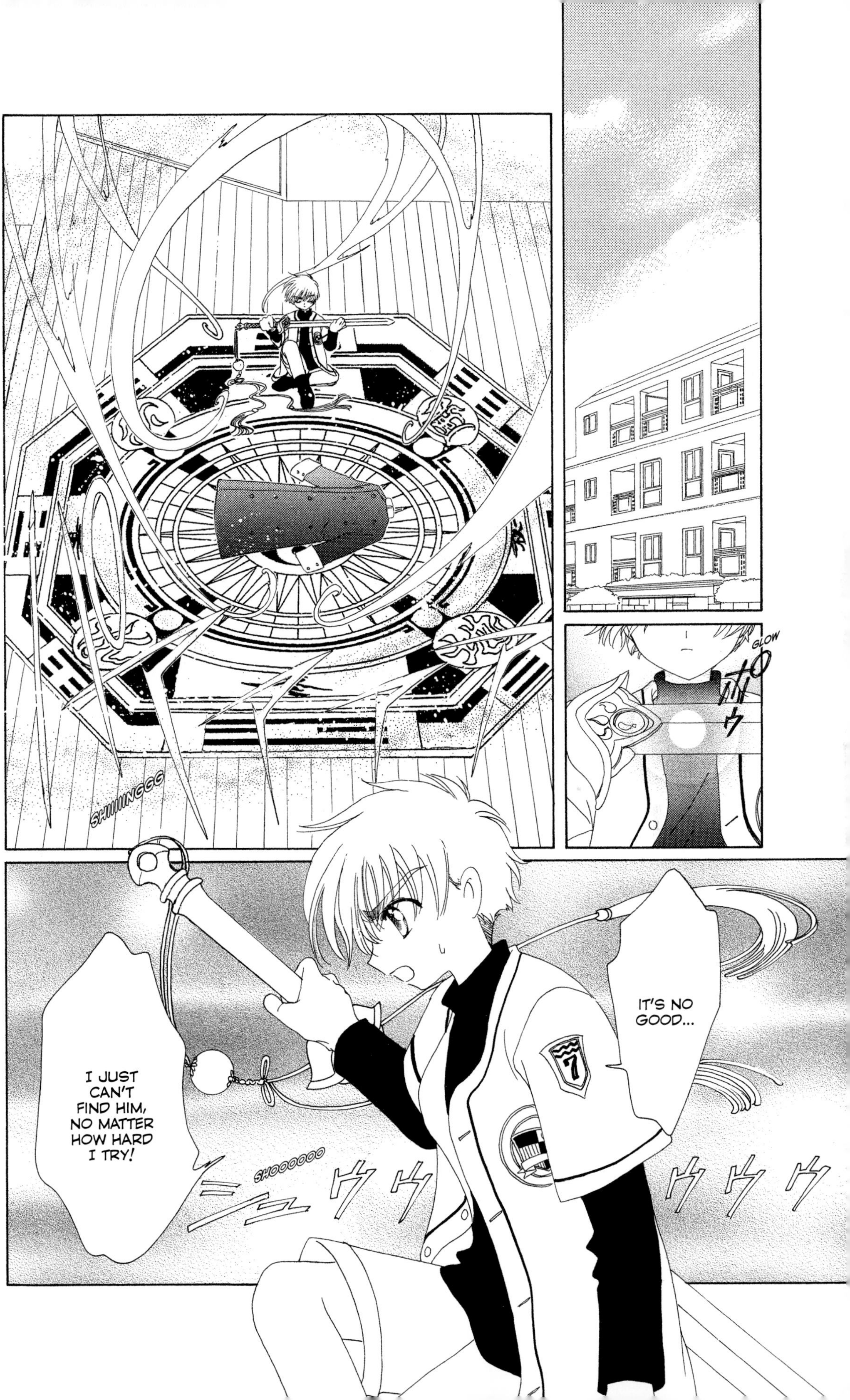
GLOW
SHIIIIINGGG
IT'S NO GOOD...
I JUST CAN'T FIND HIM, NO MATTER HOW HARD I TRY!
SHOOOOOO

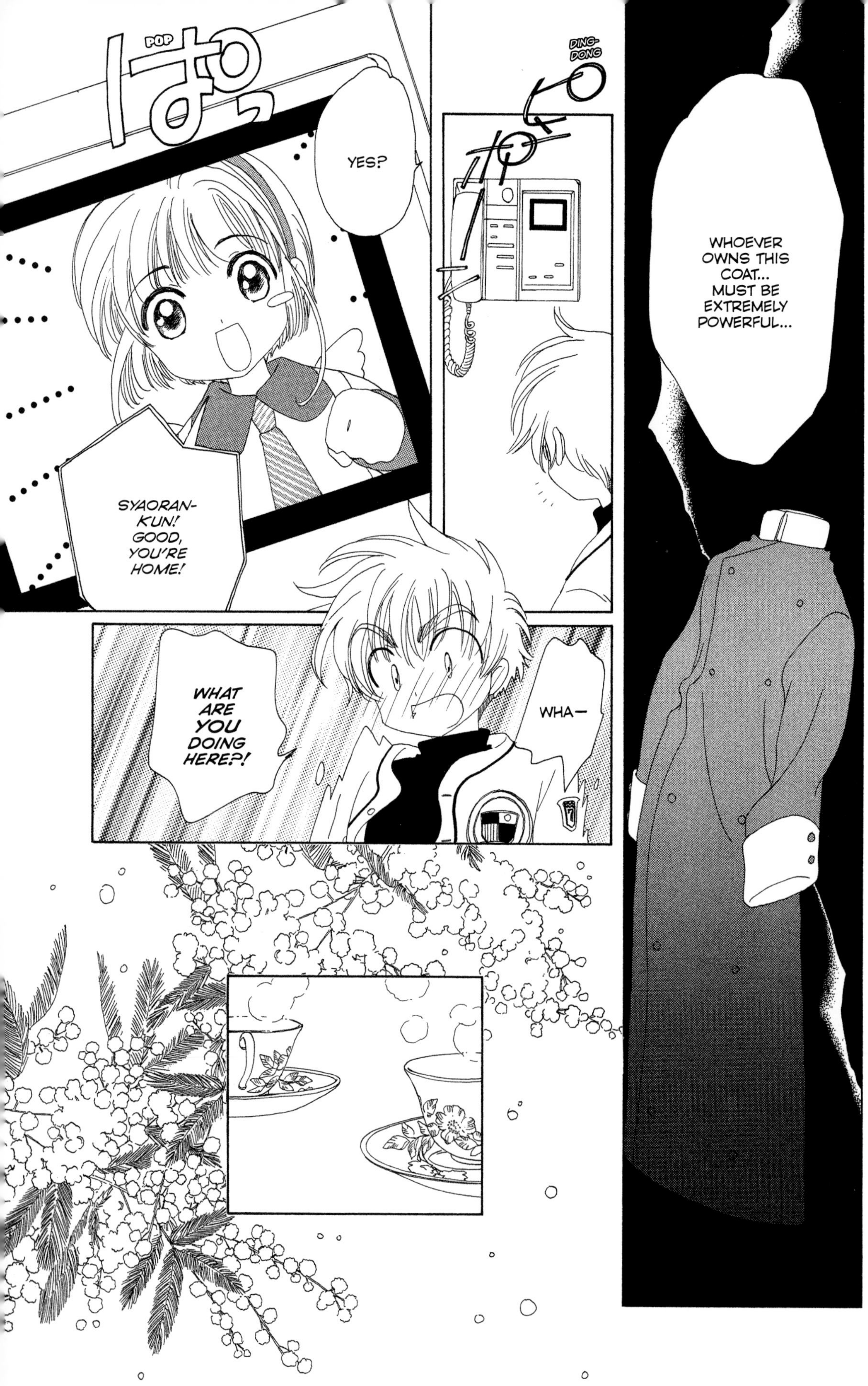
WHOEVER OWNS THIS COAT... MUST BE EXTREMELY POWERFUL...
DING-DONG
POP
ぱっ
YES?
SYAORAN-KUN! GOOD, YOU'RE HOME!
WHA—
WHAT ARE YOU DOING HERE?!

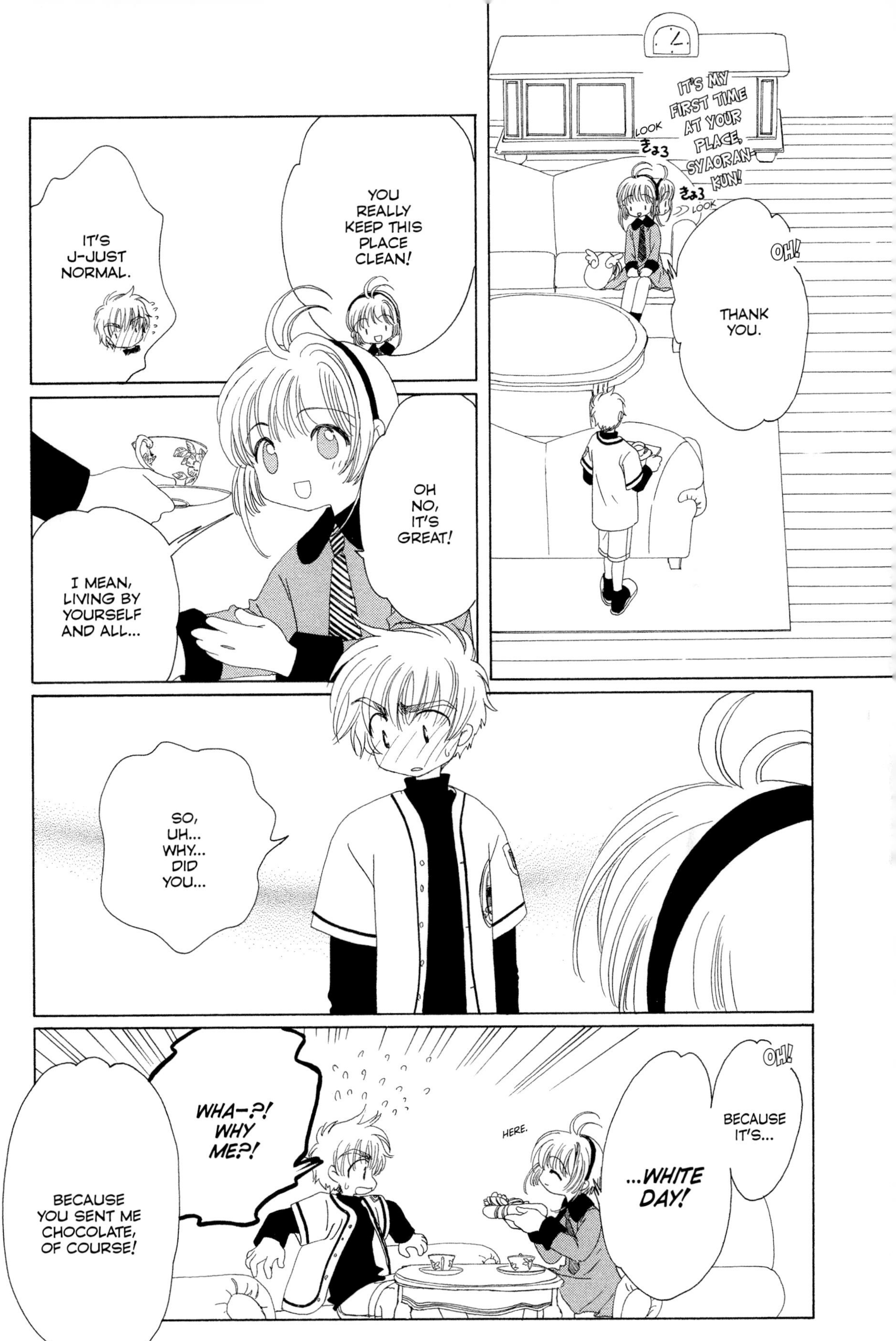

IT'S MY FIRST TIME AT YOUR PLACE, SYAORAN-KUN!
LOOK
LOOK
OH!
THANK YOU.
YOU REALLY KEEP THIS PLACE CLEAN!
IT'S J-JUST NORMAL.
OH NO, IT'S GREAT!
I MEAN, LIVING BY YOURSELF AND ALL...
SO, UH... WHY... DID YOU...
OH!
BECAUSE IT'S...
...WHITE DAY!
HERE.
WHA-?! WHY ME?!
BECAUSE YOU SENT ME CHOCOLATE, OF COURSE!

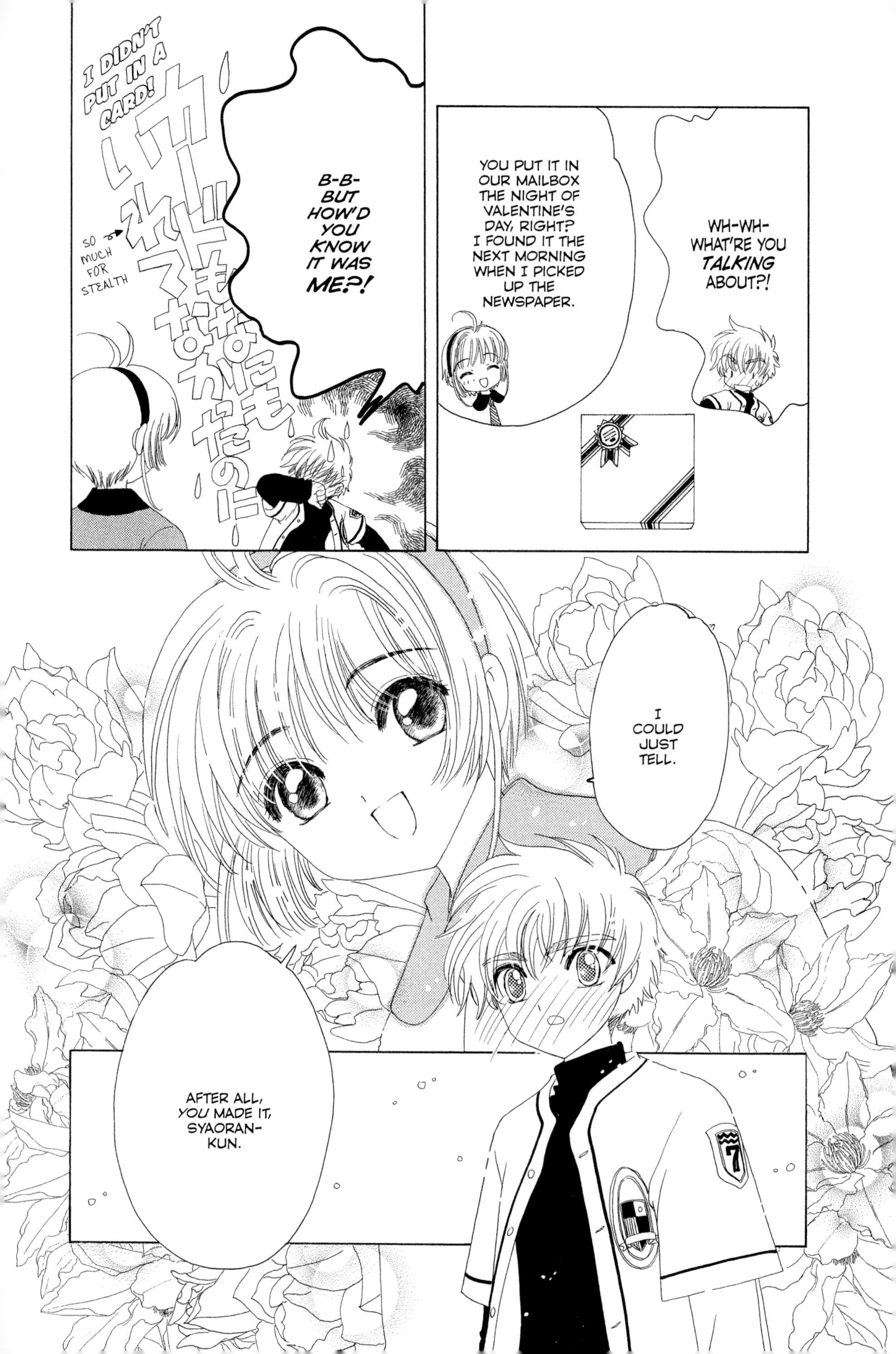
WH-WH-WHAT'RE YOU TALKING ABOUT?!
YOU PUT IT IN OUR MAILBOX THE NIGHT OF VALENTINE'S DAY, RIGHT? I FOUND IT THE NEXT MORNING WHEN I PICKED UP THE NEWSPAPER.
B-B-BUT HOW'D YOU KNOW IT WAS ME?!
I DIDN'T PUT IN A CARD!
カードもなにもなかったのに
SO MUCH FOR STEALTH
I COULD JUST TELL.
AFTER ALL, YOU MADE IT, SYAORAN-KUN.

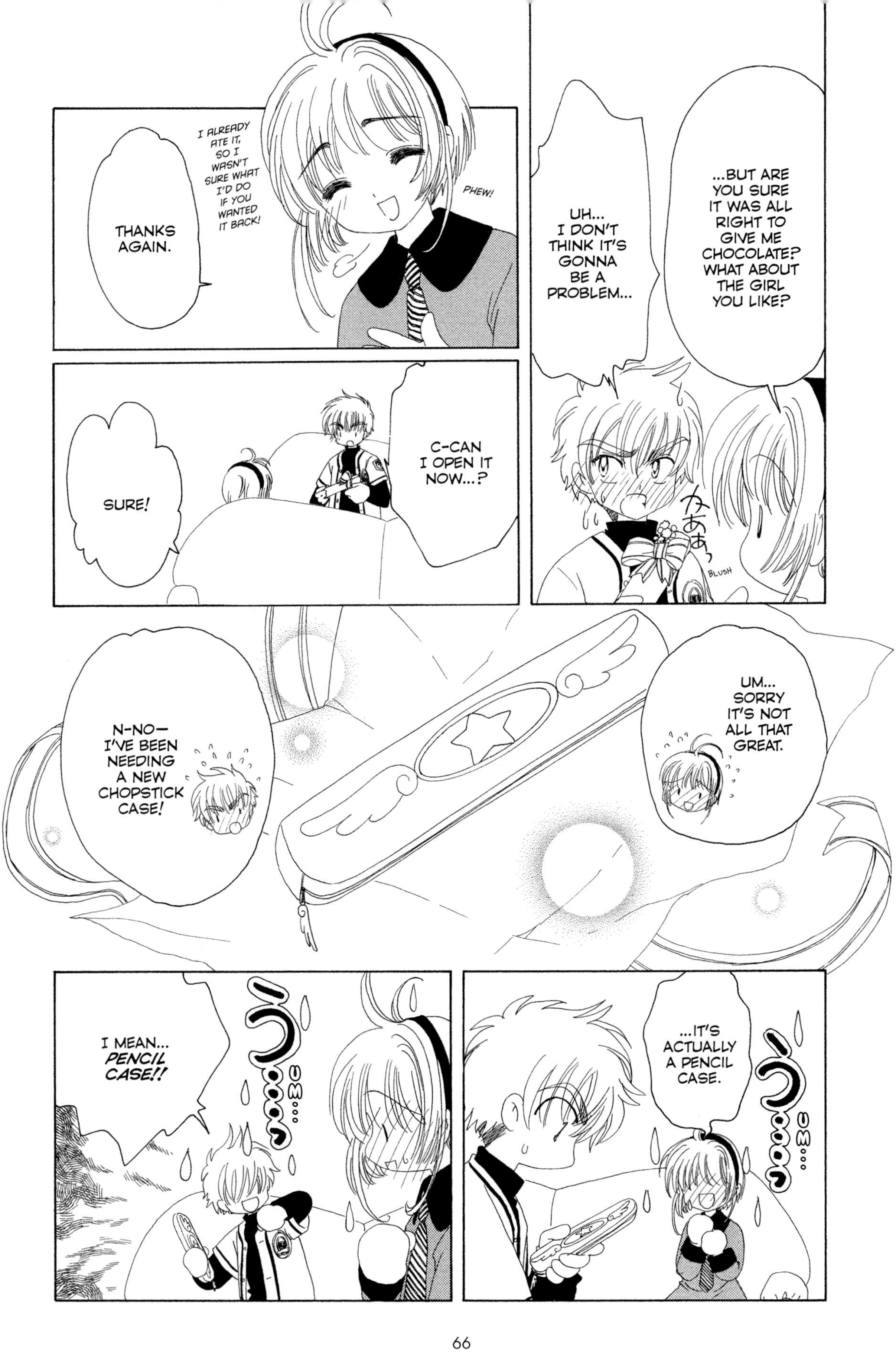

...BUT ARE YOU SURE IT WAS ALL RIGHT TO GIVE ME CHOCOLATE? WHAT ABOUT THE GIRL YOU LIKE?
UH... I DON'T THINK IT'S GONNA BE A PROBLEM...
かあぁっ
BLUSH
PHEW!
I ALREADY ATE IT, SO I WASN'T SURE WHAT I'D DO IF YOU WANTED IT BACK!
THANKS AGAIN.
C-CAN I OPEN IT NOW...?
SURE!
UM... SORRY IT'S NOT ALL THAT GREAT.
N-NO— I'VE BEEN NEEDING A NEW CHOPSTICK CASE!
...IT'S ACTUALLY A PENCIL CASE.
う…
UM...
う…
UM...
I MEAN... *PENCIL CASE!!*

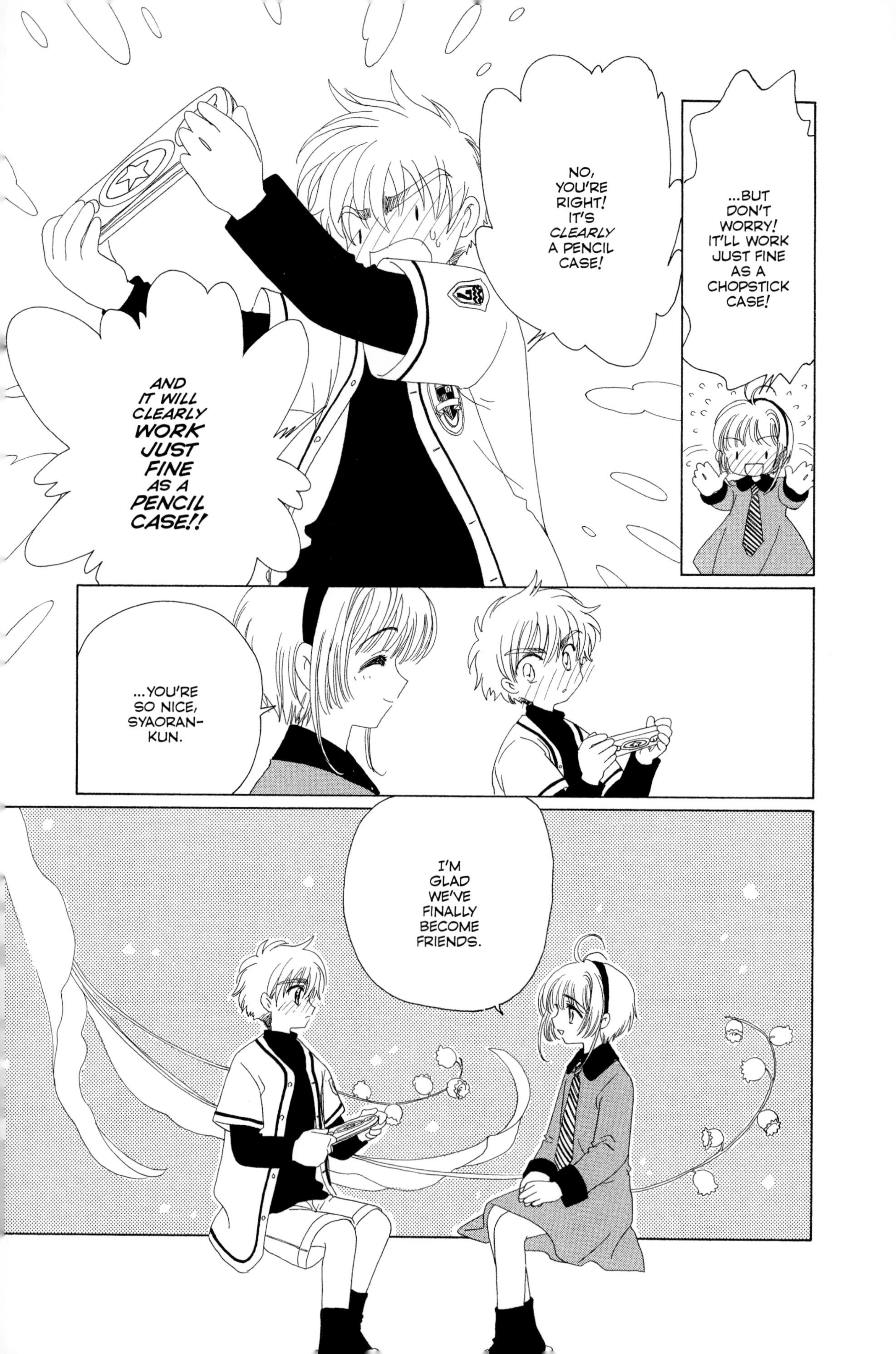
...BUT DON'T WORRY! IT'LL WORK JUST FINE AS A CHOPSTICK CASE!
NO, YOU'RE RIGHT! IT'S *CLEARLY* A PENCIL CASE!
AND IT WILL CLEARLY ***WORK JUST FINE*** *AS A* ***PENCIL CASE!!***
...YOU'RE SO NICE, SYAORAN-KUN.
I'M GLAD WE'VE FINALLY BECOME FRIENDS.

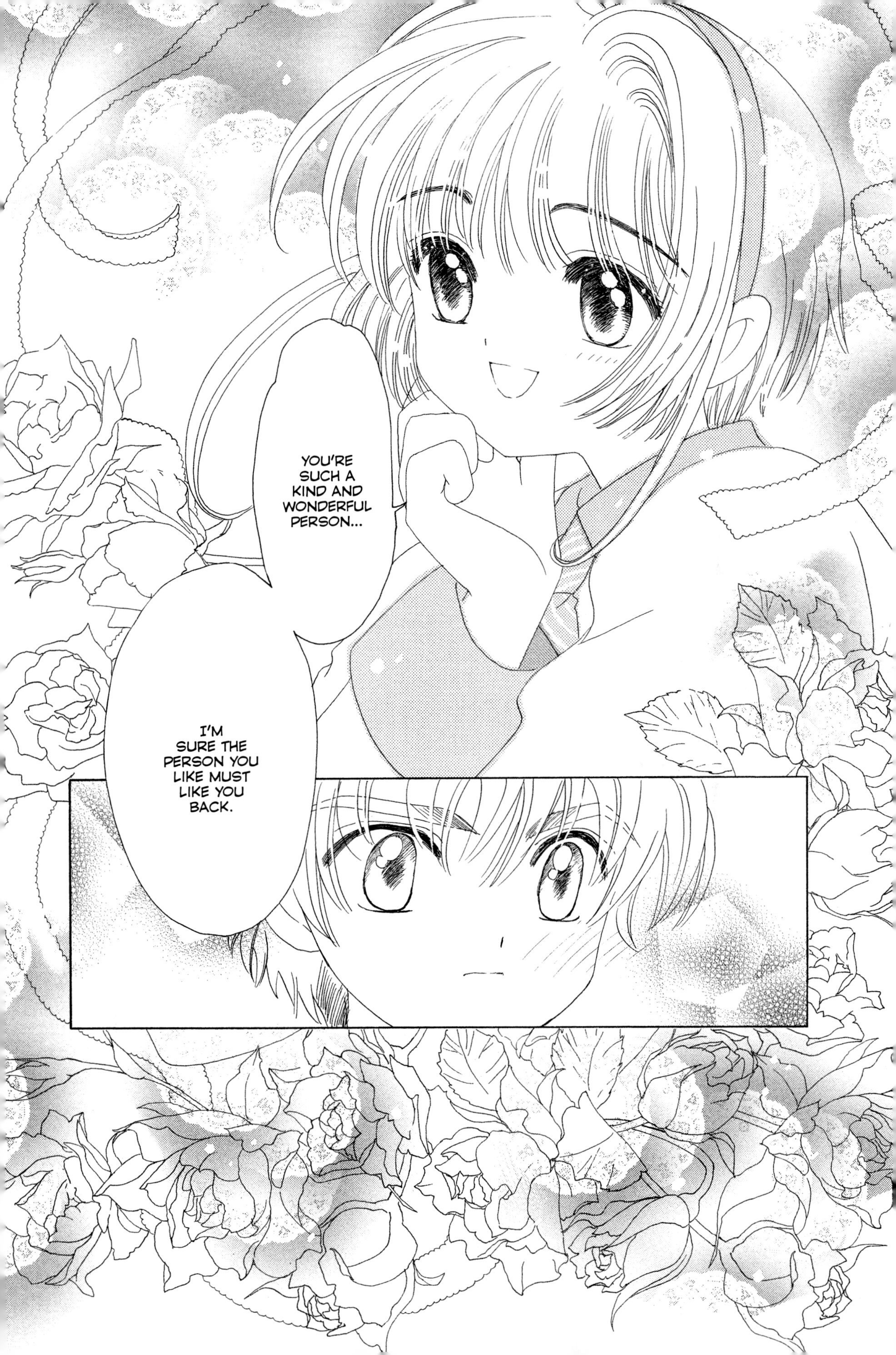
YOU'RE SUCH A KIND AND WONDERFUL PERSON...
I'M SURE THE PERSON YOU LIKE MUST LIKE YOU BACK.

25

MASAKI AMAMIYA

BIRTHDATE:
NOVEMBER 18

JOB:
PRESIDENT OF THE AMAMIYA CORPORATION

FAVORITE FOOD:
JAPANESE

LEAST FAVORITE FOOD:
NONE, REALLY

FAVORITE THING:
RAINBOWS

LEAST FAVORITE THING:
LONG CAR RIDES

FAVORITE COLOR:
BROWN

FAVORITE FLOWERS:
NADESHIKO BLOSSOMS, CHERRY BLOSSOMS

FAVORITE COOKING STYLE:
JAPANESE

HOBBY:
COLLECTING CHESS SETS

SPECIAL TALENT:
NOTHING IN PARTICULAR

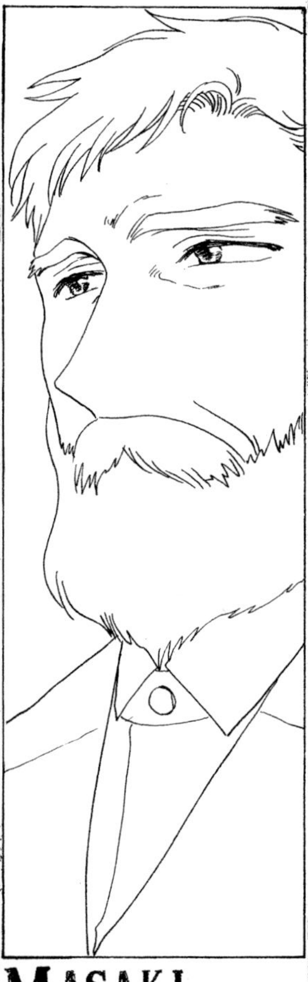

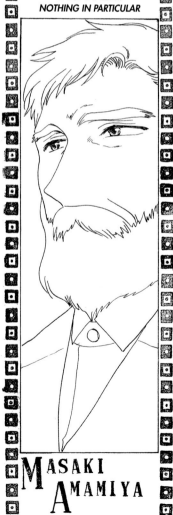

MASAKI AMAMIYA

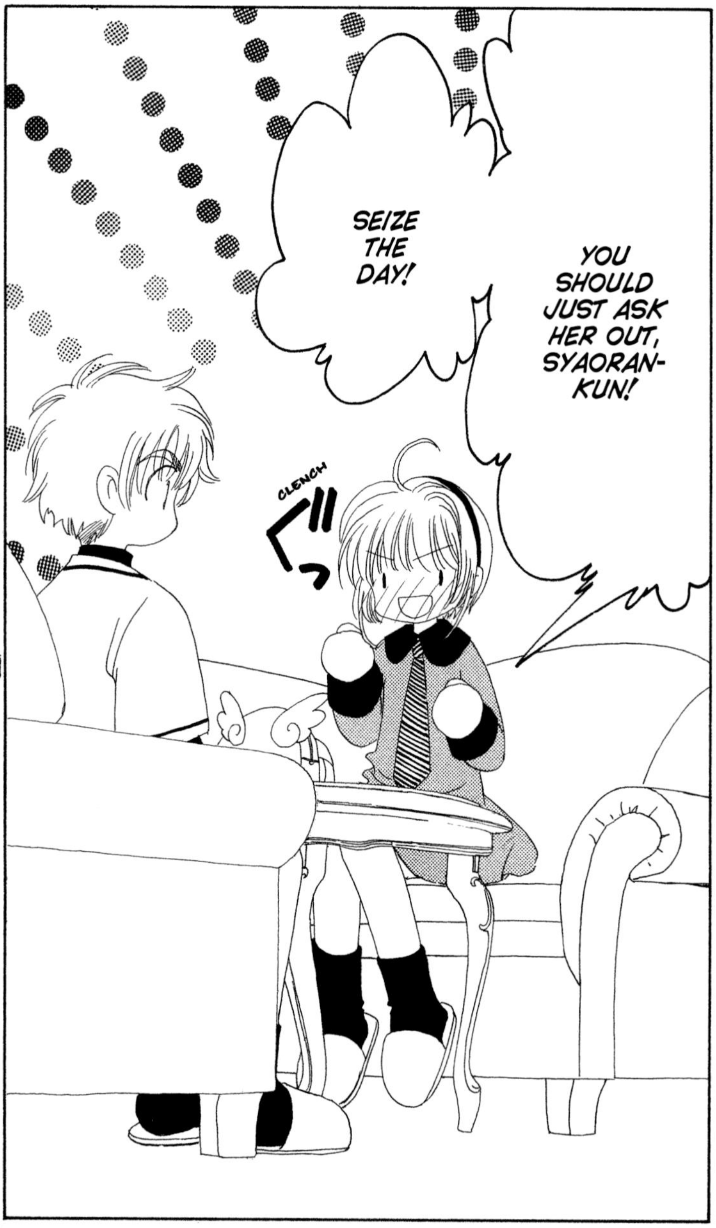
SEIZE THE DAY!
YOU SHOULD JUST ASK HER OUT, SYAORAN-KUN!
CLENCH

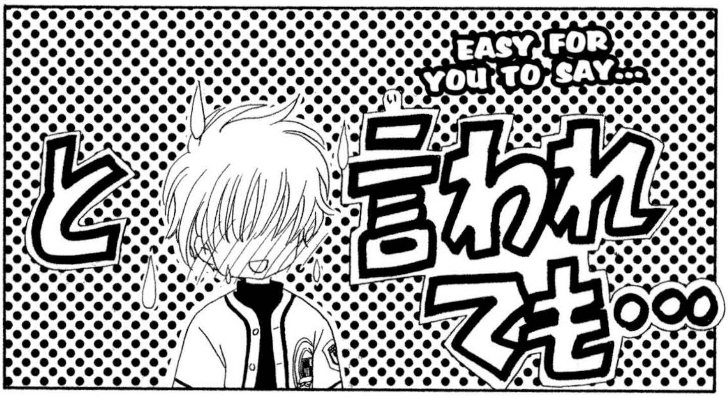
EASY FOR YOU TO SAY...
と言われても・・・

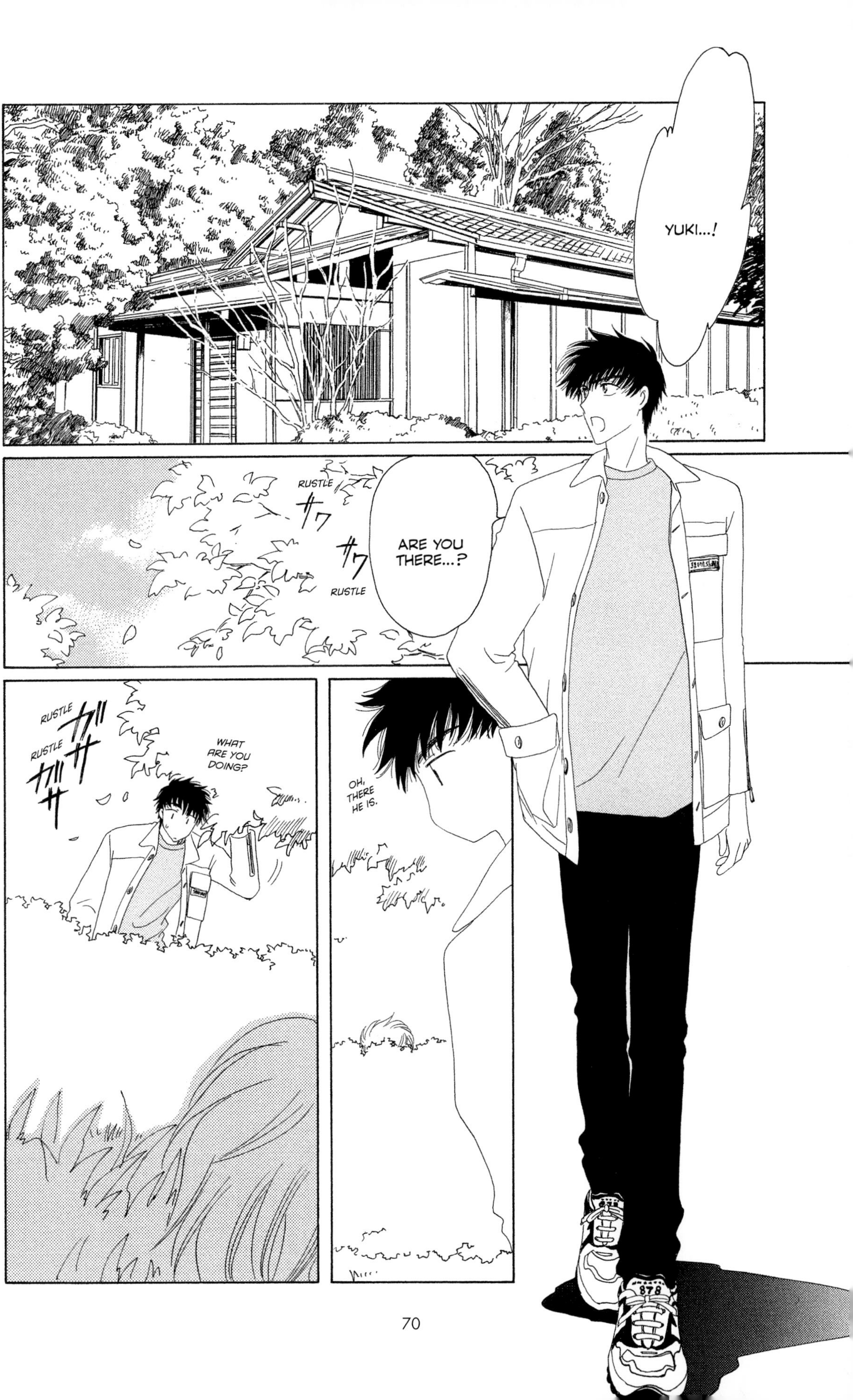
YUKI...!
ARE YOU THERE...?
RUSTLE
RUSTLE
OH, THERE HE IS.
RUSTLE
RUSTLE
WHAT ARE YOU DOING?

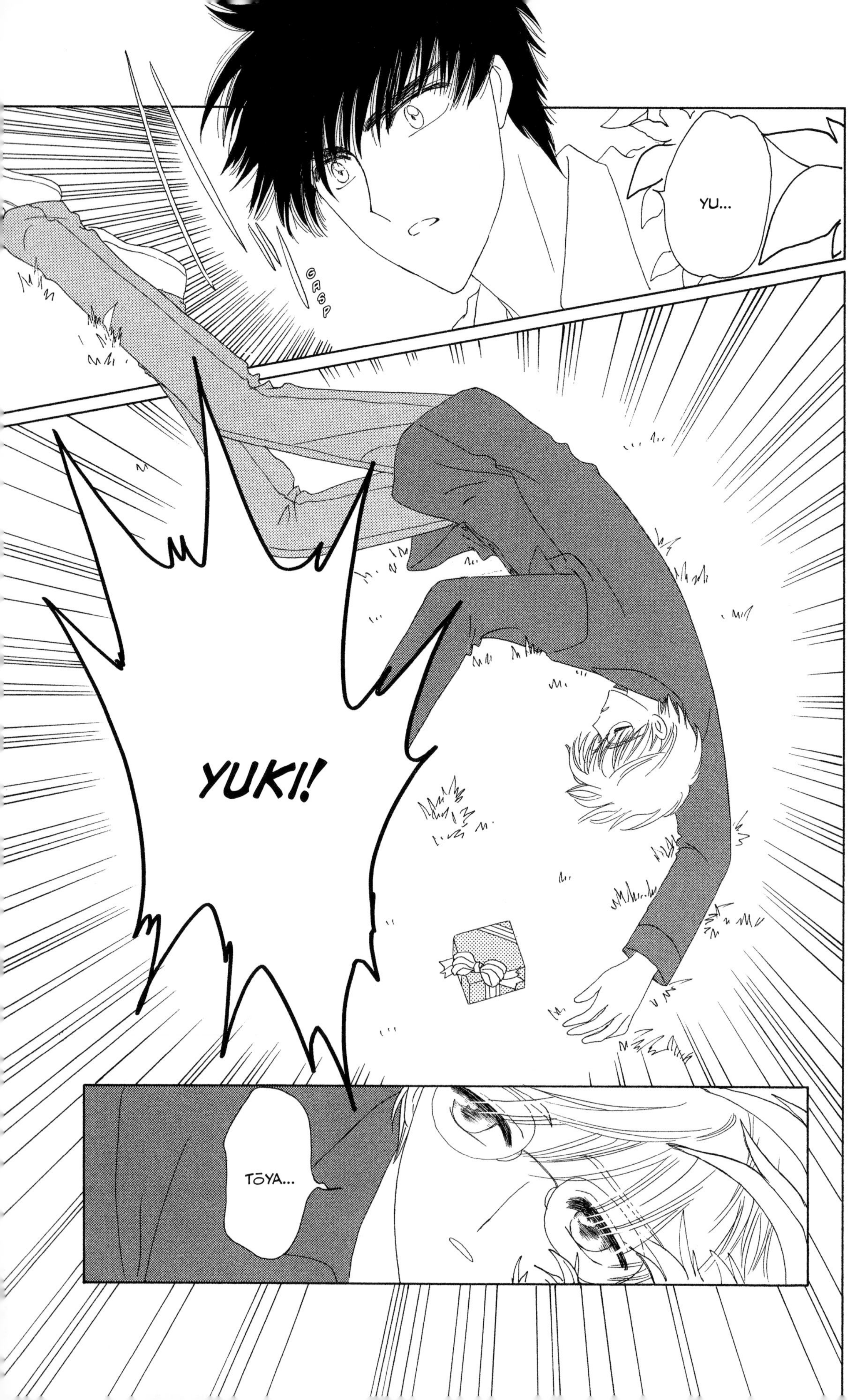
YU...
GASP
YUKI!
TŌYA...

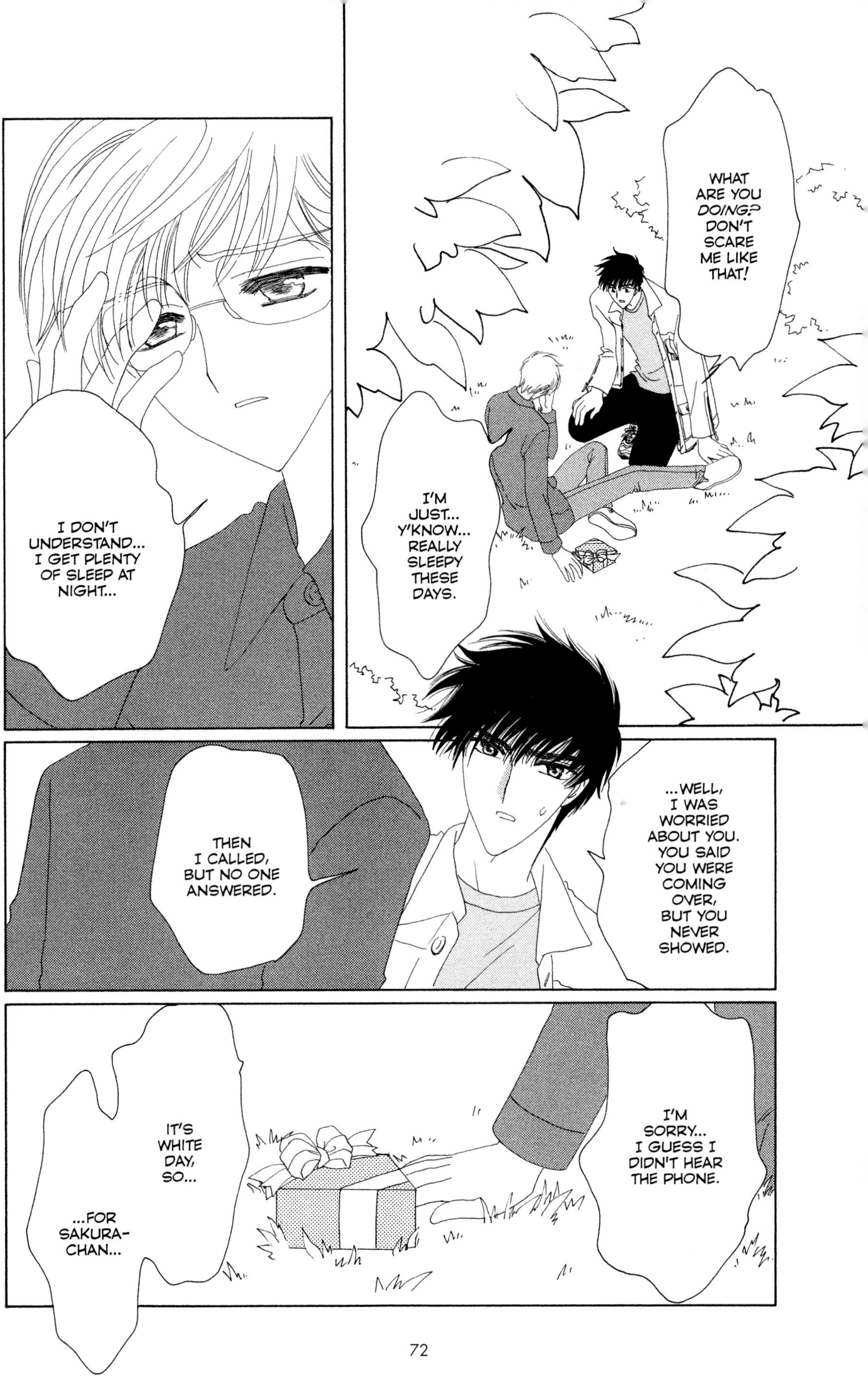
WHAT ARE YOU *DOING?* DON'T SCARE ME LIKE THAT!
I'M JUST... Y'KNOW... REALLY SLEEPY THESE DAYS.
I DON'T UNDERSTAND... I GET PLENTY OF SLEEP AT NIGHT...
...WELL, I WAS WORRIED ABOUT YOU. YOU SAID YOU WERE COMING OVER, BUT YOU NEVER SHOWED.
THEN I CALLED, BUT NO ONE ANSWERED.
I'M SORRY... I GUESS I DIDN'T HEAR THE PHONE.
IT'S WHITE DAY, SO...
...FOR SAKURA-CHAN...

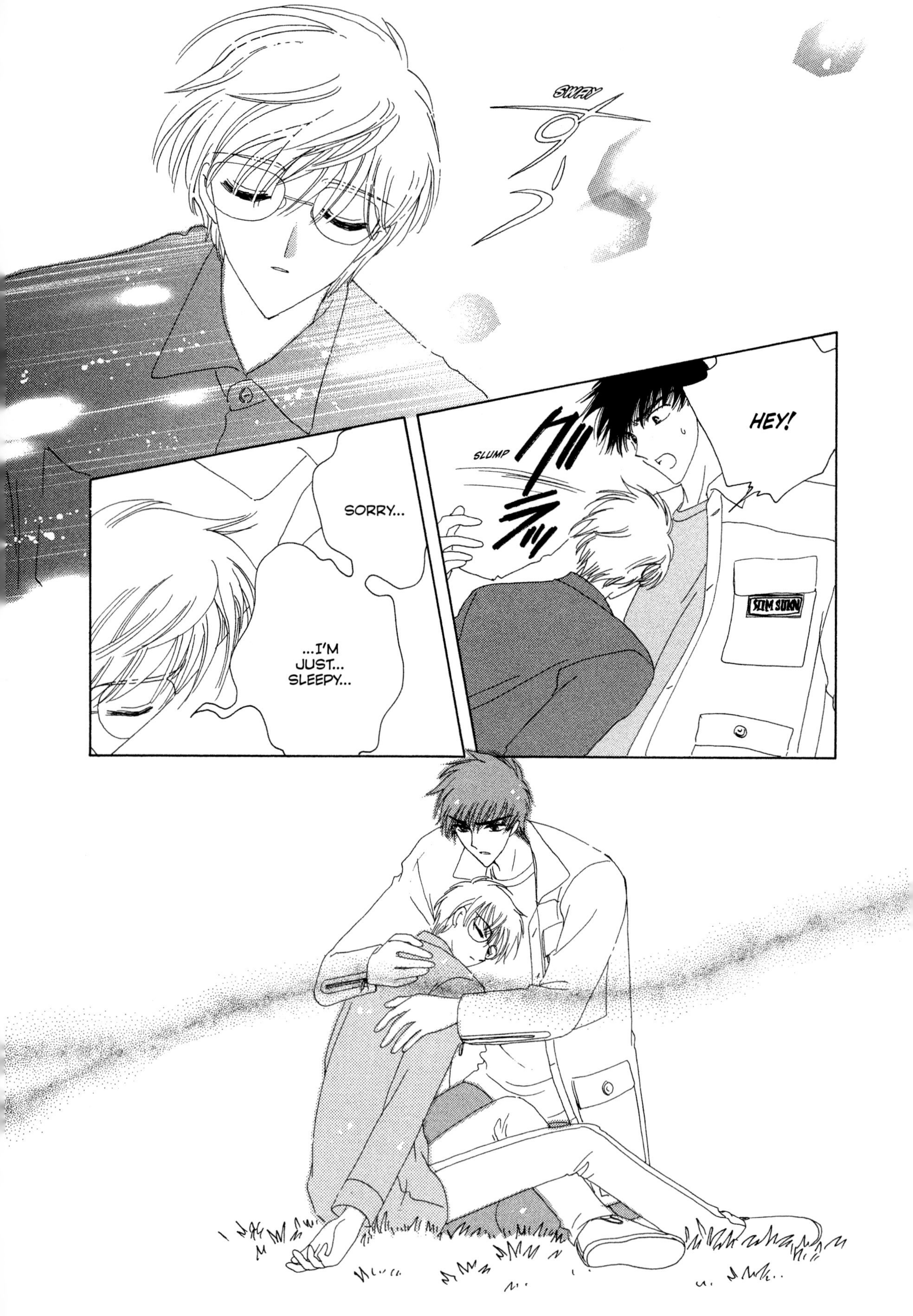
SWAY
SLUMP
HEY!
SORRY...
...I'M JUST... SLEEPY...

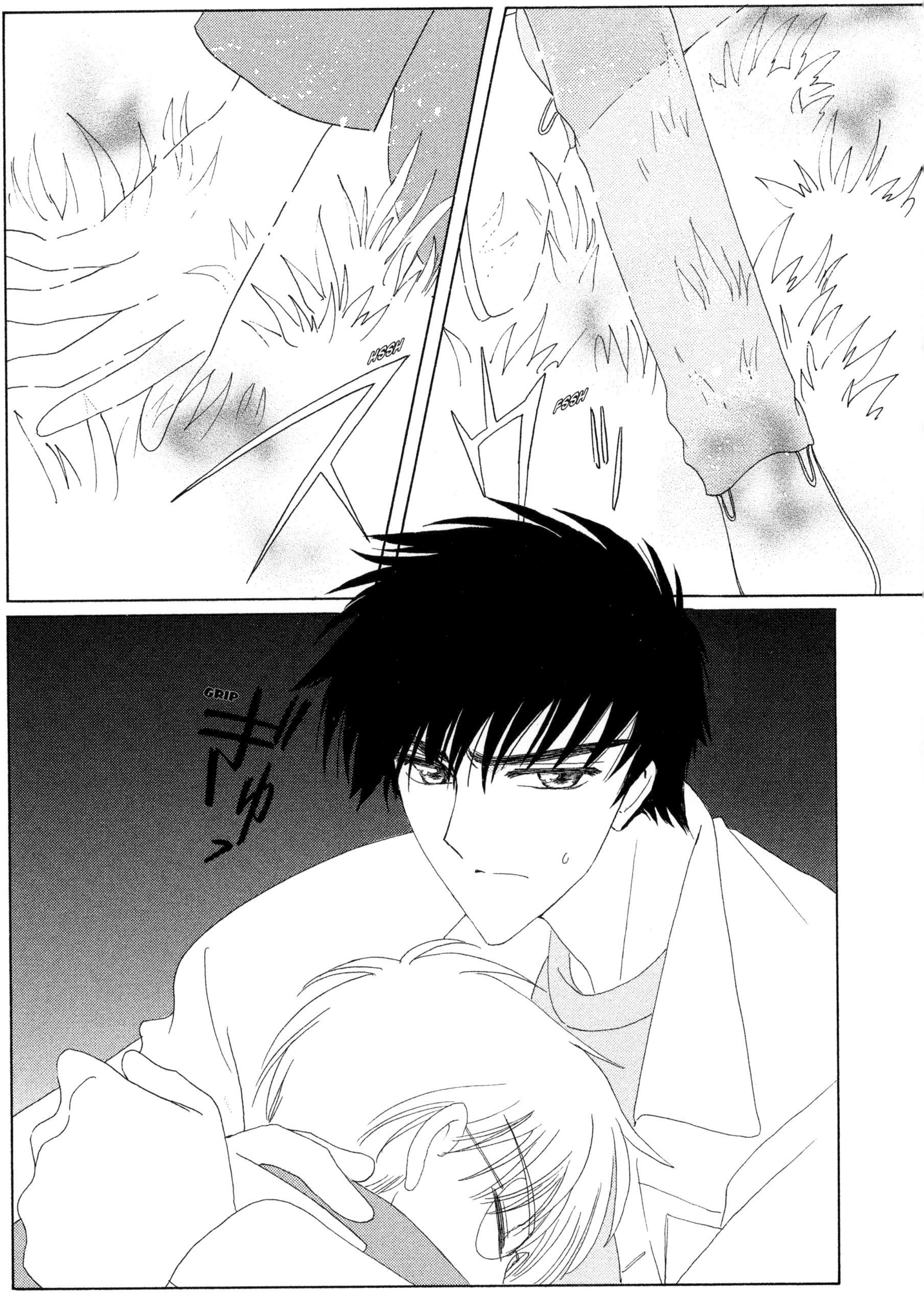
FSSH
HSSH
GRIP
ぎゅっ

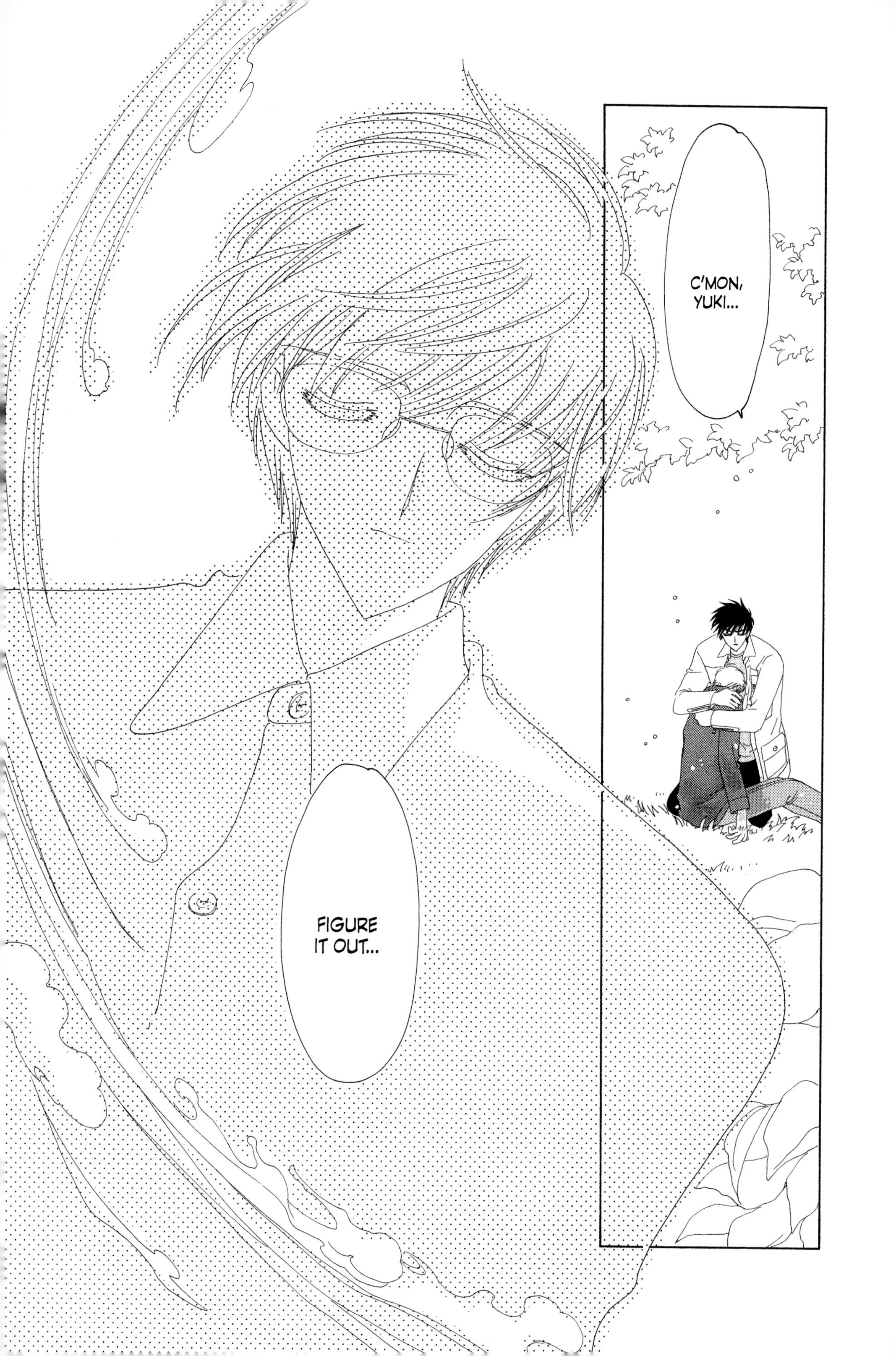
C'MON, YUKI...
FIGURE IT OUT...

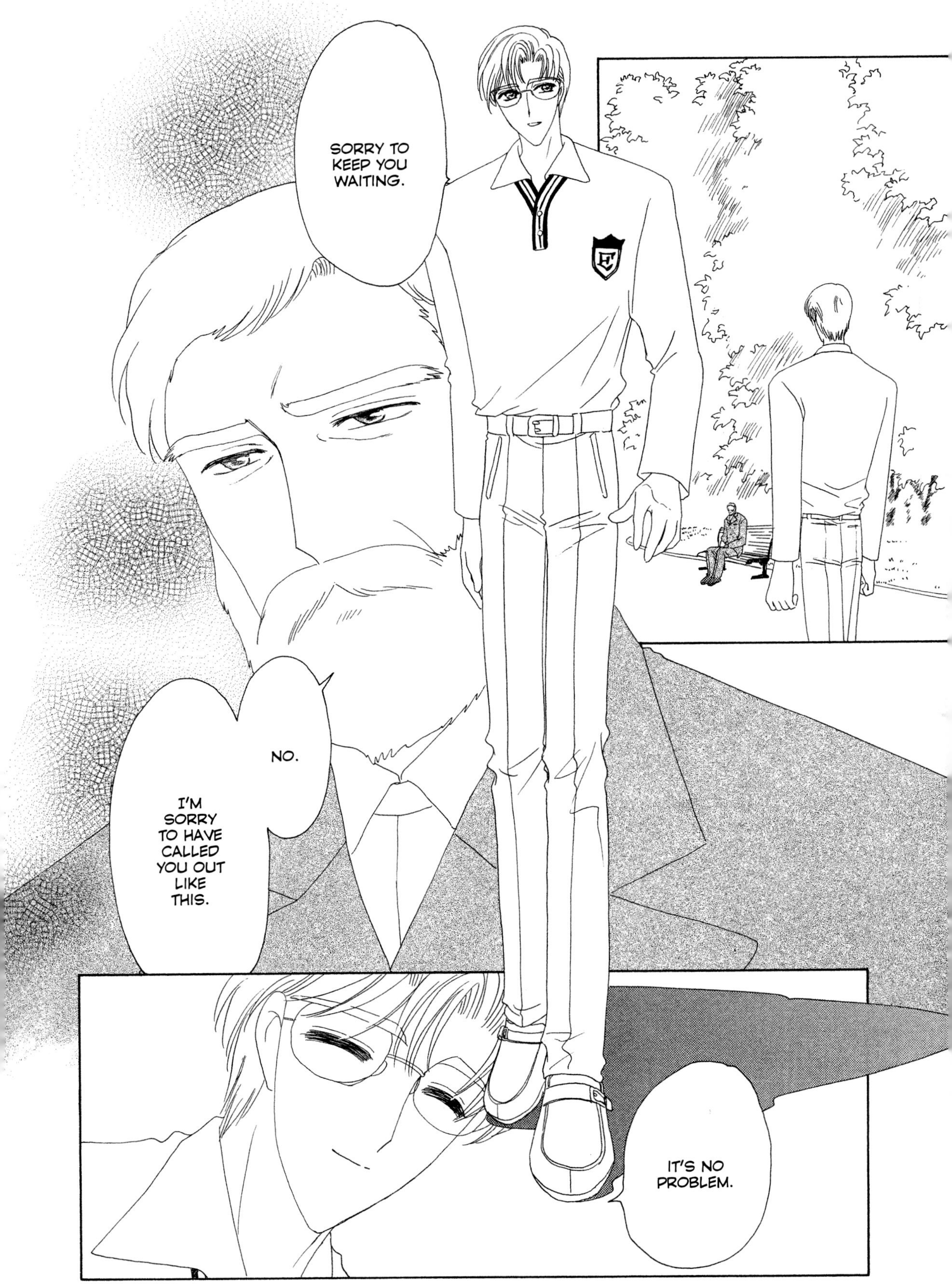
SORRY TO KEEP YOU WAITING.
NO.
I'M SORRY TO HAVE CALLED YOU OUT LIKE THIS.
IT'S NO PROBLEM.

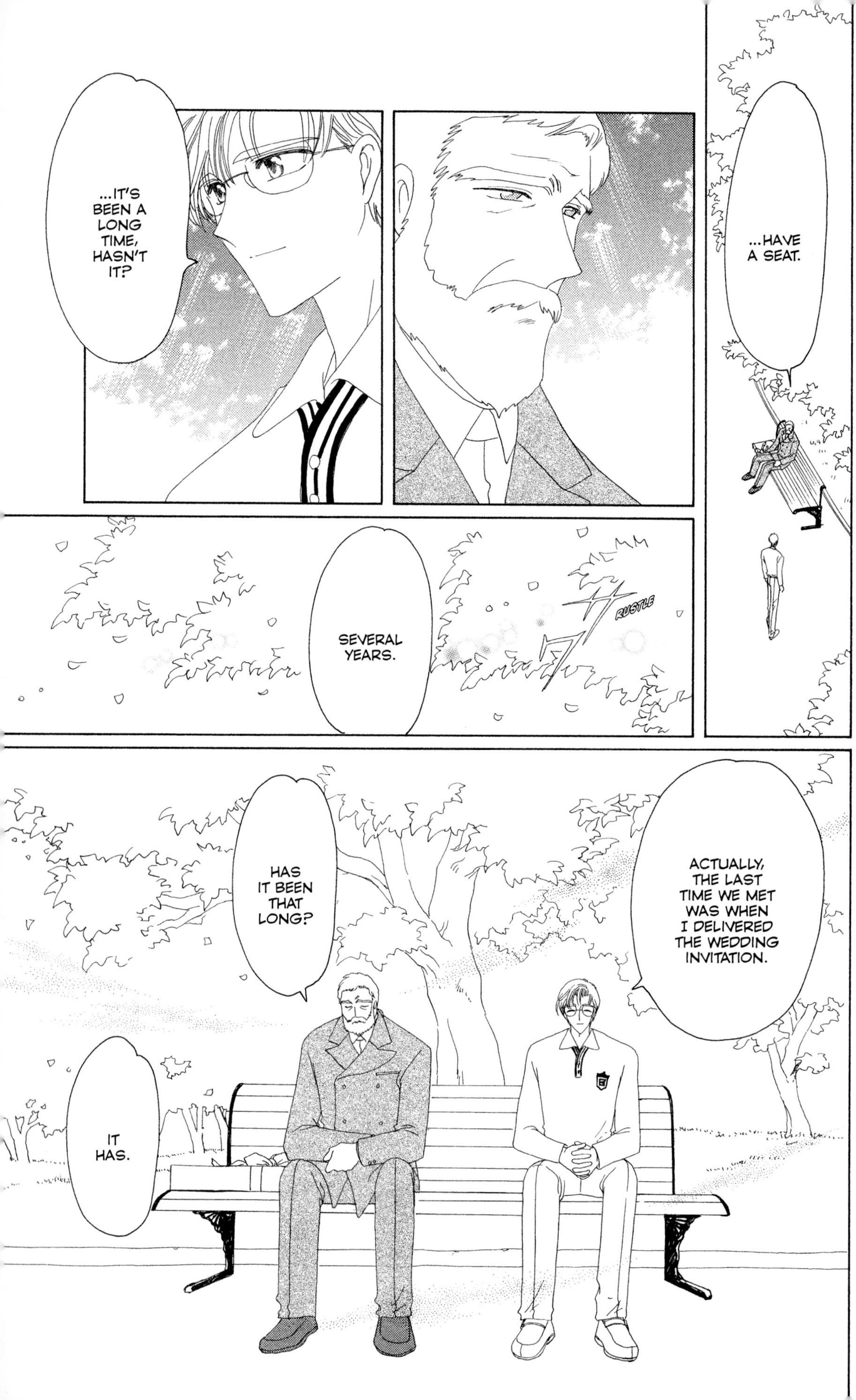
...HAVE A SEAT.
...IT'S BEEN A LONG TIME, HASN'T IT?
RUSTLE
SEVERAL YEARS.
ACTUALLY, THE LAST TIME WE MET WAS WHEN I DELIVERED THE WEDDING INVITATION.
HAS IT BEEN THAT LONG?
IT HAS.

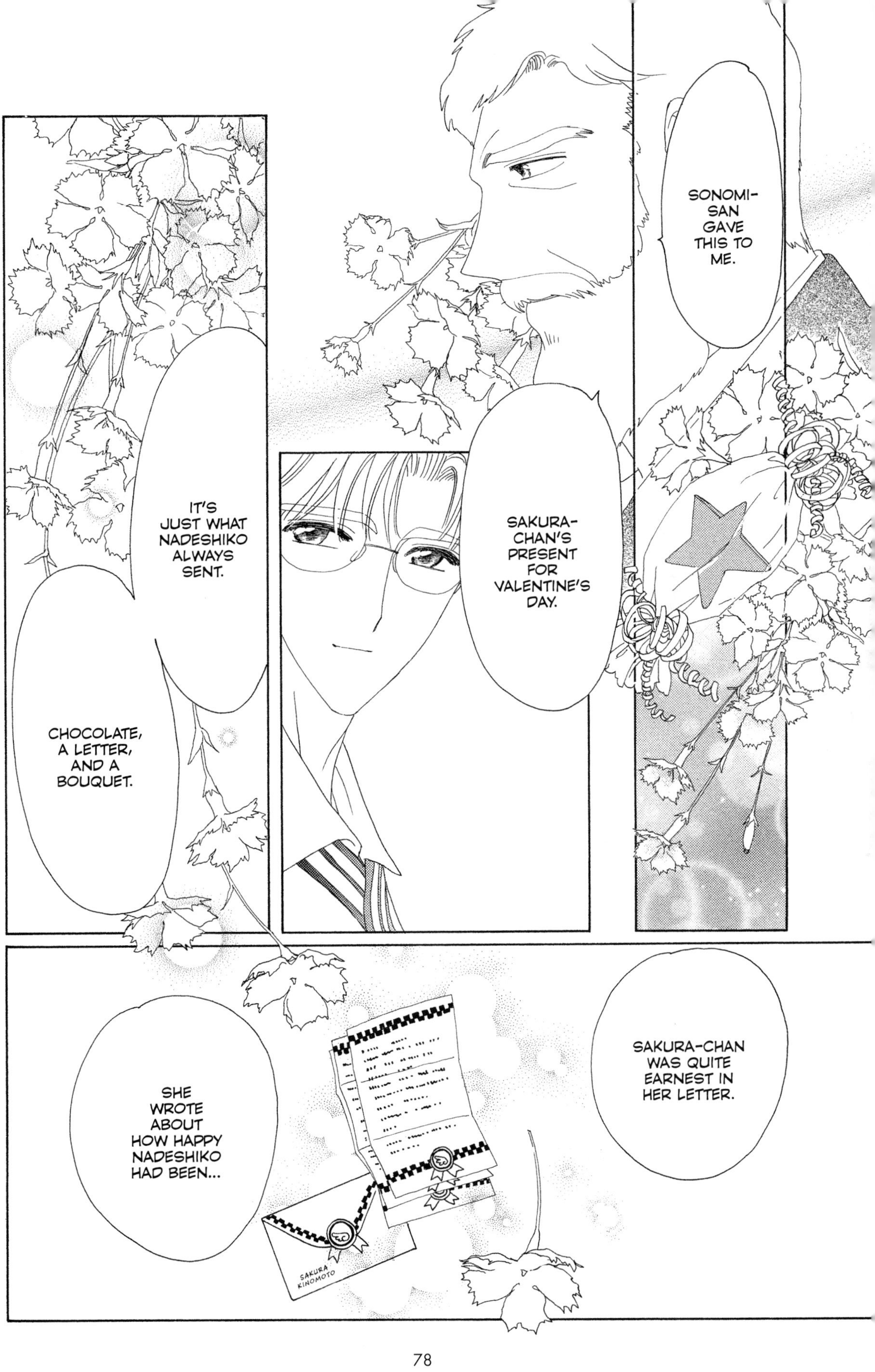
SONOMI-SAN GAVE THIS TO ME.
SAKURA-CHAN'S PRESENT FOR VALENTINE'S DAY.
IT'S JUST WHAT NADESHIKO ALWAYS SENT.
CHOCOLATE, A LETTER, AND A BOUQUET.
SAKURA-CHAN WAS QUITE EARNEST IN HER LETTER.
SHE WROTE ABOUT HOW HAPPY NADESHIKO HAD BEEN...
SAKURA KINOMOTO

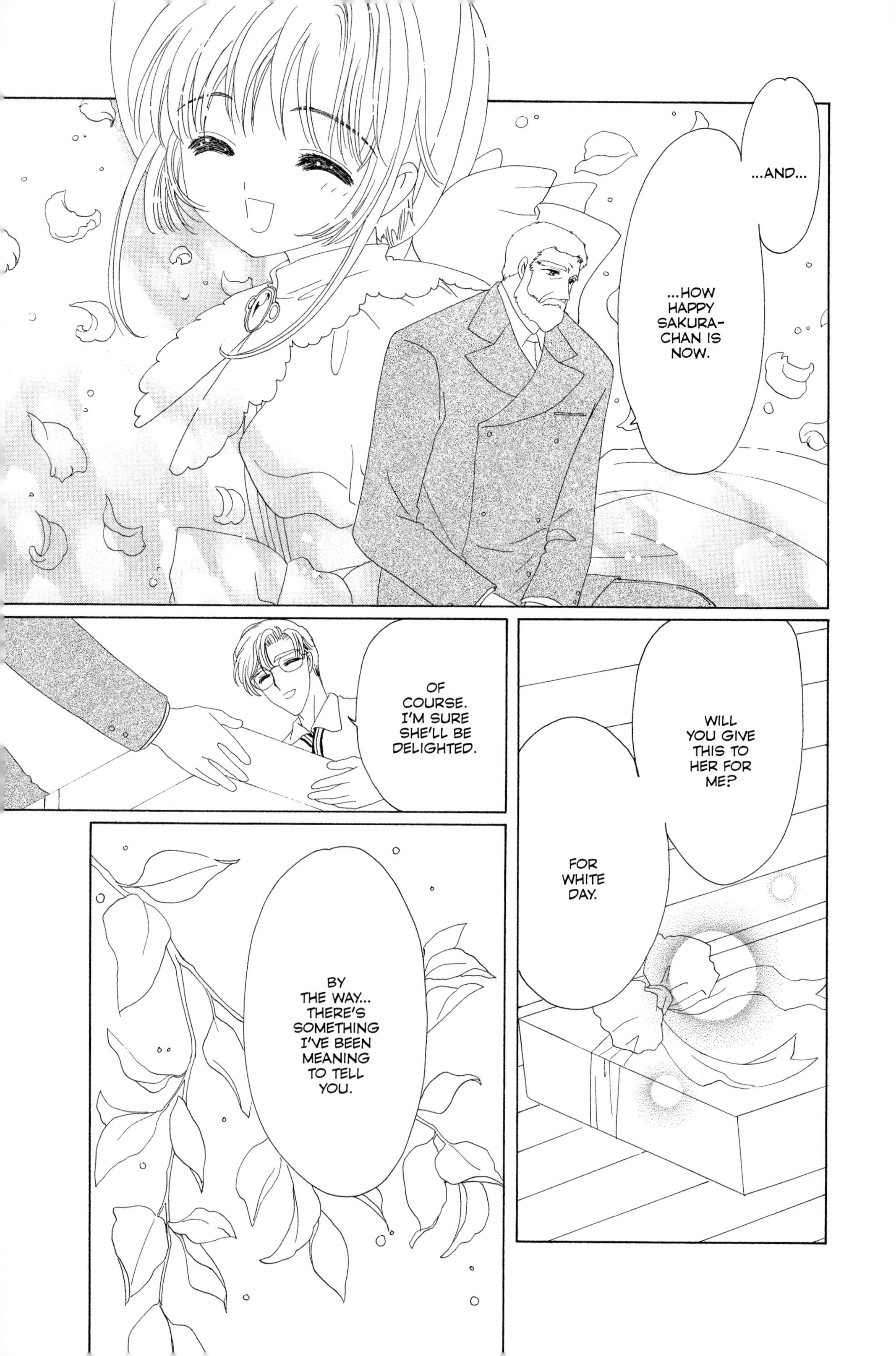
...AND...
...HOW HAPPY SAKURA-CHAN IS NOW.
WILL YOU GIVE THIS TO HER FOR ME?
FOR WHITE DAY.
OF COURSE. I'M SURE SHE'LL BE DELIGHTED.
BY THE WAY... THERE'S SOMETHING I'VE BEEN MEANING TO TELL YOU.

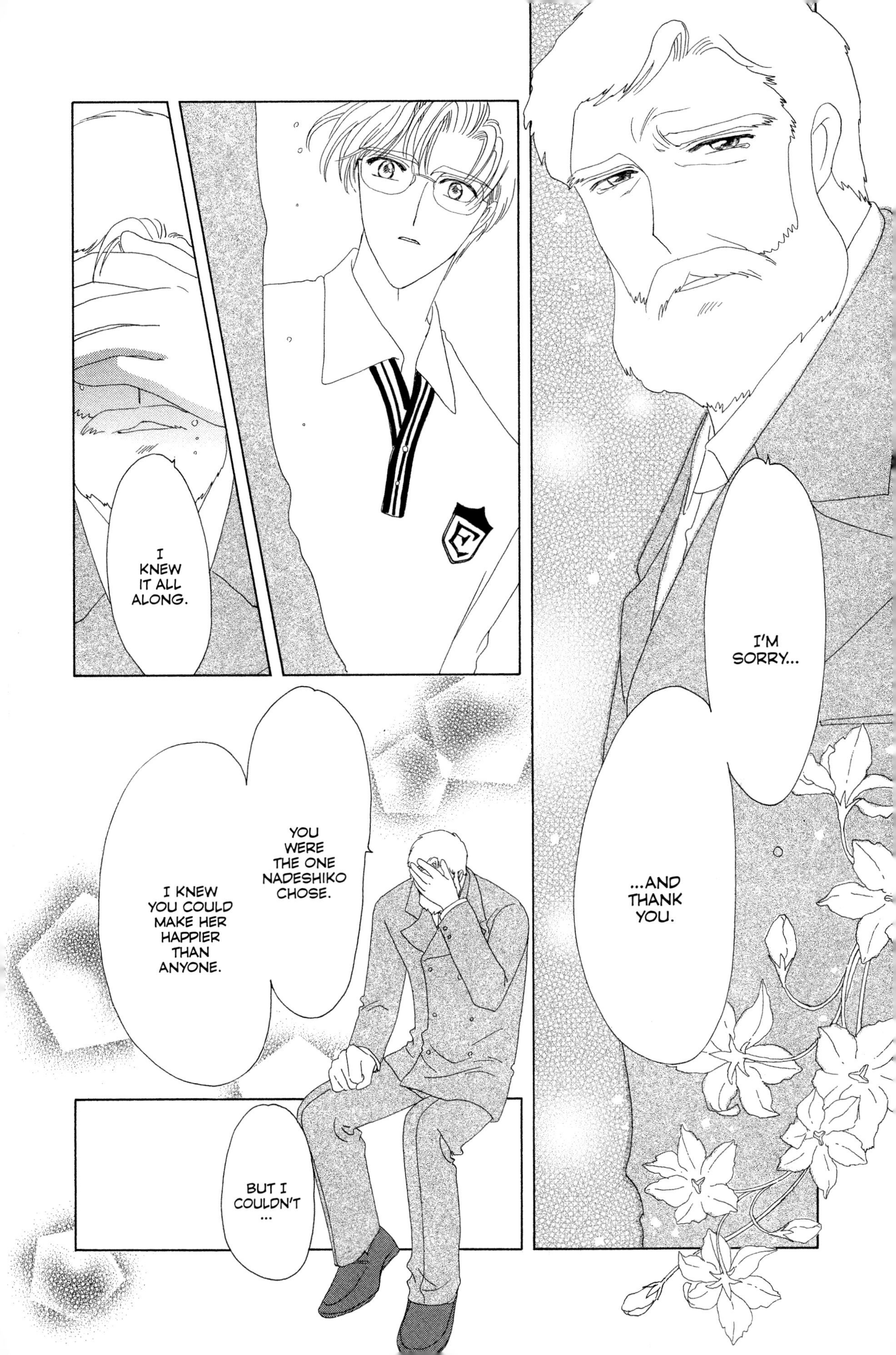
I'M SORRY...
...AND THANK YOU.
I KNEW IT ALL ALONG.
YOU WERE THE ONE NADESHIKO CHOSE.
I KNEW YOU COULD MAKE HER HAPPIER THAN ANYONE.
BUT I COULDN'T ...

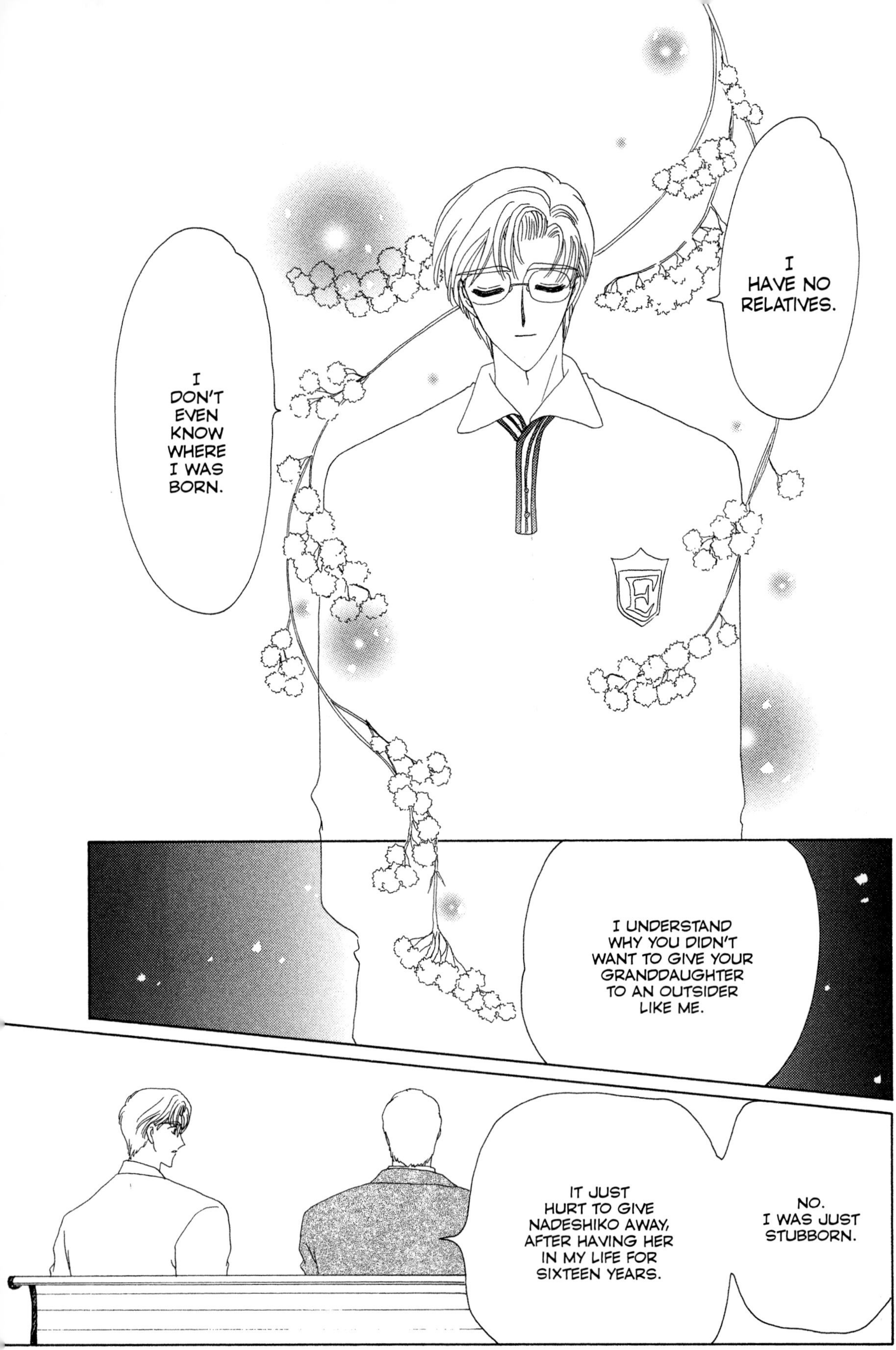
I HAVE NO RELATIVES.
I DON'T EVEN KNOW WHERE I WAS BORN.
I UNDERSTAND WHY YOU DIDN'T WANT TO GIVE YOUR GRANDDAUGHTER TO AN OUTSIDER LIKE ME.
NO. I WAS JUST STUBBORN.
IT JUST HURT TO GIVE NADESHIKO AWAY, AFTER HAVING HER IN MY LIFE FOR SIXTEEN YEARS.

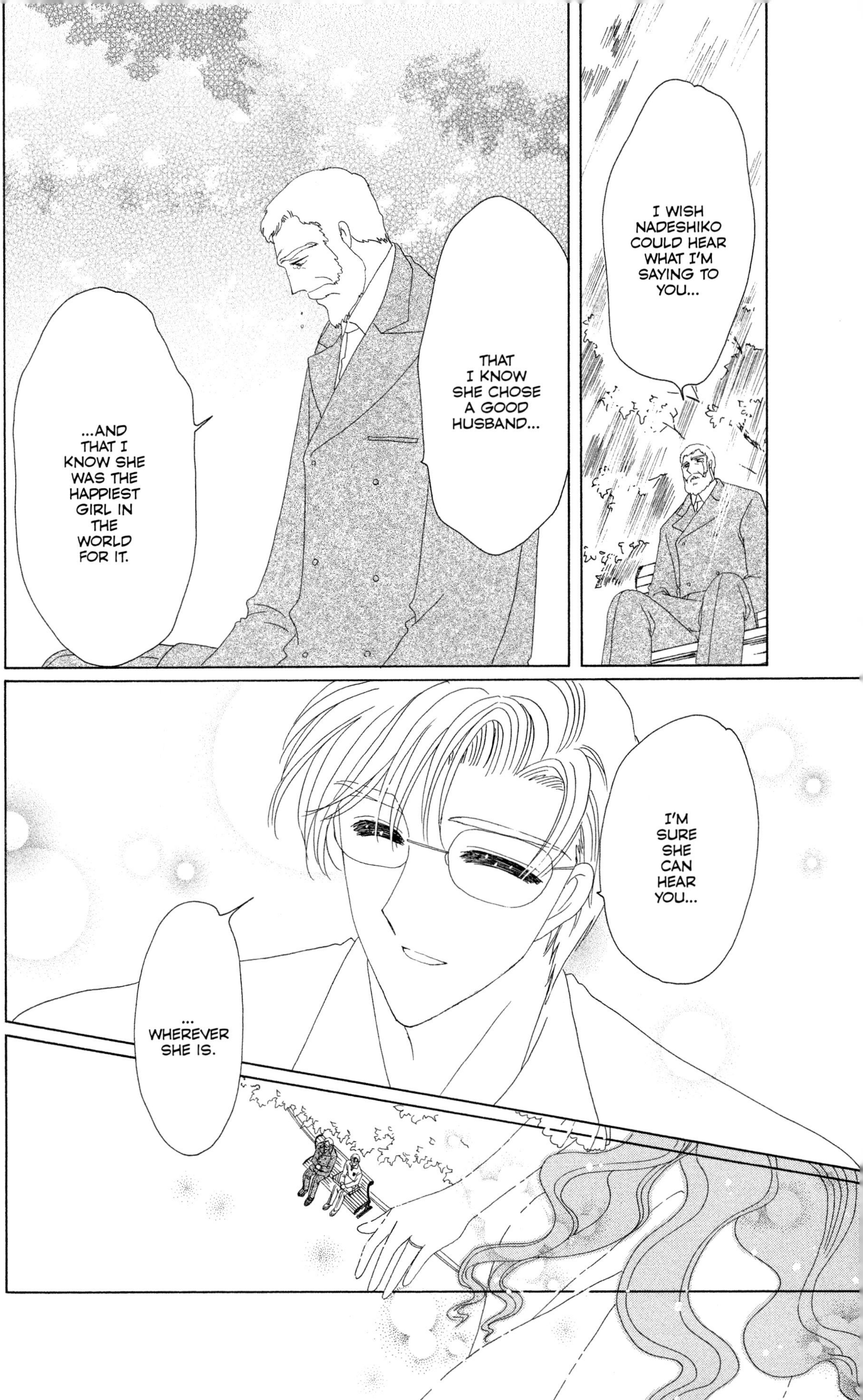
I WISH NADESHIKO COULD HEAR WHAT I'M SAYING TO YOU...
THAT I KNOW SHE CHOSE A GOOD HUSBAND...
...AND THAT I KNOW SHE WAS THE HAPPIEST GIRL IN THE WORLD FOR IT.
I'M SURE SHE CAN HEAR YOU...
... WHEREVER SHE IS.

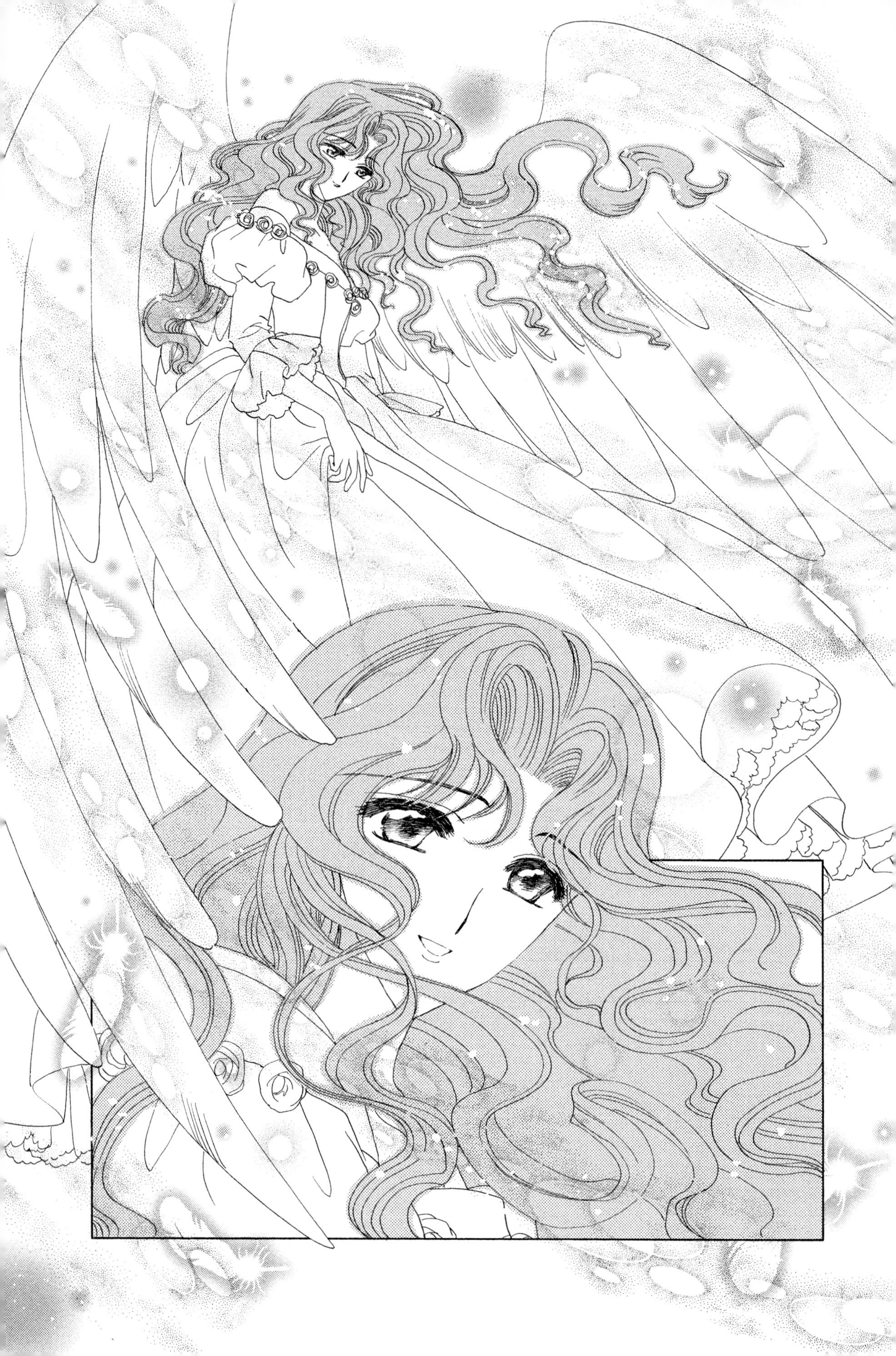

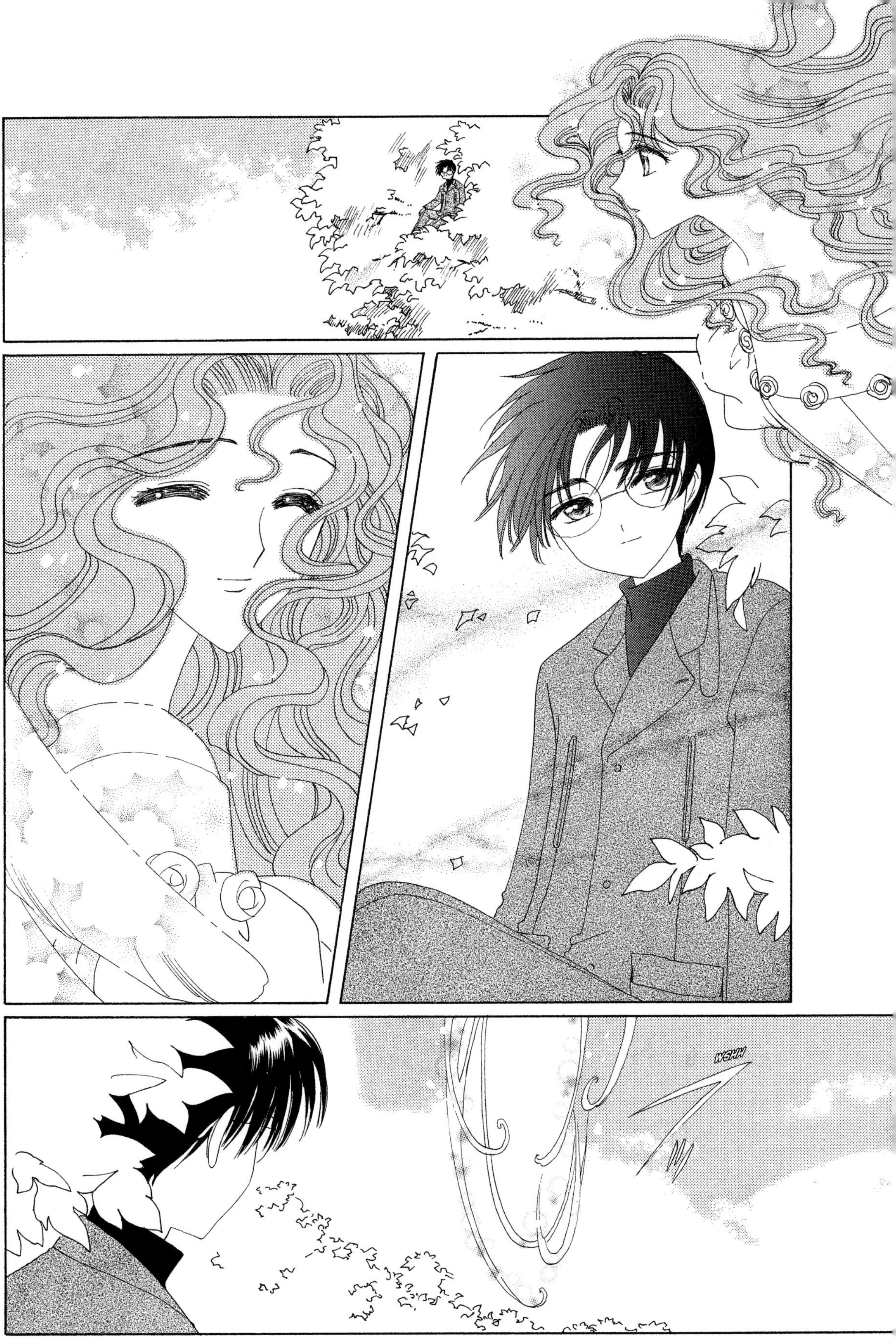
WSHH

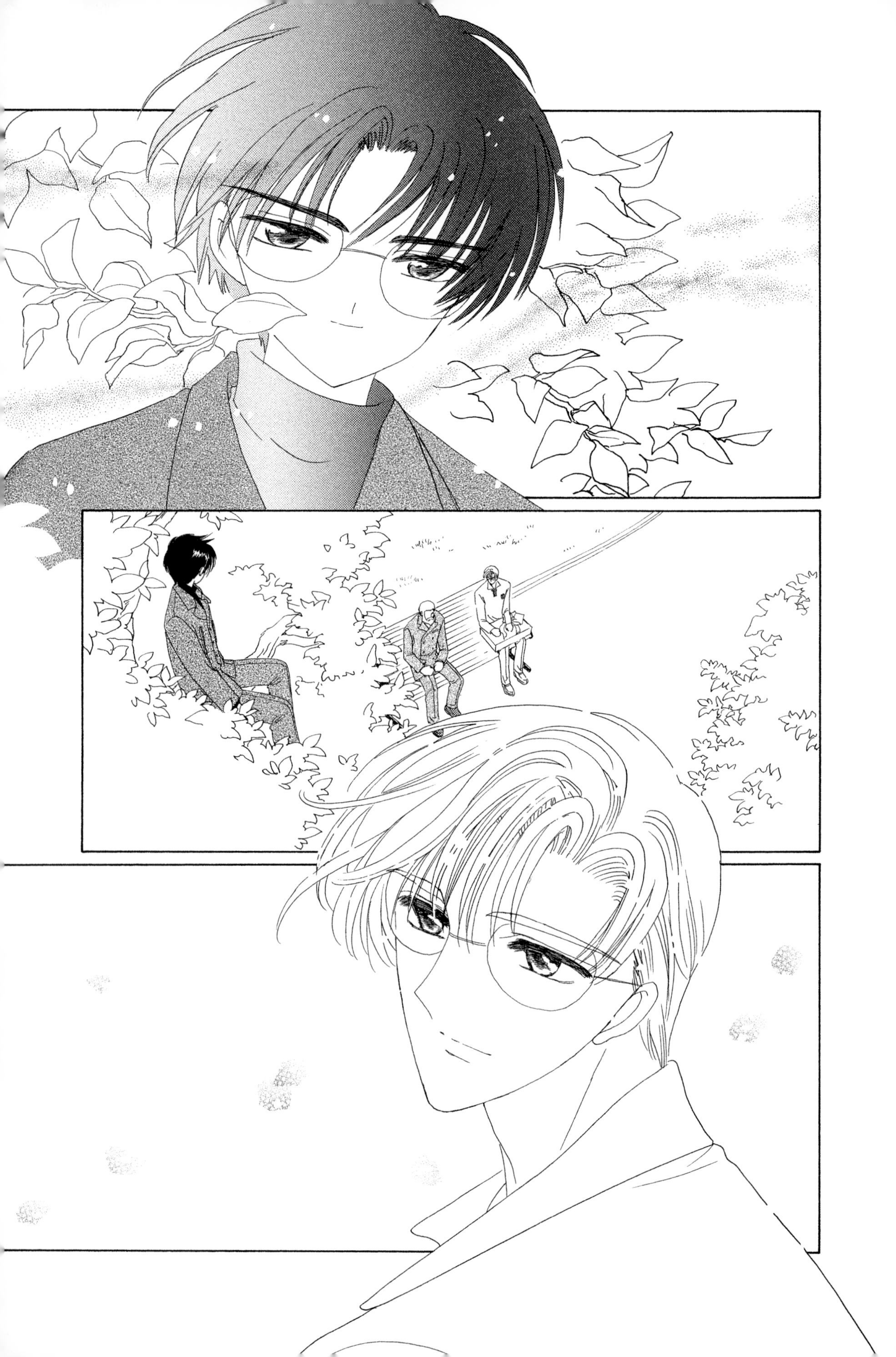

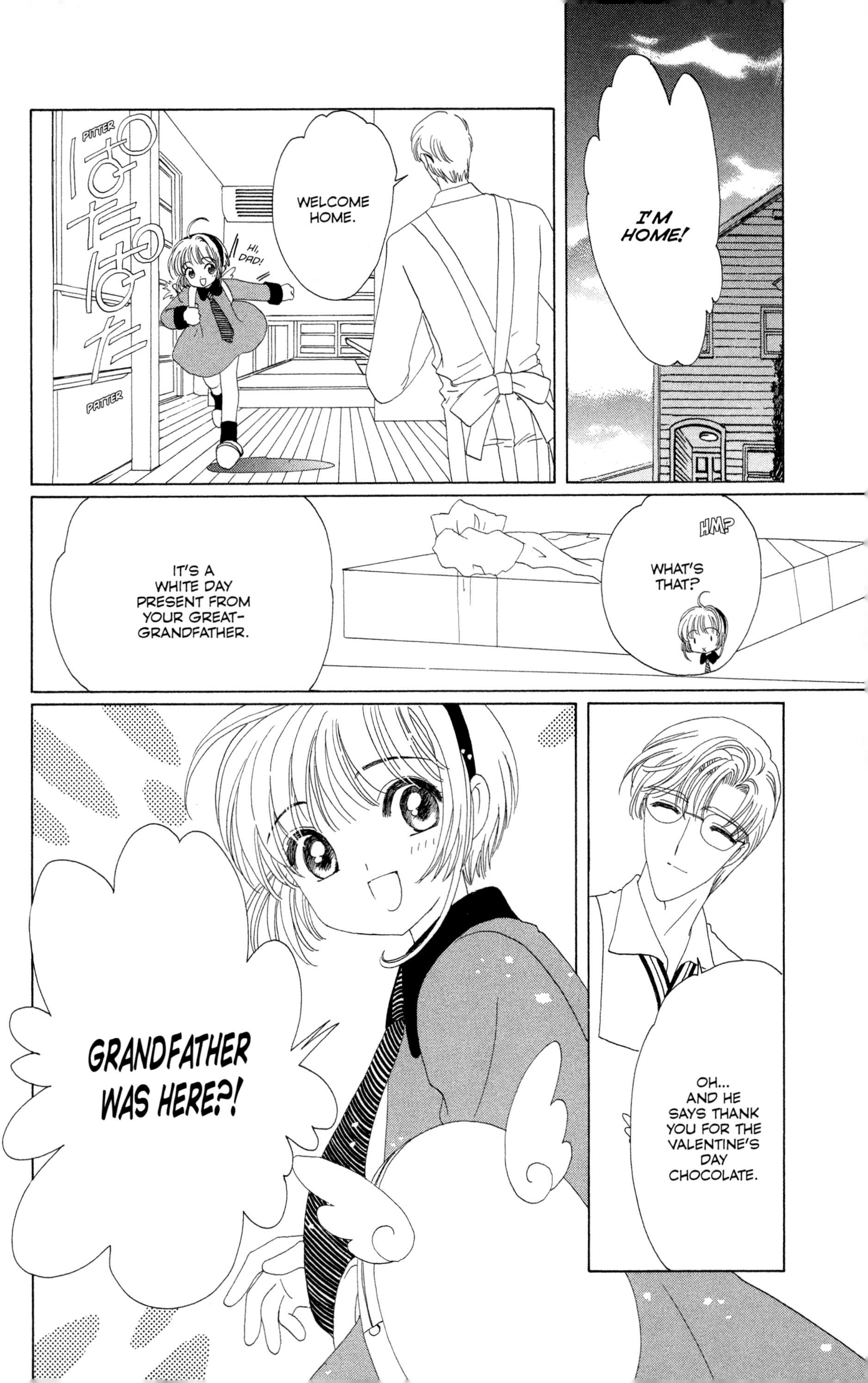
I'M HOME!
WELCOME HOME.
HI, DAD!
PITTER
PATTER
HM?
WHAT'S THAT?
IT'S A WHITE DAY PRESENT FROM YOUR GREAT-GRANDFATHER.
OH... AND HE SAYS THANK YOU FOR THE VALENTINE'S DAY CHOCOLATE.
GRANDFATHER WAS HERE?!

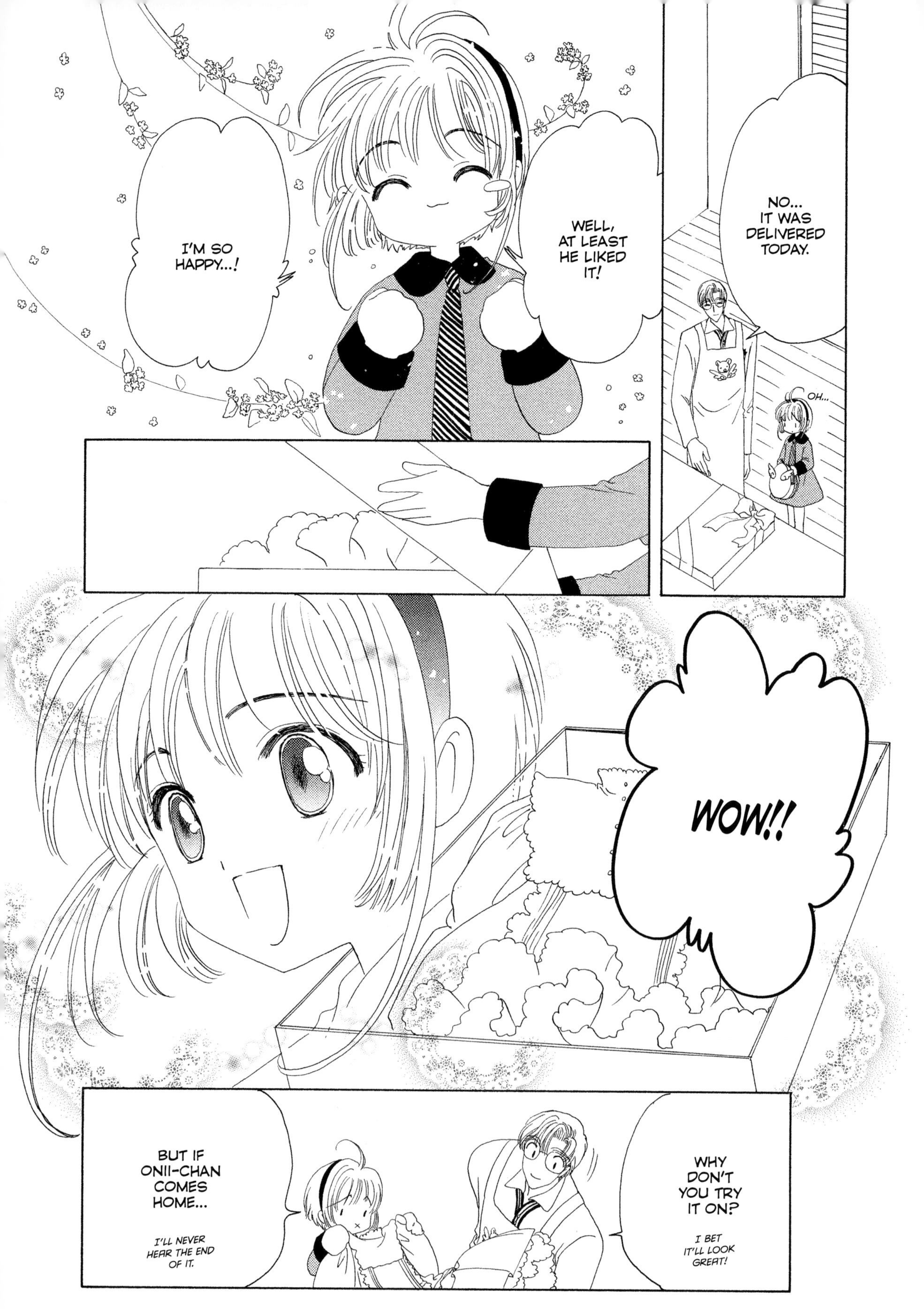
NO... IT WAS DELIVERED TODAY.
OH...
WELL, AT LEAST HE LIKED IT!
I'M SO HAPPY...!
WOW!!
WHY DON'T YOU TRY IT ON?
I BET IT'LL LOOK GREAT!
BUT IF ONII-CHAN COMES HOME...
I'LL NEVER HEAR THE END OF IT.

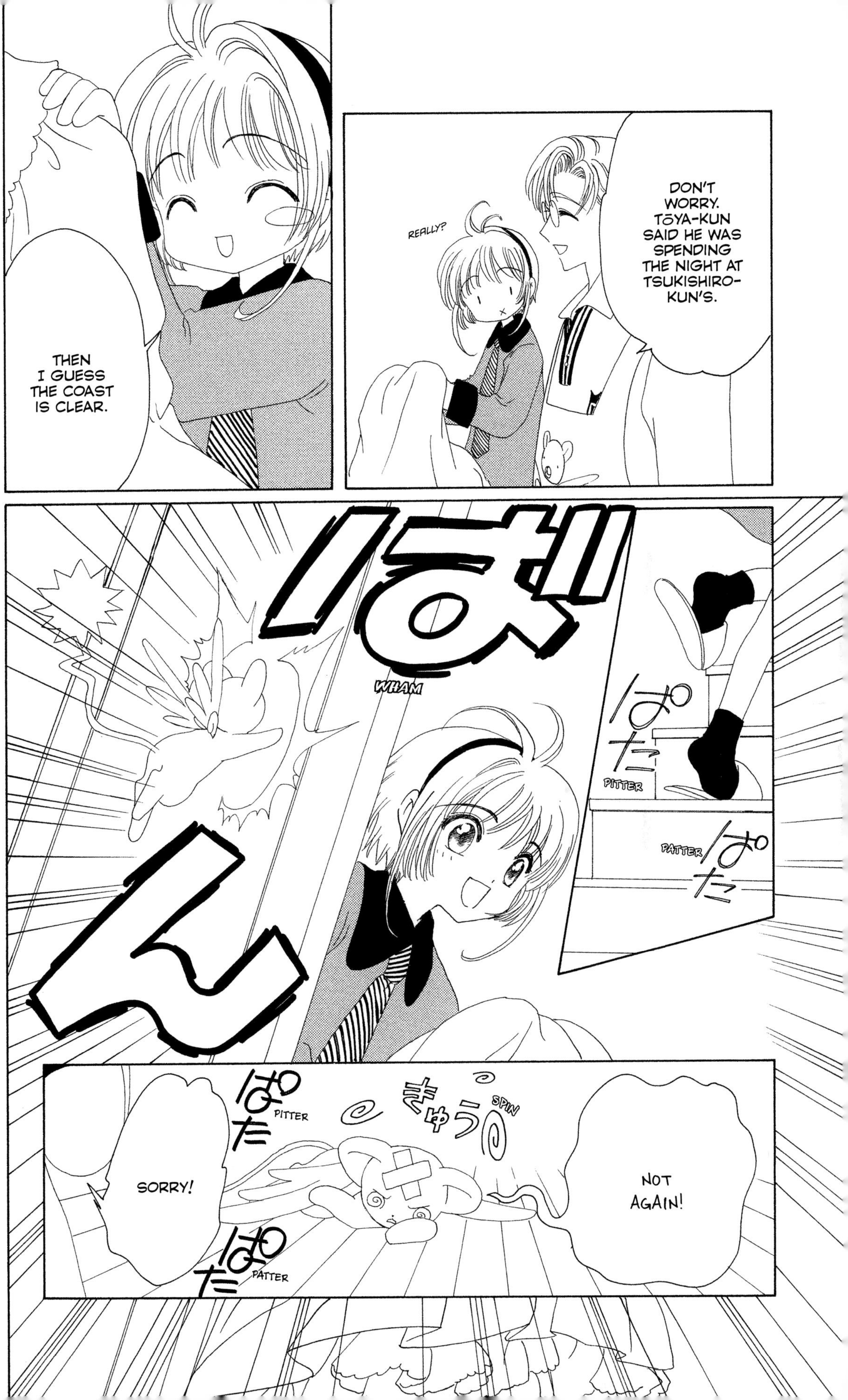

DON'T WORRY. TŌYA-KUN SAID HE WAS SPENDING THE NIGHT AT TSUKISHIRO-KUN'S.
REALLY?
THEN I GUESS THE COAST IS CLEAR.
ばん
WHAM
ぱた
PITTER
ぱた
PATTER
NOT AGAIN!
きゅう
SPIN
ぱた
PITTER
SORRY!
ぱた
PATTER

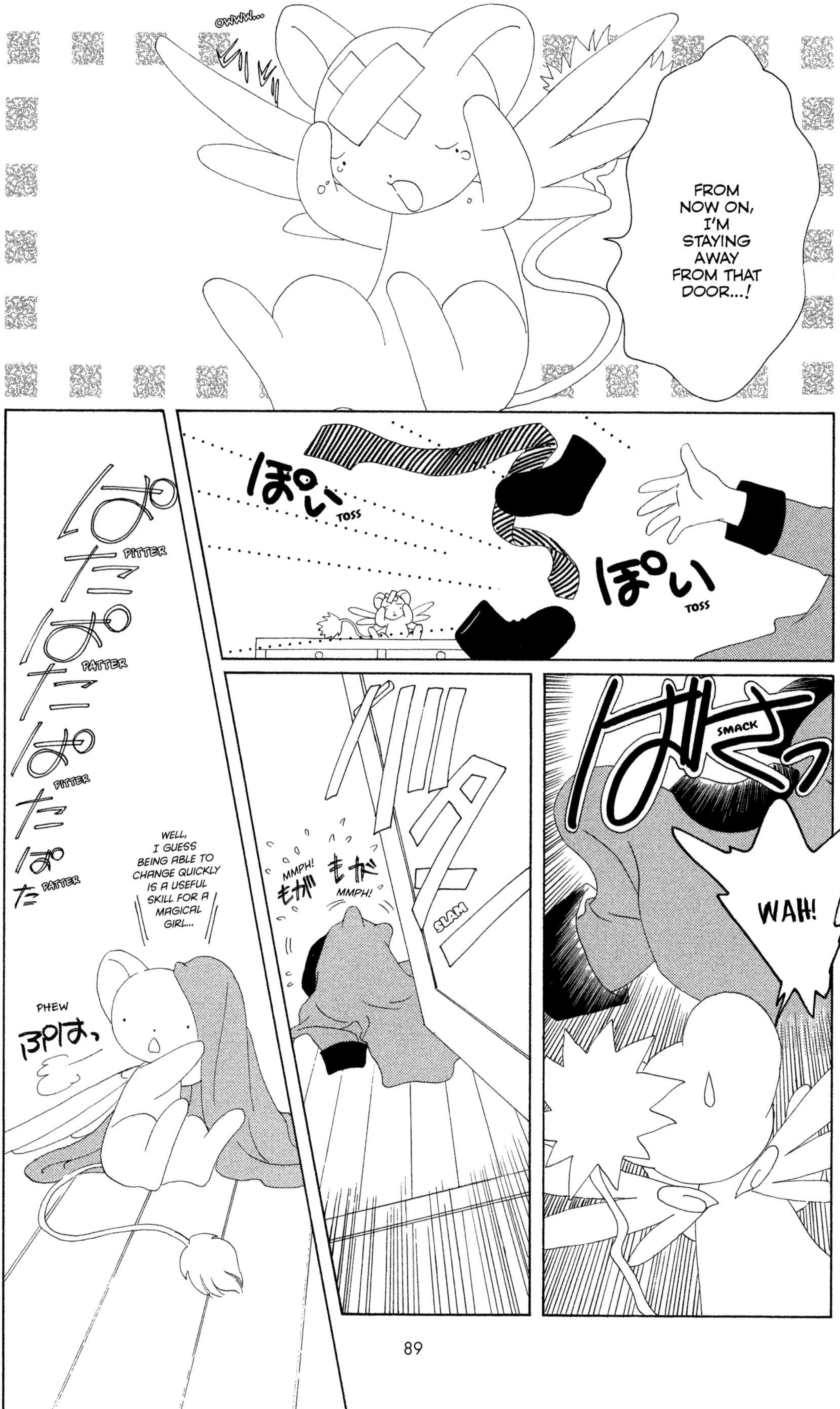
OWWW...
FROM NOW ON, I'M STAYING AWAY FROM THAT DOOR...!
ぽい TOSS
ぽい TOSS
ばさっ SMACK
WAH!
もが MMPH!
もが MMPH!
SLAM
ぱたぱたぱたぱた
PITTER PATTER PITTER PATTER
WELL, I GUESS BEING ABLE TO CHANGE QUICKLY IS A USEFUL SKILL FOR A MAGICAL GIRL...
ぷはっ PHEW

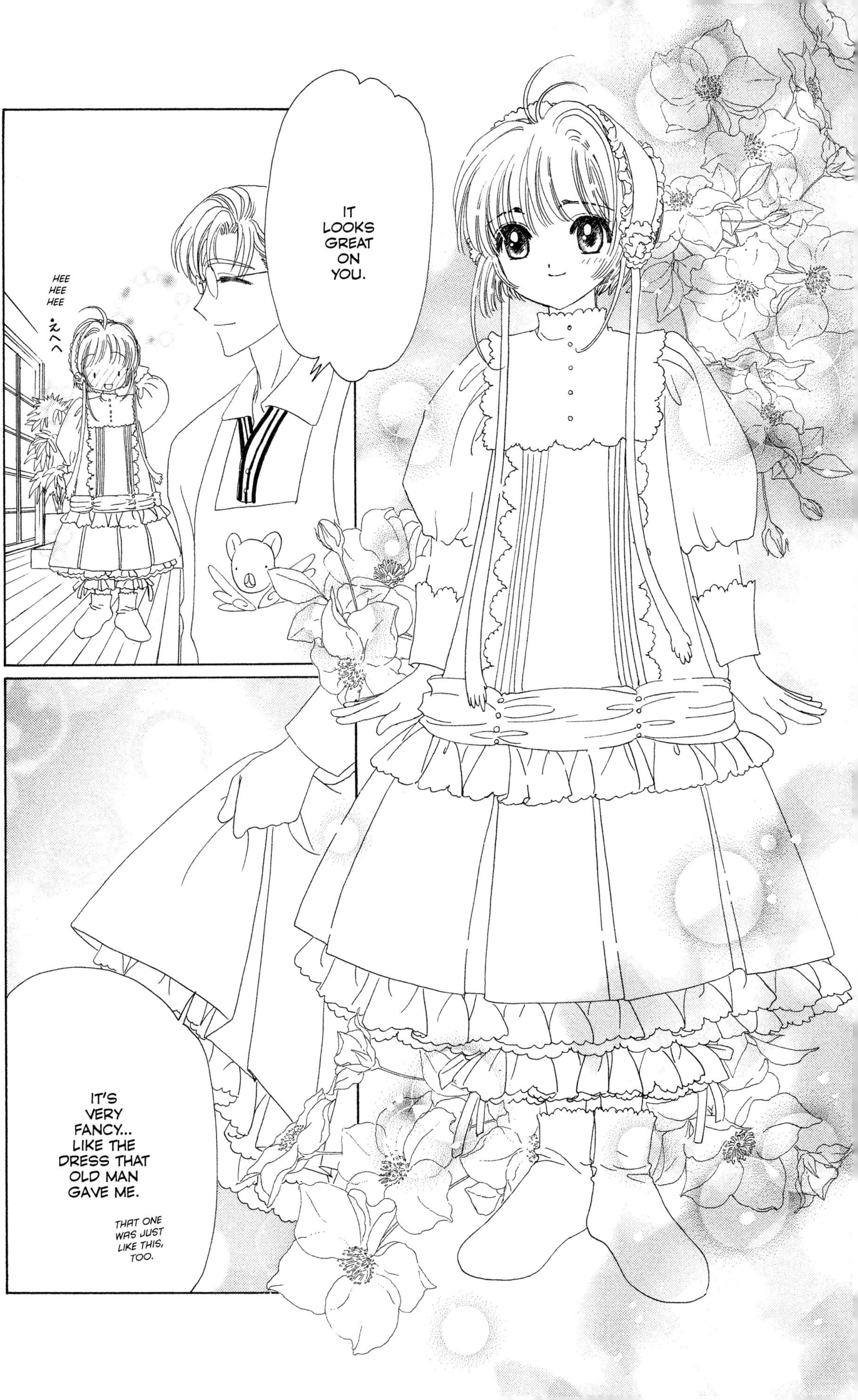
IT LOOKS GREAT ON YOU.
HEE HEE HEE
えへへ
IT'S VERY FANCY... LIKE THE DRESS THAT OLD MAN GAVE ME.
THAT ONE WAS JUST LIKE THIS, TOO.

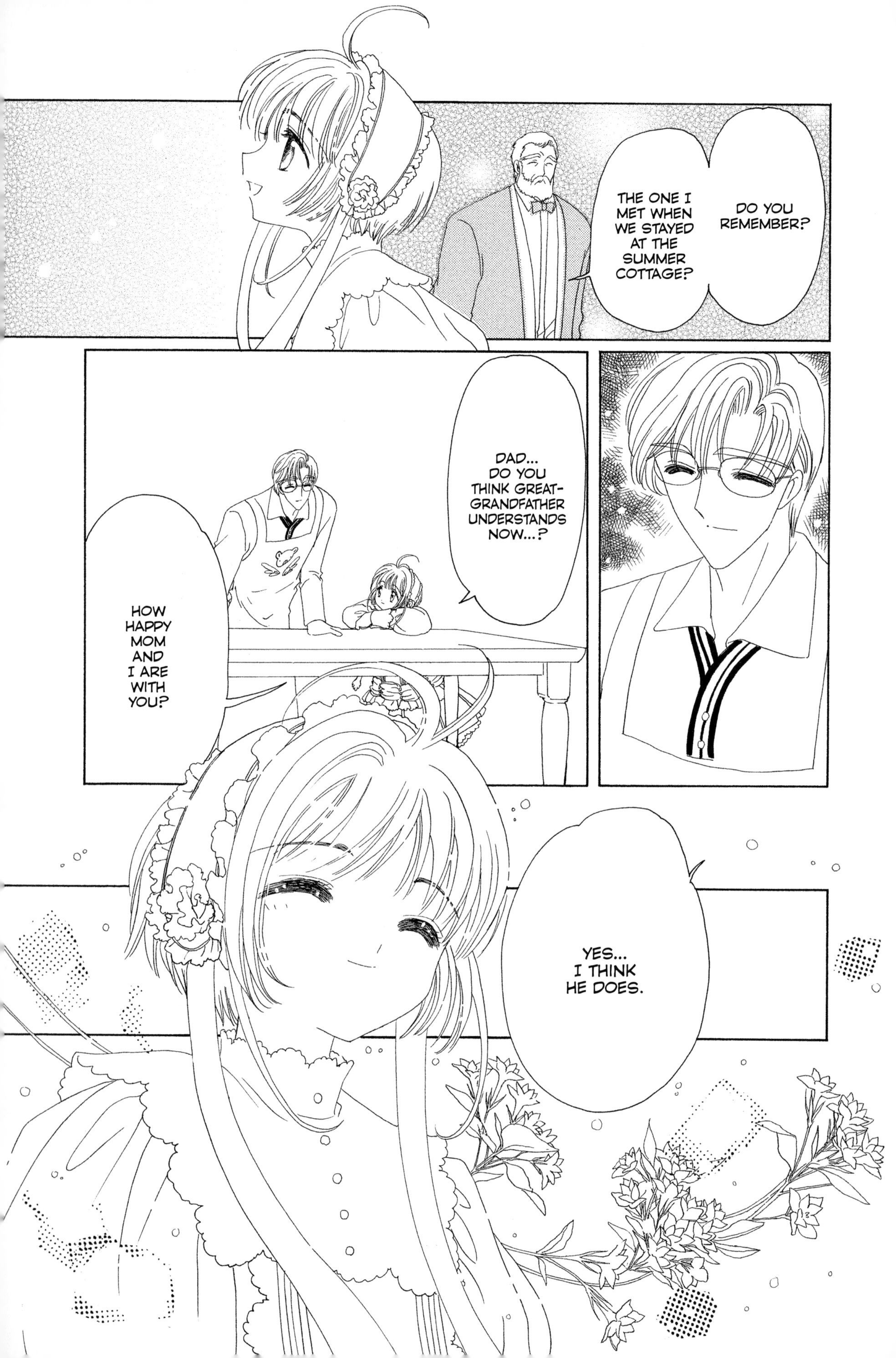
DO YOU REMEMBER?
THE ONE I MET WHEN WE STAYED AT THE SUMMER COTTAGE?
DAD... DO YOU THINK GREAT-GRANDFATHER UNDERSTANDS NOW...?
HOW HAPPY MOM AND I ARE WITH YOU?
YES... I THINK HE DOES.

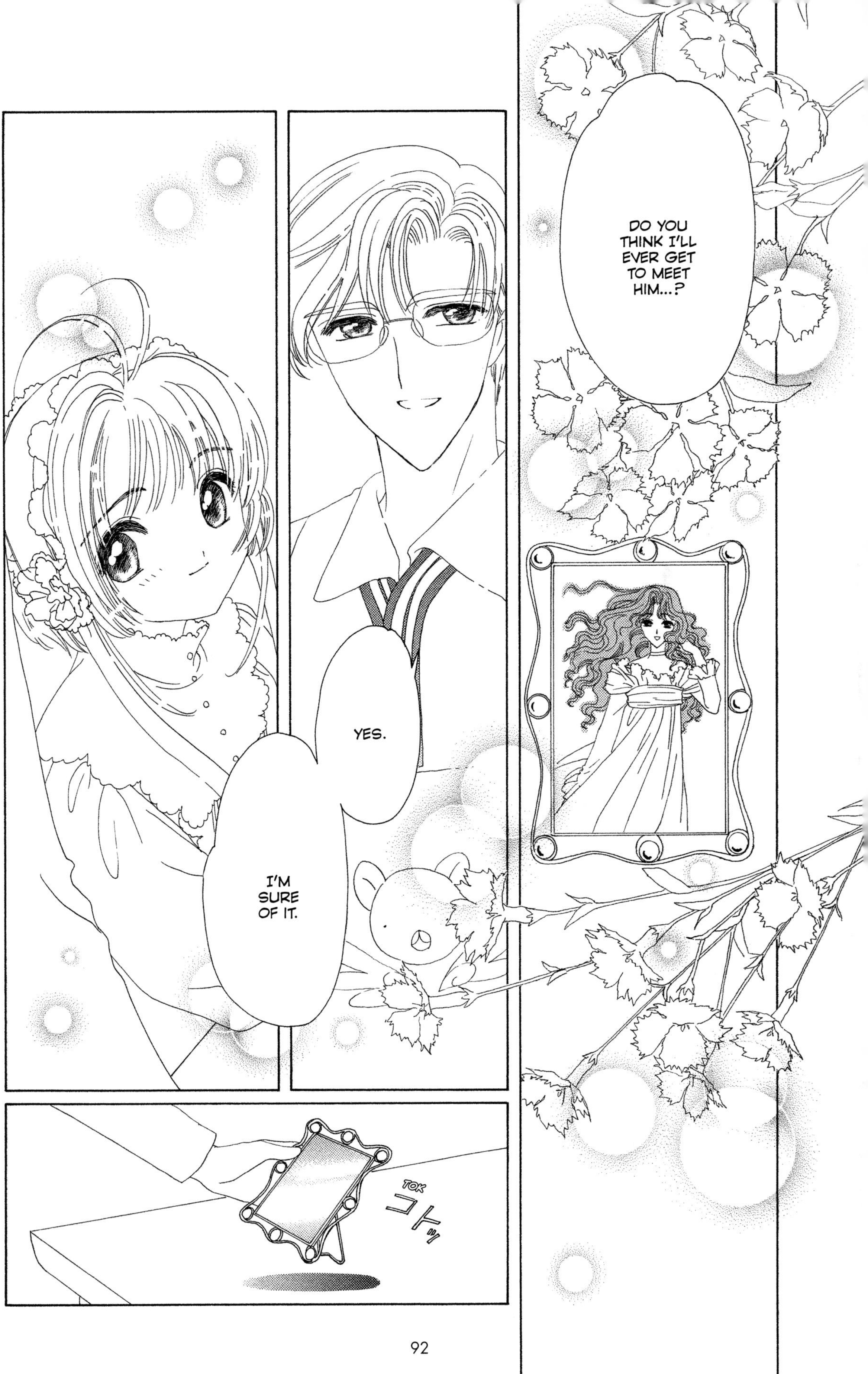
DO YOU THINK I'LL EVER GET TO MEET HIM...?
YES.
I'M SURE OF IT.
TOK
コトッ

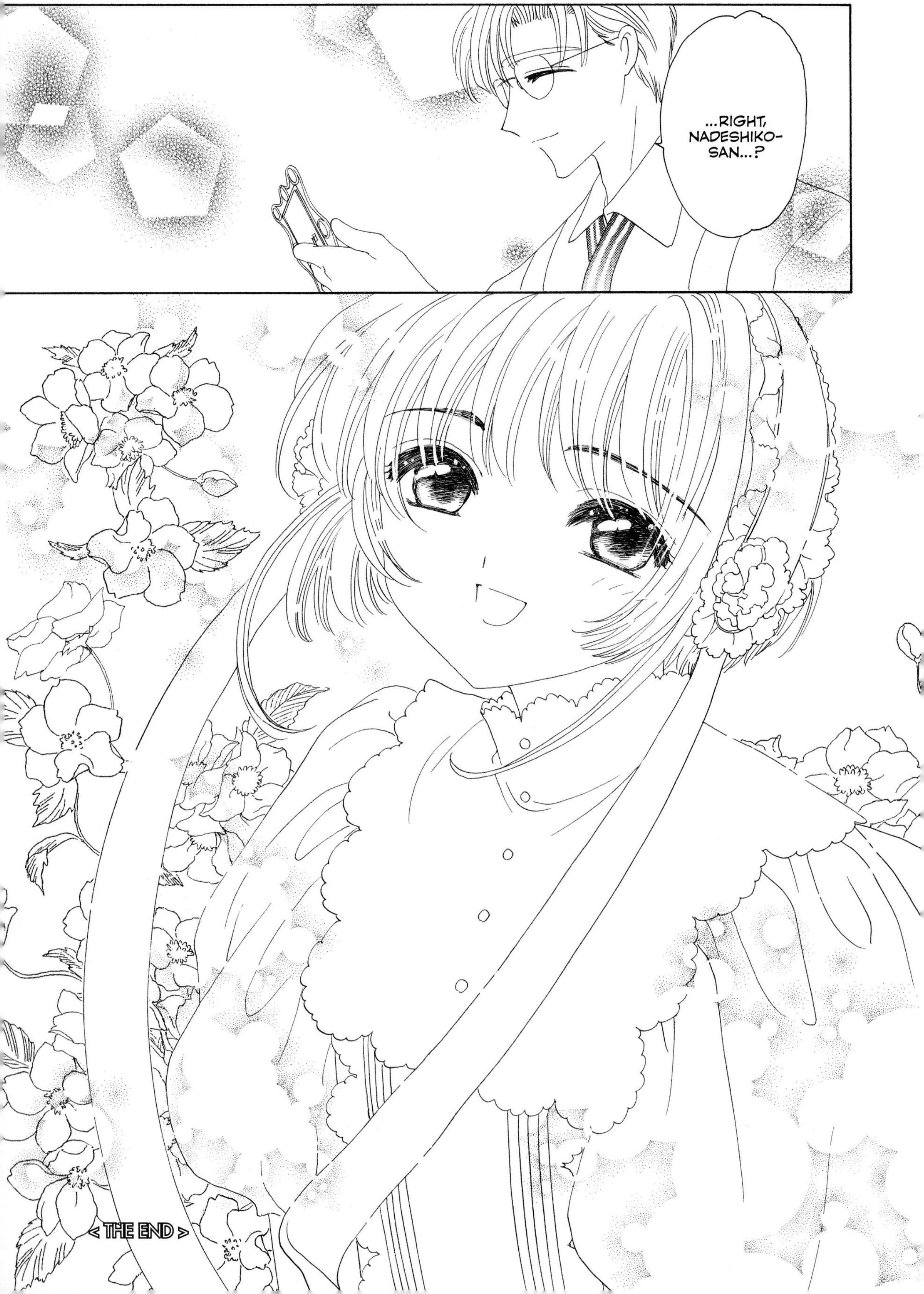
...RIGHT, NADESHIKO-SAN...?
< THE END >

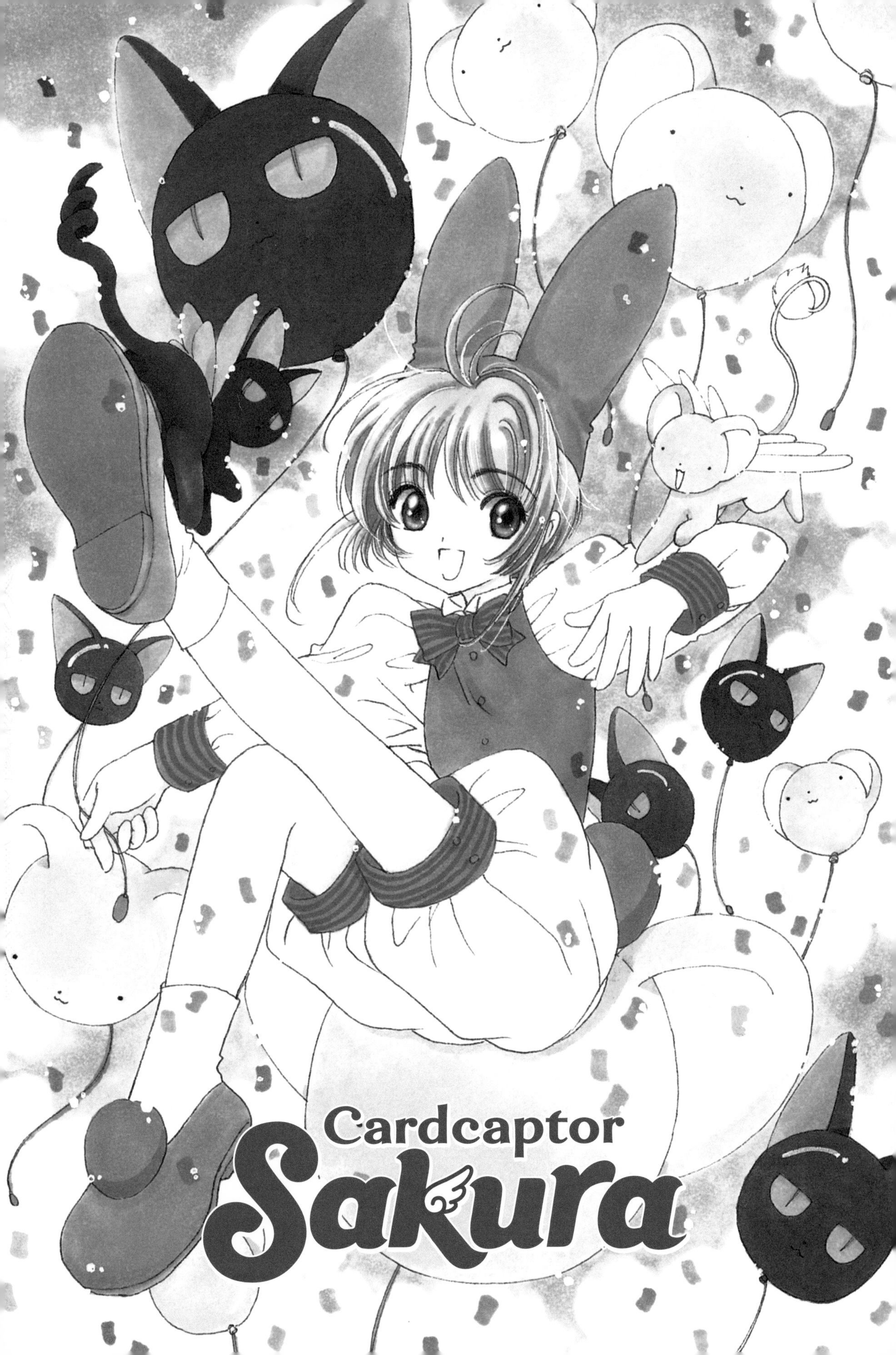
Cardcaptor
Sakura

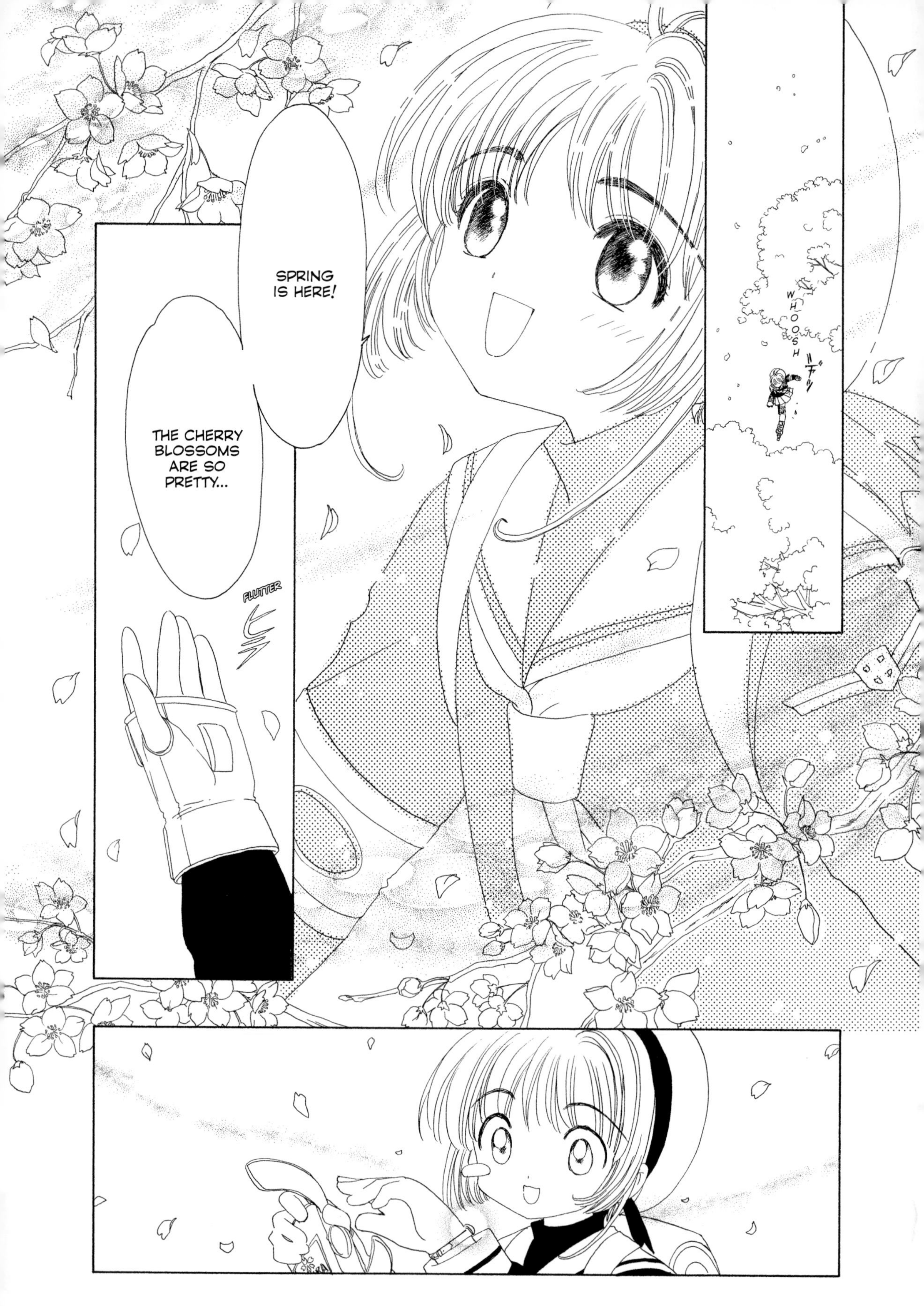
WHOOSH
SPRING IS HERE!
THE CHERRY BLOSSOMS ARE SO PRETTY...
FLUTTER

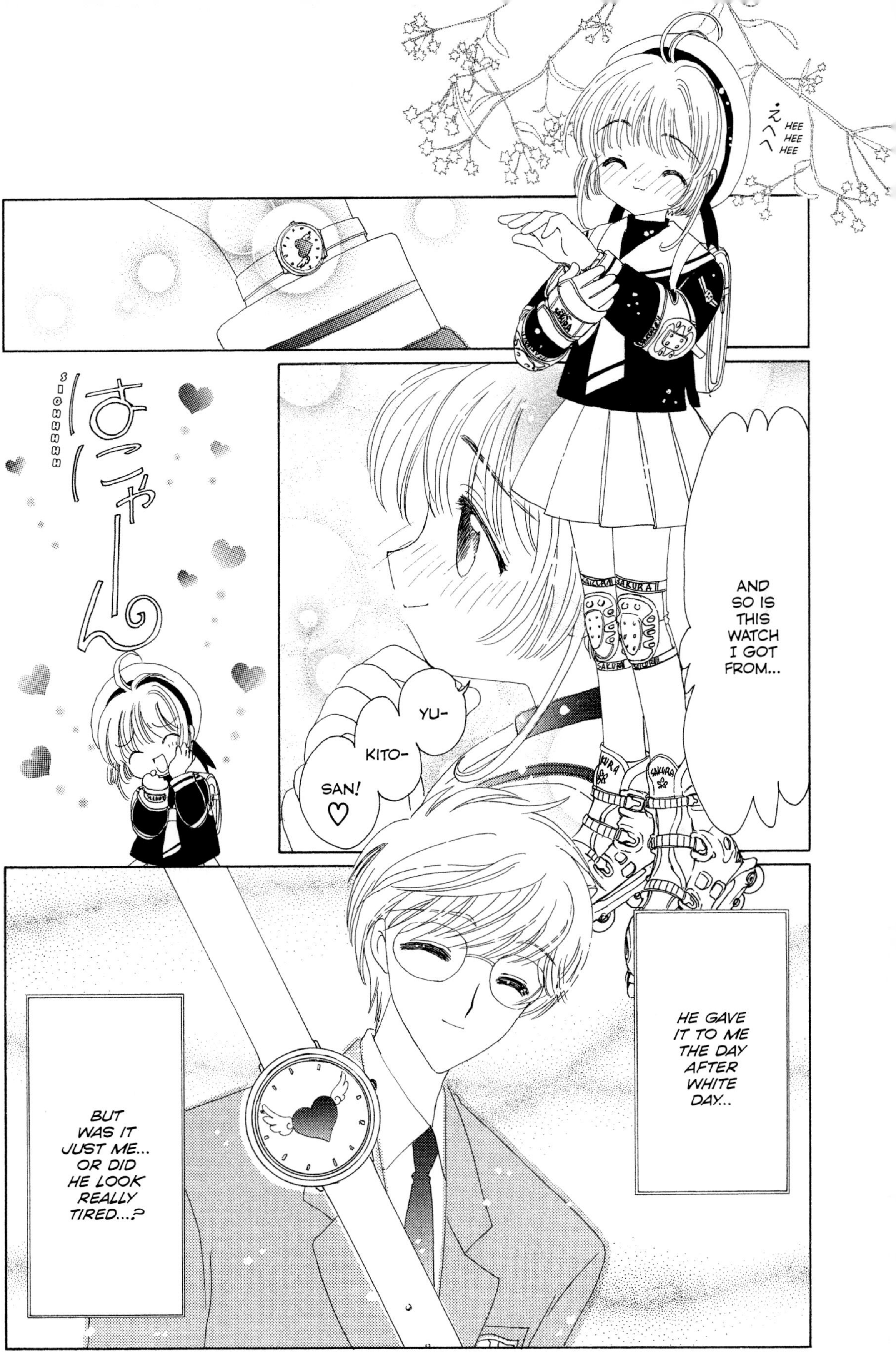
えへへ
HEE HEE HEE
AND SO IS THIS WATCH I GOT FROM...
YU-KITO-SAN! ♡
はにゃーん
SIGHHHHHH
HE GAVE IT TO ME THE DAY AFTER WHITE DAY...
BUT WAS IT JUST ME... OR DID HE LOOK REALLY TIRED...?

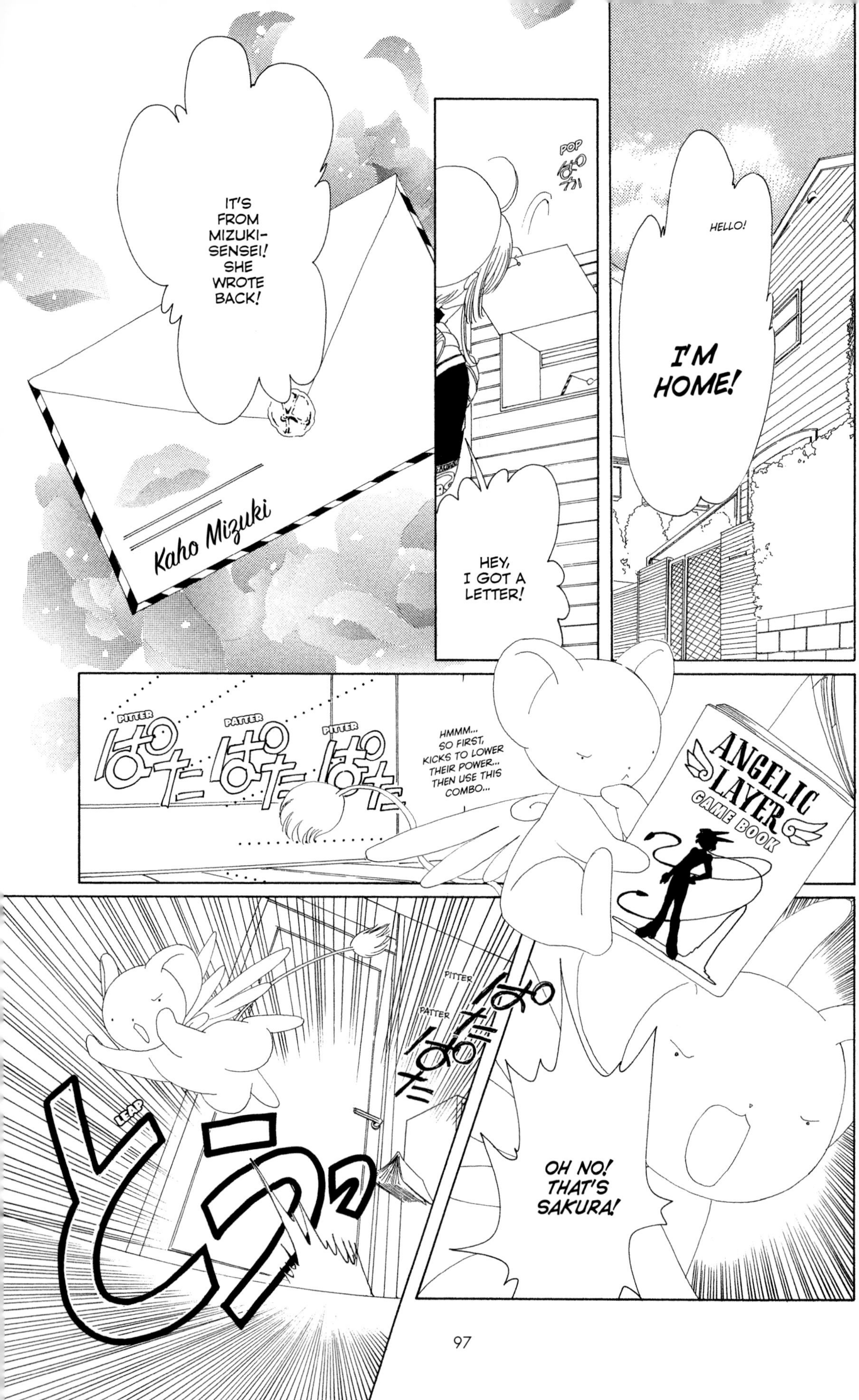

HELLO!
I'M HOME!
POP
HEY, I GOT A LETTER!
IT'S FROM MIZUKI-SENSEI! SHE WROTE BACK!
Kaho Mizuki
ANGELIC LAYER
GAME BOOK
HMMM... SO FIRST, KICKS TO LOWER THEIR POWER... THEN USE THIS COMBO...
PITTER
PATTER
PITTER
PITTER
PATTER
OH NO! THAT'S SAKURA!
LEAP

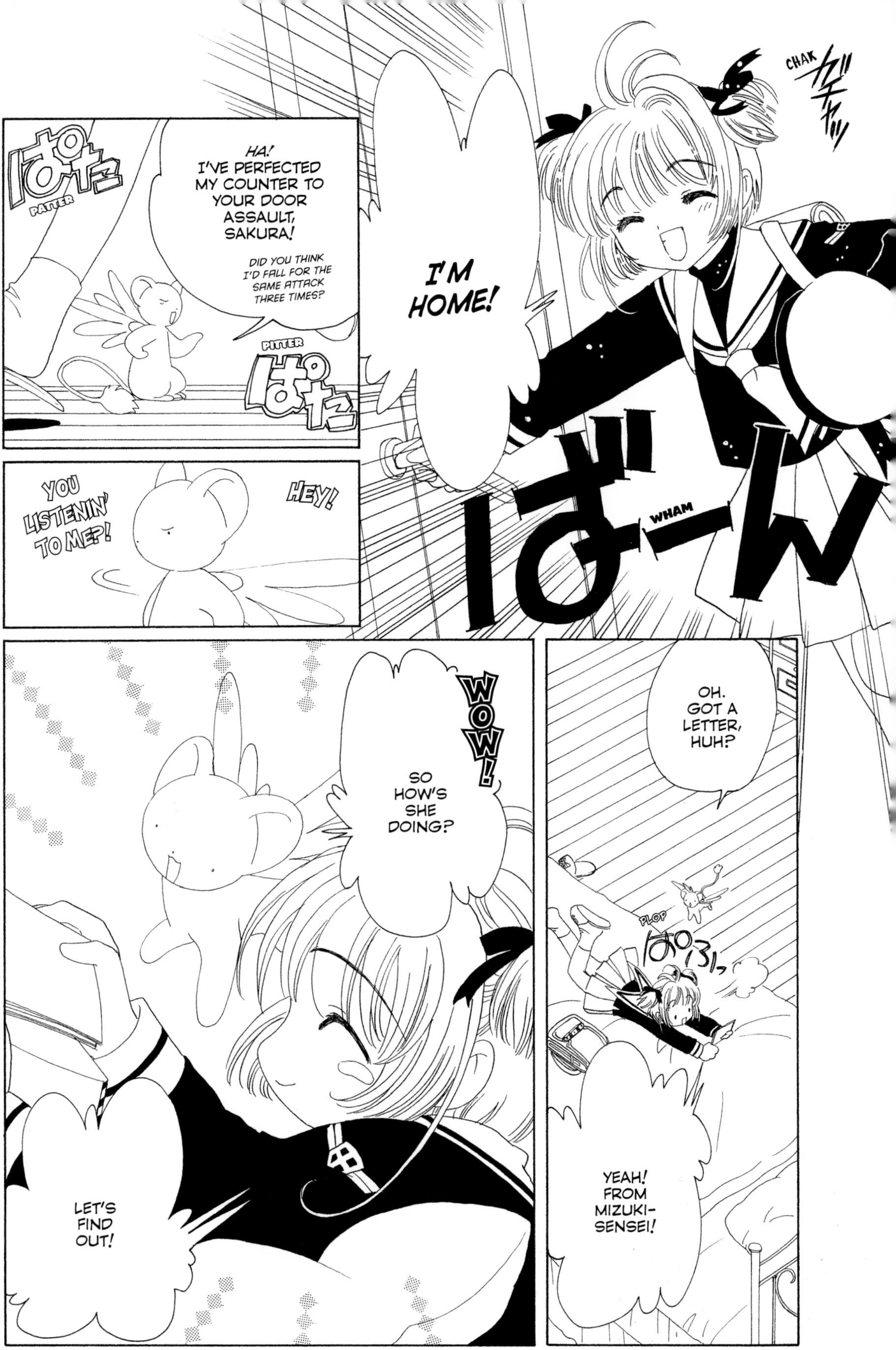
CHAK
I'M HOME!
WHAM
HA! I'VE PERFECTED MY COUNTER TO YOUR DOOR ASSAULT, SAKURA!
DID YOU THINK I'D FALL FOR THE SAME ATTACK THREE TIMES?
PATTER
PITTER
HEY!
YOU LISTENIN' TO ME?!
OH. GOT A LETTER, HUH?
PLOP
YEAH! FROM MIZUKI-SENSEI!
WOW!
SO HOW'S SHE DOING?
LET'S FIND OUT!

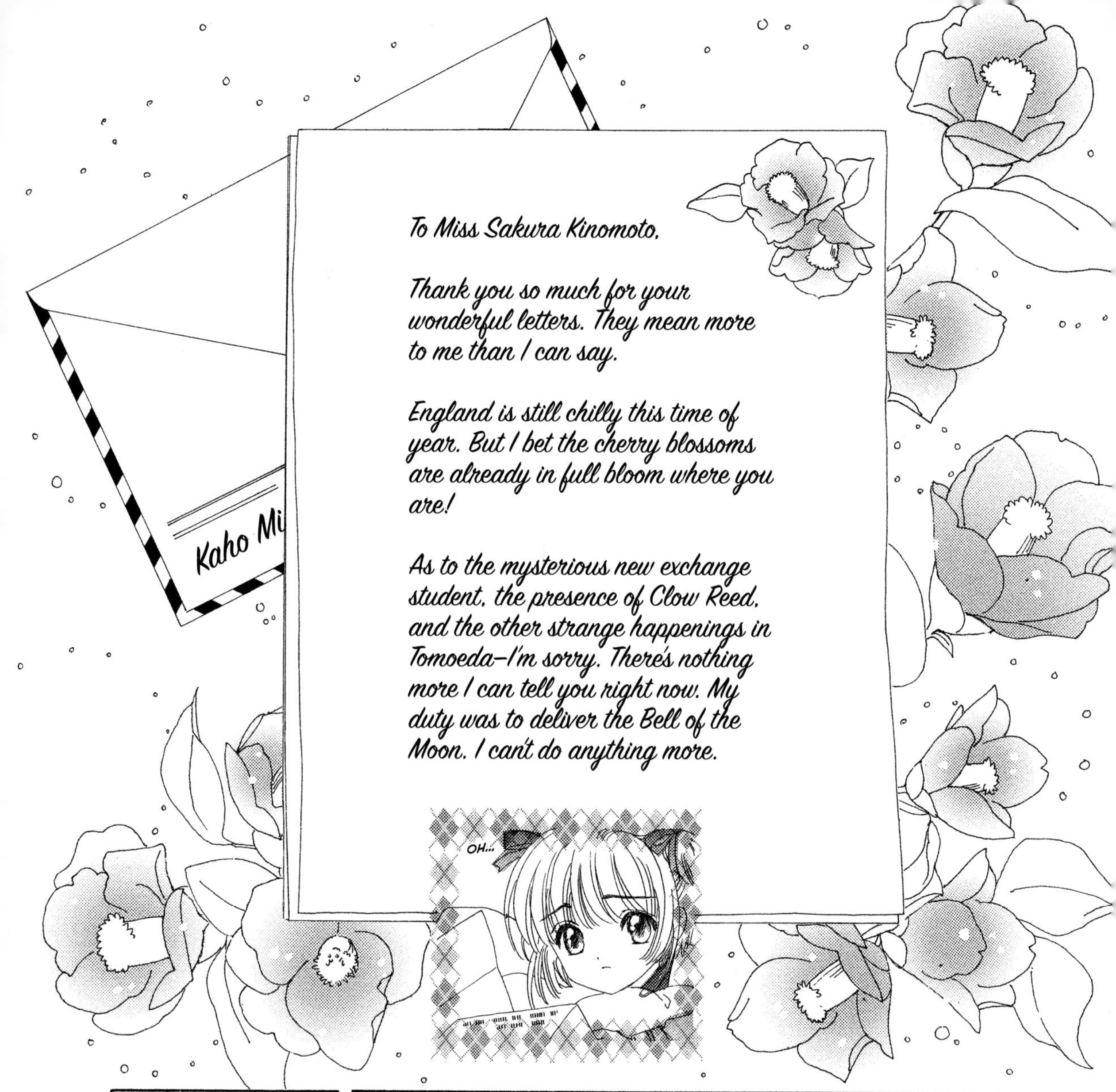
To Miss Sakura Kinomoto,
Thank you so much for your wonderful letters. They mean more to me than I can say.
England is still chilly this time of year. But I bet the cherry blossoms are already in full bloom where you are!
As to the mysterious new exchange student, the presence of Clow Reed, and the other strange happenings in Tomoeda—I'm sorry. There's nothing more I can tell you right now. My duty was to deliver the Bell of the Moon. I can't do anything more.
OH...

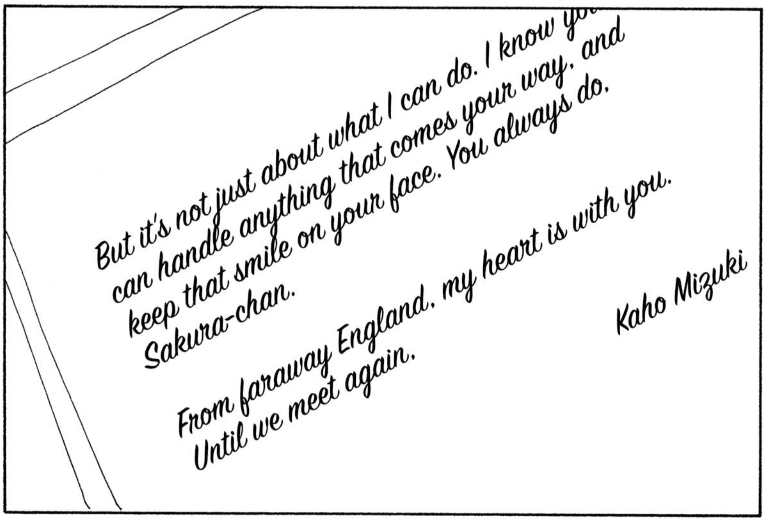
But it's not just about what I can do. I know you can handle anything that comes your way, and keep that smile on your face. You always do, Sakura-chan.
From faraway England, my heart is with you. Until we meet again,
Kaho Mizuki

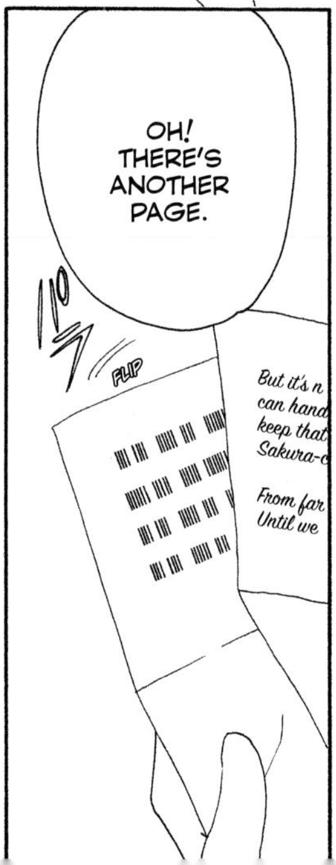
OH! THERE'S ANOTHER PAGE.
FLIP

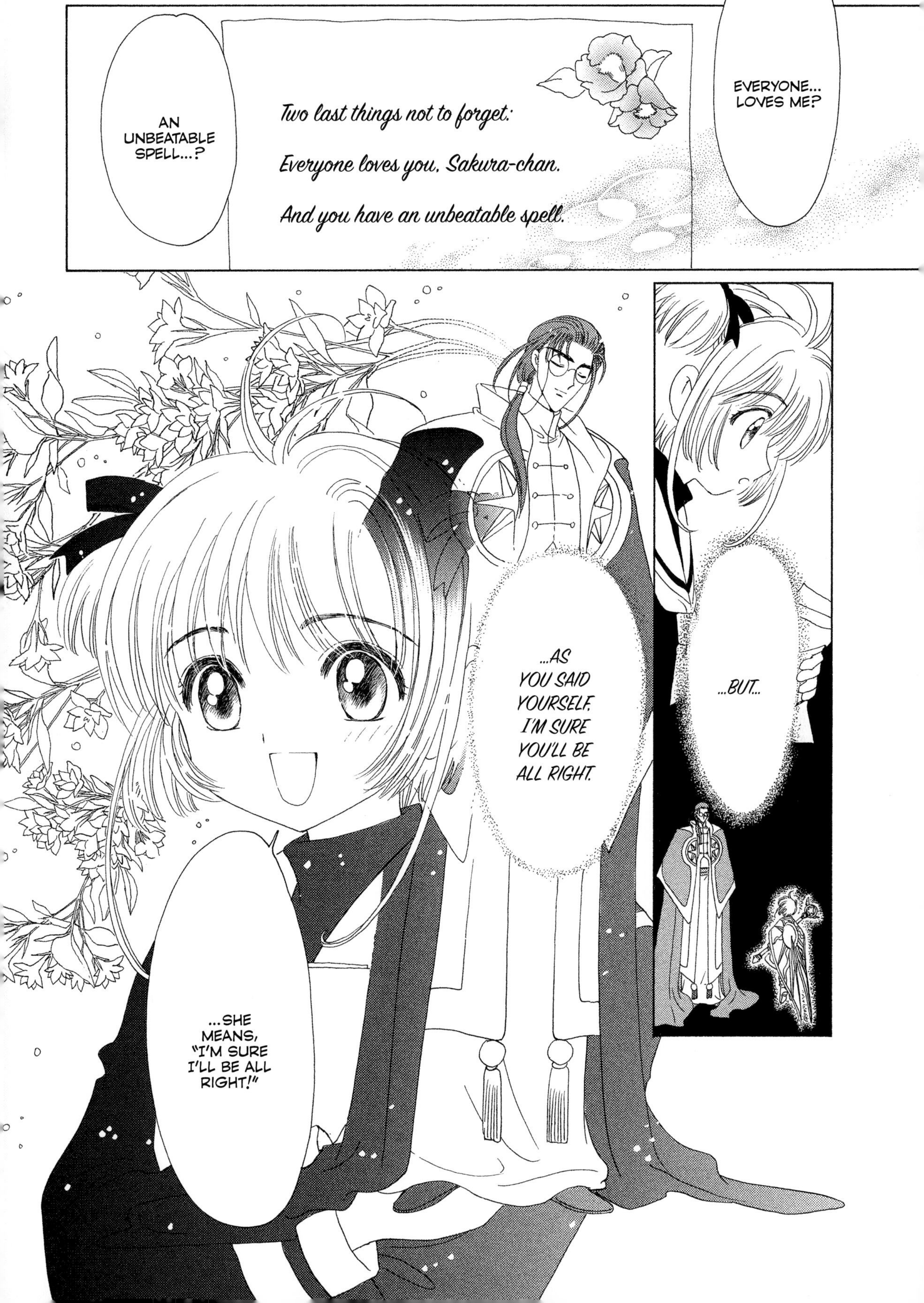
EVERYONE... LOVES ME?
Two last things not to forget:
Everyone loves you, Sakura-chan.
And you have an unbeatable spell.
AN UNBEATABLE SPELL...?
...BUT...
...AS YOU SAID YOURSELF, I'M SURE YOU'LL BE ALL RIGHT.
...SHE MEANS, "I'M SURE I'LL BE ALL RIGHT!"

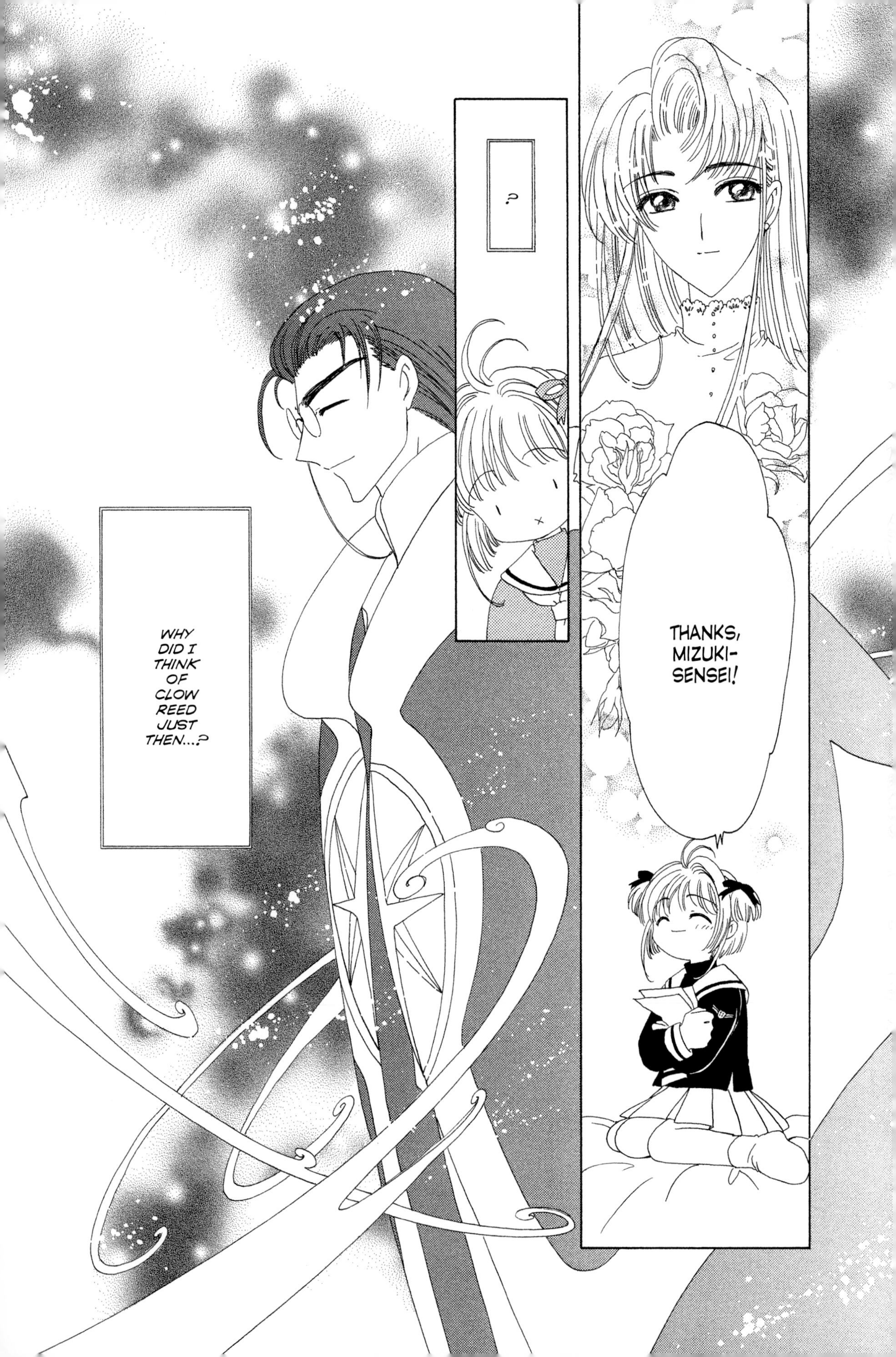
THANKS, MIZUKI-SENSEI!
?
WHY DID I THINK OF CLOW REED JUST THEN...?

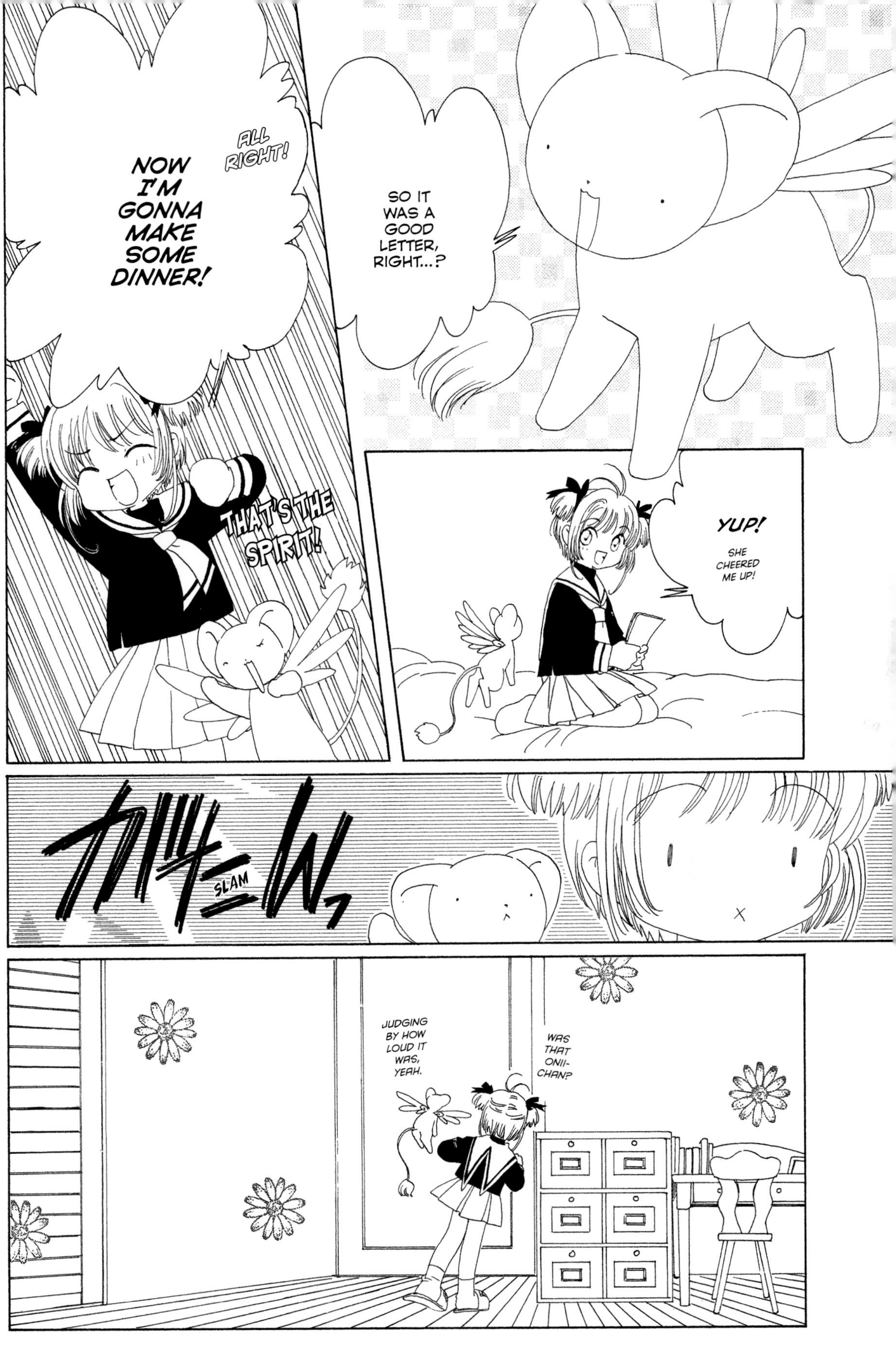
SO IT WAS A GOOD LETTER, RIGHT...?
YUP!
SHE CHEERED ME UP!
ALL RIGHT!
NOW I'M GONNA MAKE SOME DINNER!
THAT'S THE SPIRIT!
SLAM
WAS THAT ONII-CHAN?
JUDGING BY HOW LOUD IT WAS, YEAH.

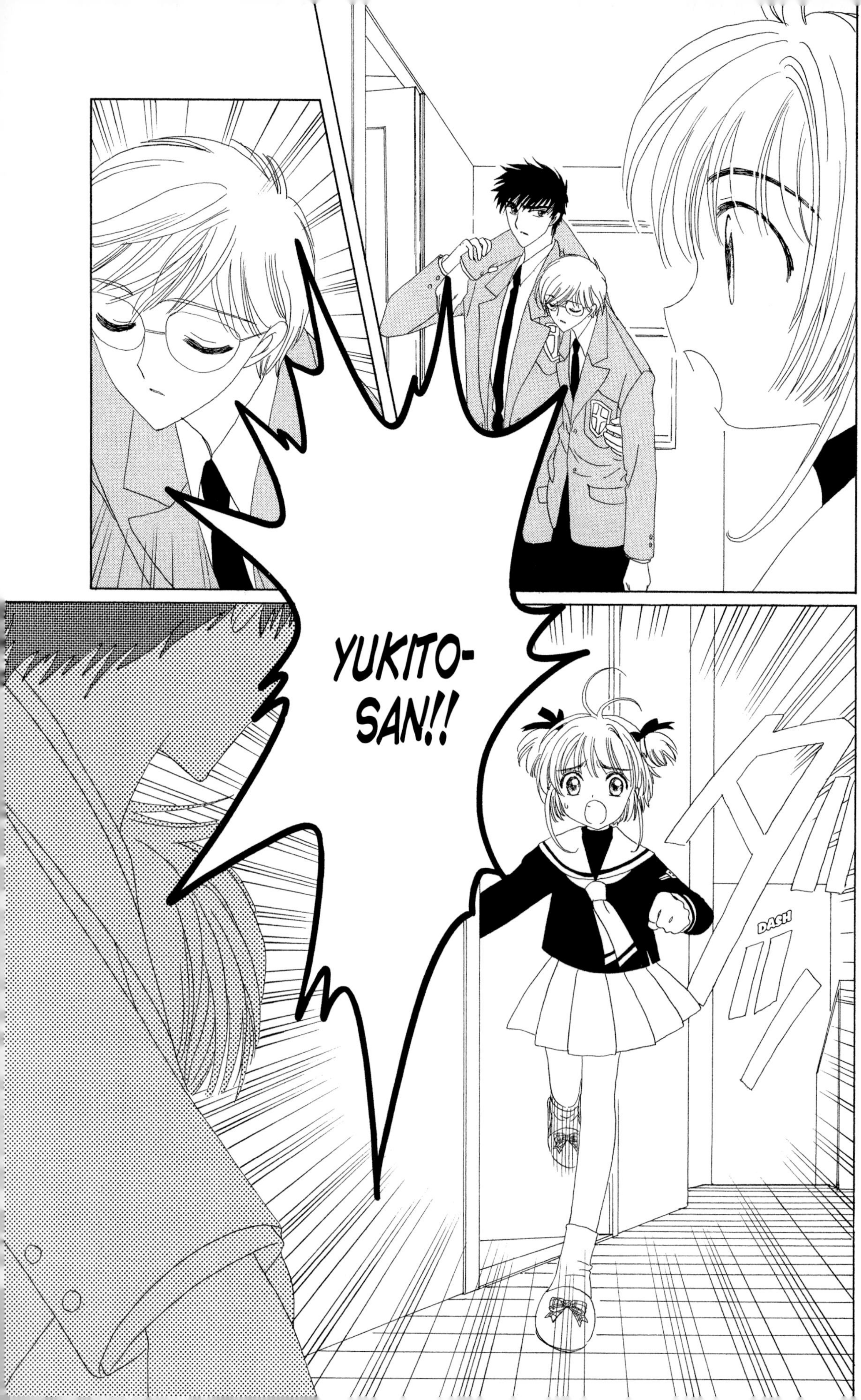
YUKITO-SAN!!
DASH

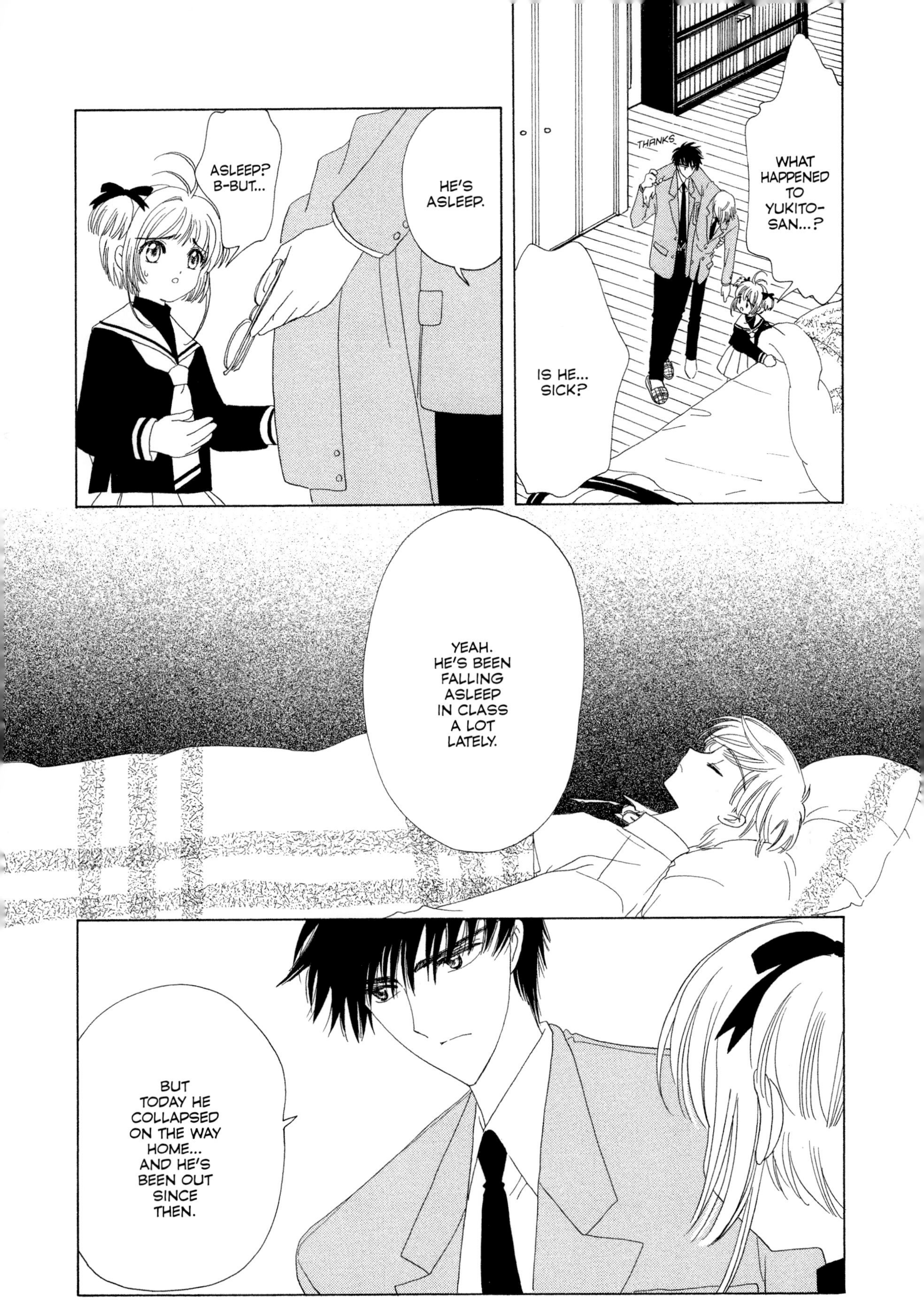
WHAT HAPPENED TO YUKITO-SAN...?
THANKS
IS HE... SICK?
HE'S ASLEEP.
ASLEEP? B-BUT...
YEAH. HE'S BEEN FALLING ASLEEP IN CLASS A LOT LATELY.
BUT TODAY HE COLLAPSED ON THE WAY HOME... AND HE'S BEEN OUT SINCE THEN.

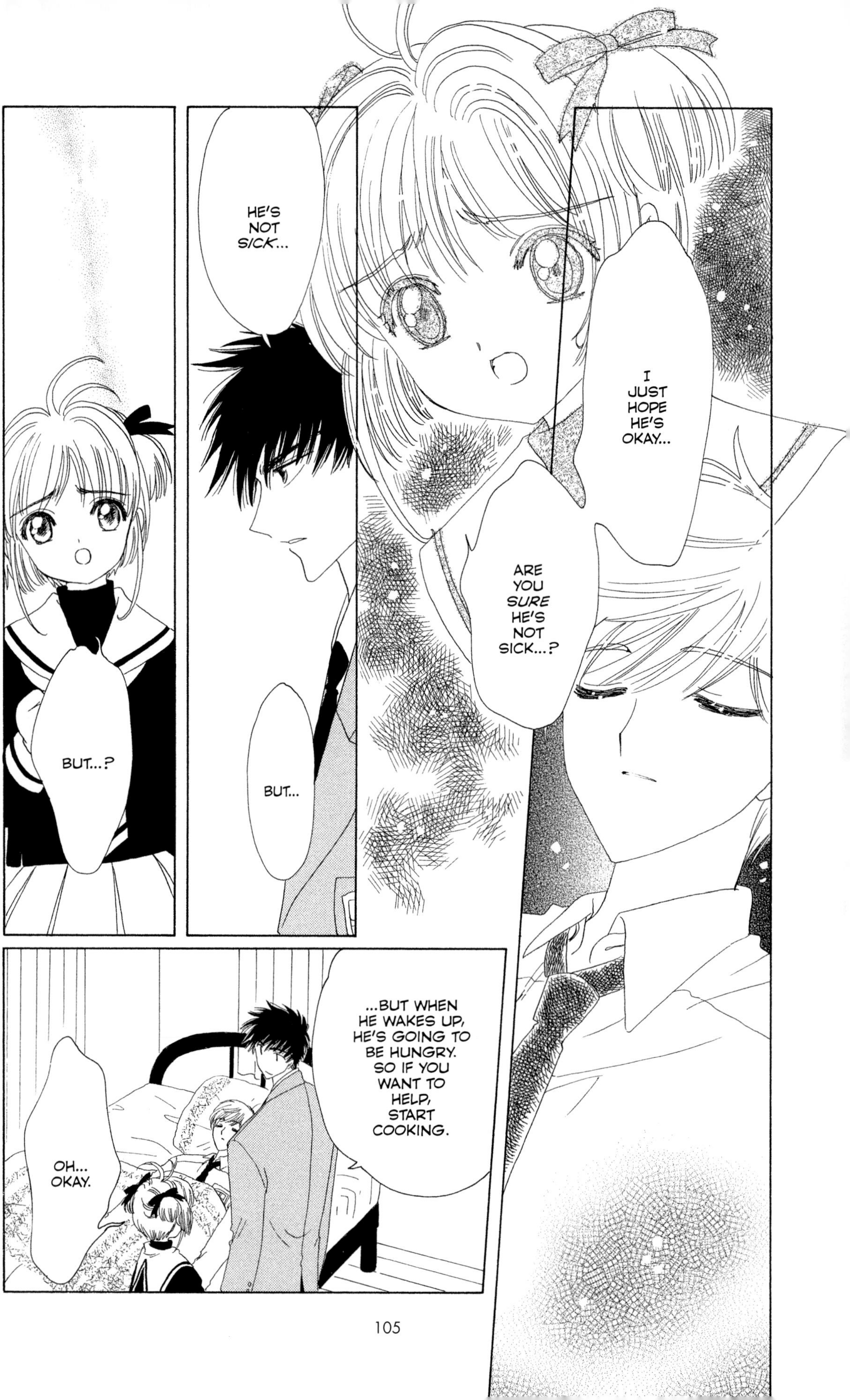
I JUST HOPE HE'S OKAY...
ARE YOU *SURE* HE'S NOT SICK...?
HE'S NOT *SICK*...
BUT...
BUT...?
...BUT WHEN HE WAKES UP, HE'S GOING TO BE HUNGRY. SO IF YOU WANT TO HELP, START COOKING.
OH... OKAY.

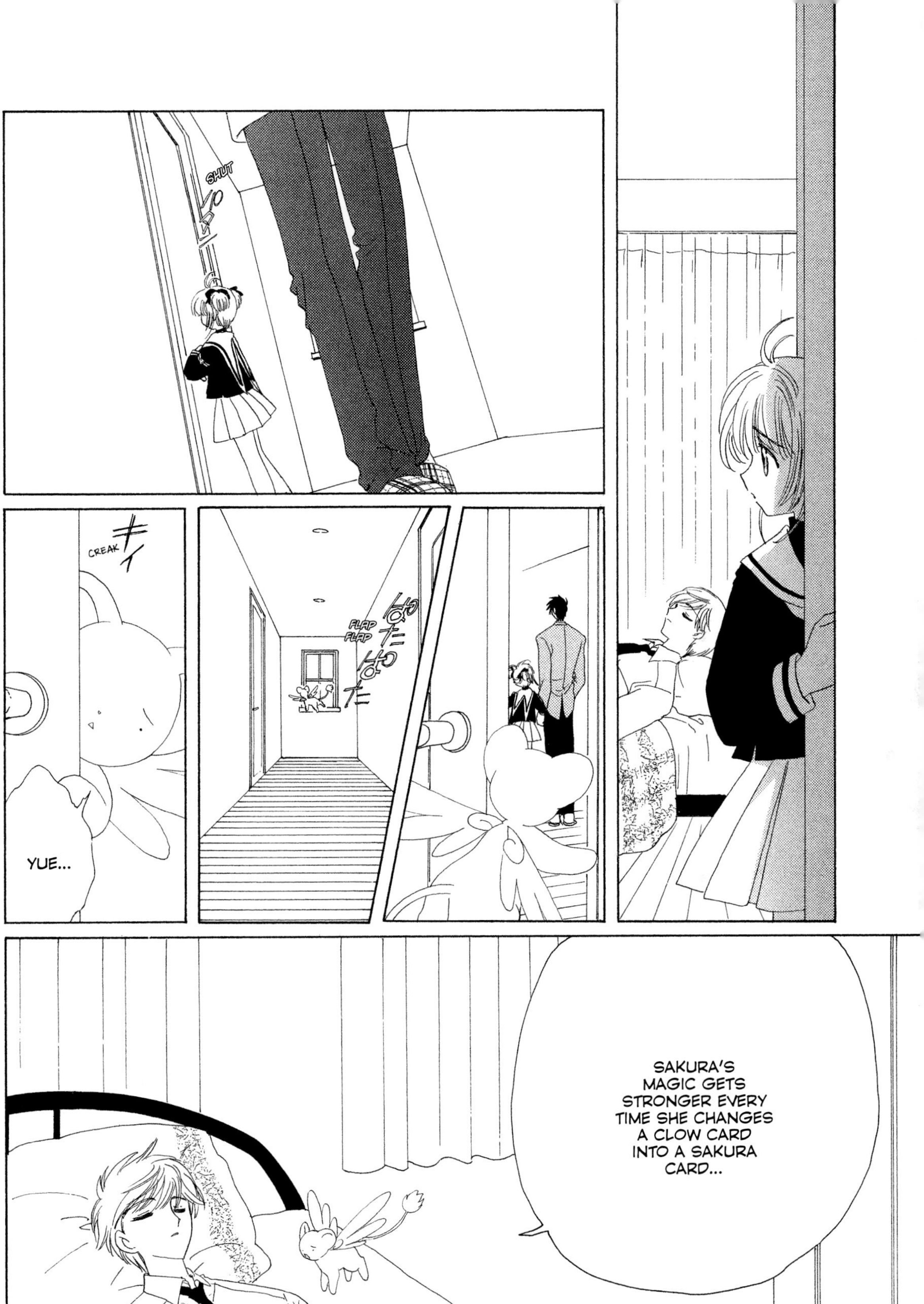
SHUT
FLAP FLAP
CREAK
YUE...
SAKURA'S MAGIC GETS STRONGER EVERY TIME SHE CHANGES A CLOW CARD INTO A SAKURA CARD...

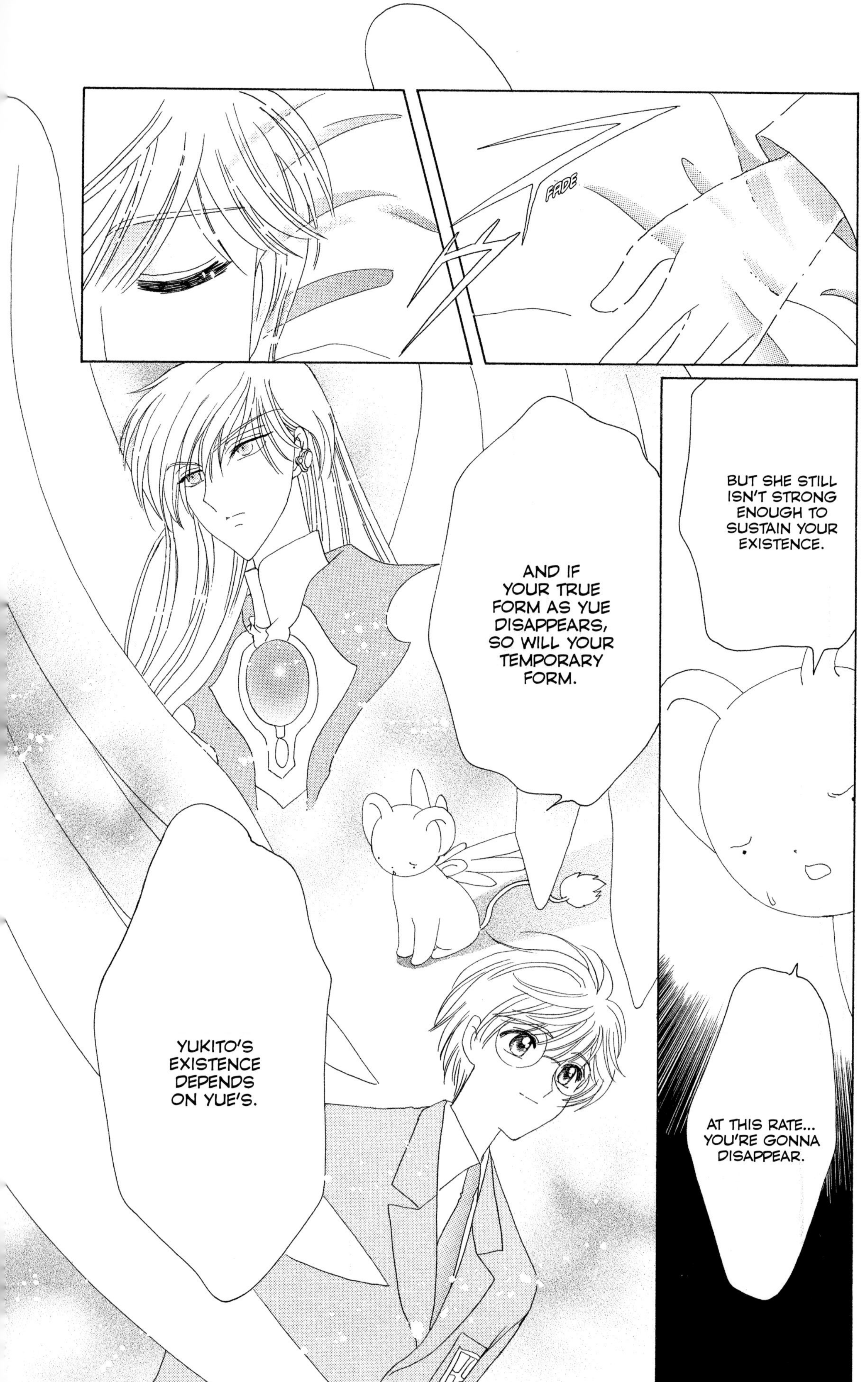
FADE
BUT SHE STILL ISN'T STRONG ENOUGH TO SUSTAIN YOUR EXISTENCE.
AT THIS RATE... YOU'RE GONNA DISAPPEAR.
AND IF YOUR TRUE FORM AS YUE DISAPPEARS, SO WILL YOUR TEMPORARY FORM.
YUKITO'S EXISTENCE DEPENDS ON YUE'S.

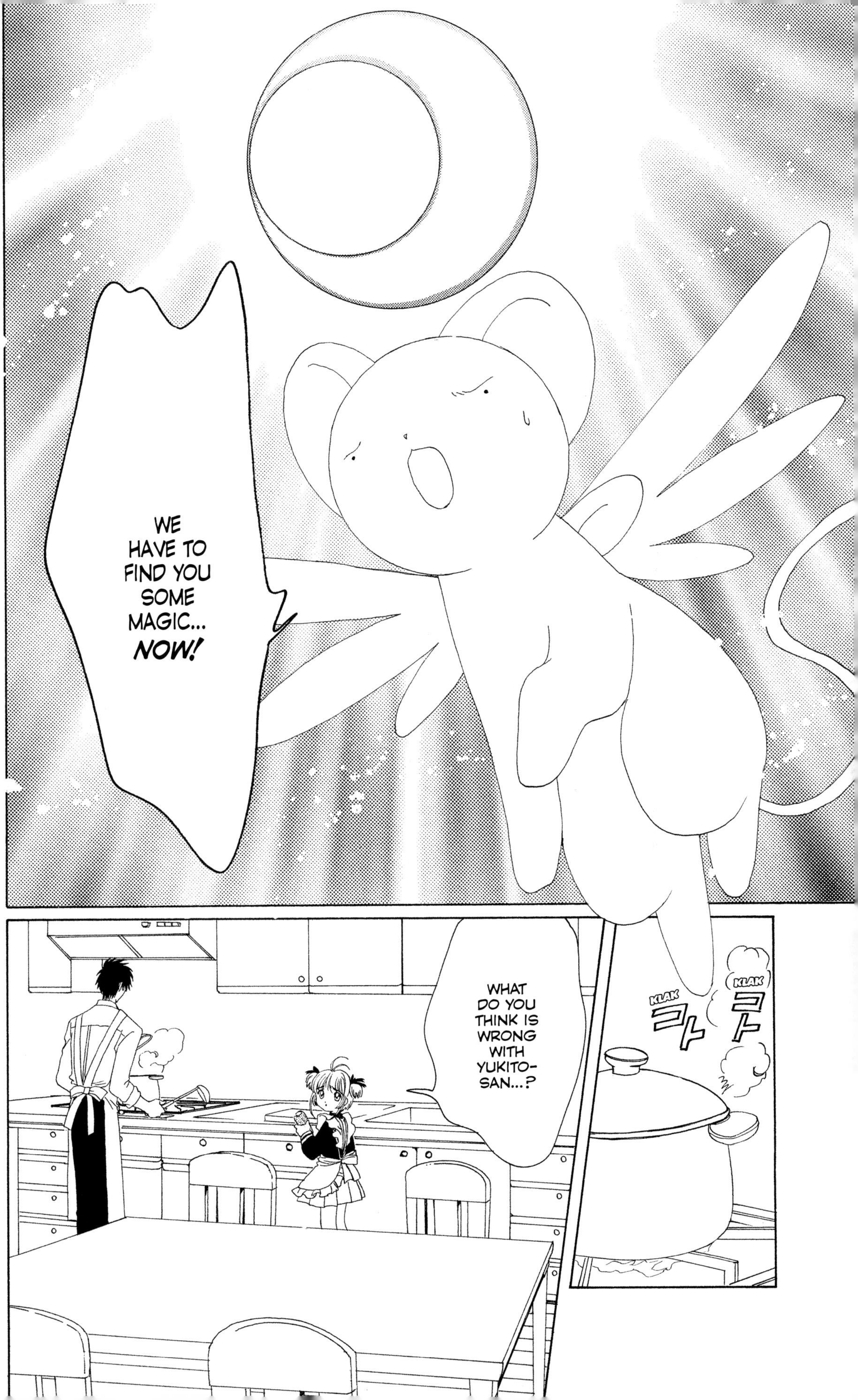
WE HAVE TO FIND YOU SOME MAGIC... NOW!
KLAK
KLAK
WHAT DO YOU THINK IS WRONG WITH YUKITO-SAN...?

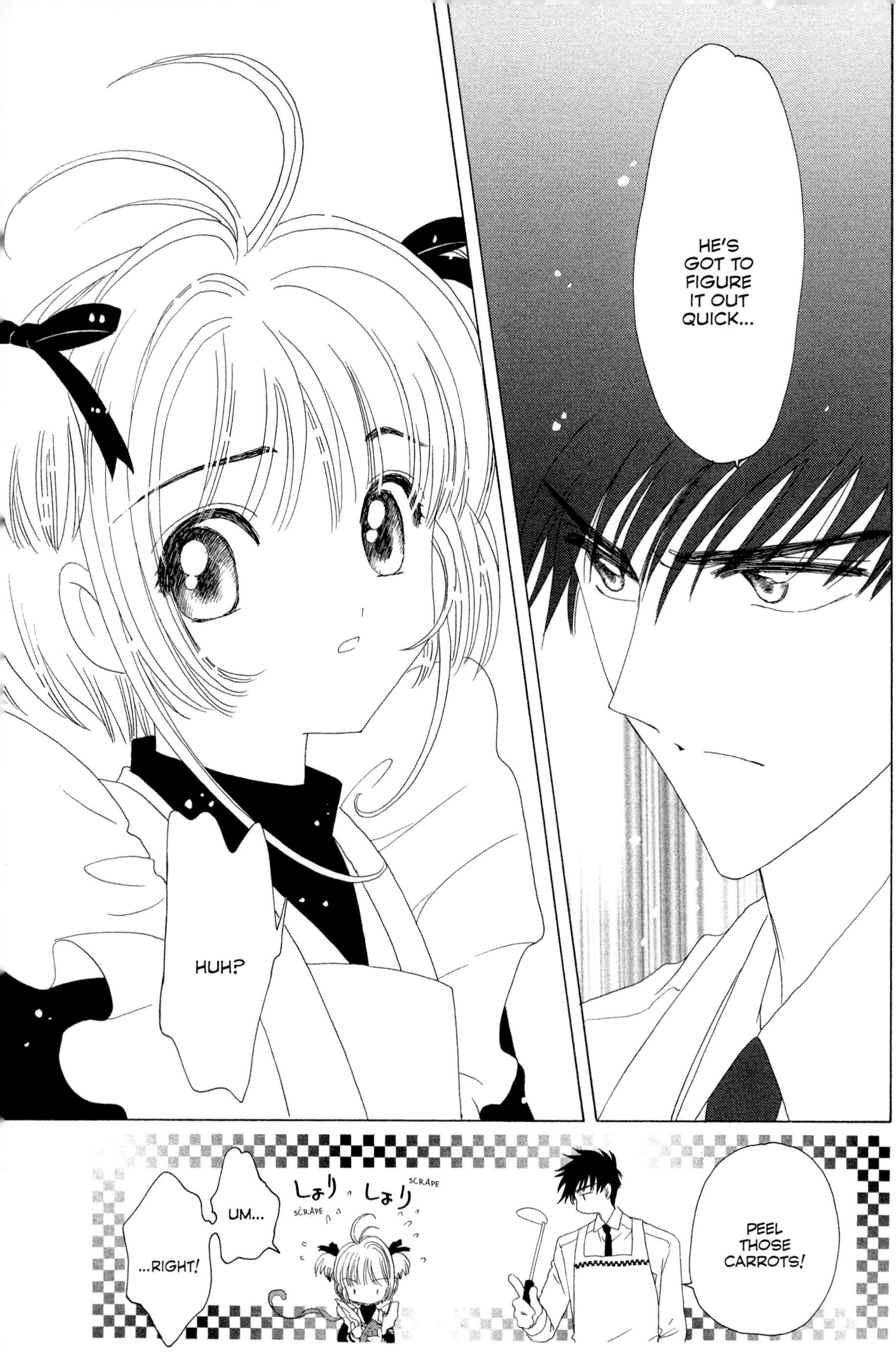
HE'S GOT TO FIGURE IT OUT QUICK...
HUH?
PEEL THOSE CARROTS!
しょり SCRAPE
しょり SCRAPE
UM...
...RIGHT!

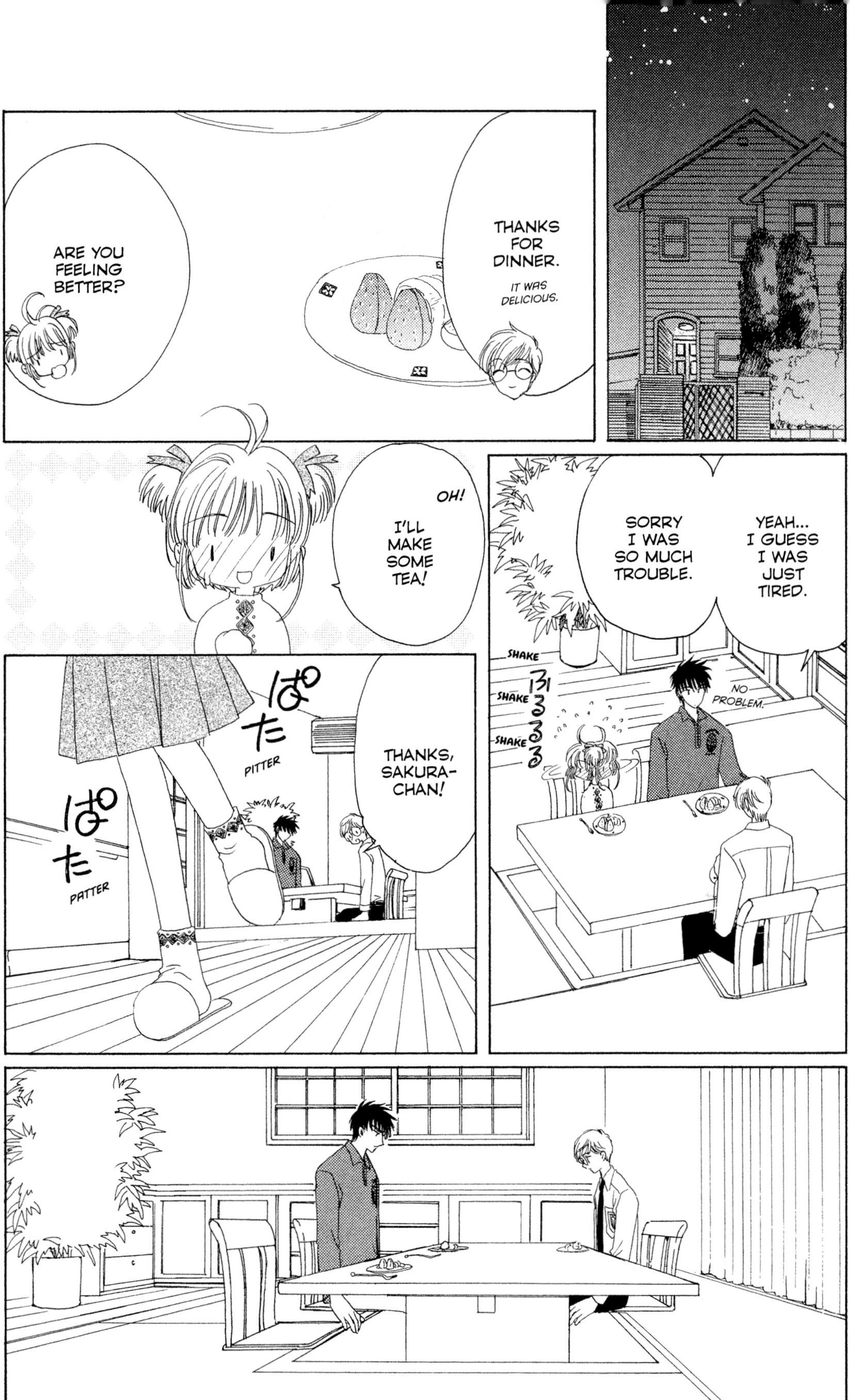

THANKS FOR DINNER.
IT WAS DELICIOUS.
ARE YOU FEELING BETTER?
YEAH... I GUESS I WAS JUST TIRED.
SORRY I WAS SO MUCH TROUBLE.
NO PROBLEM.
ふるるる
SHAKE
SHAKE
SHAKE
OH!
I'LL MAKE SOME TEA!
THANKS, SAKURA-CHAN!
ぱた
PITTER
ぱた
PATTER

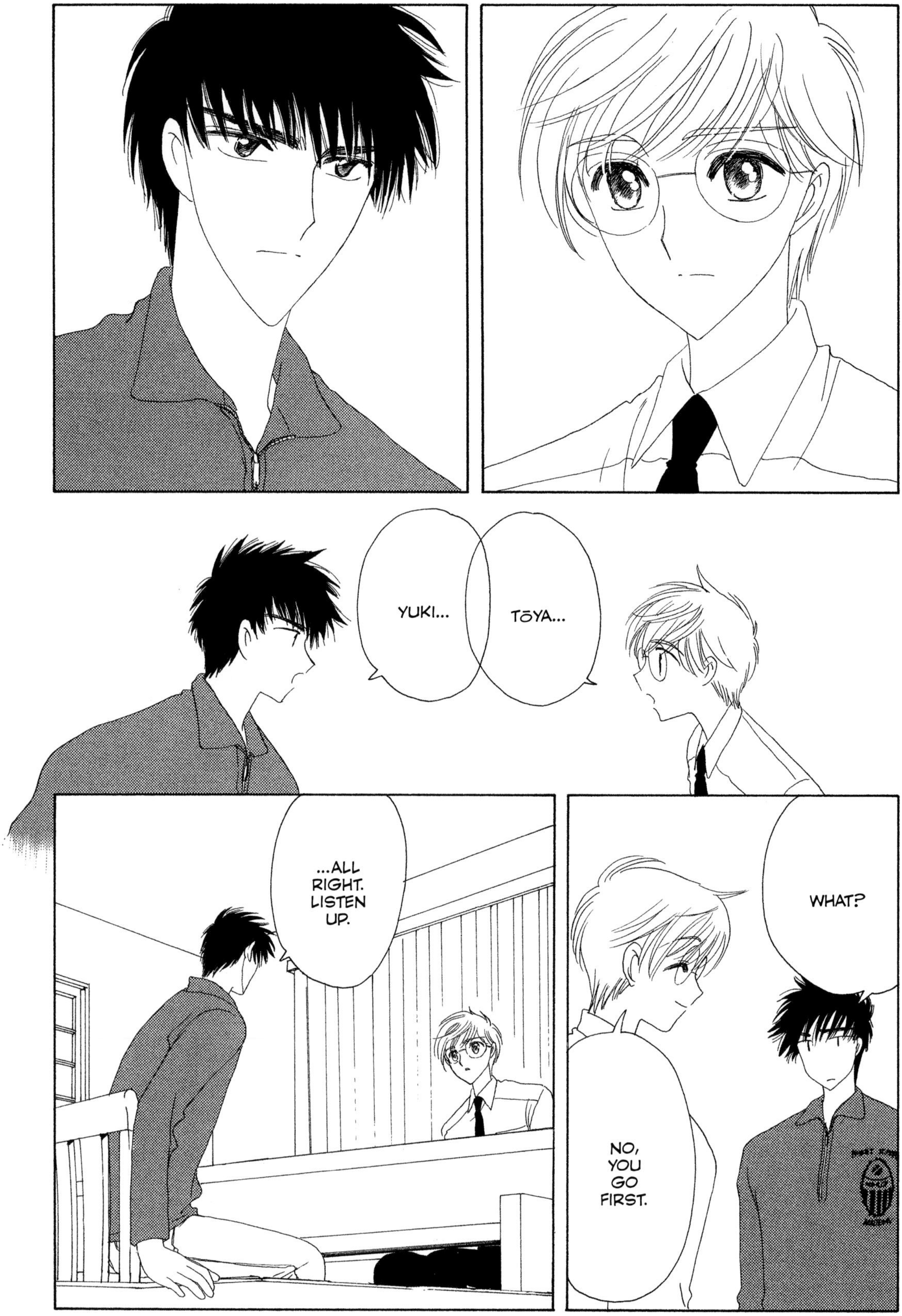
TŌYA...
YUKI...
WHAT?
NO, YOU GO FIRST.
...ALL RIGHT. LISTEN UP.

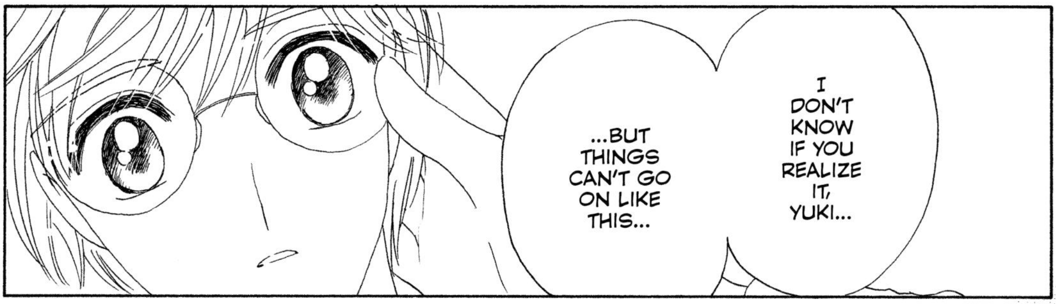
I DON'T KNOW IF YOU REALIZE IT, YUKI...
...BUT THINGS CAN'T GO ON LIKE THIS...

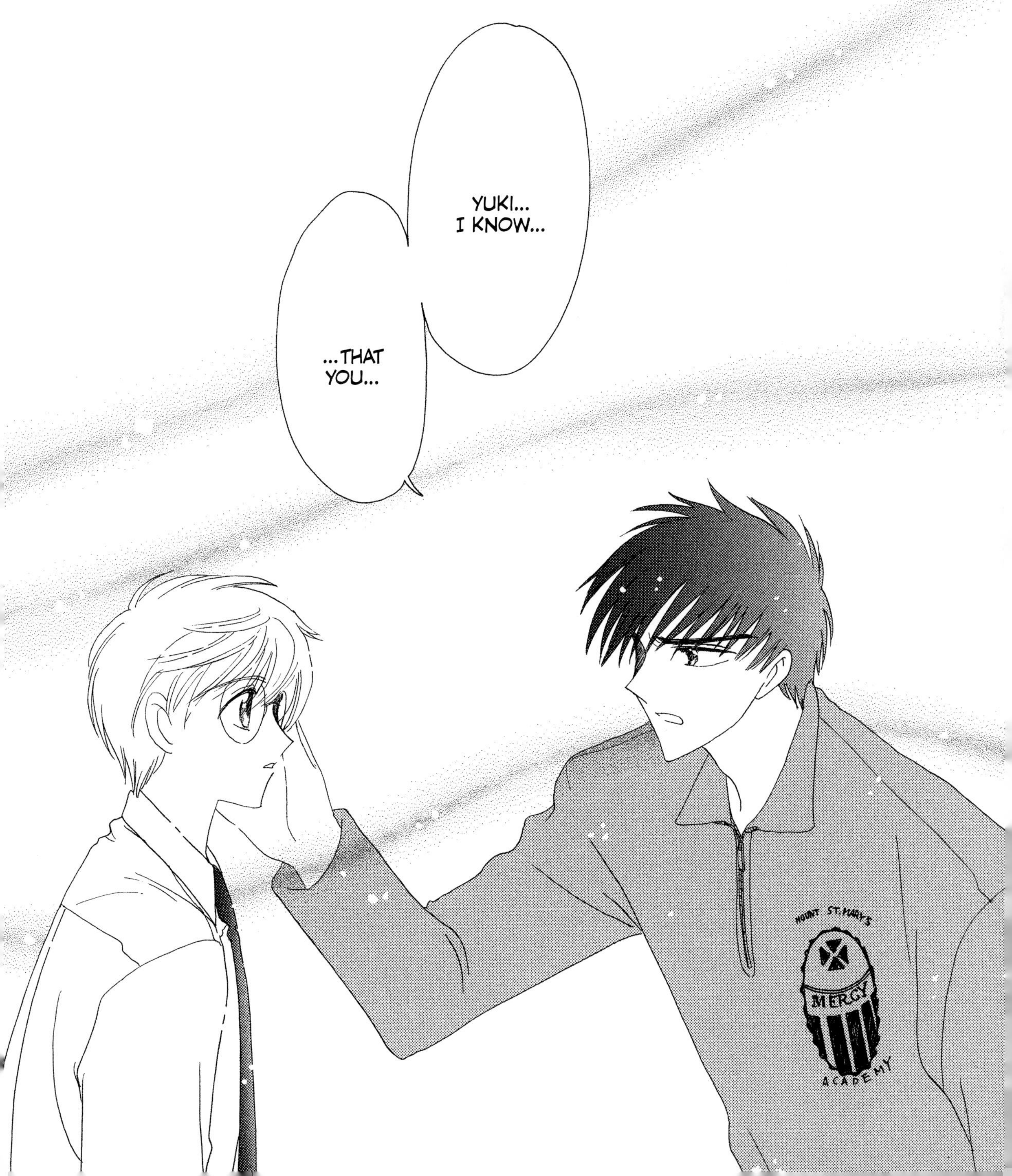
YUKI... I KNOW...
...THAT YOU...
MOUNT ST. MARY'S
MERCY
ACADEMY

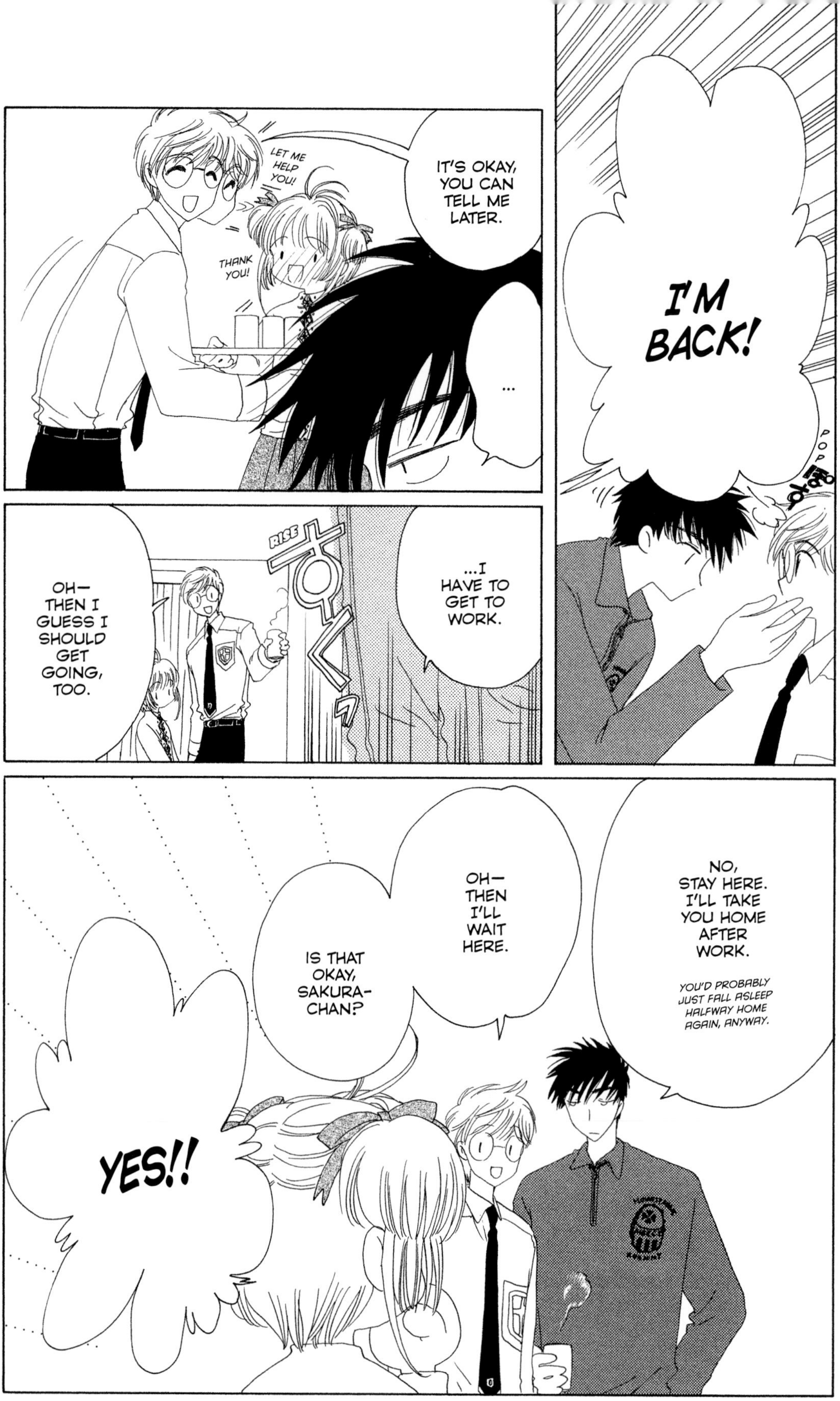
I'M BACK!
POP
IT'S OKAY, YOU CAN TELL ME LATER.
LET ME HELP YOU!
THANK YOU!
...
...I HAVE TO GET TO WORK.
RISE
OH— THEN I GUESS I SHOULD GET GOING, TOO.
NO, STAY HERE. I'LL TAKE YOU HOME AFTER WORK.
YOU'D PROBABLY JUST FALL ASLEEP HALFWAY HOME AGAIN, ANYWAY.
OH— THEN I'LL WAIT HERE.
IS THAT OKAY, SAKURA-CHAN?
YES!!

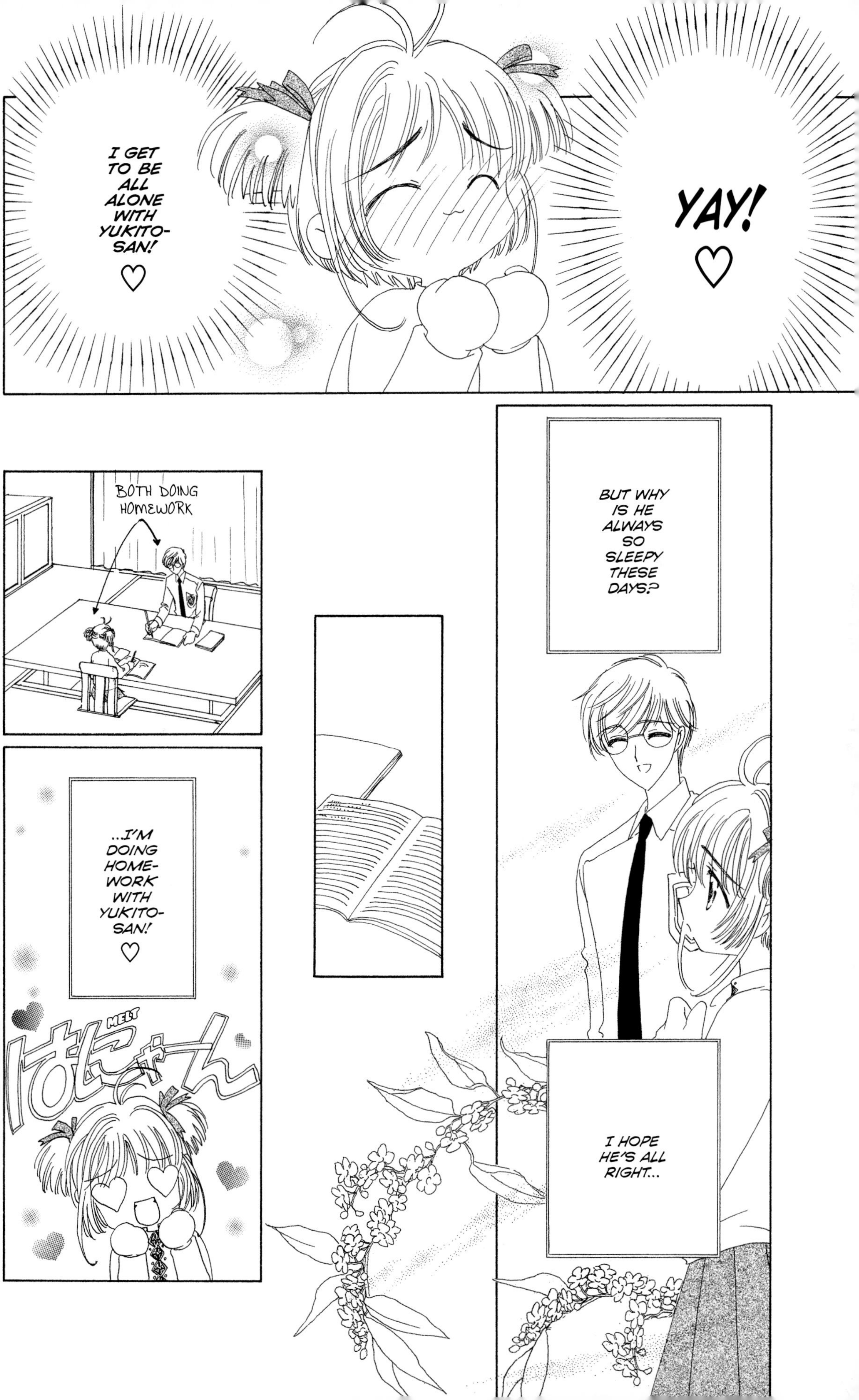
YAY! ♡
I GET TO BE ALL ALONE WITH YUKITO-SAN! ♡
BUT WHY IS HE ALWAYS SO SLEEPY THESE DAYS?
I HOPE HE'S ALL RIGHT...
BOTH DOING HOMEWORK
...I'M DOING HOME-WORK WITH YUKITO-SAN! ♡
MELT
はにゃん

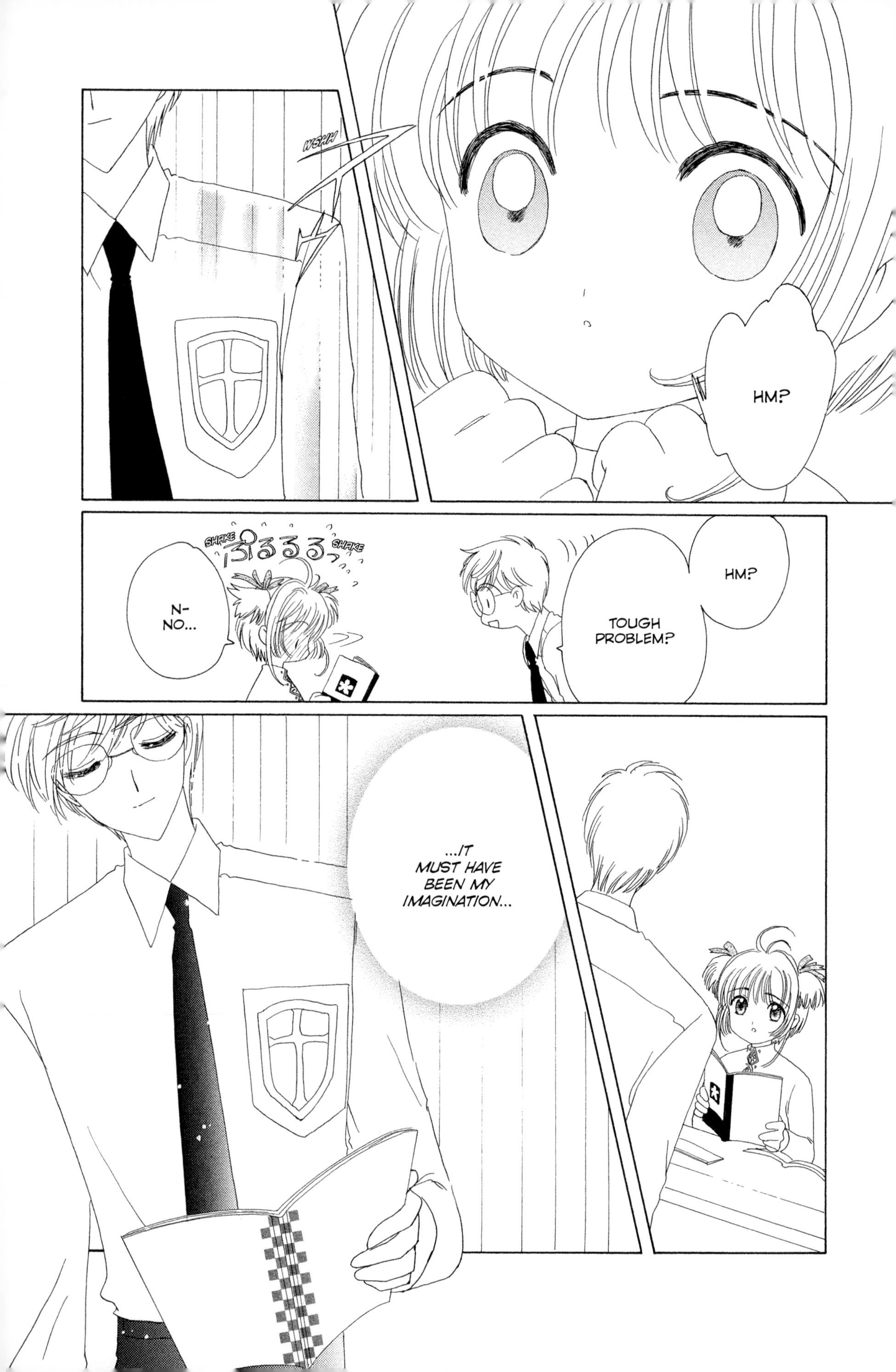
HM?
WSHH
HM?
TOUGH PROBLEM?
SHAKE ぷるるる SHAKE
N- NO...
...IT MUST HAVE BEEN MY IMAGINATION...

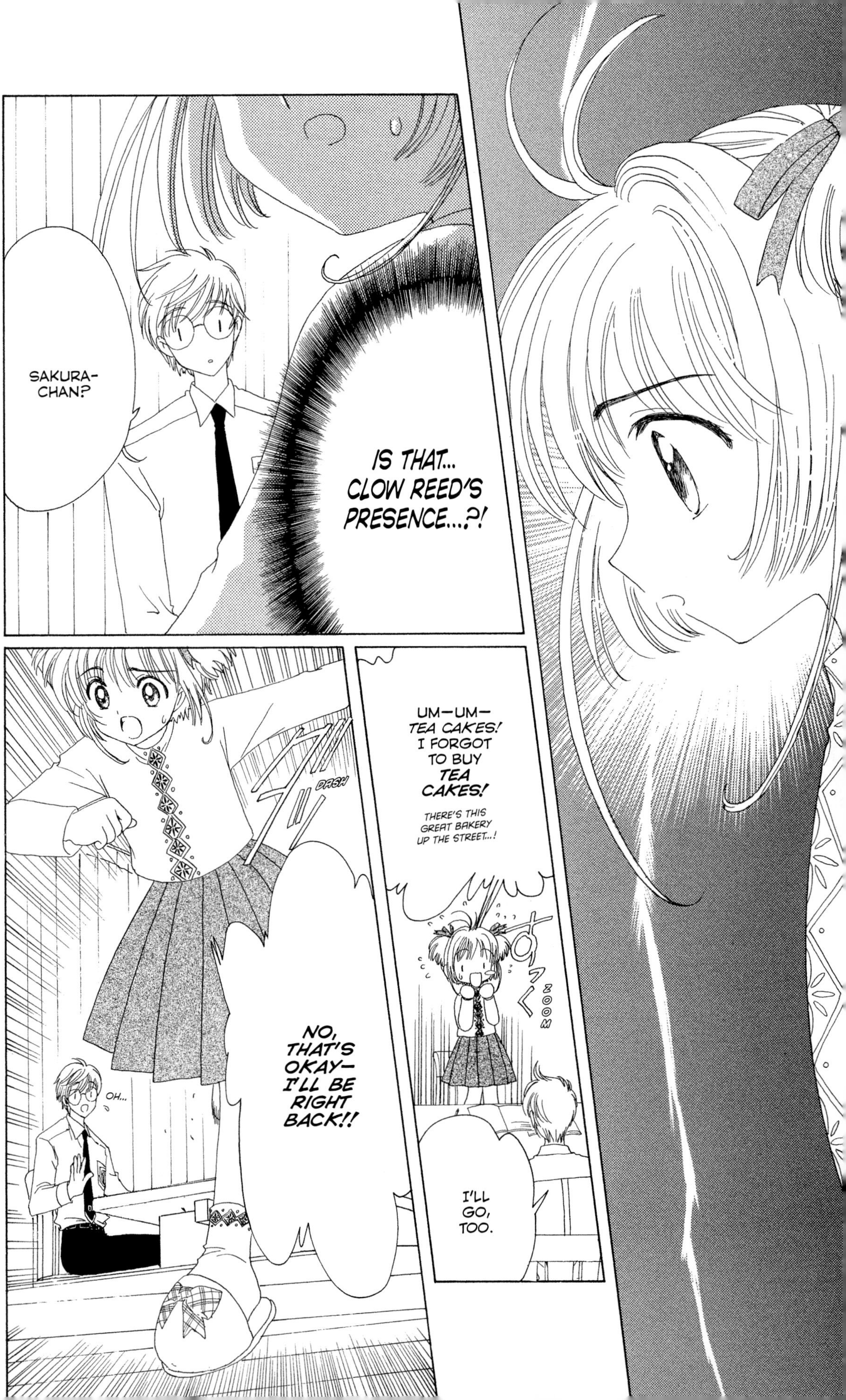
IS THAT... CLOW REED'S PRESENCE...?!
SAKURA-CHAN?
UM—UM— TEA CAKES! I FORGOT TO BUY TEA CAKES!
THERE'S THIS GREAT BAKERY UP THE STREET...!
ZOOM
I'LL GO, TOO.
DASH
NO, THAT'S OKAY— I'LL BE RIGHT BACK!!
OH...

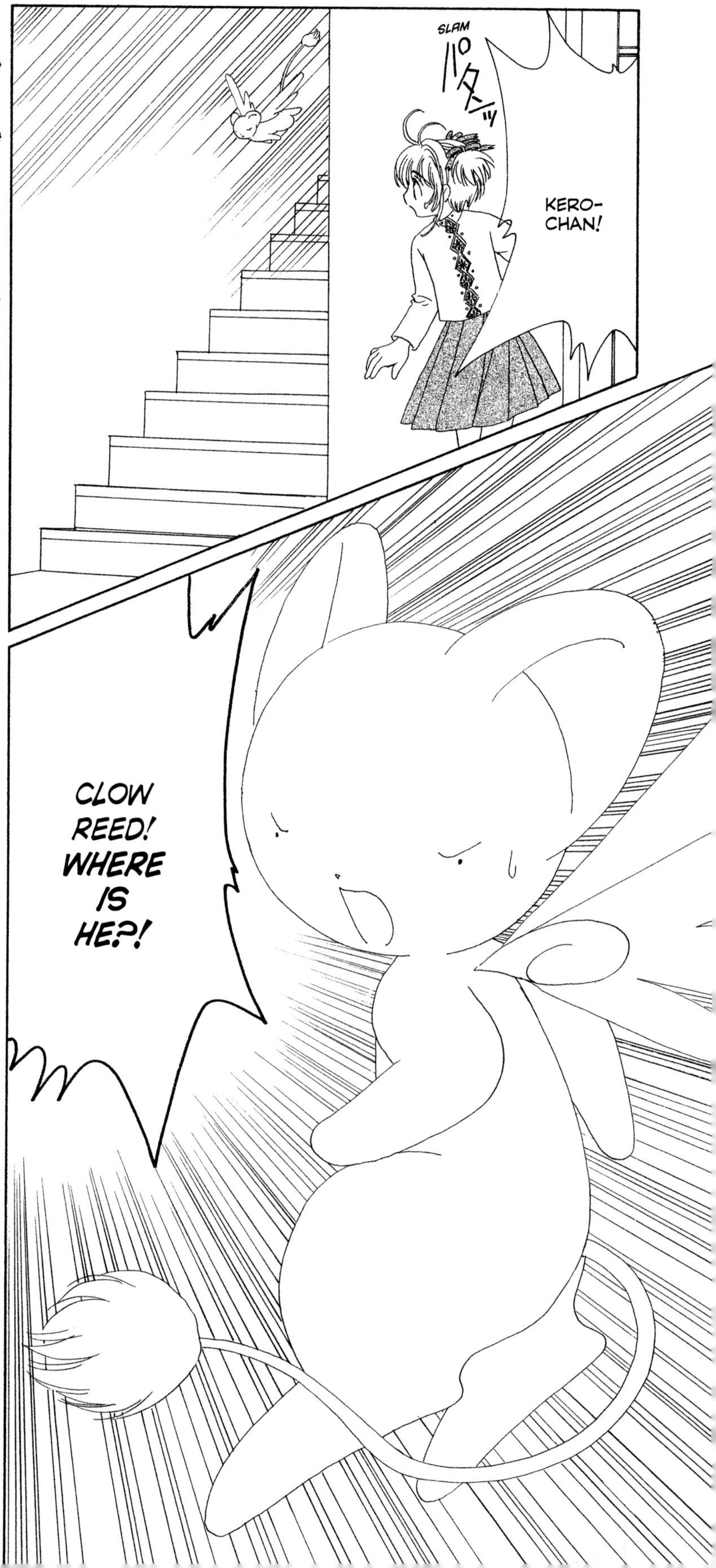
SLAM
パタンッ
KERO-CHAN!
CLOW REED! WHERE IS HE?!

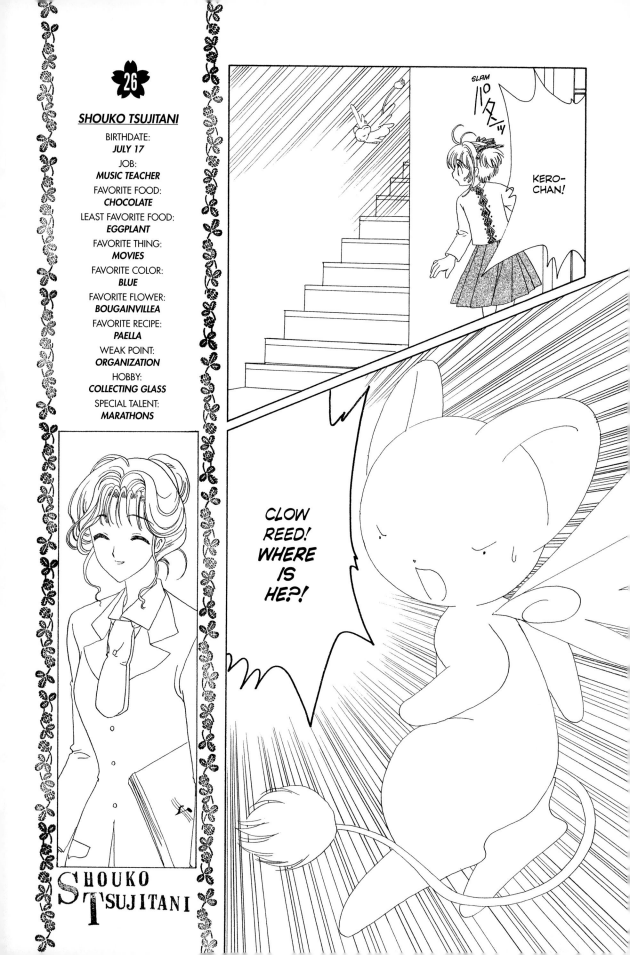

26

SHOUKO TSUJITANI

BIRTHDATE:
JULY 17
JOB:
MUSIC TEACHER
FAVORITE FOOD:
CHOCOLATE
LEAST FAVORITE FOOD:
EGGPLANT
FAVORITE THING:
MOVIES
FAVORITE COLOR:
BLUE
FAVORITE FLOWER:
BOUGAINVILLEA
FAVORITE RECIPE:
PAELLA
WEAK POINT:
ORGANIZATION
HOBBY:
COLLECTING GLASS
SPECIAL TALENT:
MARATHONS

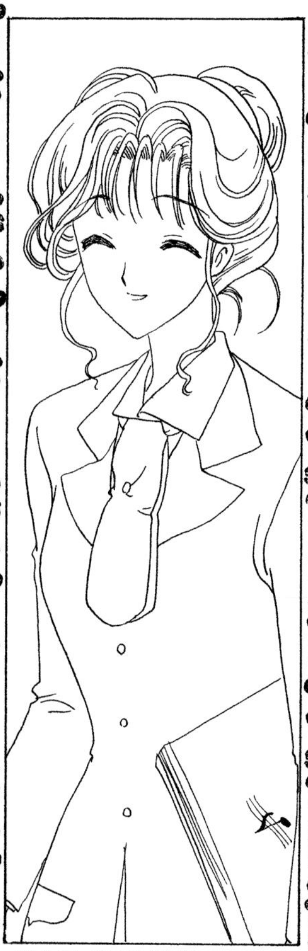

SHOUKO TSUJITANI

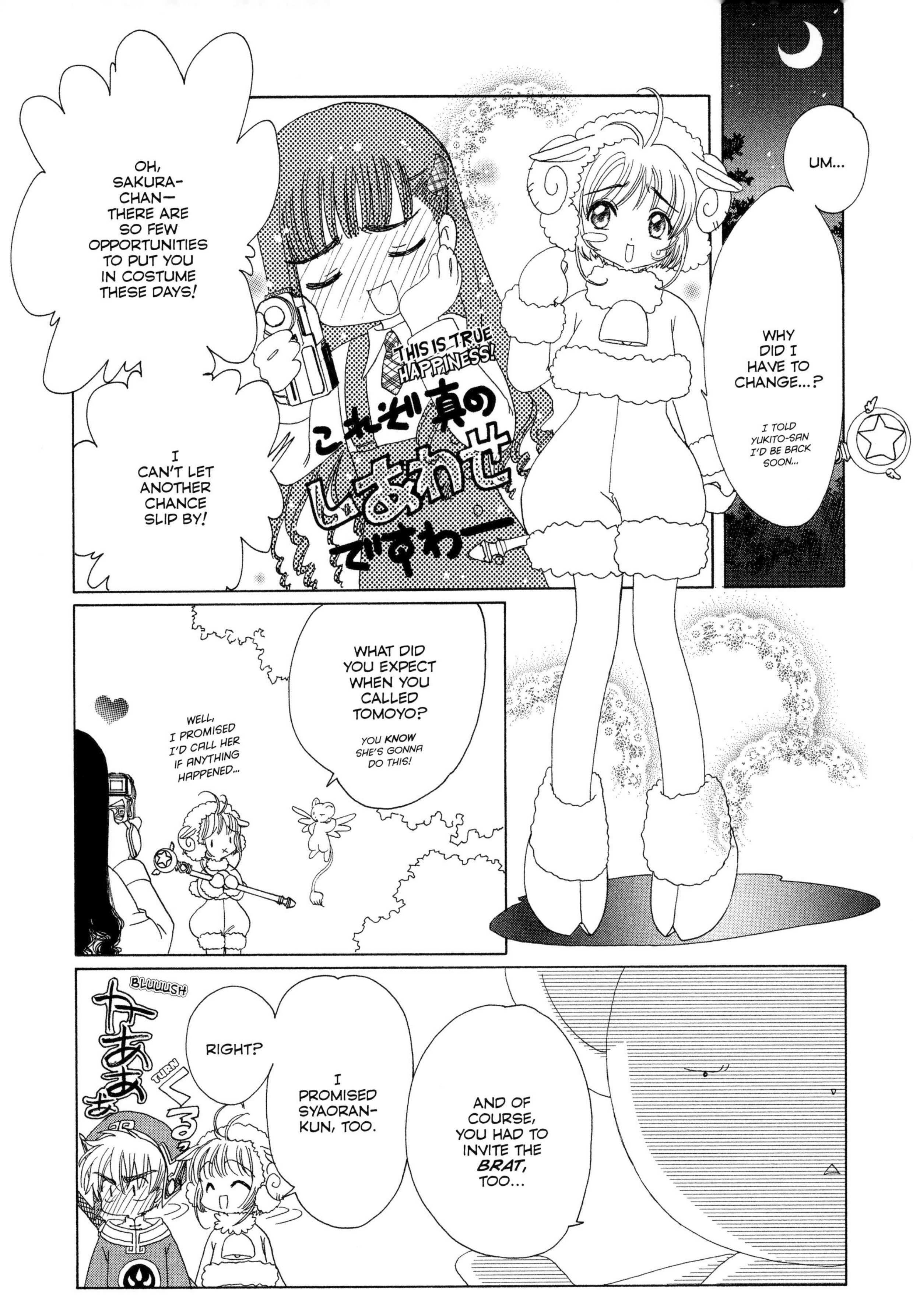

UM...
WHY DID I HAVE TO CHANGE...?
I TOLD YUKITO-SAN I'D BE BACK SOON...
OH, SAKURA-CHAN— THERE ARE SO FEW OPPORTUNITIES TO PUT YOU IN COSTUME THESE DAYS!
THIS IS TRUE HAPPINESS!
これぞ真のしあわせですわー
I CAN'T LET ANOTHER CHANCE SLIP BY!
WHAT DID YOU EXPECT WHEN YOU CALLED TOMOYO?
YOU KNOW SHE'S GONNA DO THIS!
WELL, I PROMISED I'D CALL HER IF ANYTHING HAPPENED...
AND OF COURSE, YOU HAD TO INVITE THE BRAT, TOO...
I PROMISED SYAORAN-KUN, TOO.
RIGHT?
TURN
くる
BLUUUSH
かあああ

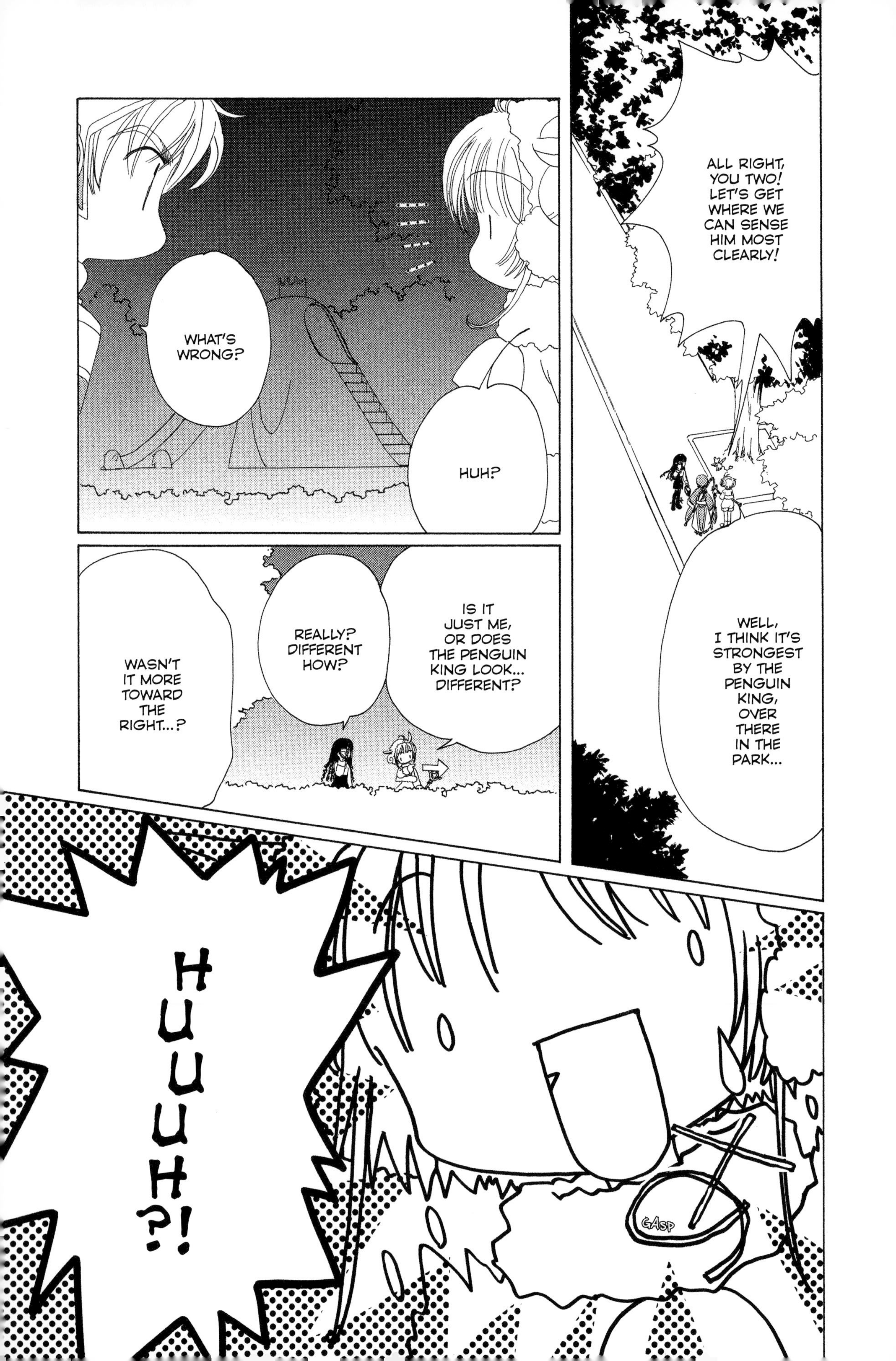

ALL RIGHT, YOU TWO! LET'S GET WHERE WE CAN SENSE HIM MOST CLEARLY!
WELL, I THINK IT'S STRONGEST BY THE PENGUIN KING, OVER THERE IN THE PARK...
WHAT'S WRONG?
HUH?
IS IT JUST ME, OR DOES THE PENGUIN KING LOOK... DIFFERENT?
REALLY? DIFFERENT HOW?
WASN'T IT MORE TOWARD THE RIGHT...?
GASP
HUUUH?!

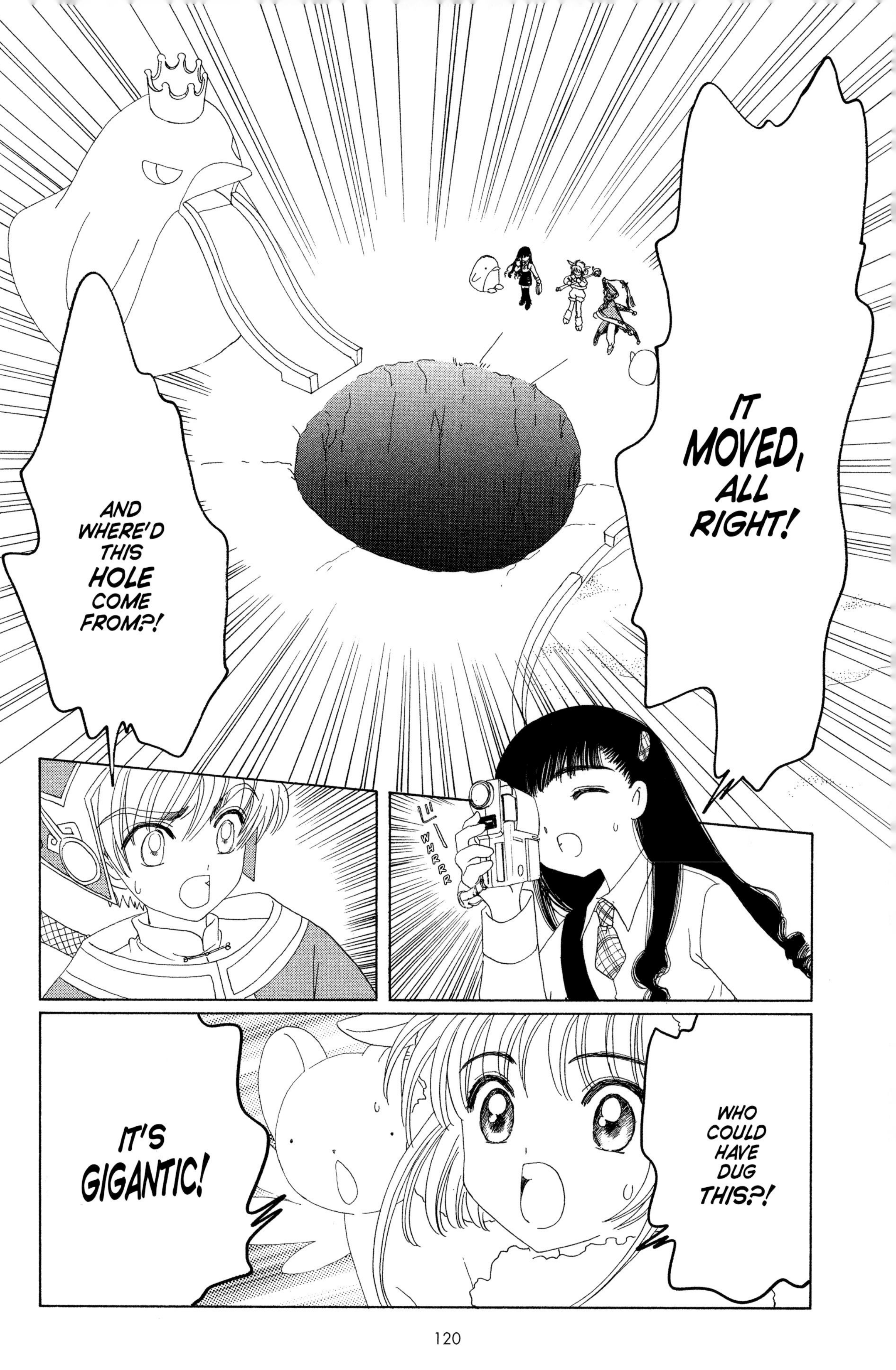
IT MOVED, ALL RIGHT!
AND WHERE'D THIS HOLE COME FROM?!
WHRRR
WHO COULD HAVE DUG THIS?!
IT'S GIGANTIC!

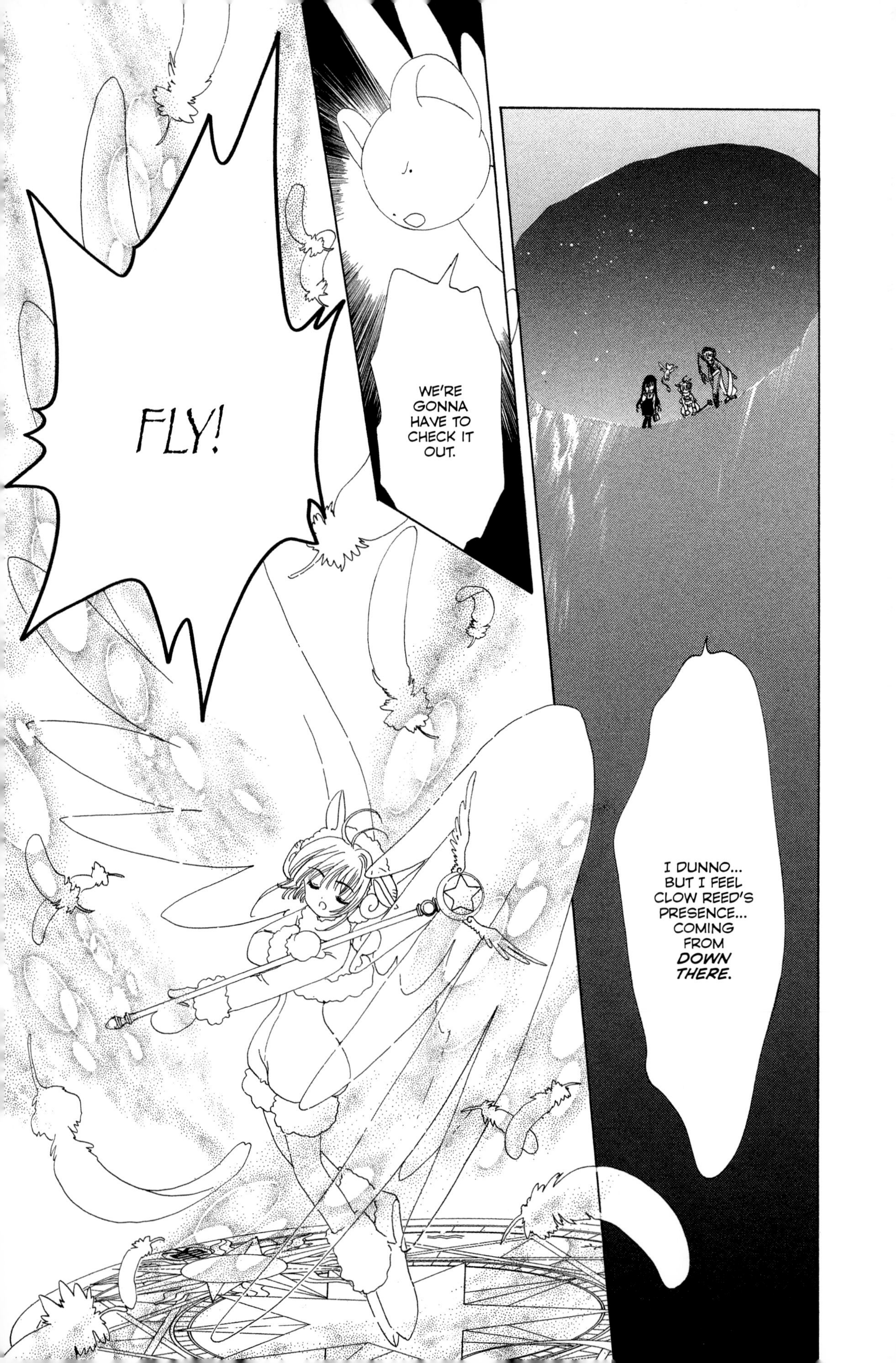
I DUNNO... BUT I FEEL CLOW REED'S PRESENCE... COMING FROM DOWN THERE.
WE'RE GONNA HAVE TO CHECK IT OUT.
FLY!

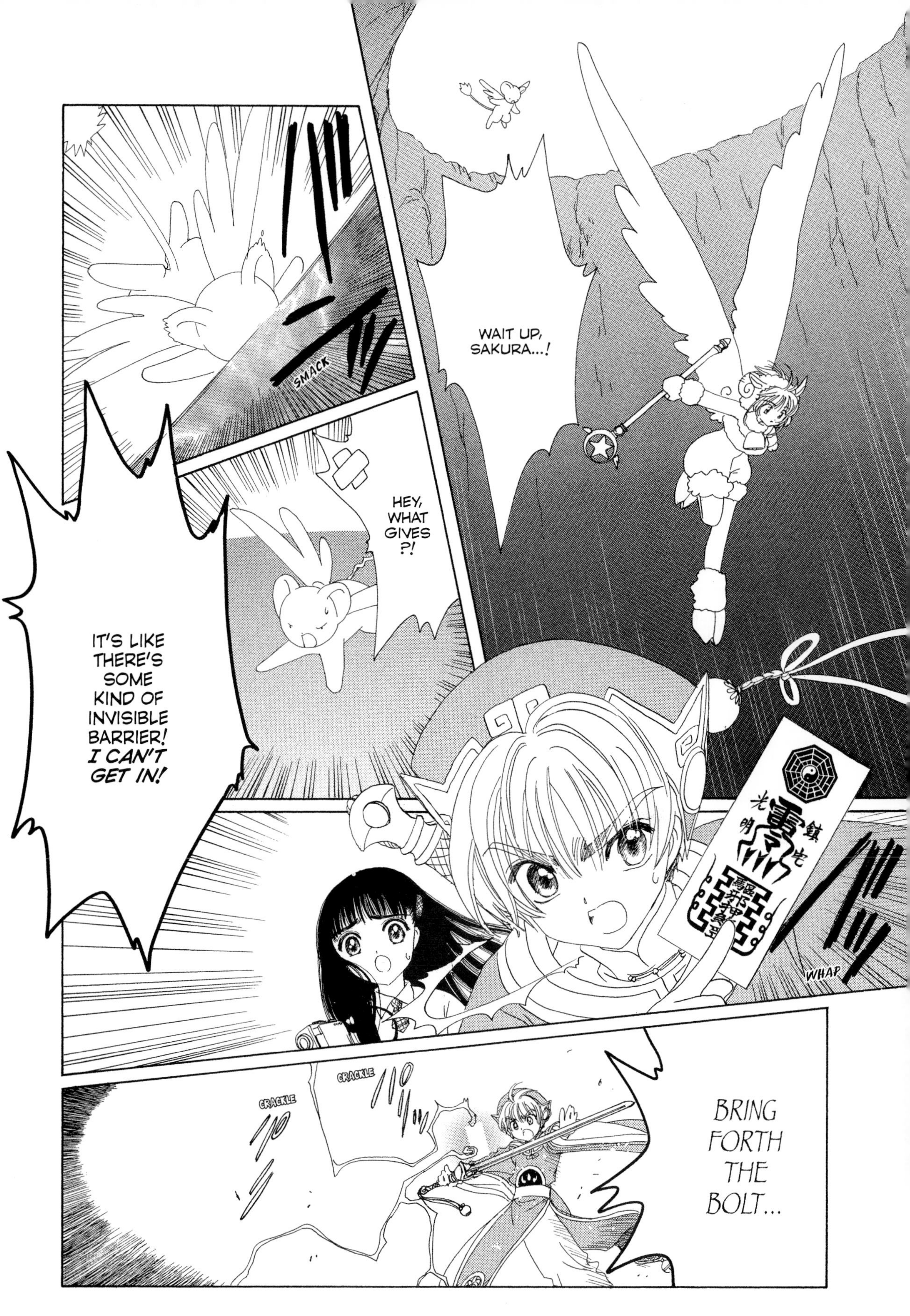

WAIT UP, SAKURA...!
SMACK
HEY, WHAT GIVES?!
IT'S LIKE THERE'S SOME KIND OF INVISIBLE BARRIER! I CAN'T GET IN!
WHAP
BRING FORTH THE BOLT...
CRACKLE
CRACKLE

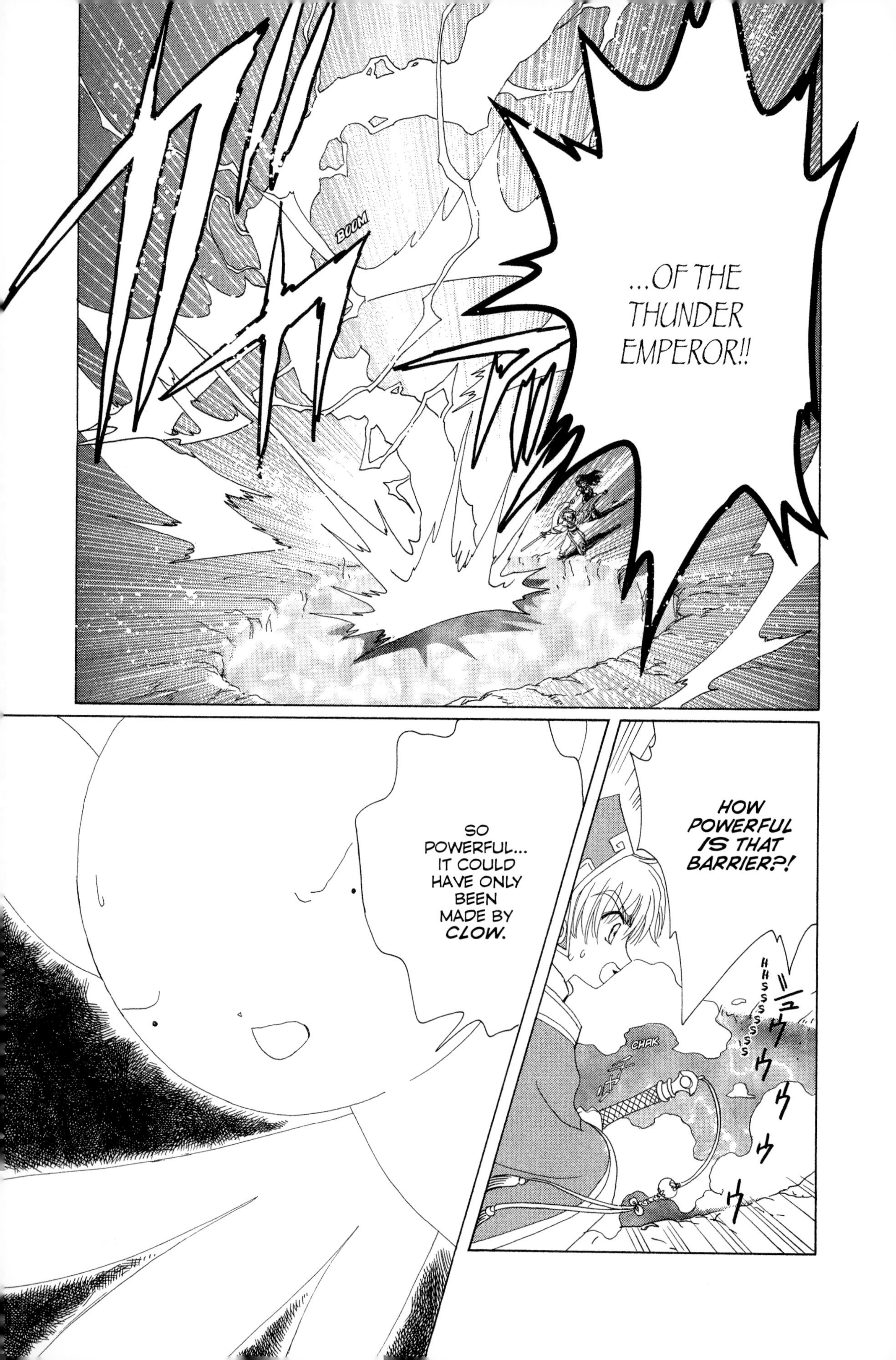
BOOM
...OF THE THUNDER EMPEROR!!
HOW POWERFUL IS THAT BARRIER?!
HHSSSSSSS
CHAK
SO POWERFUL... IT COULD HAVE ONLY BEEN MADE BY CLOW.

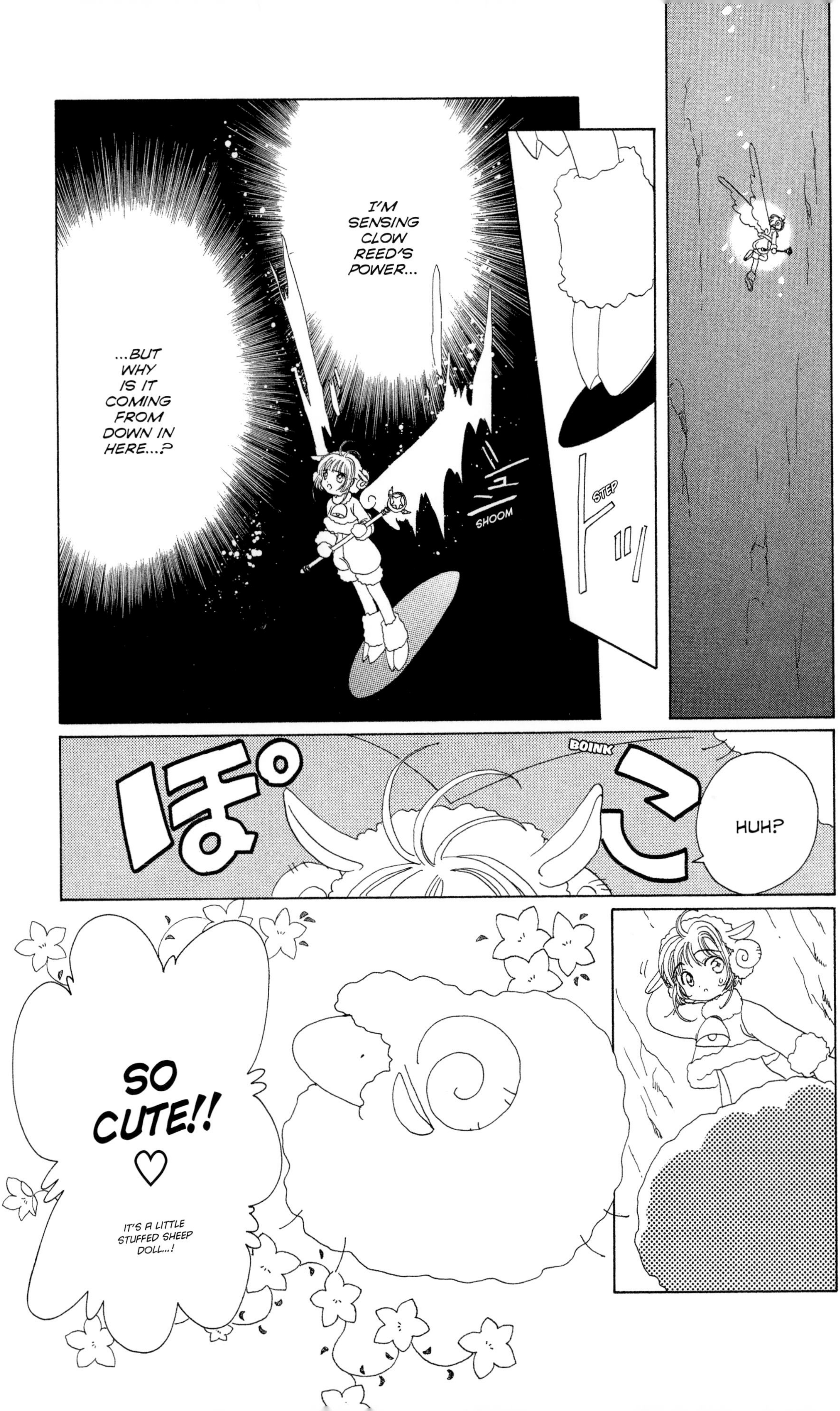

STEP
I'M SENSING CLOW REED'S POWER...
...BUT WHY IS IT COMING FROM DOWN IN HERE...?
SHOOM
BOINK
HUH?
SO CUTE!! ♡
IT'S A LITTLE STUFFED SHEEP DOLL...!

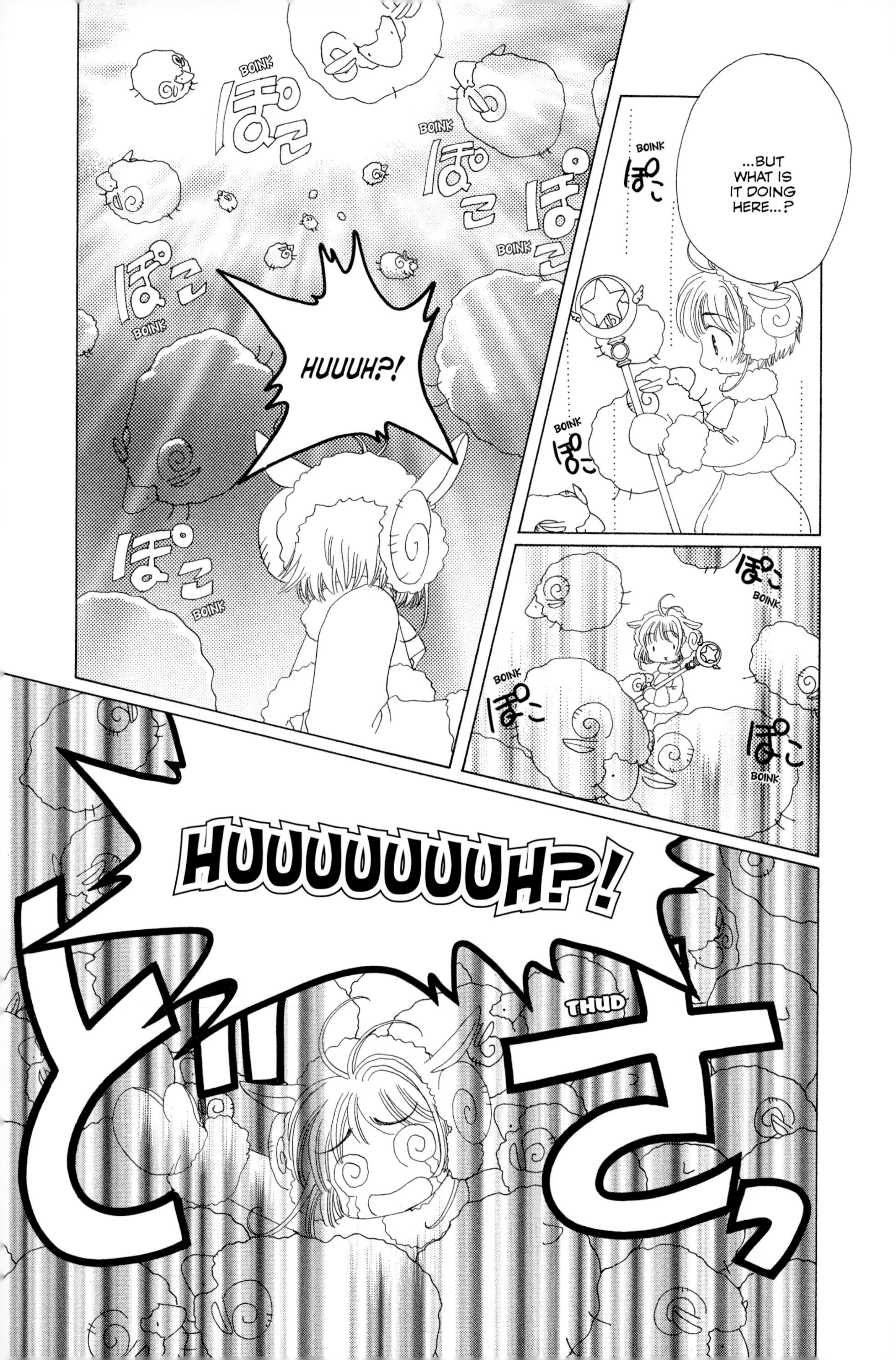
BOINK
ぽこ
...BUT WHAT IS IT DOING HERE...?
BOINK
ぽこ
ぽこ
BOINK
BOINK
ぽこ
ぽこ
BOINK
BOINK
ぽこ
BOINK
ぽこ
BOINK
ぽこ
BOINK
ぽこ
ぽこ
BOINK
HUUUH?!
HUUUUUUUUH?!
THUD
どさっ

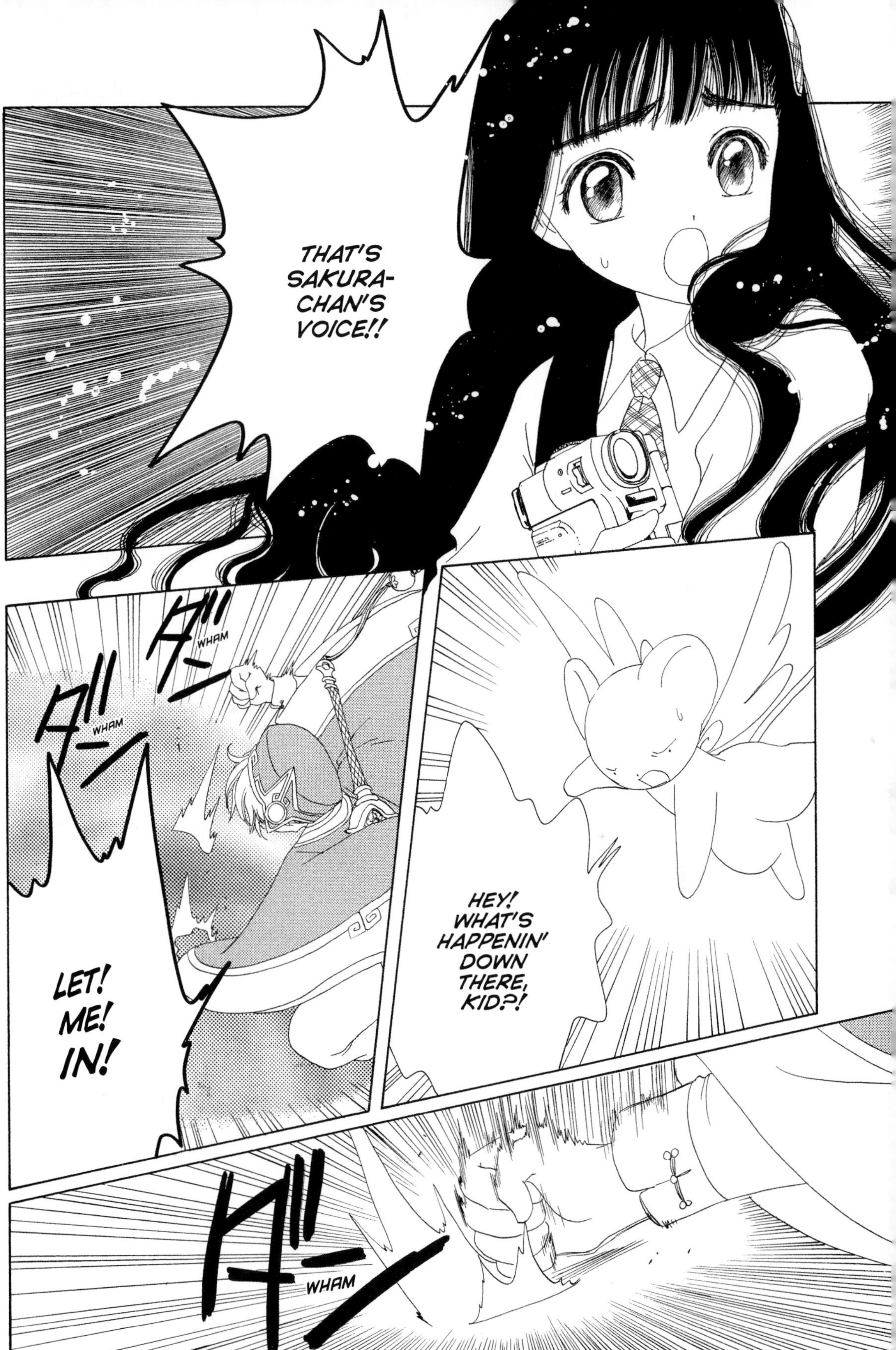
THAT'S SAKURA-CHAN'S VOICE!!
HEY! WHAT'S HAPPENIN' DOWN THERE, KID?!
WHAM
WHAM
LET! ME! IN!
WHAM

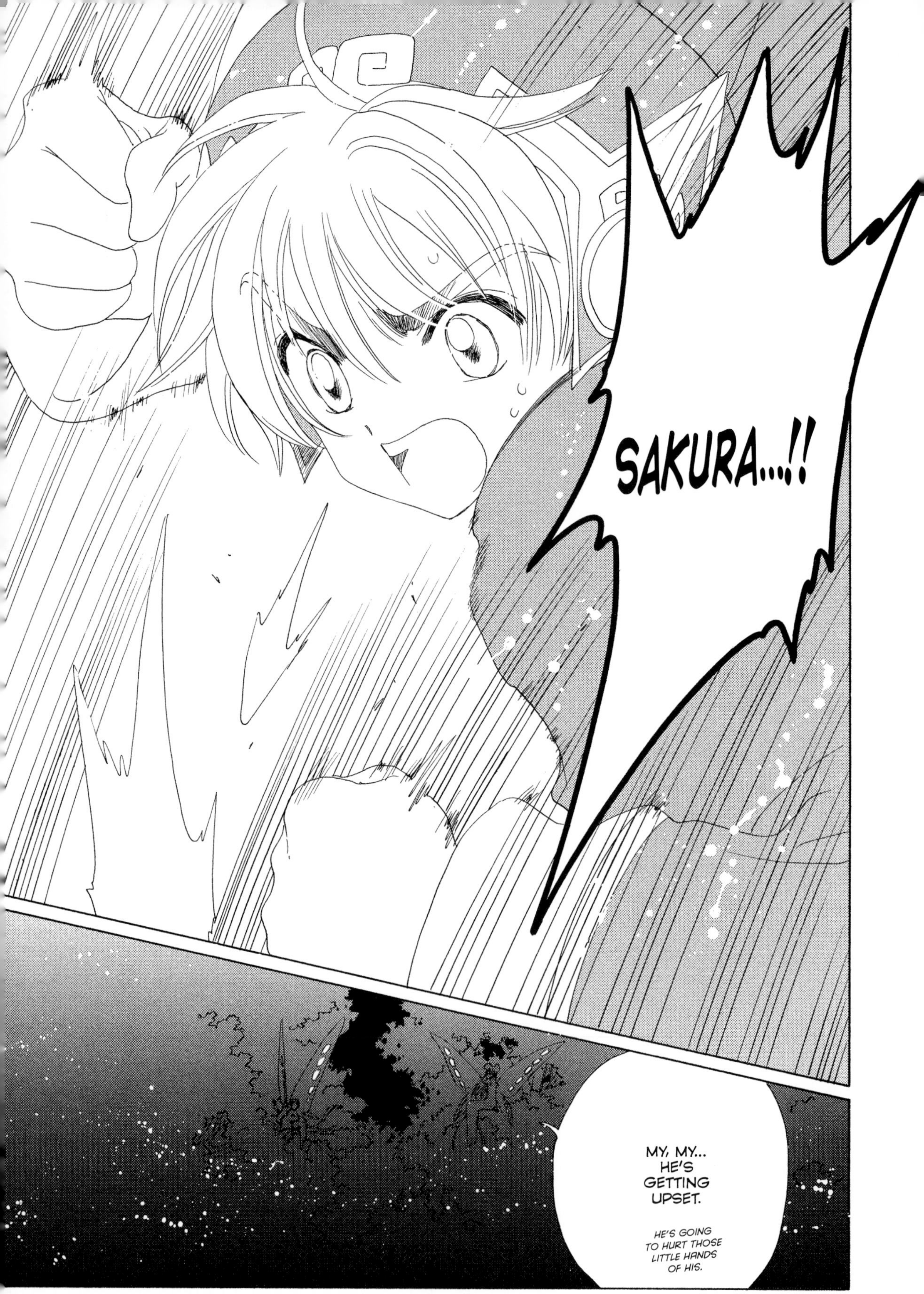
SAKURA...!!
MY, MY... HE'S GETTING UPSET.
HE'S GOING TO HURT THOSE LITTLE HANDS OF HIS.

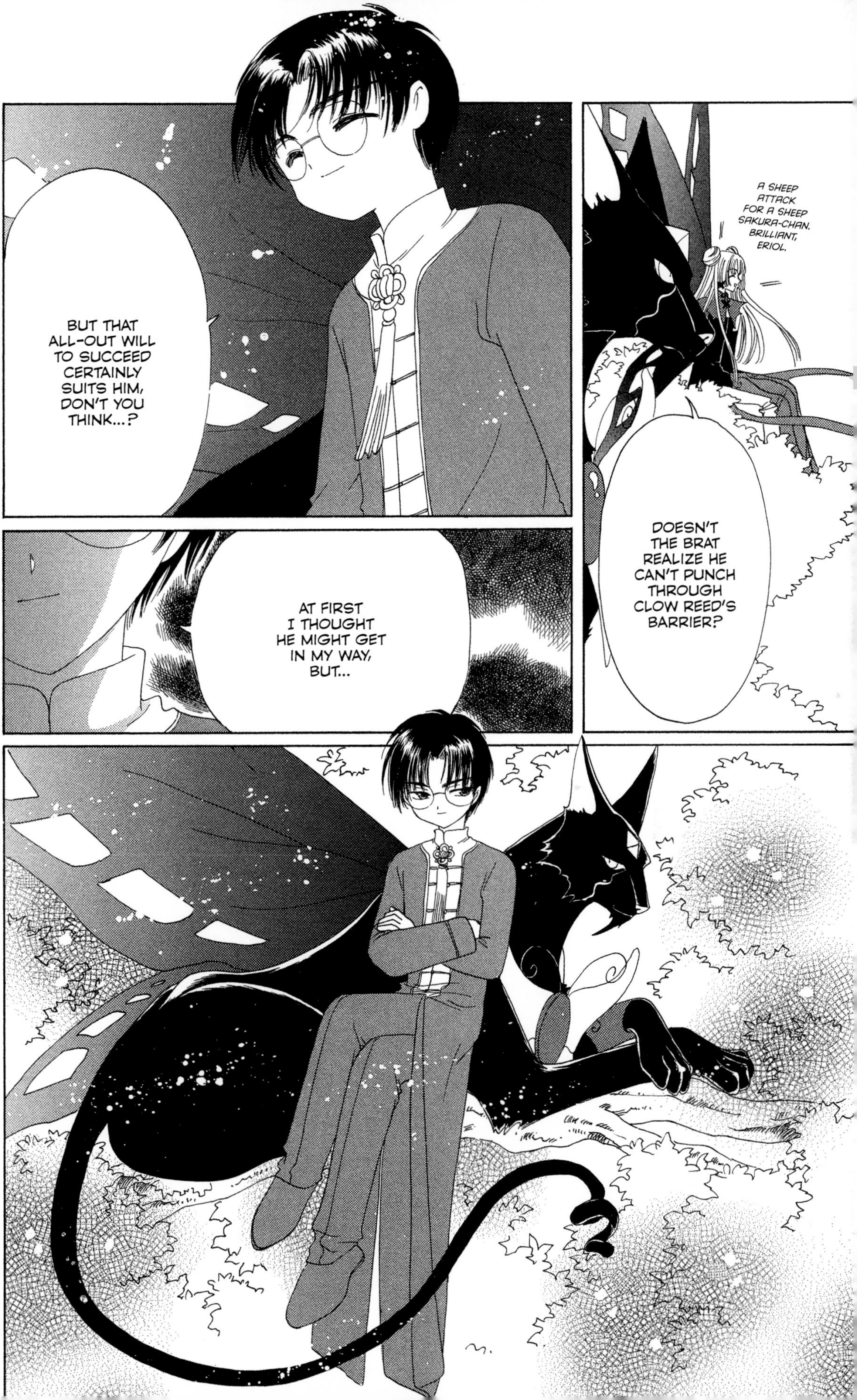
A SHEEP ATTACK FOR A SHEEP SAKURA-CHAN. BRILLIANT, ERIOL.
DOESN'T THE BRAT REALIZE HE CAN'T PUNCH THROUGH CLOW REED'S BARRIER?
BUT THAT ALL-OUT WILL TO SUCCEED CERTAINLY SUITS HIM, DON'T YOU THINK...?
AT FIRST I THOUGHT HE MIGHT GET IN MY WAY, BUT...

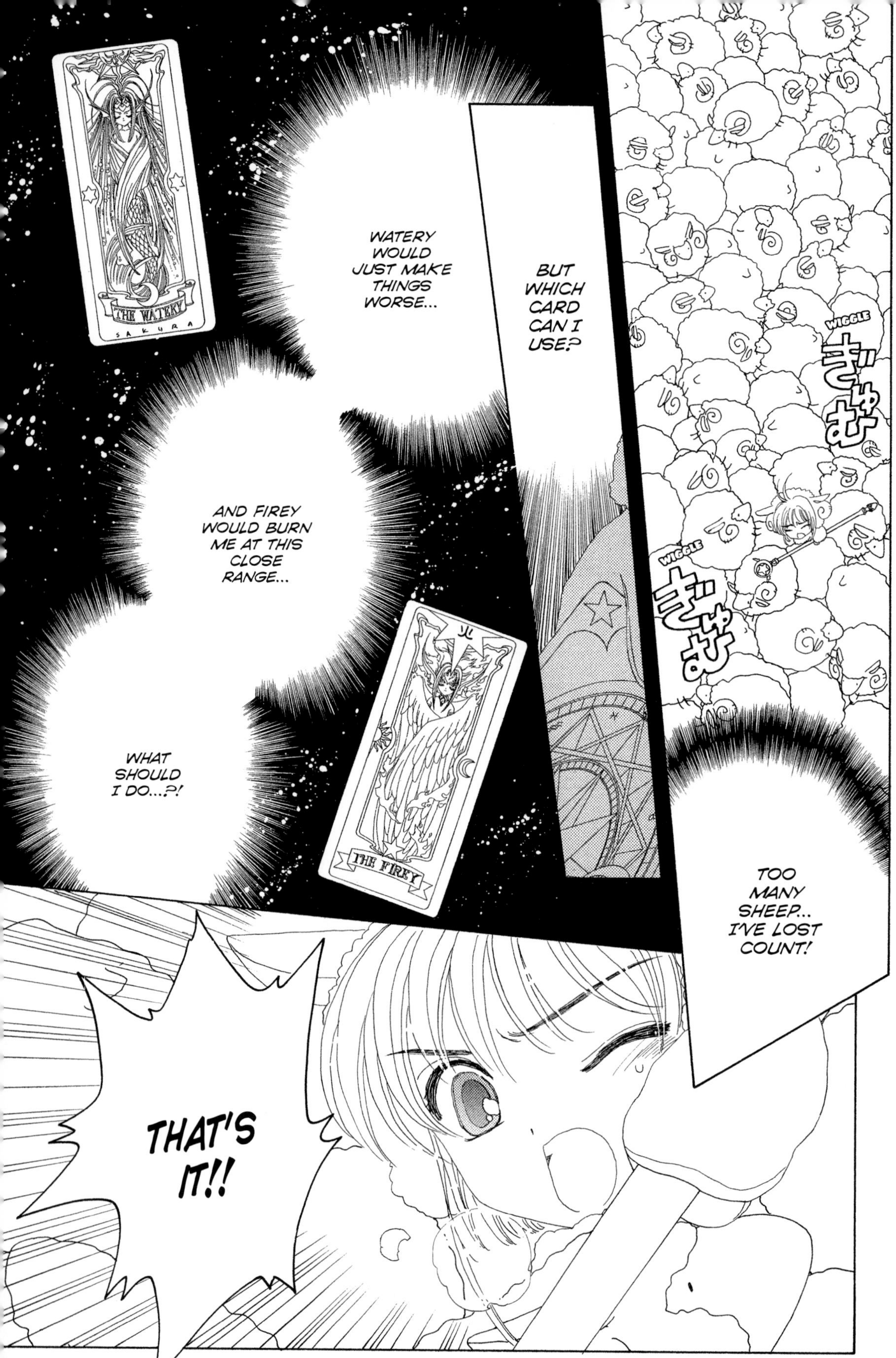
WIGGLE
ぎゅむ
WIGGLE
ぎゅむ
TOO MANY SHEEP... I'VE LOST COUNT!
BUT WHICH CARD CAN I USE?
WATERY WOULD JUST MAKE THINGS WORSE...
THE WATERY
SAKURA
AND FIREY WOULD BURN ME AT THIS CLOSE RANGE...
火
THE FIREY
WHAT SHOULD I DO...?!
THAT'S IT!!

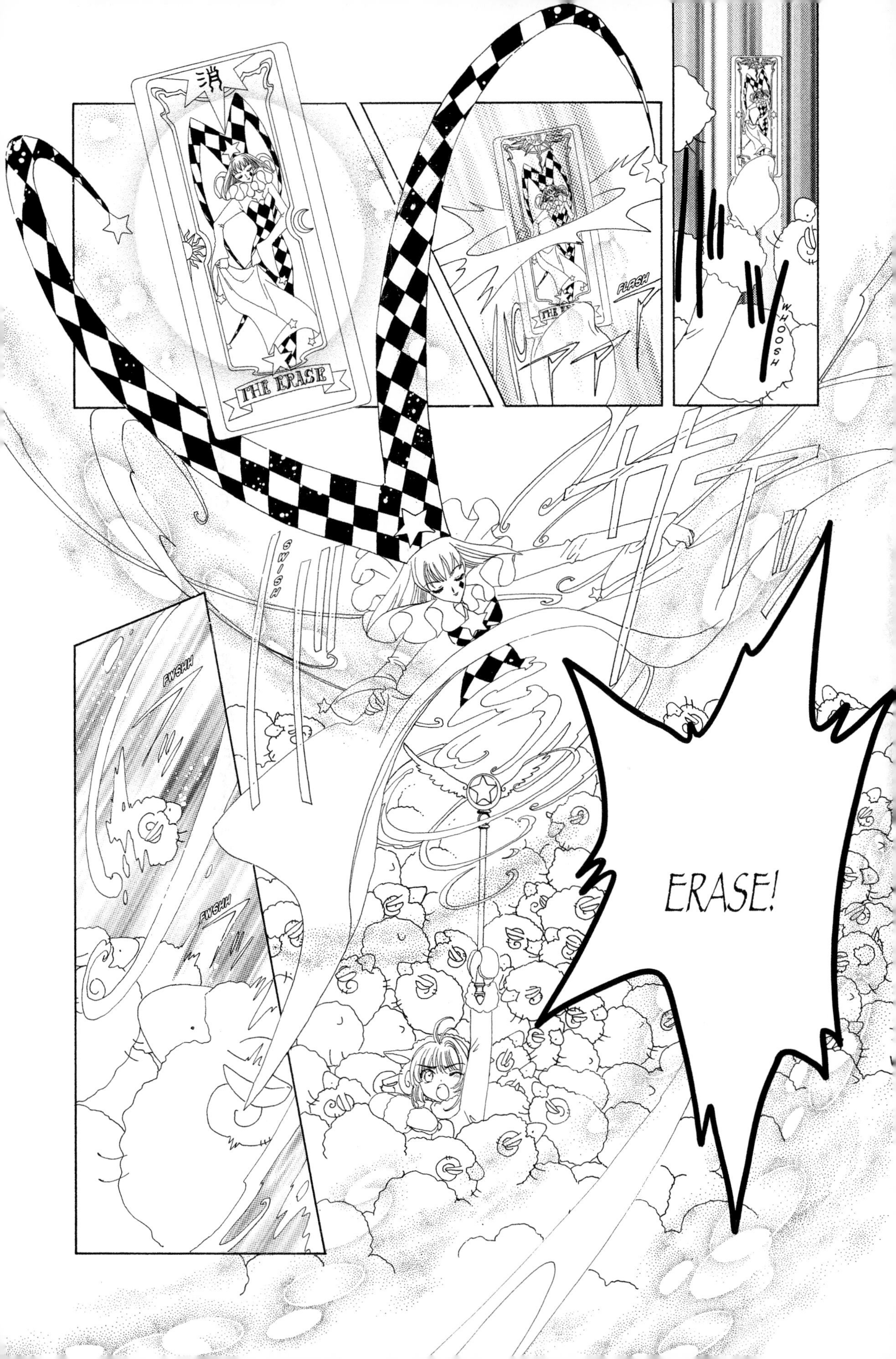
WHOOSH
FLASH
消
THE ERASE
SWISH
ERASE!
FWSHH
FWSHH

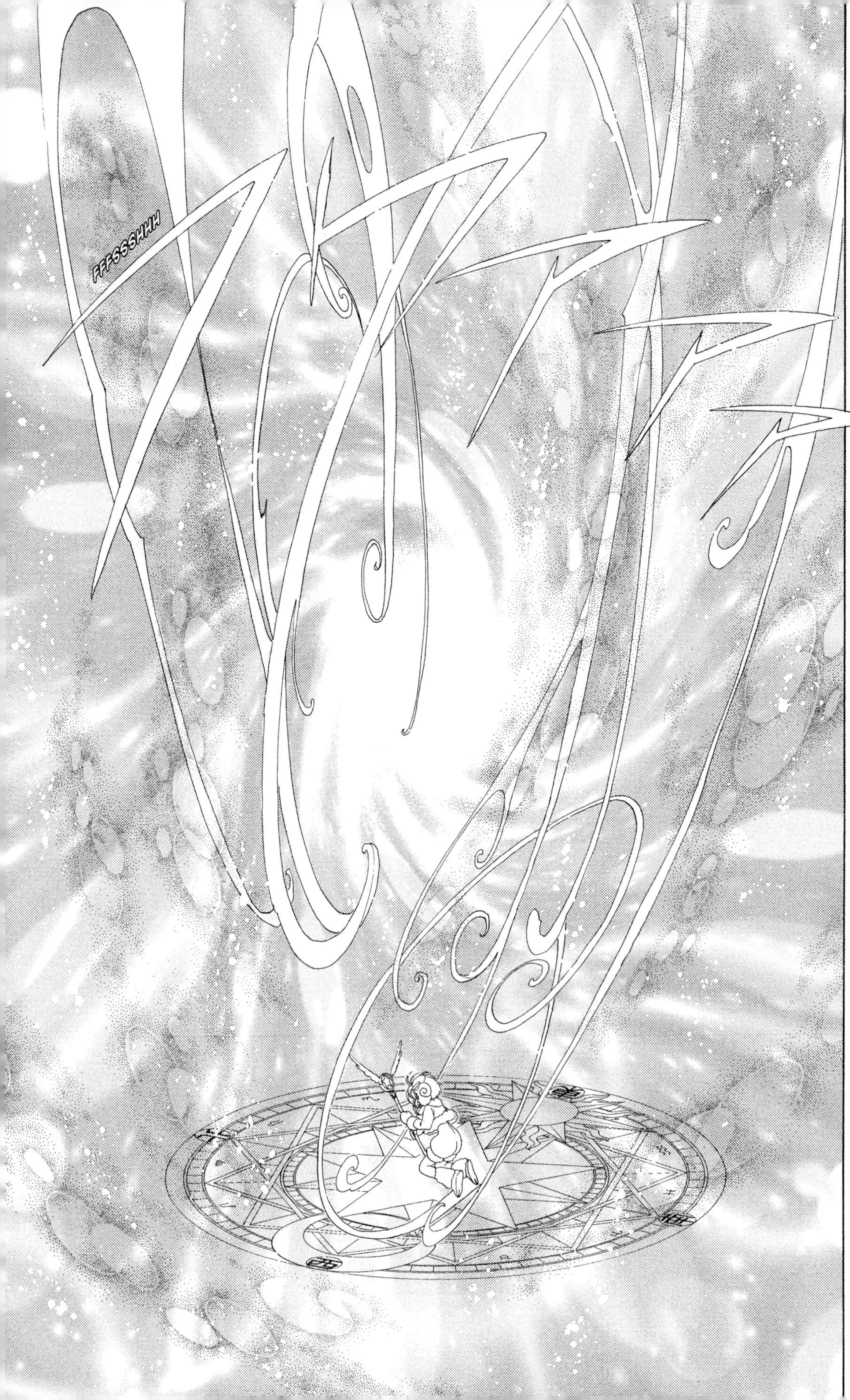
FFFSSSHHH

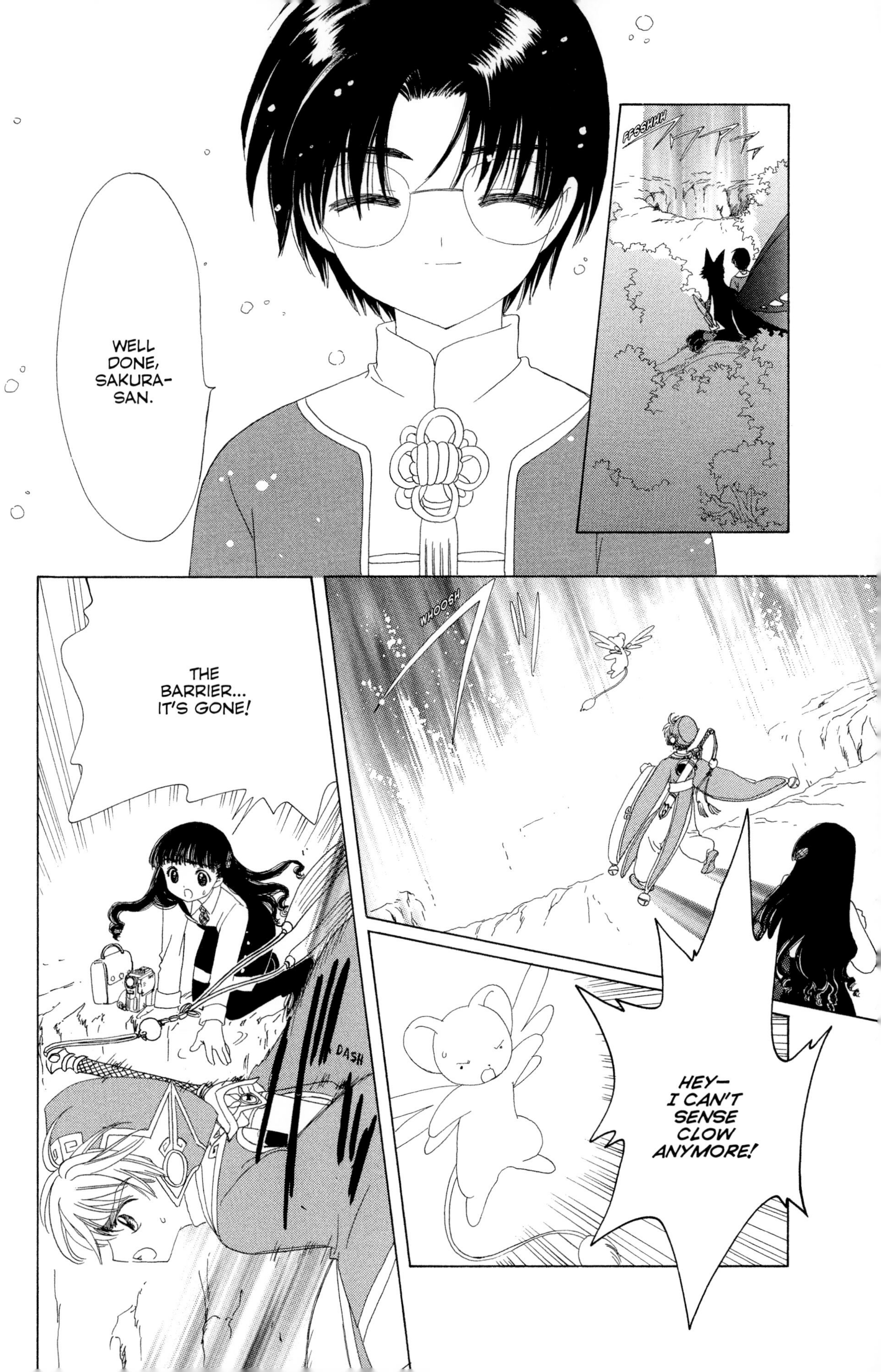
FFSSHHH
WELL DONE, SAKURA-SAN.
WHOOSH
HEY— I CAN'T SENSE CLOW ANYMORE!
THE BARRIER... IT'S GONE!
DASH

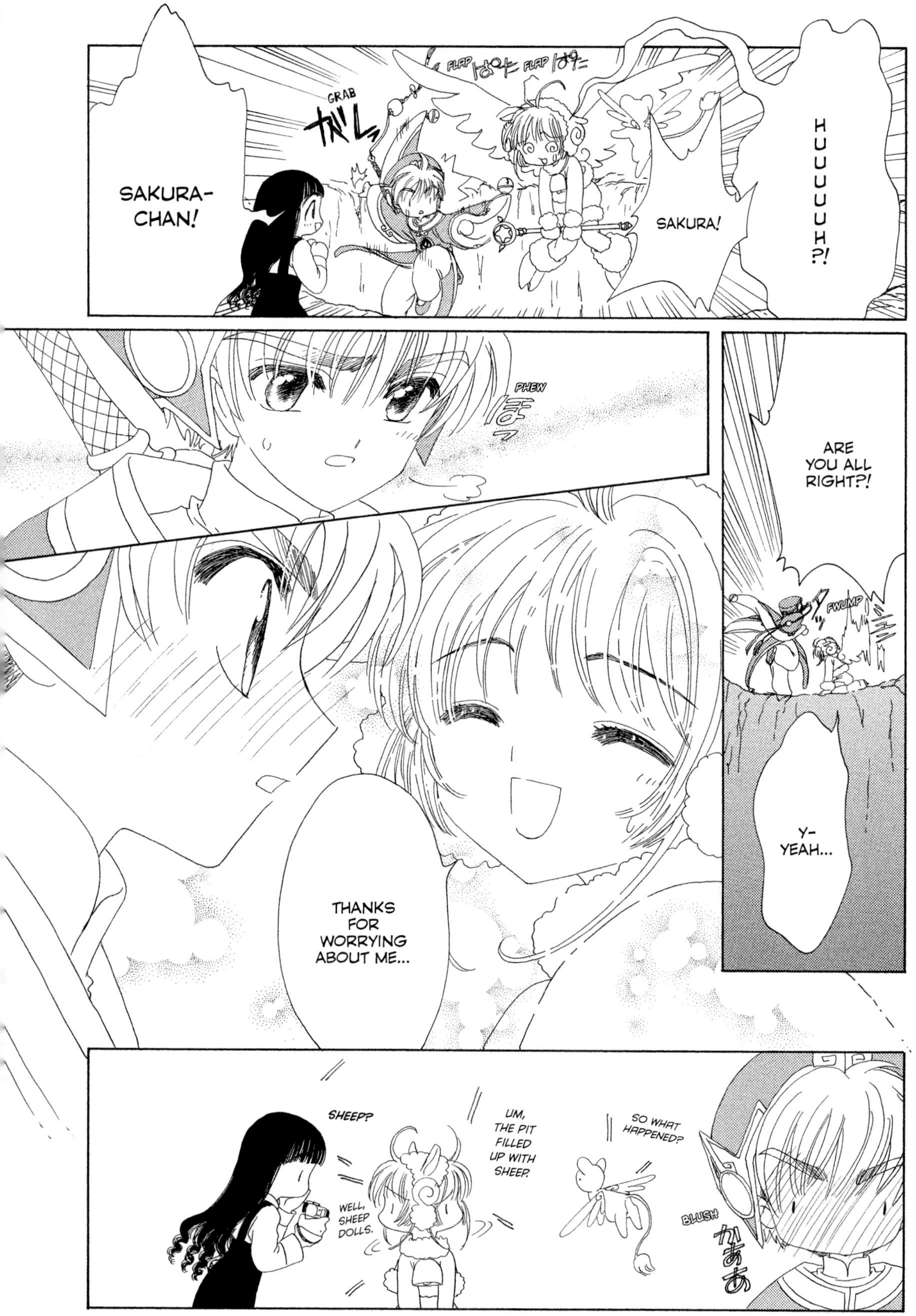
HUUUUUUH?!
FLAP
FLAP
SAKURA!
GRAB
SAKURA-CHAN!
ARE YOU ALL RIGHT?!
FWUMP
Y-YEAH...
PHEW
THANKS FOR WORRYING ABOUT ME...
BLUSH
SO WHAT HAPPENED?
UM, THE PIT FILLED UP WITH SHEEP.
SHEEP?
WELL, SHEEP DOLLS.

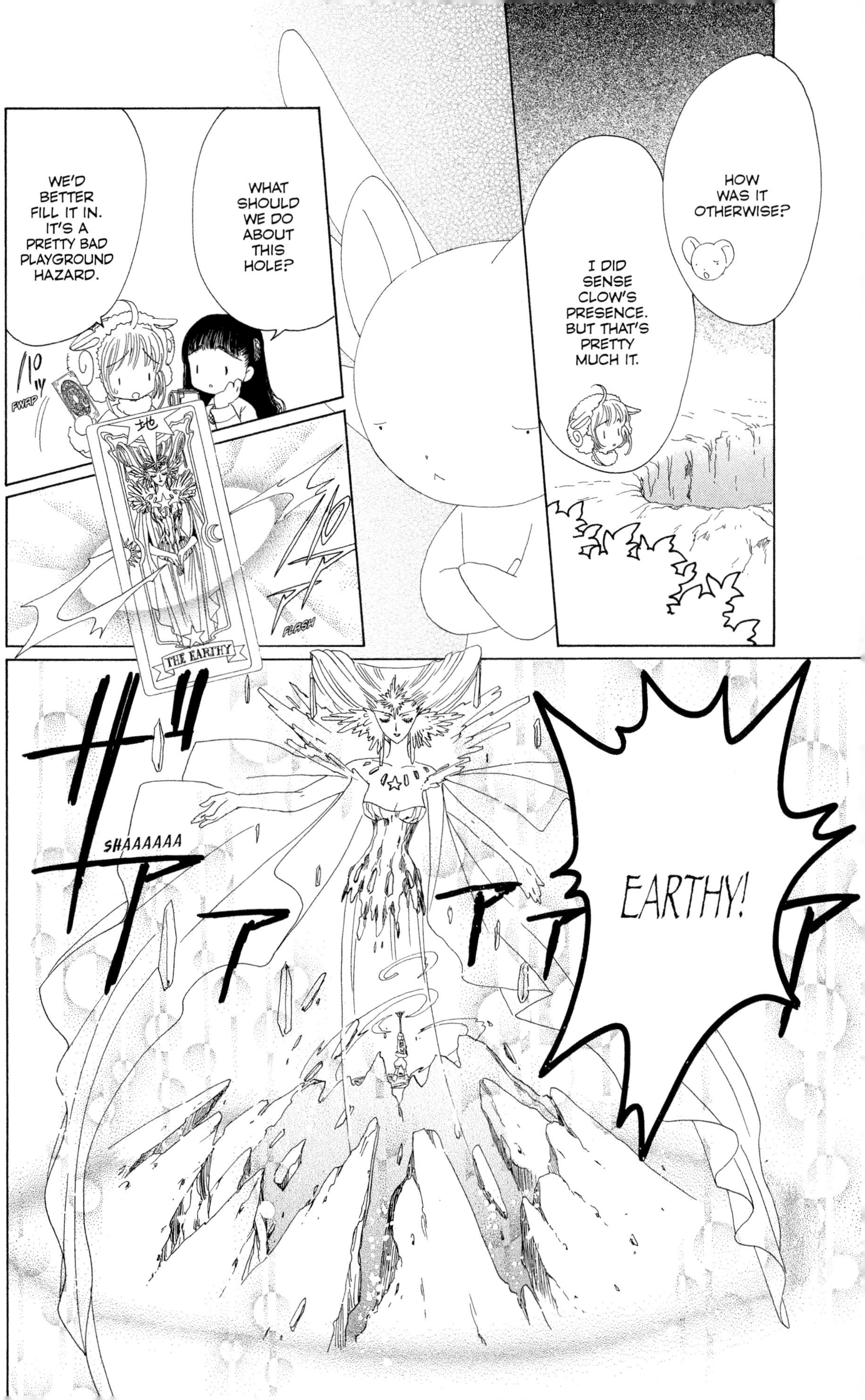
HOW WAS IT OTHERWISE?
I DID SENSE CLOW'S PRESENCE. BUT THAT'S PRETTY MUCH IT.
WHAT SHOULD WE DO ABOUT THIS HOLE?
WE'D BETTER FILL IT IN. IT'S A PRETTY BAD PLAYGROUND HAZARD.
FWAP
FLASH
THE EARTHY
EARTHY!
SHAAAAAA

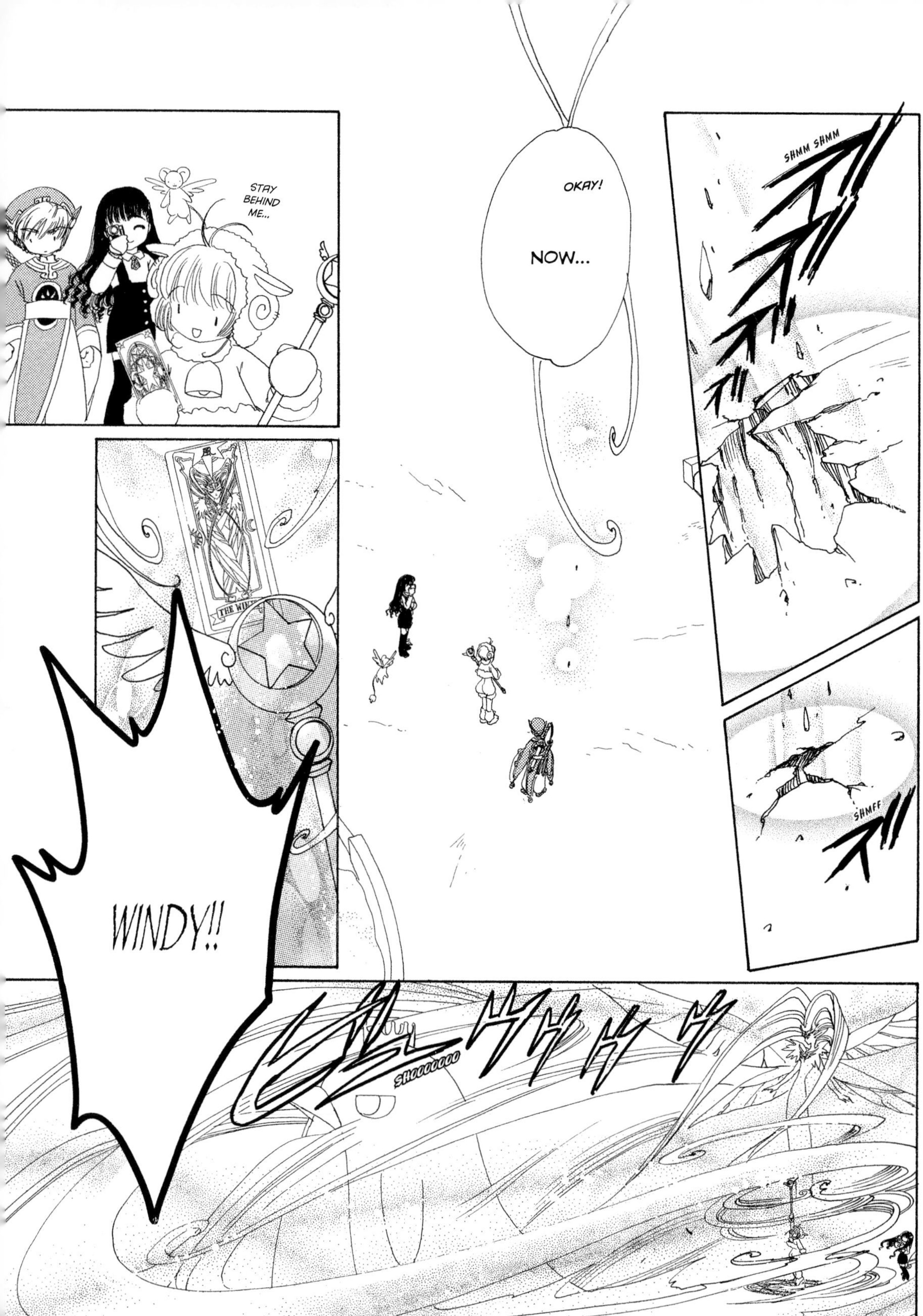
SHMM SHMM
SHMFF
OKAY!
NOW...
STAY BEHIND ME...
WINDY!!
SHOOOOOOO

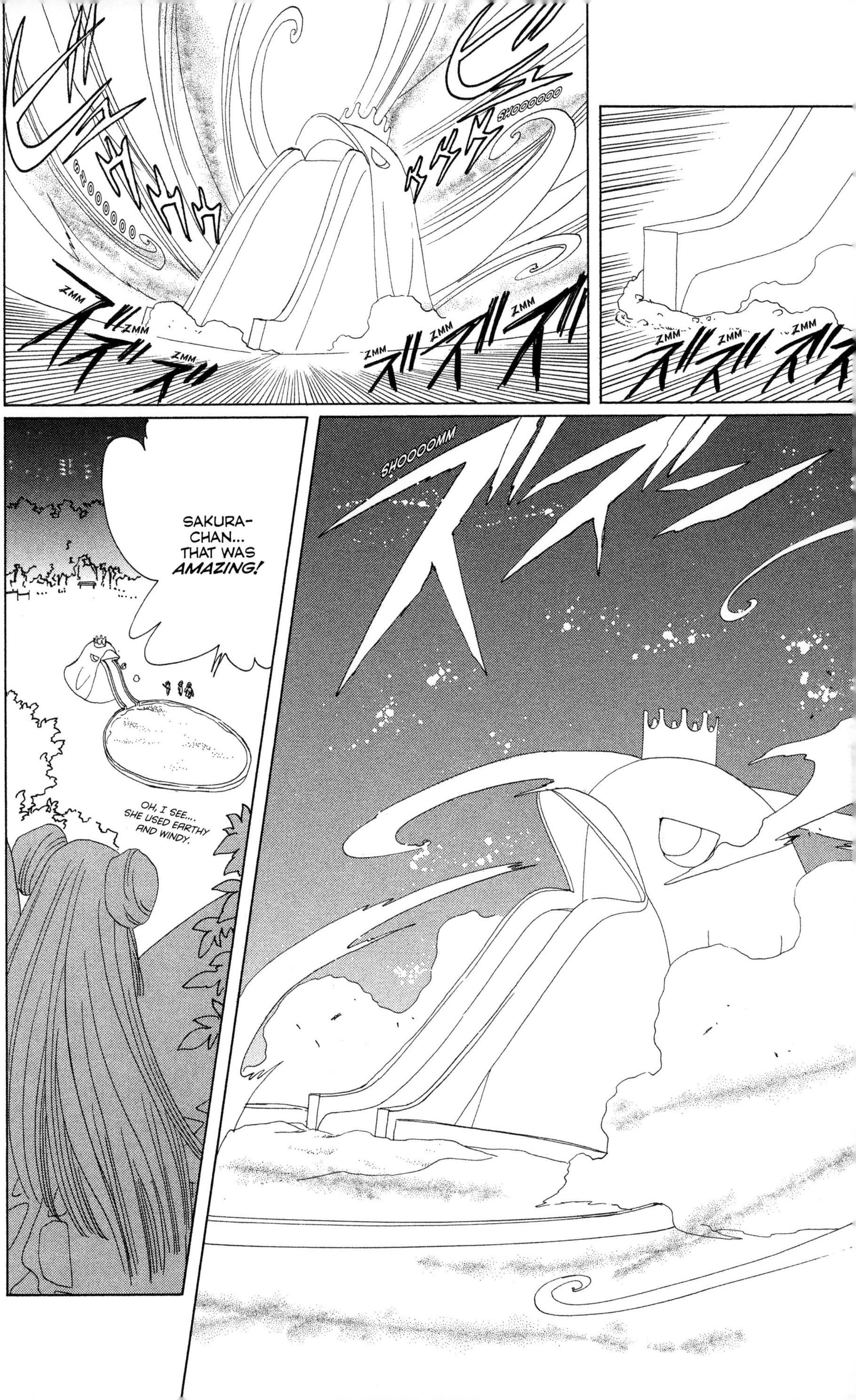
ZMM ZMM ZMM
SHOOOOOO
SHOOOOOO
ZMM ZMM ZMM ZMM ZMM ZMM
SHOOOOMM
SAKURA-CHAN... THAT WAS *AMAZING!*
OH, I SEE... SHE USED EARTHY AND WINDY.

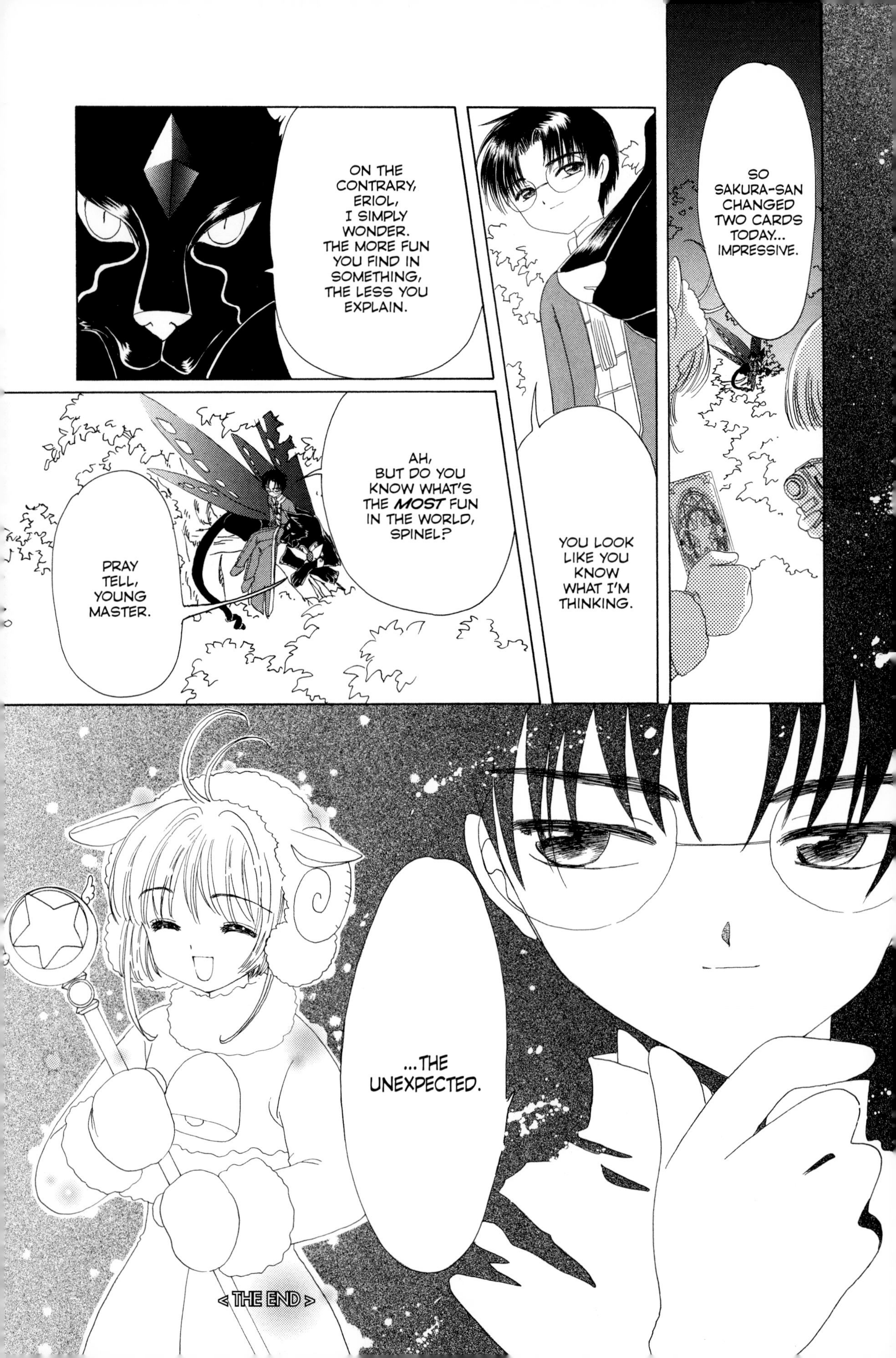
SO SAKURA-SAN CHANGED TWO CARDS TODAY... IMPRESSIVE.
YOU LOOK LIKE YOU KNOW WHAT I'M THINKING.
ON THE CONTRARY, ERIOL, I SIMPLY WONDER. THE MORE FUN YOU FIND IN SOMETHING, THE LESS YOU EXPLAIN.
AH, BUT DO YOU KNOW WHAT'S THE ***MOST*** FUN IN THE WORLD, SPINEL?
PRAY TELL, YOUNG MASTER.
...THE UNEXPECTED.
< THE END >

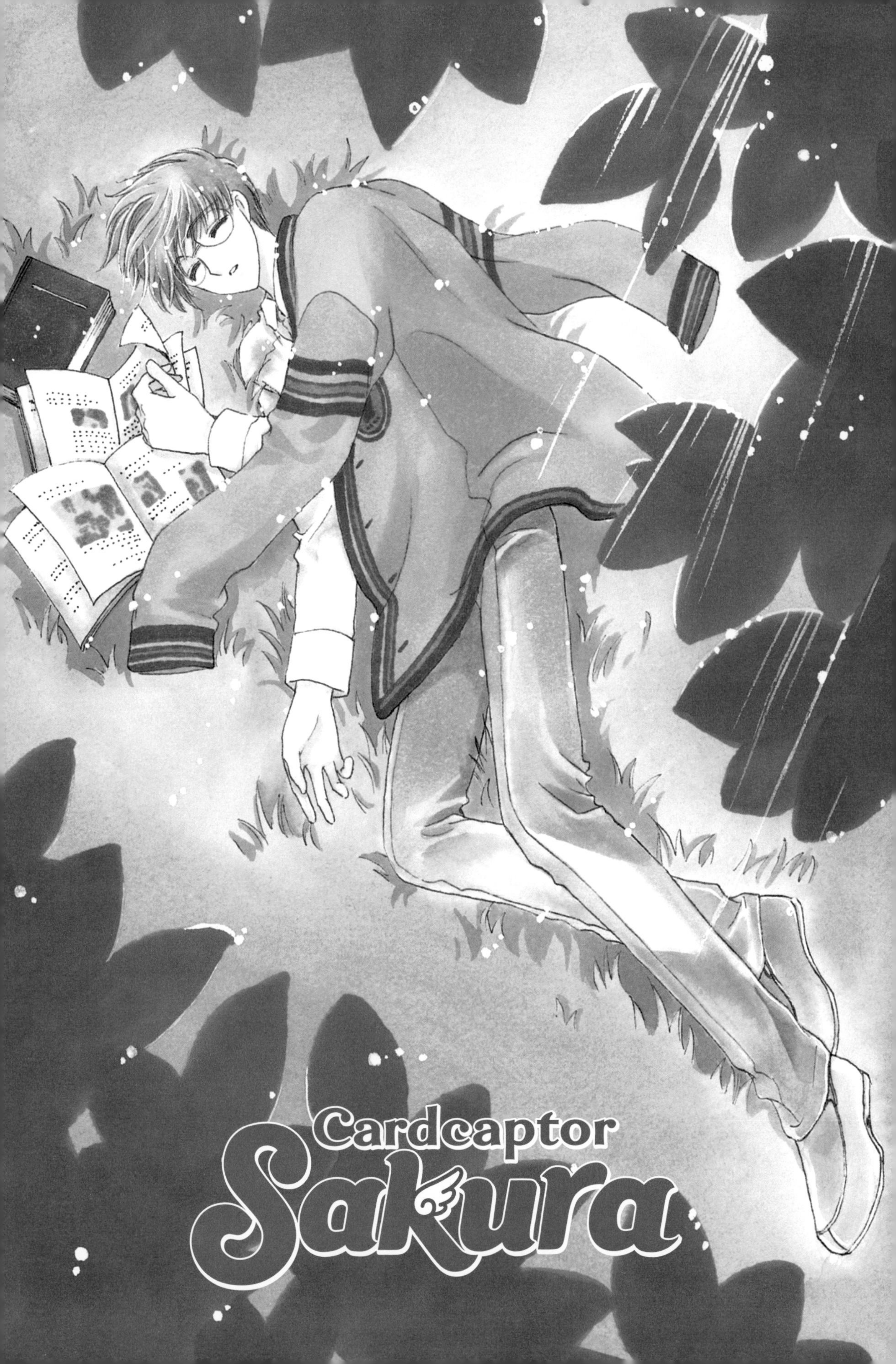
Cardcaptor
Sakura

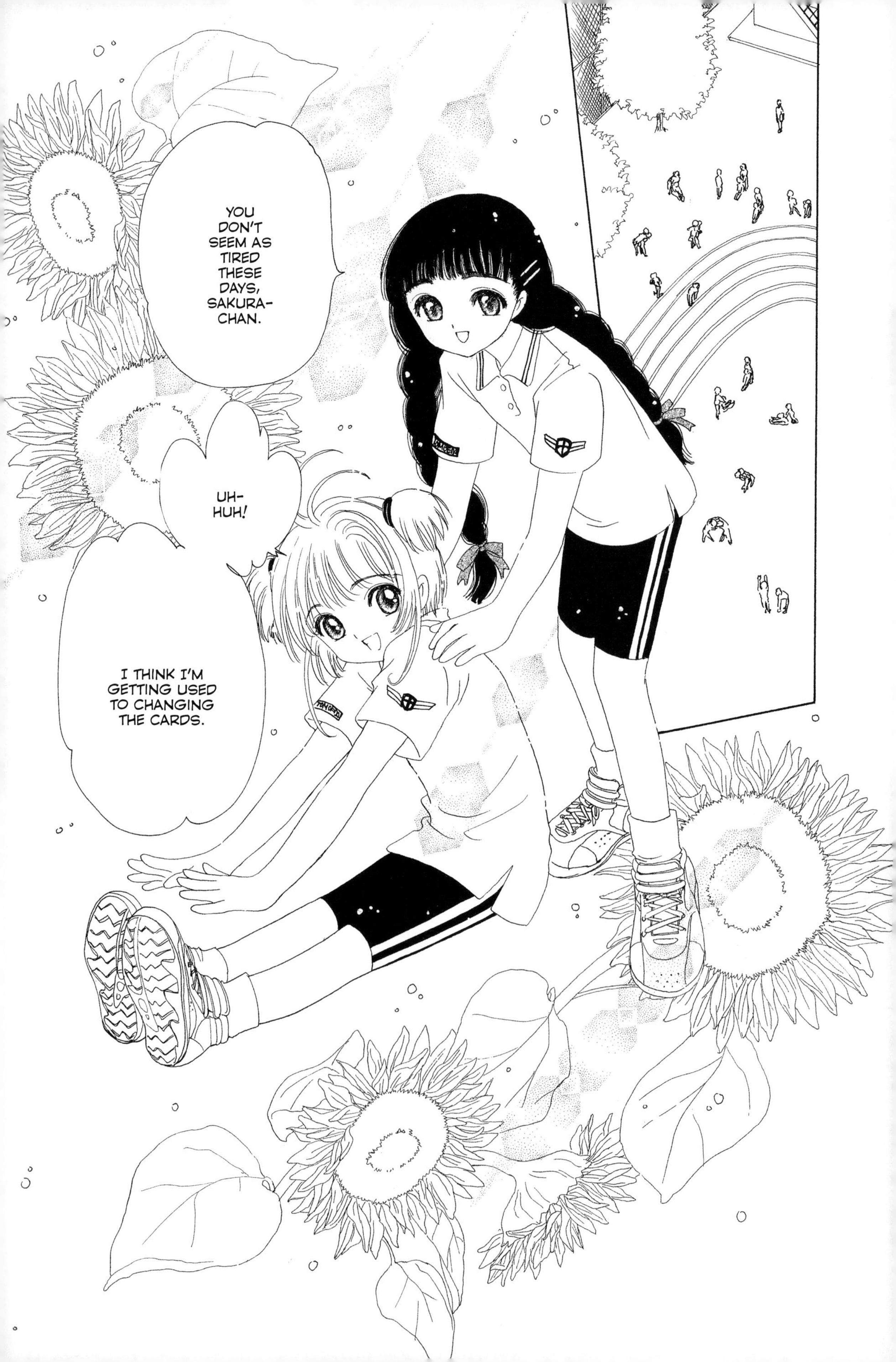
YOU DON'T SEEM AS TIRED THESE DAYS, SAKURA-CHAN.
UH-HUH!
I THINK I'M GETTING USED TO CHANGING THE CARDS.

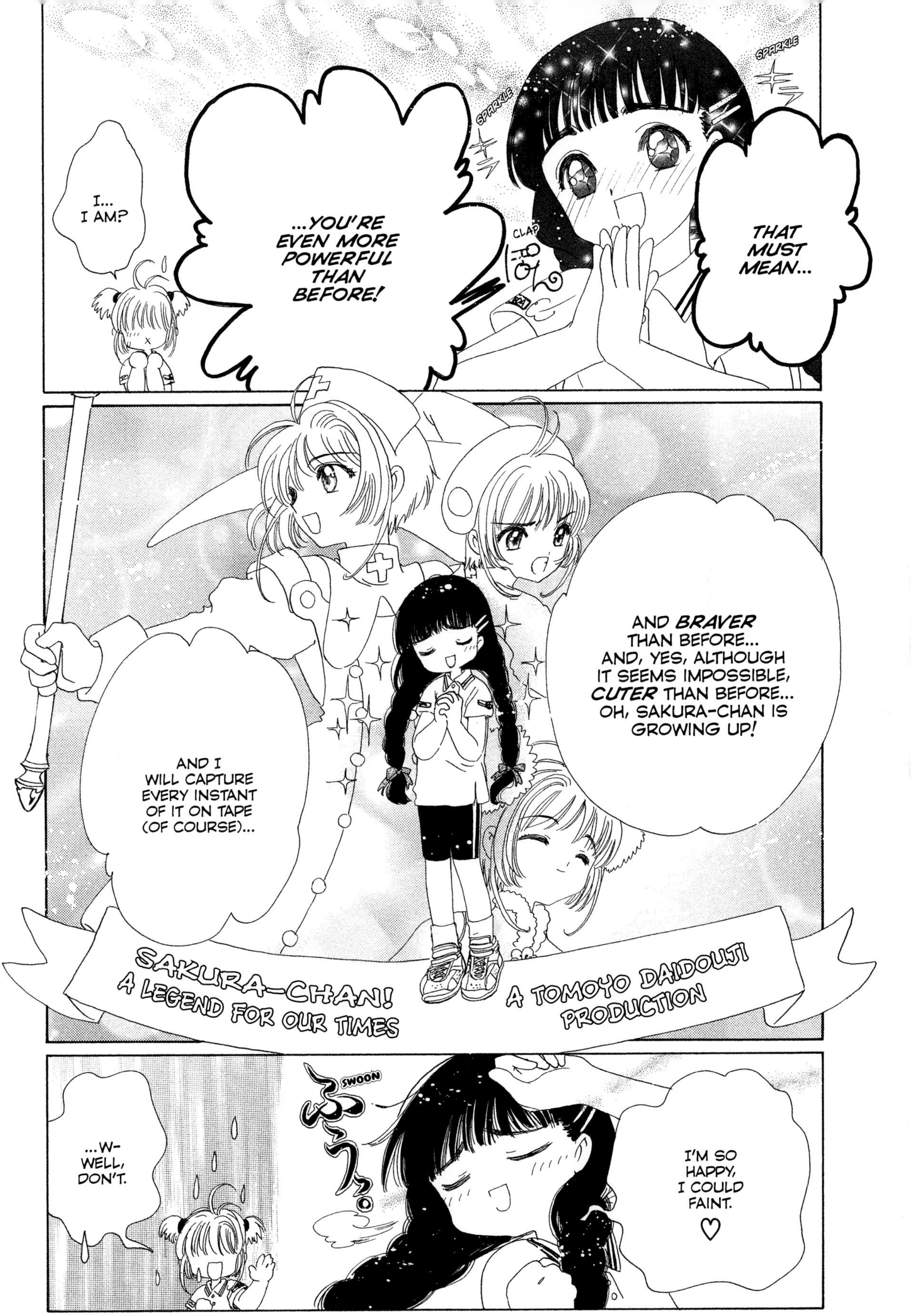
SPARKLE
SPARKLE
THAT MUST MEAN...
CLAP
...YOU'RE EVEN MORE POWERFUL THAN BEFORE!
I... I AM?
AND BRAVER THAN BEFORE... AND, YES, ALTHOUGH IT SEEMS IMPOSSIBLE, CUTER THAN BEFORE... OH, SAKURA-CHAN IS GROWING UP!
AND I WILL CAPTURE EVERY INSTANT OF IT ON TAPE (OF COURSE)...
SAKURA-CHAN! A LEGEND FOR OUR TIMES
A TOMOYO DAIDOUJI PRODUCTION
I'M SO HAPPY, I COULD FAINT. ♡
SWOON
...W-WELL, DON'T.

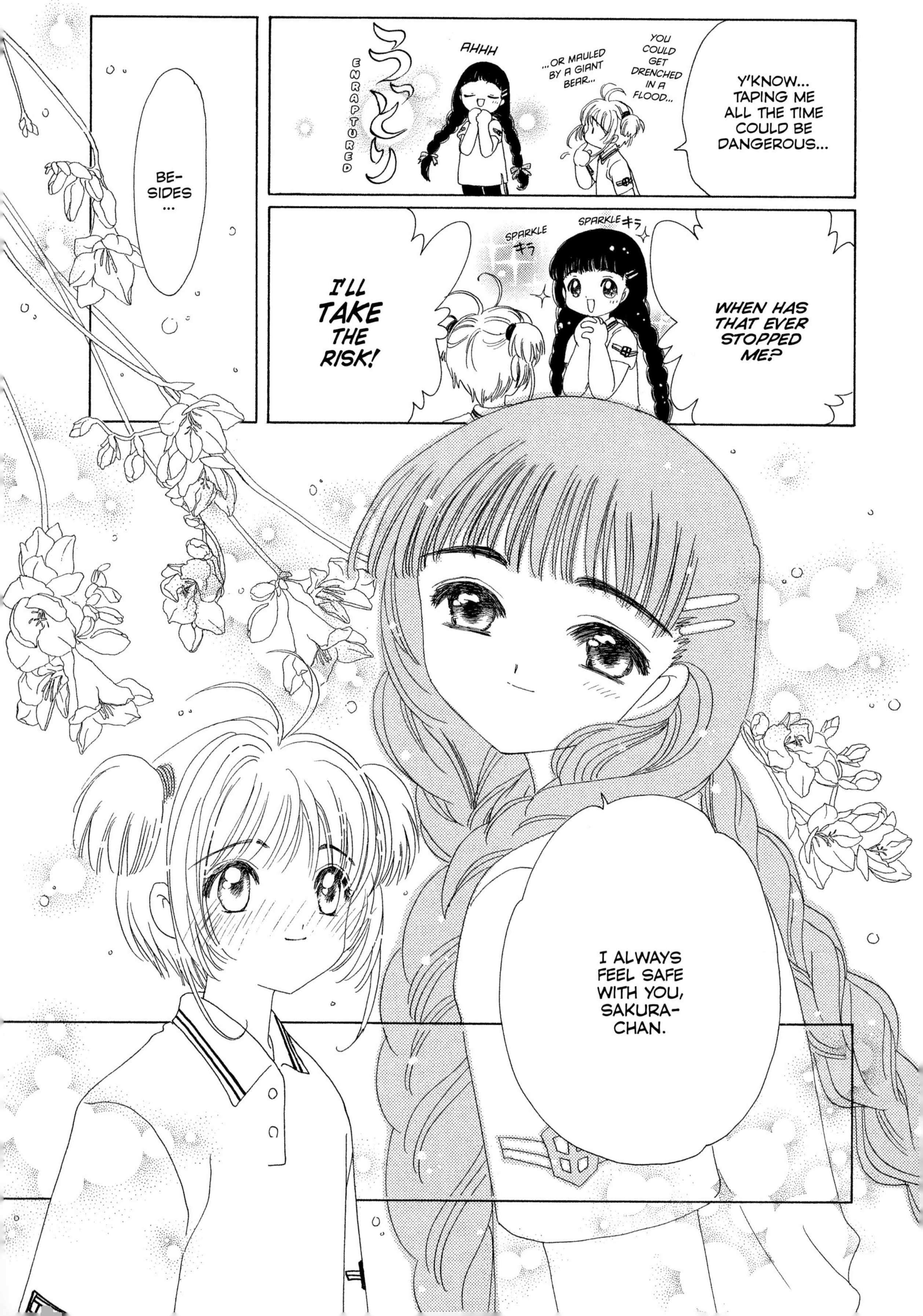

Y'KNOW... TAPING ME ALL THE TIME COULD BE DANGEROUS...
YOU COULD GET DRENCHED IN A FLOOD...
...OR MAULED BY A GIANT BEAR...
AHHH
うっとり
ENRAPTURED
WHEN HAS THAT EVER STOPPED ME?
SPARKLE キラ
SPARKLE キラ
I'LL TAKE THE RISK!
BE-SIDES...
I ALWAYS FEEL SAFE WITH YOU, SAKURA-CHAN.

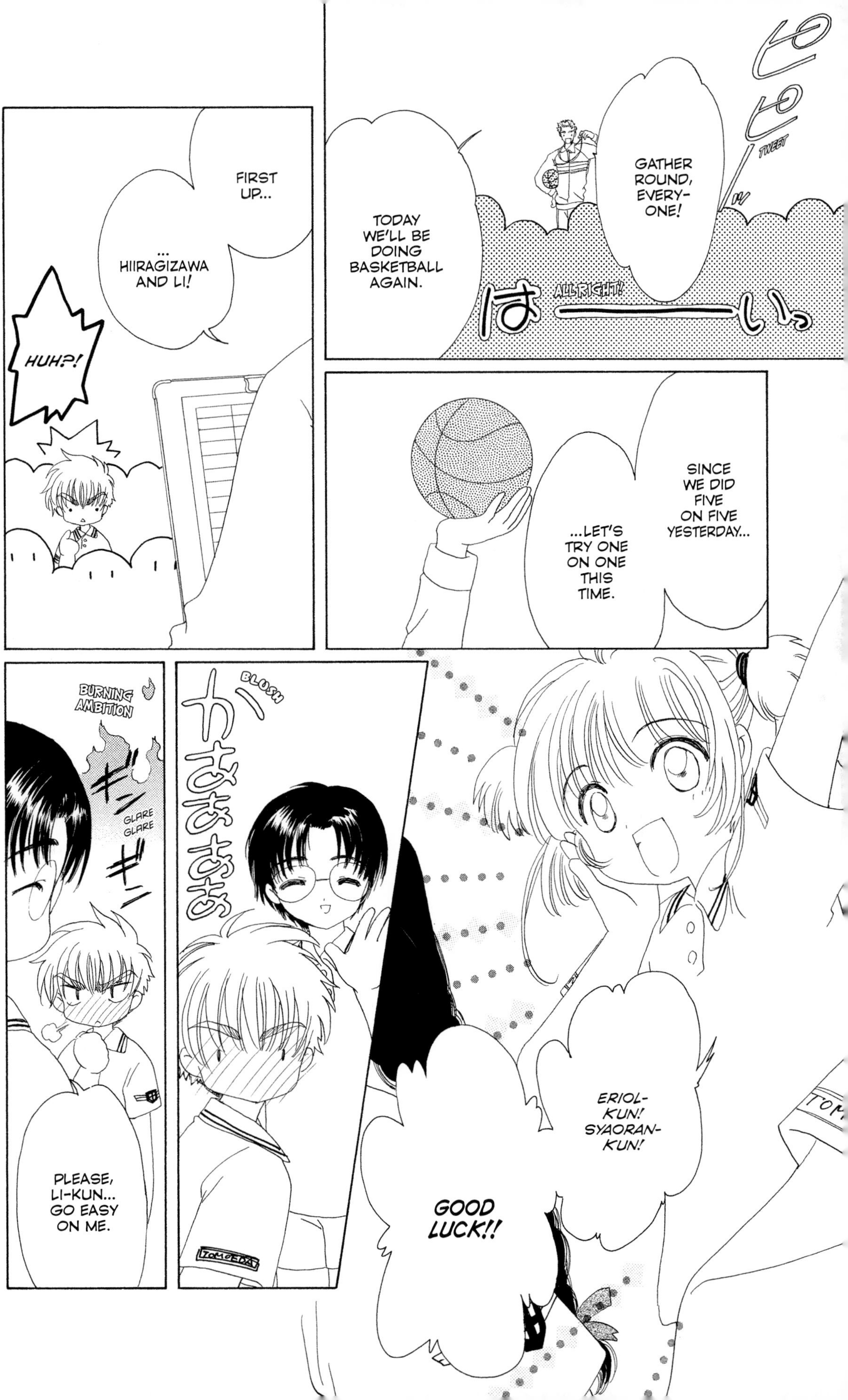

TWEET
GATHER ROUND, EVERY-ONE!
TODAY WE'LL BE DOING BASKETBALL AGAIN.
はーい
ALL RIGHT!
SINCE WE DID FIVE ON FIVE YESTERDAY...
...LET'S TRY ONE ON ONE THIS TIME.
FIRST UP...
... HIIRAGIZAWA AND LI!
HUH?!
ERIOL-KUN! SYAORAN-KUN!
GOOD LUCK!!
かあああああ
BLUSH
BURNING AMBITION
ギン ギン
GLARE GLARE
PLEASE, LI-KUN... GO EASY ON ME.
TOMOEDA

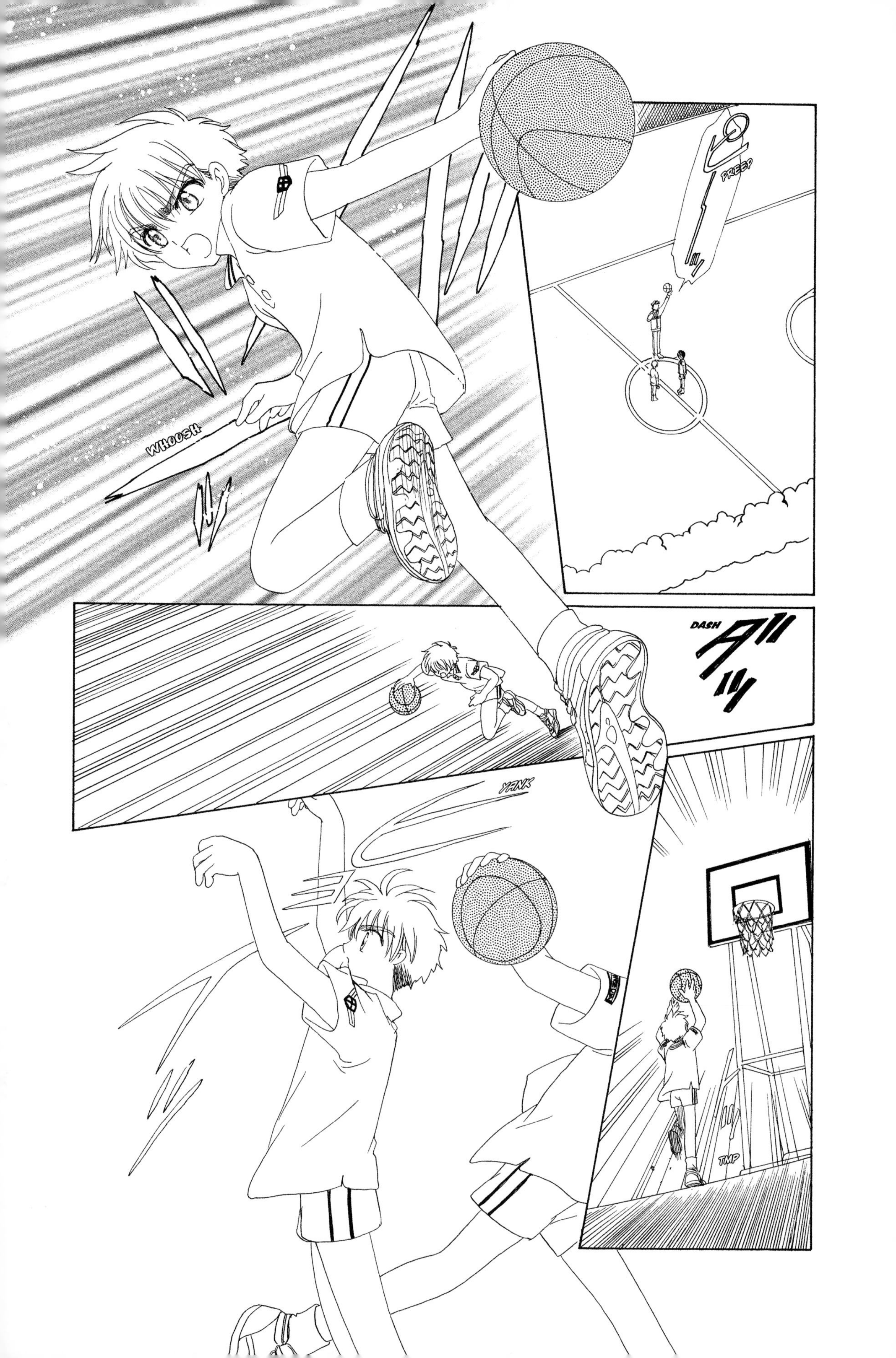
PREEP
WHOOSH
DASH
TMP
YANK

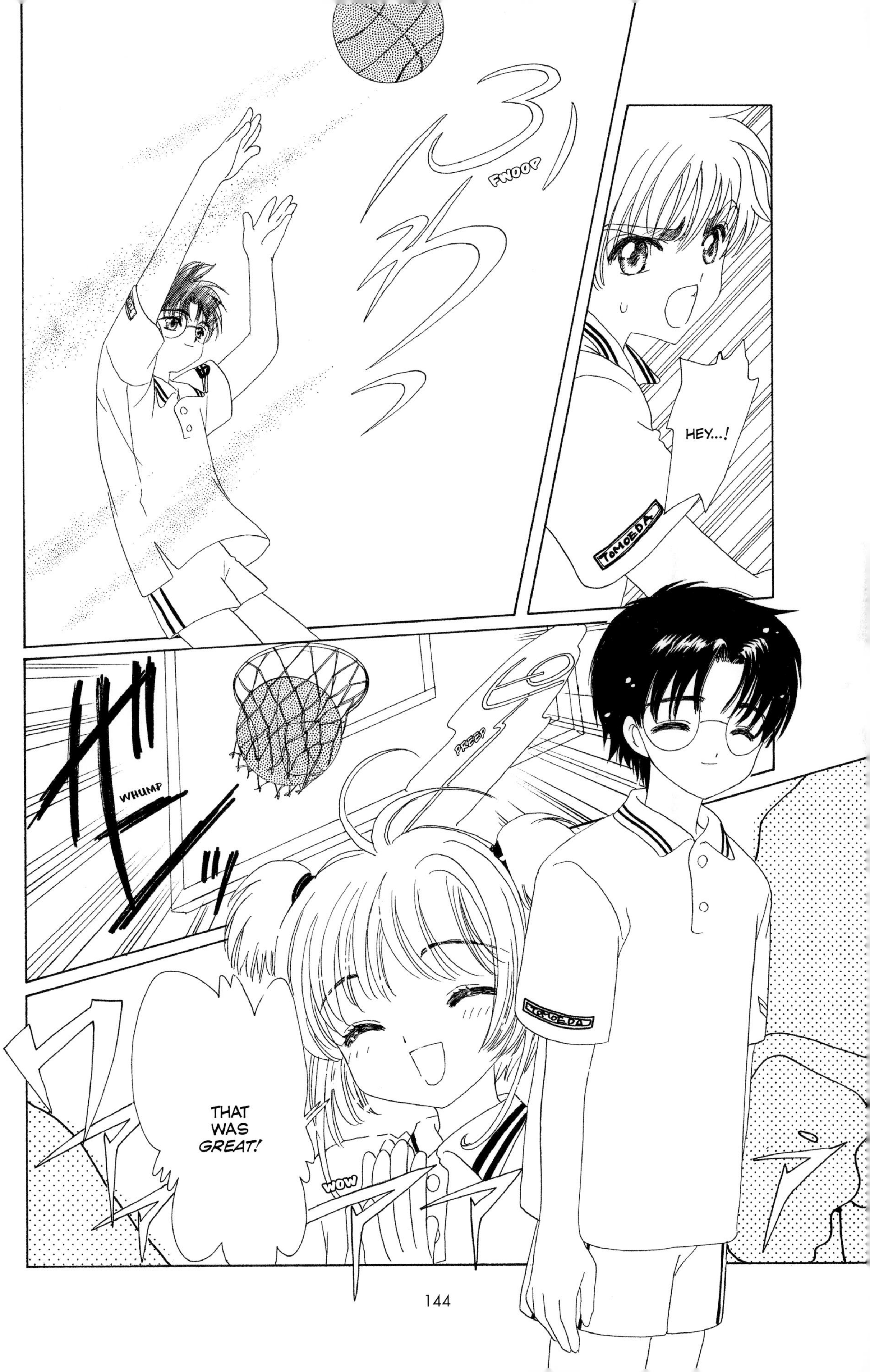
HEY...!
FWOOP
PREEP
WHUMP
TOMOEDA
THAT WAS GREAT!
WOW

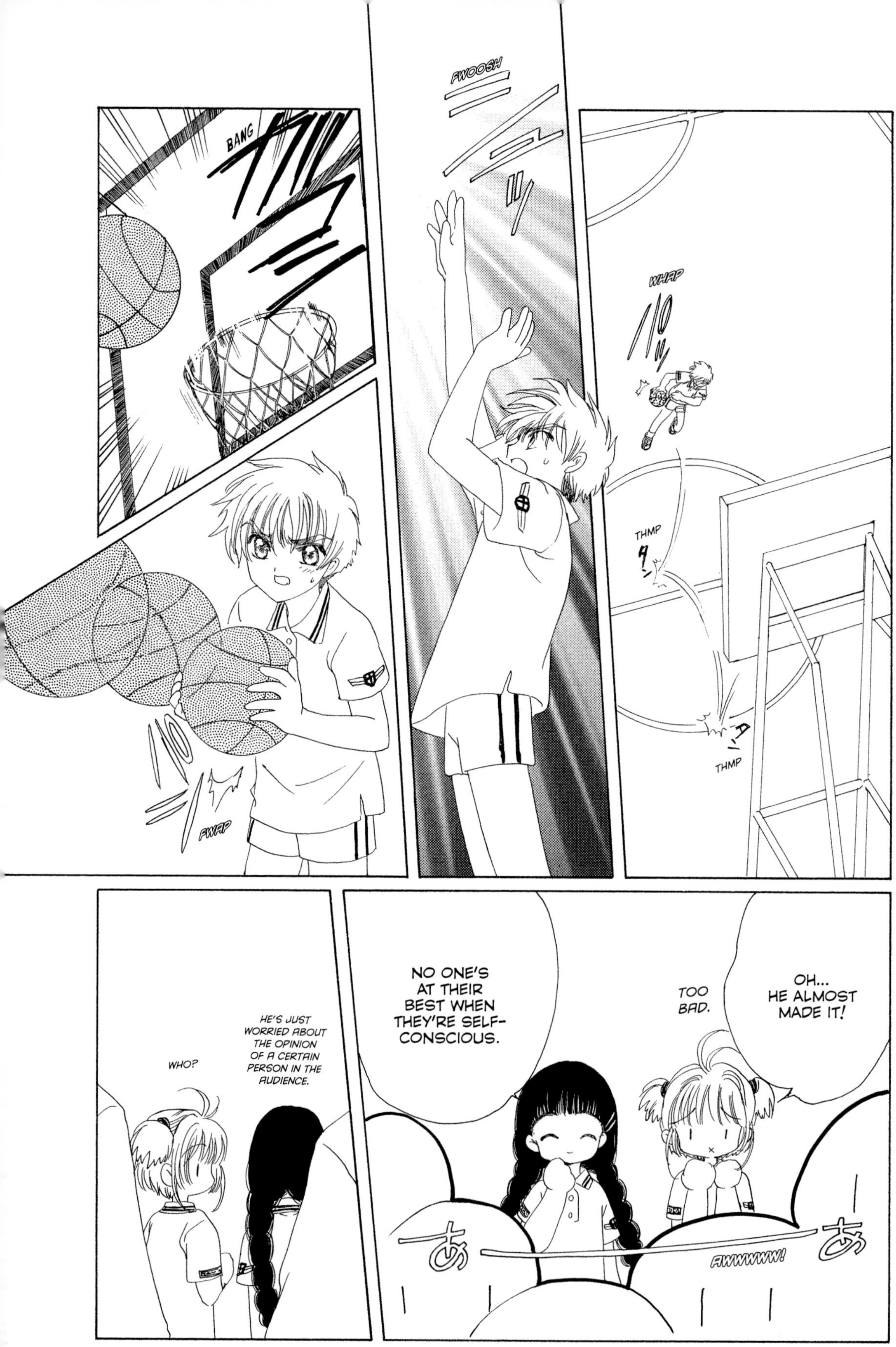
WHAP
THMP
THMP
FWOOSH
BANG
FWAP
OH... HE ALMOST MADE IT!
TOO BAD.
NO ONE'S AT THEIR BEST WHEN THEY'RE SELF-CONSCIOUS.
あ
AWWWWW!
あ
HE'S JUST WORRIED ABOUT THE OPINION OF A CERTAIN PERSON IN THE AUDIENCE.
WHO?

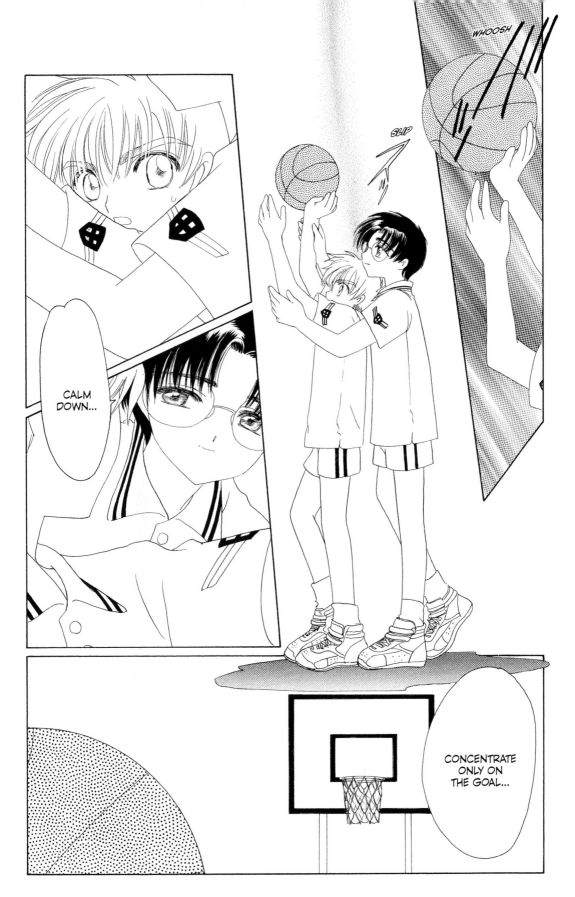

CALM DOWN...

WHOOSH

SLAP

CONCENTRATE ONLY ON THE GOAL...

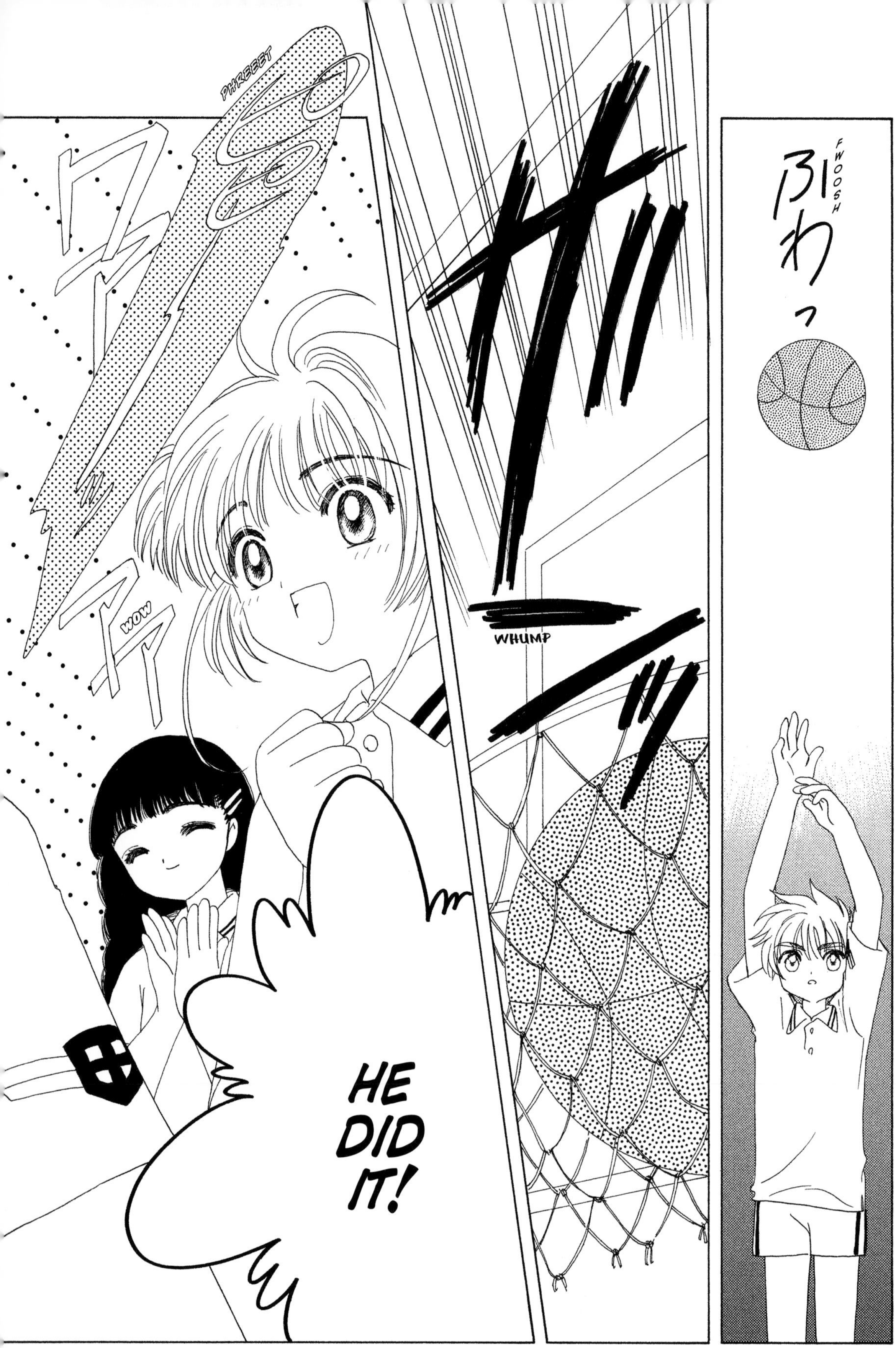
FWOOSH
ふわっ
WHUMP
PHREEET
WOW
HE DID IT!

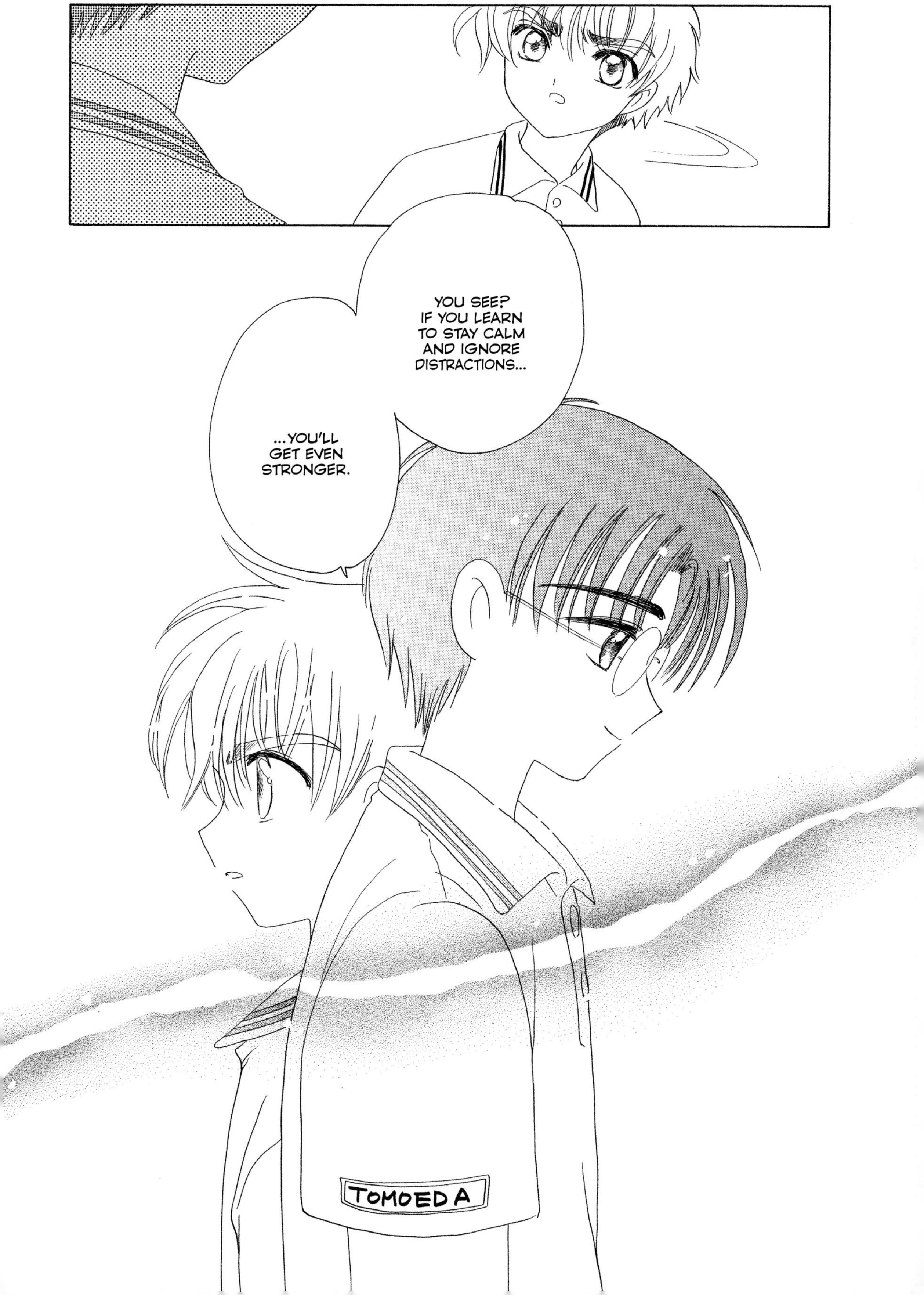
YOU SEE? IF YOU LEARN TO STAY CALM AND IGNORE DISTRACTIONS...
...YOU'LL GET EVEN STRONGER.
TOMOEDA

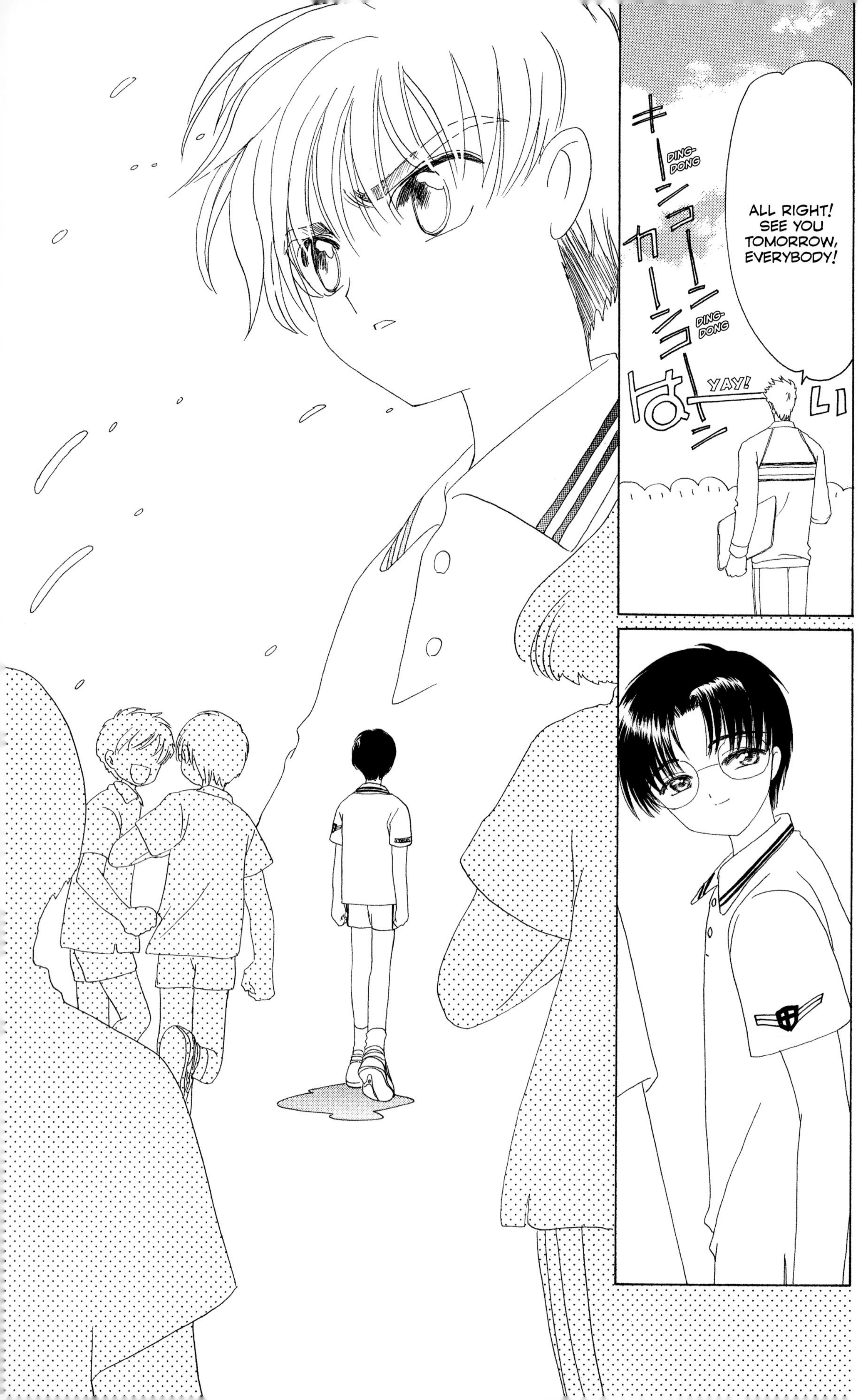
ALL RIGHT! SEE YOU TOMORROW, EVERYBODY!
キーンコーンカーンコーン
DING-DONG
DING-DONG
はーい
YAY!

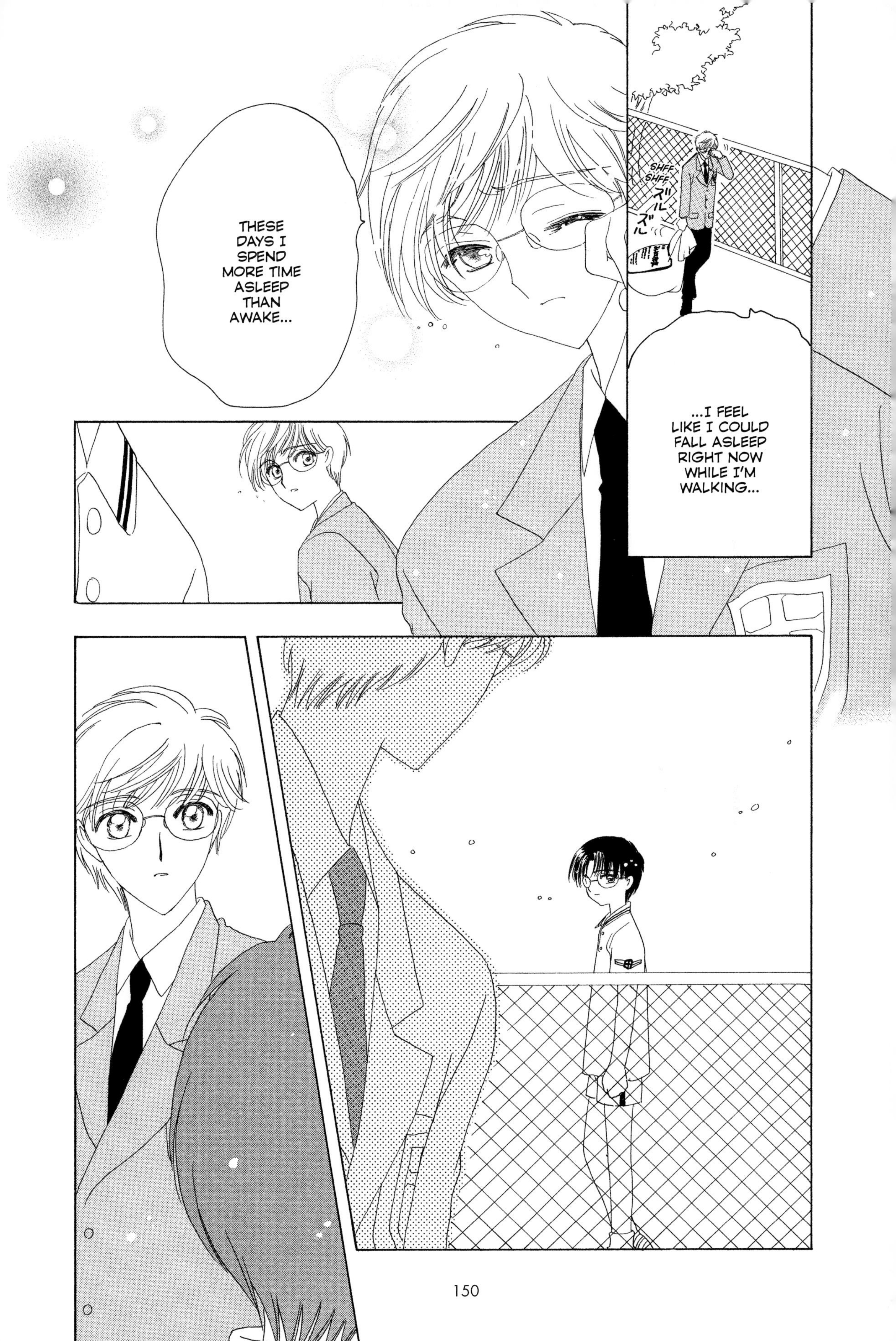
THESE DAYS I SPEND MORE TIME ASLEEP THAN AWAKE...
SHFF SHFF
ズルズル
...I FEEL LIKE I COULD FALL ASLEEP RIGHT NOW WHILE I'M WALKING...

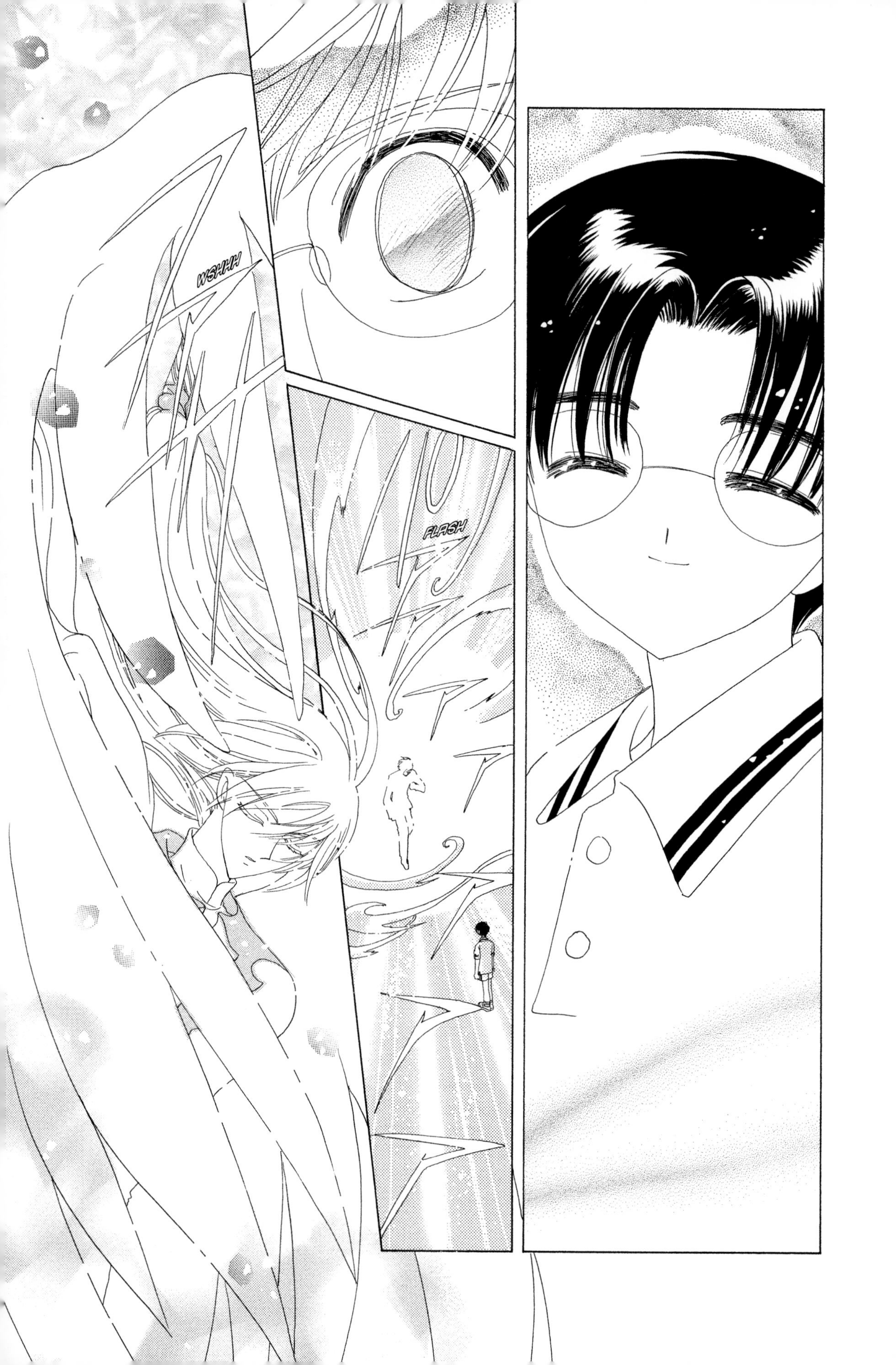
FLASH
WSHHH

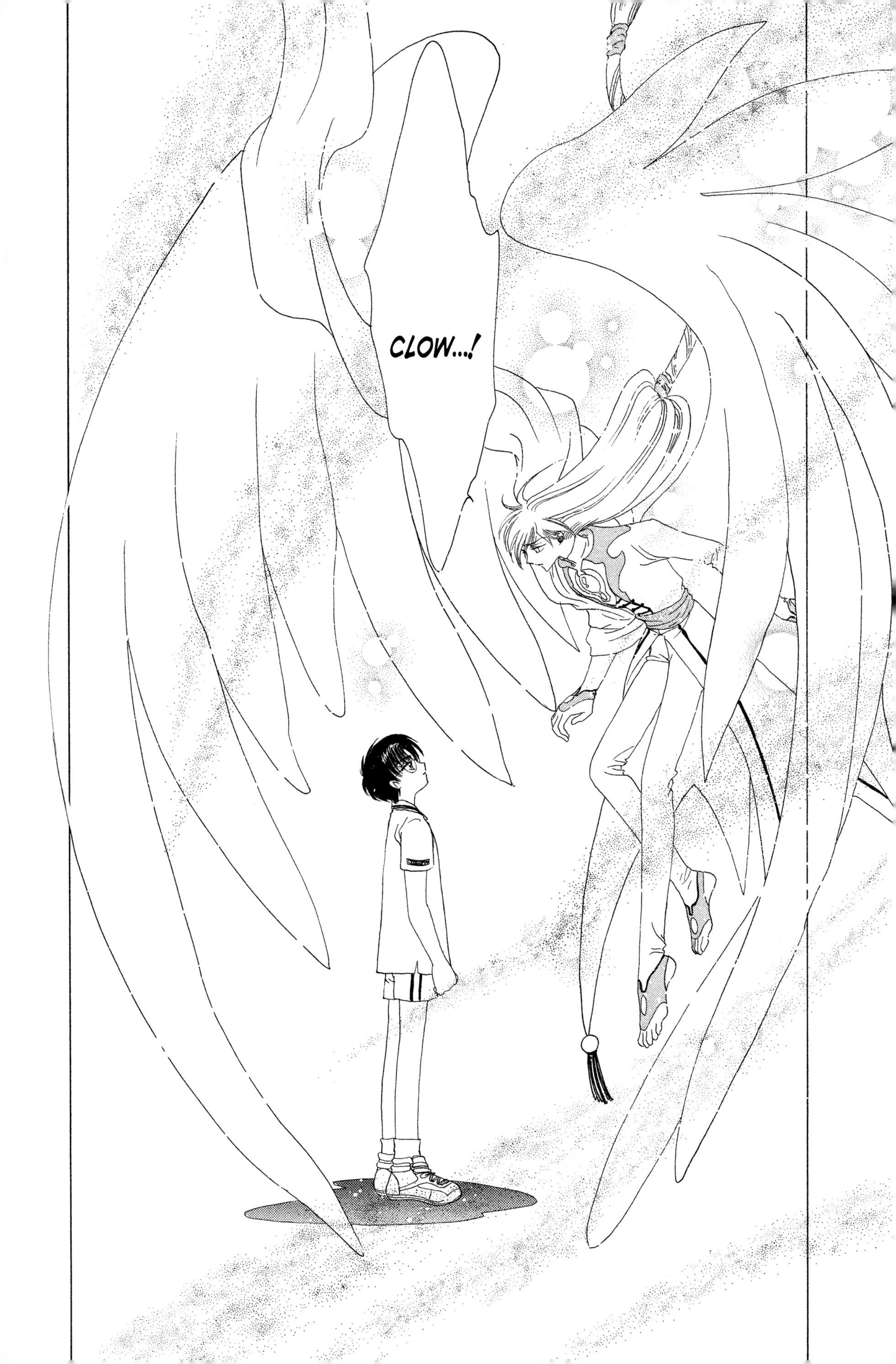
CLOW...!

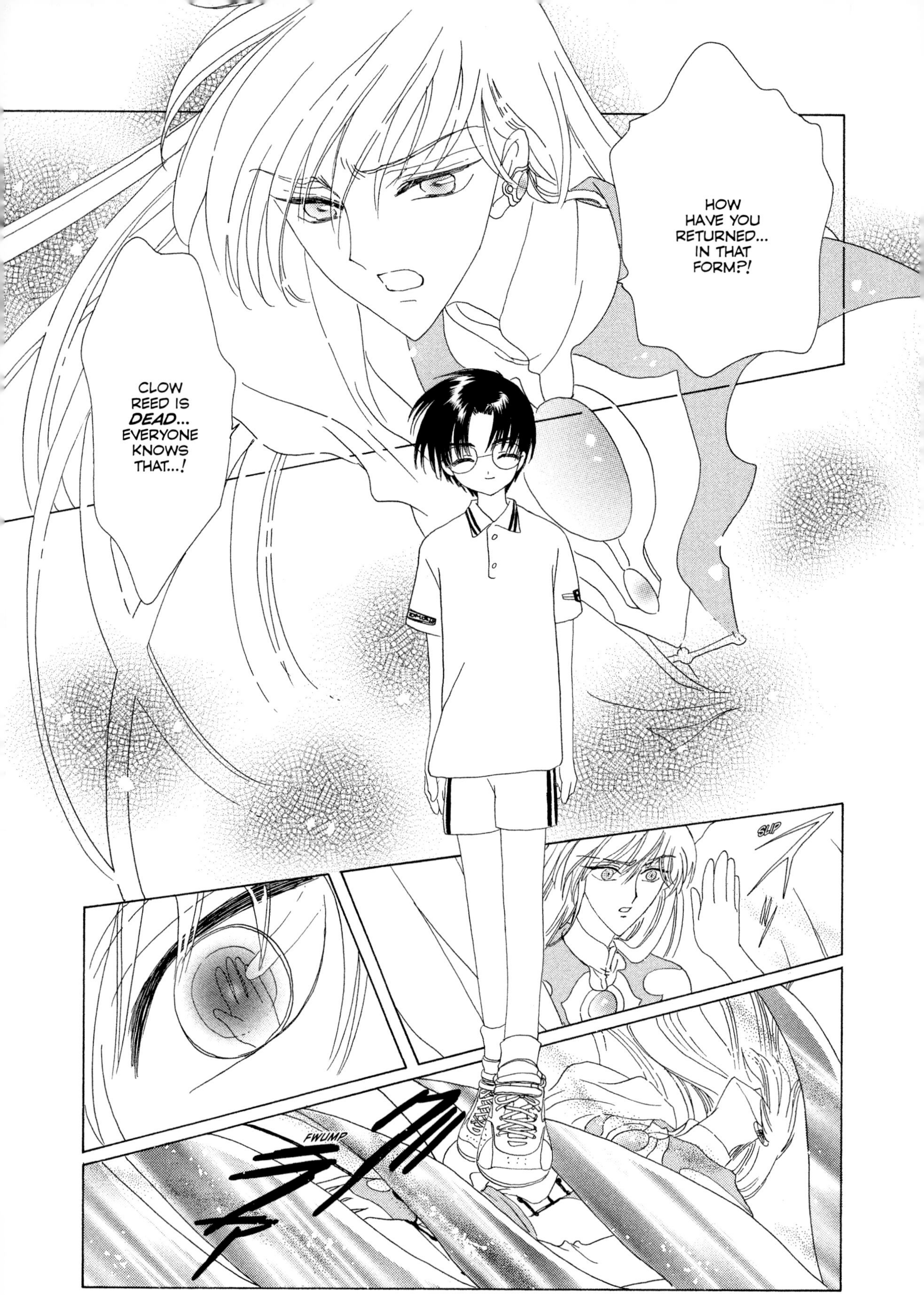
HOW HAVE YOU RETURNED... IN THAT FORM?!
CLOW REED IS **DEAD**... EVERYONE KNOWS THAT...!
SLIP
FWUMP

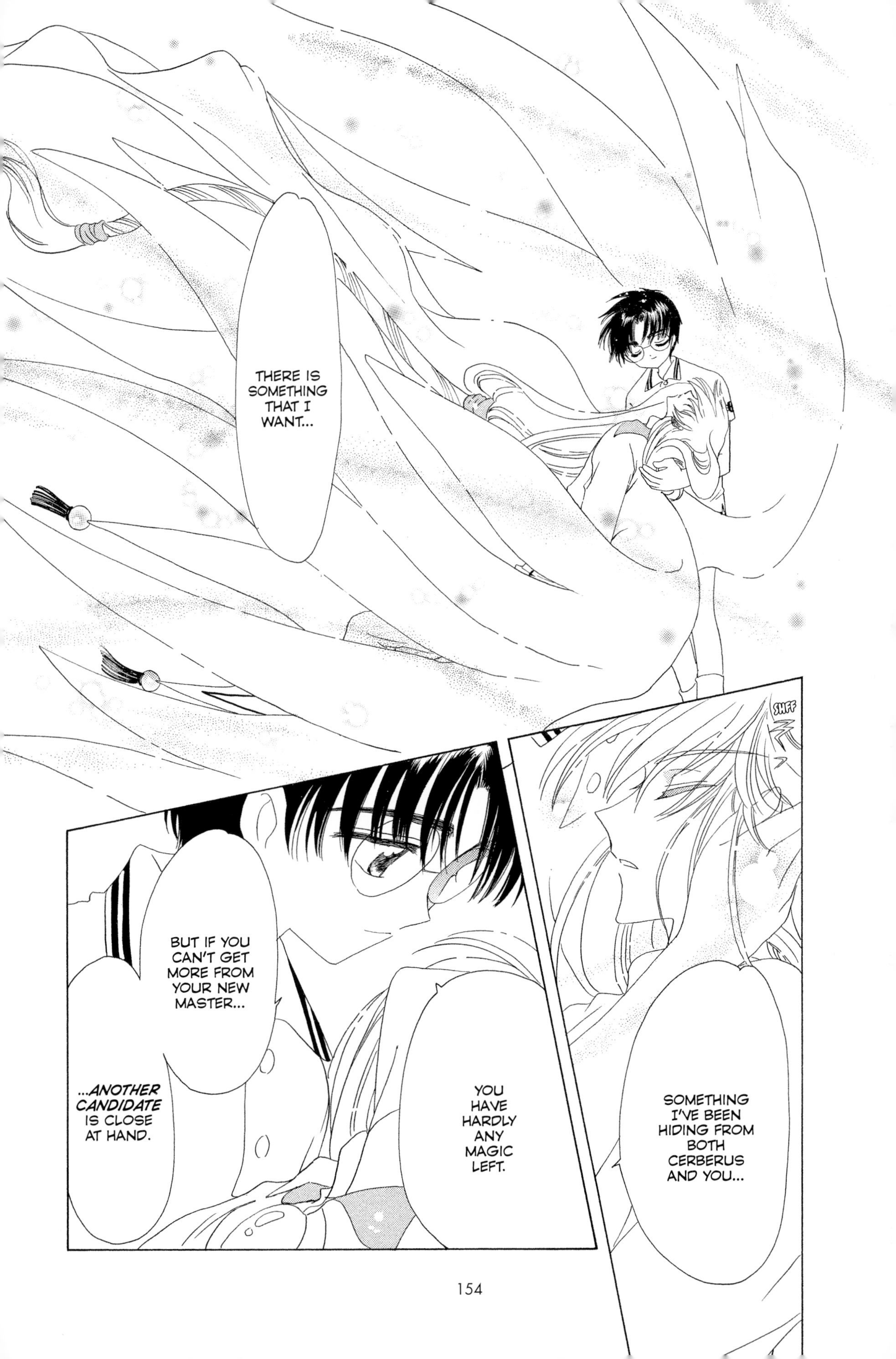
THERE IS SOMETHING THAT I WANT...
SHFF
SOMETHING I'VE BEEN HIDING FROM BOTH CERBERUS AND YOU...
YOU HAVE HARDLY ANY MAGIC LEFT.
BUT IF YOU CAN'T GET MORE FROM YOUR NEW MASTER...
...*ANOTHER CANDIDATE* IS CLOSE AT HAND.

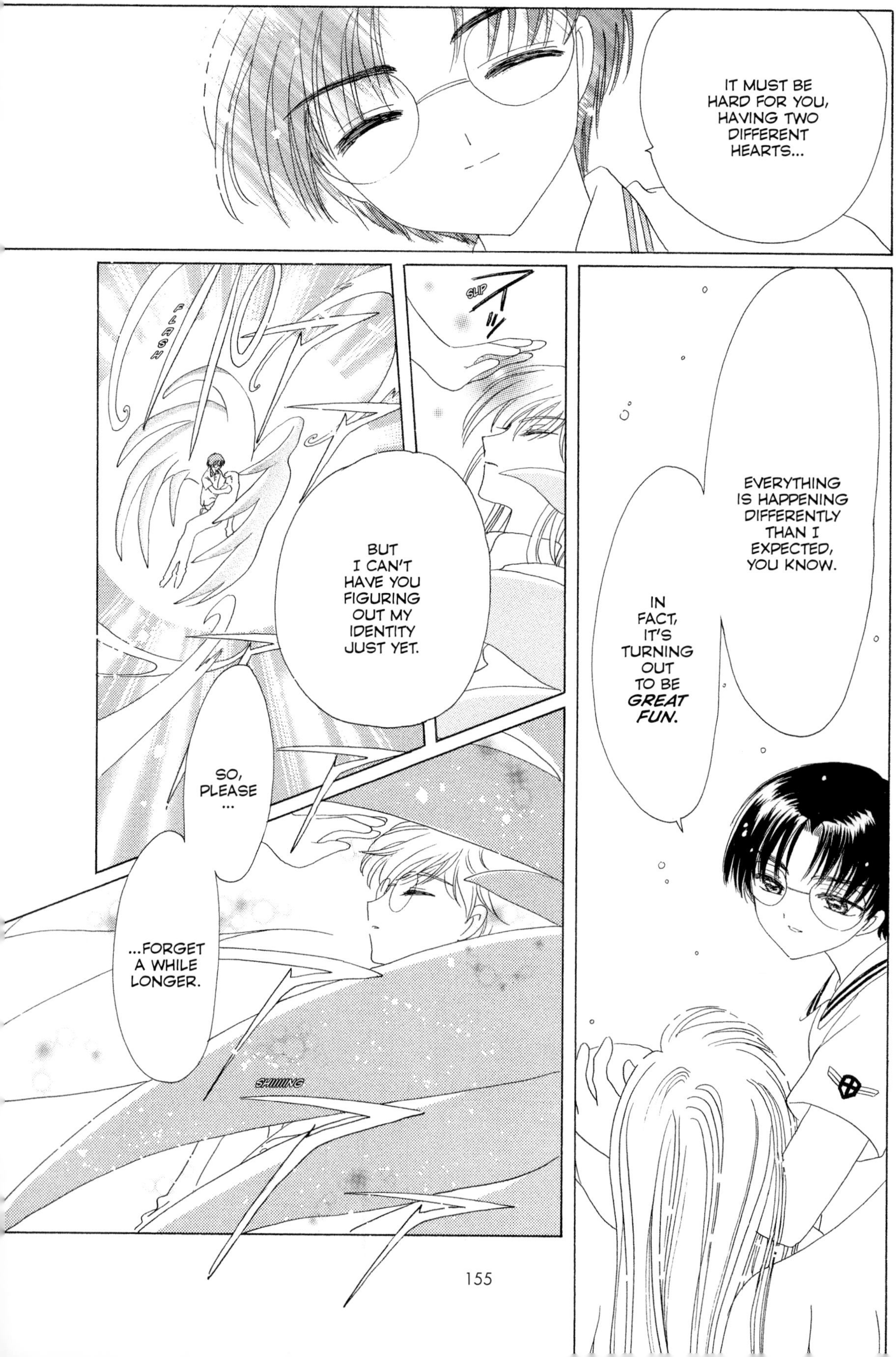
IT MUST BE HARD FOR YOU, HAVING TWO DIFFERENT HEARTS...
EVERYTHING IS HAPPENING DIFFERENTLY THAN I EXPECTED, YOU KNOW.
IN FACT, IT'S TURNING OUT TO BE ***GREAT FUN.***
SLIP
BUT I CAN'T HAVE YOU FIGURING OUT MY IDENTITY JUST YET.
FLASH
SO, PLEASE ...
...FORGET A WHILE LONGER.
SHIIIING

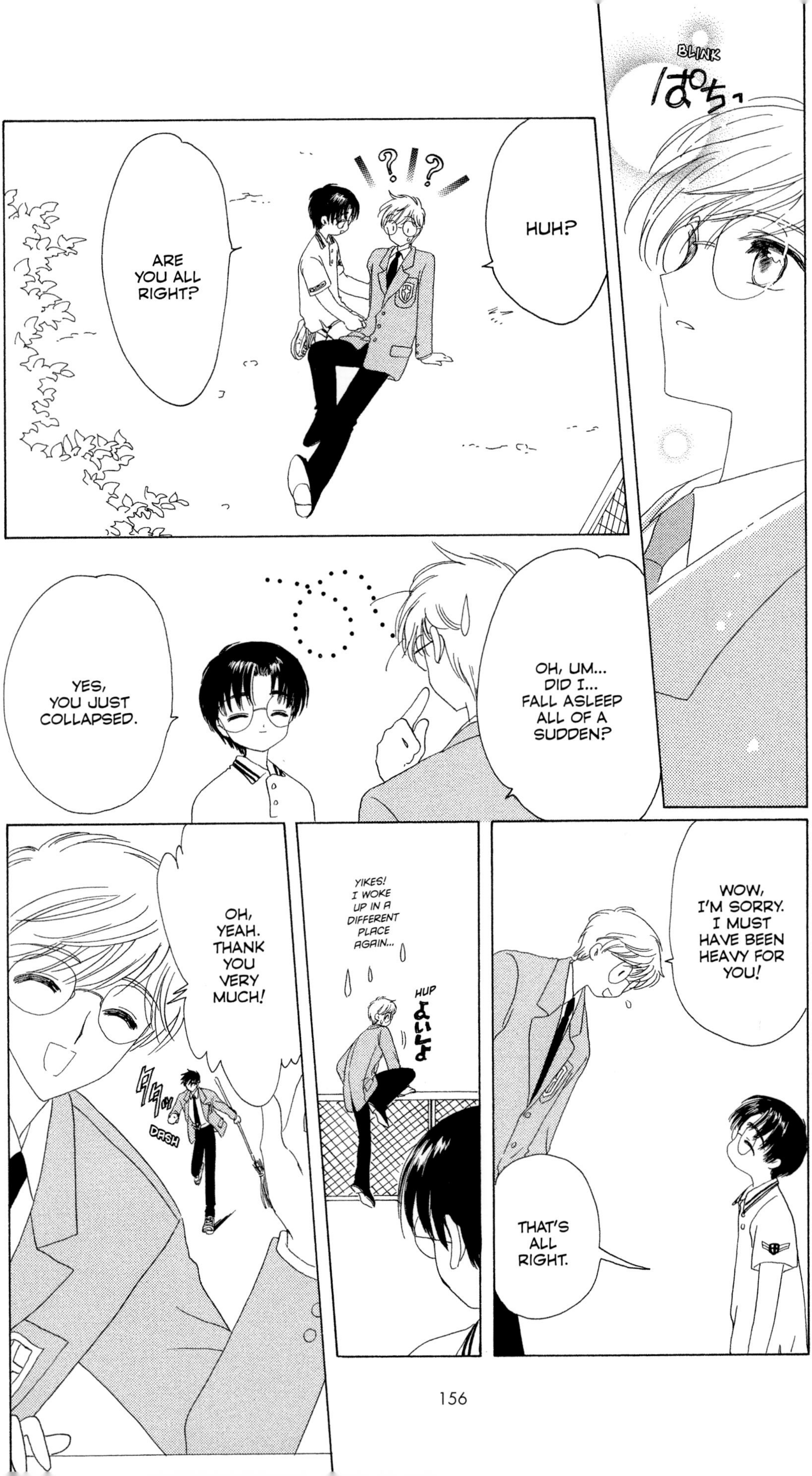
BLINK
ぱちっ
HUH?
ARE YOU ALL RIGHT?
OH, UM... DID I... FALL ASLEEP ALL OF A SUDDEN?
YES, YOU JUST COLLAPSED.
WOW, I'M SORRY. I MUST HAVE BEEN HEAVY FOR YOU!
THAT'S ALL RIGHT.
YIKES! I WOKE UP IN A DIFFERENT PLACE AGAIN...
HUP
よいしょ
OH, YEAH. THANK YOU VERY MUCH!
DASH

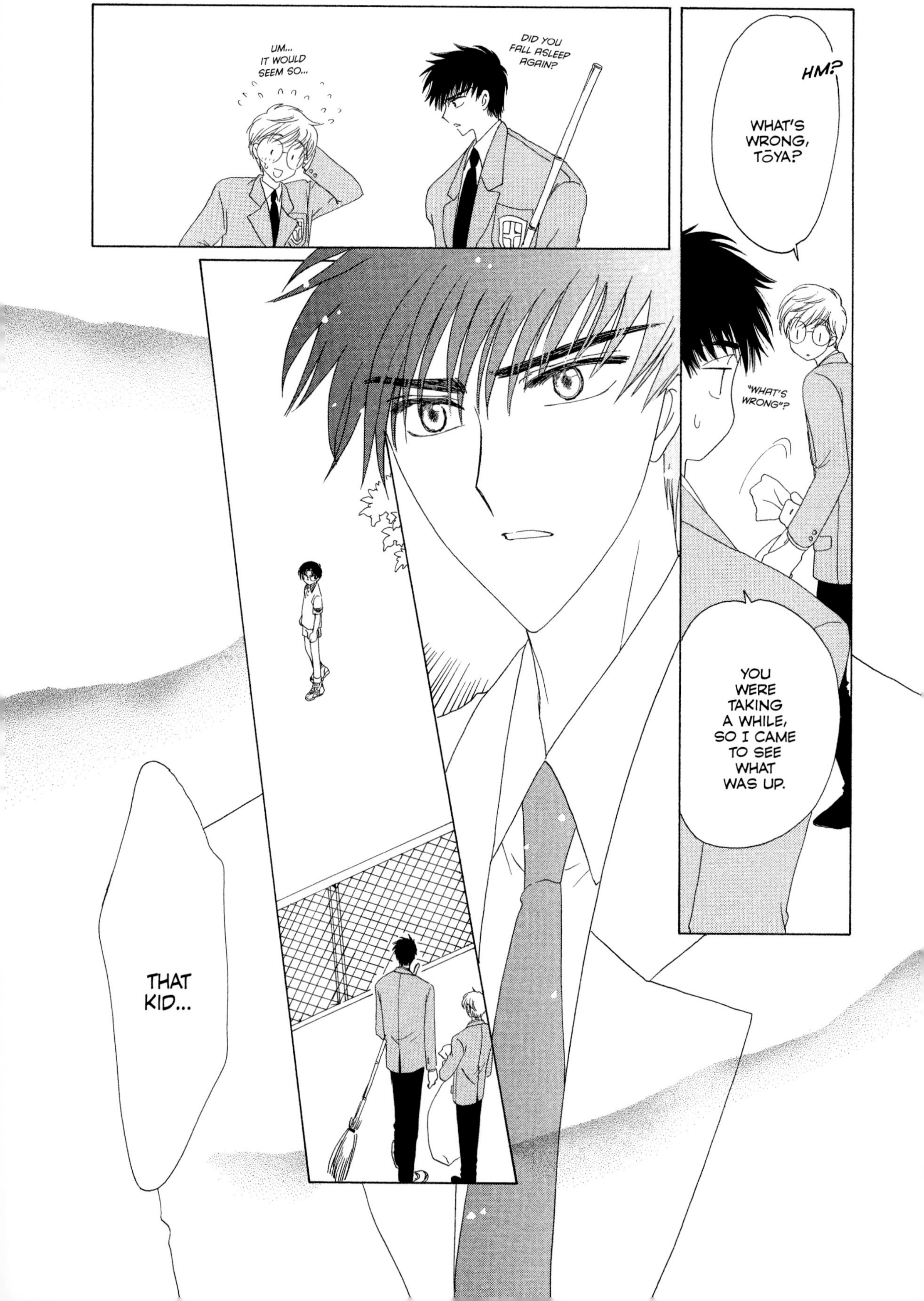
HM?
WHAT'S WRONG, TŌYA?
"WHAT'S WRONG"?
YOU WERE TAKING A WHILE, SO I CAME TO SEE WHAT WAS UP.
DID YOU FALL ASLEEP AGAIN?
UM... IT WOULD SEEM SO...
THAT KID...

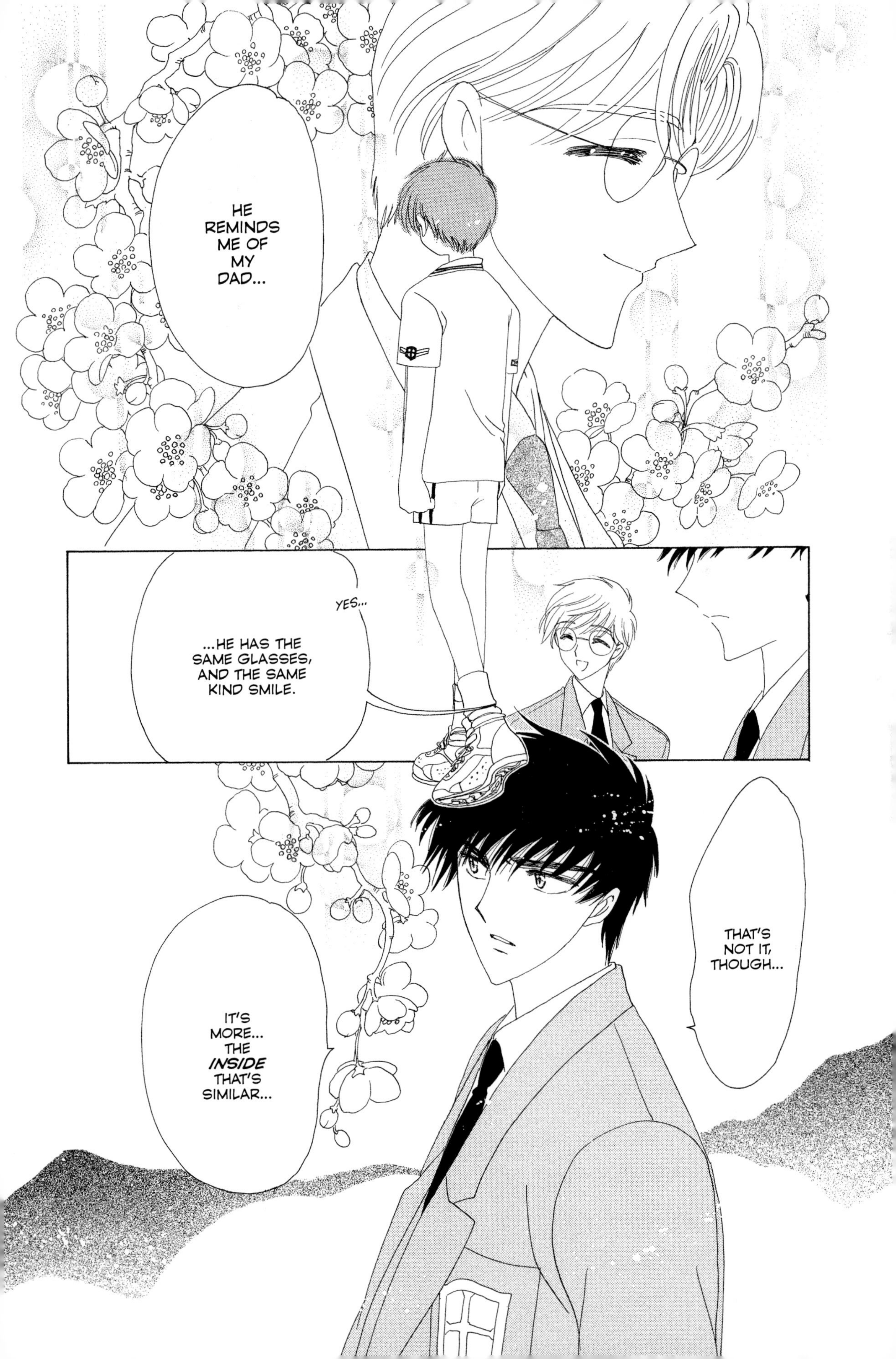
HE REMINDS ME OF MY DAD...
YES...
...HE HAS THE SAME GLASSES, AND THE SAME KIND SMILE.
THAT'S NOT IT, THOUGH...
IT'S MORE... THE *INSIDE* THAT'S SIMILAR...

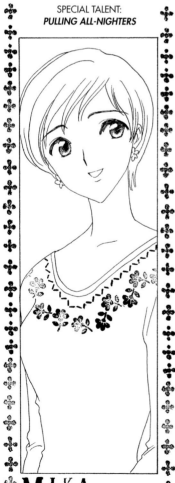

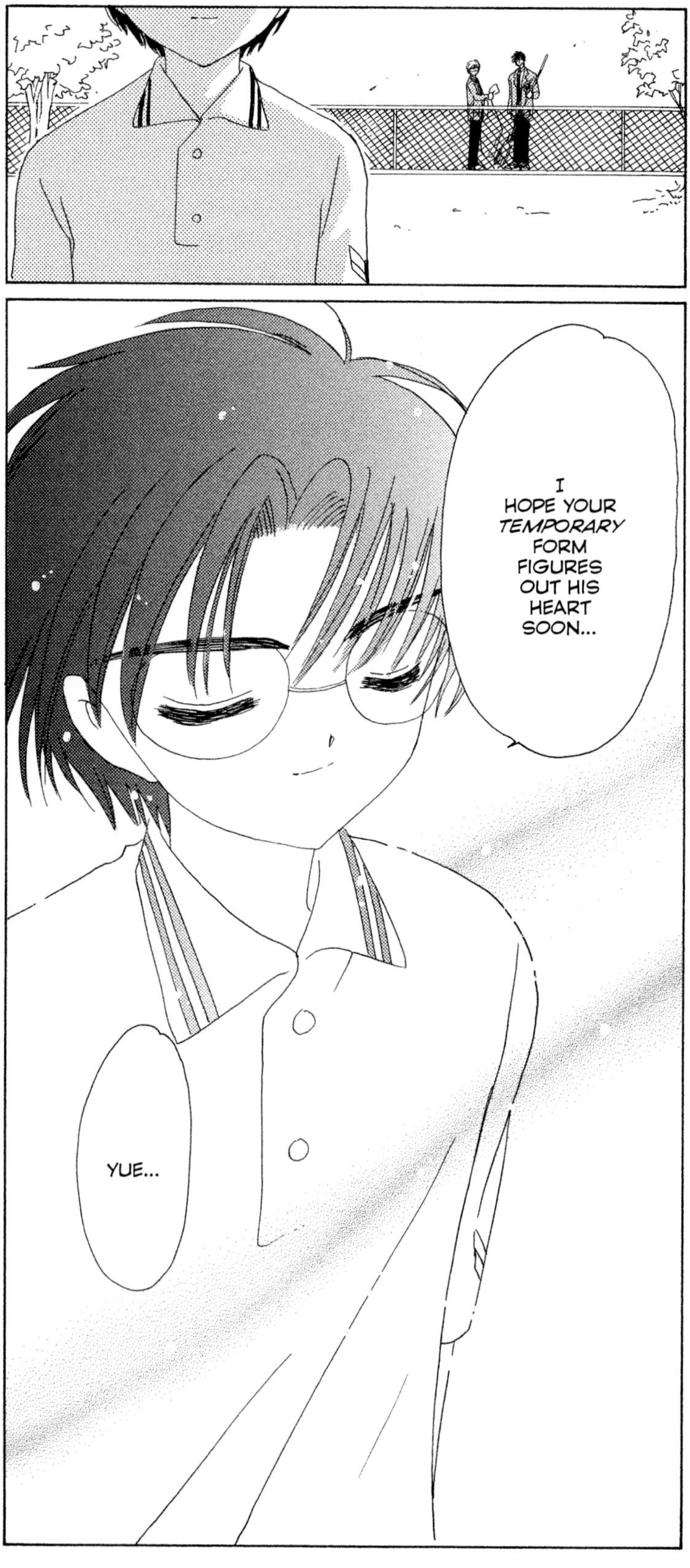
I HOPE YOUR *TEMPORARY* FORM FIGURES OUT HIS HEART SOON...
YUE...

27

MIKA TSUTSUMI

BIRTHDATE:
SEPTEMBER 26
JOB:
MATH TEACHER
FAVORITE FOOD:
UDON
LEAST FAVORITE FOOD:
CABBAGE
FAVORITE THING:
DOING LAUNDRY
LEAST FAVORITE THING:
GRADING PAPERS
FAVORITE COLOR:
YELLOW-GREEN
FAVORITE FLOWER:
CARNATION
FAVORITE RECIPE:
ANYTHING WITHOUT MILK
HOBBY:
LISTENING TO MUSIC
SPECIAL TALENT:
PULLING ALL-NIGHTERS

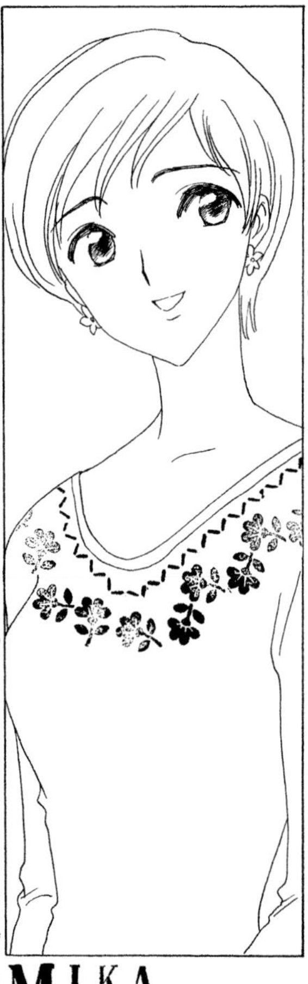

MIKA TSUTSUMI

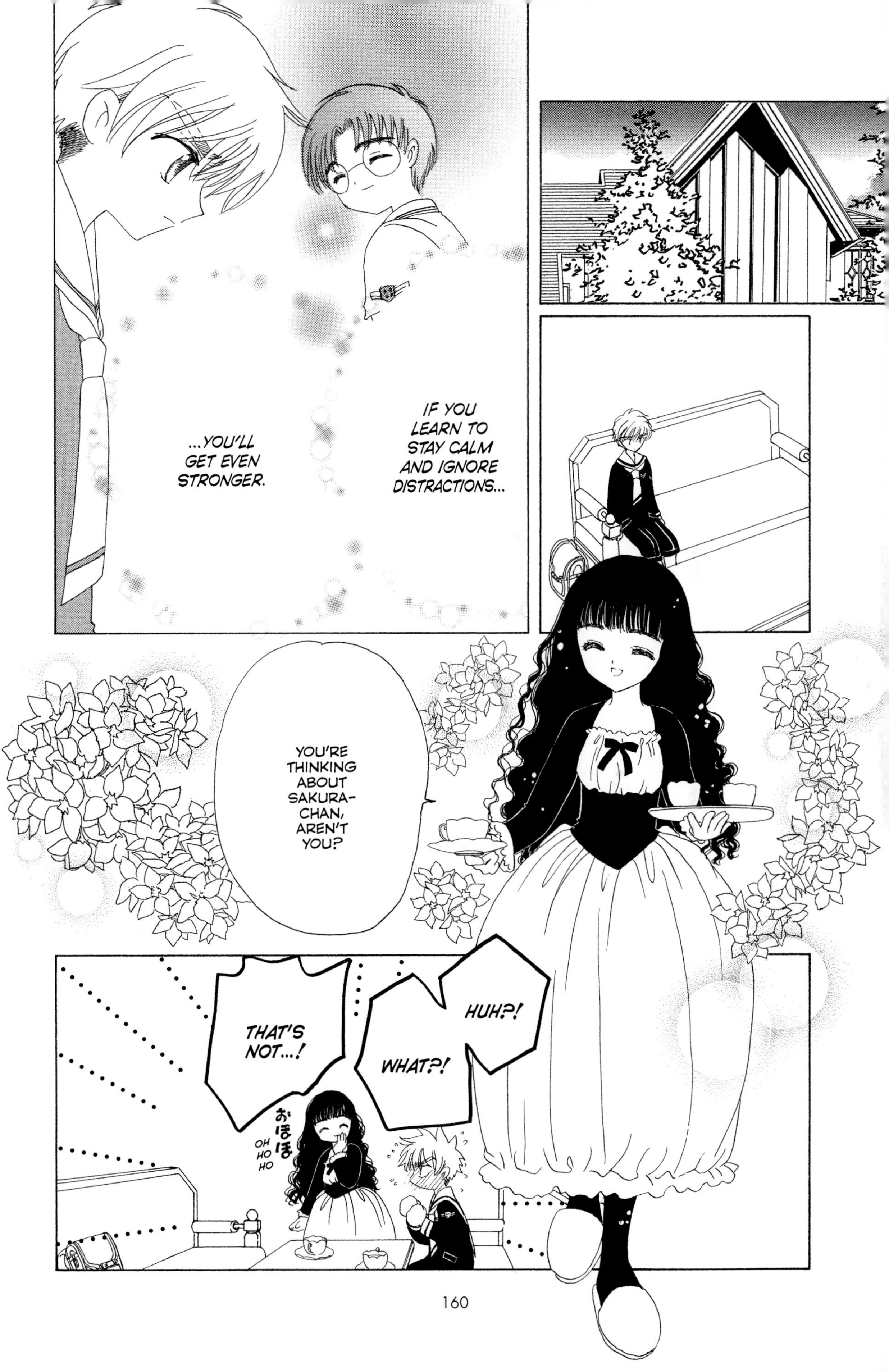
IF YOU LEARN TO STAY CALM AND IGNORE DISTRACTIONS...
...YOU'LL GET EVEN STRONGER.
YOU'RE THINKING ABOUT SAKURA-CHAN, AREN'T YOU?
HUH?!
WHAT?!
THAT'S NOT...!
おほほ
OH HO HO

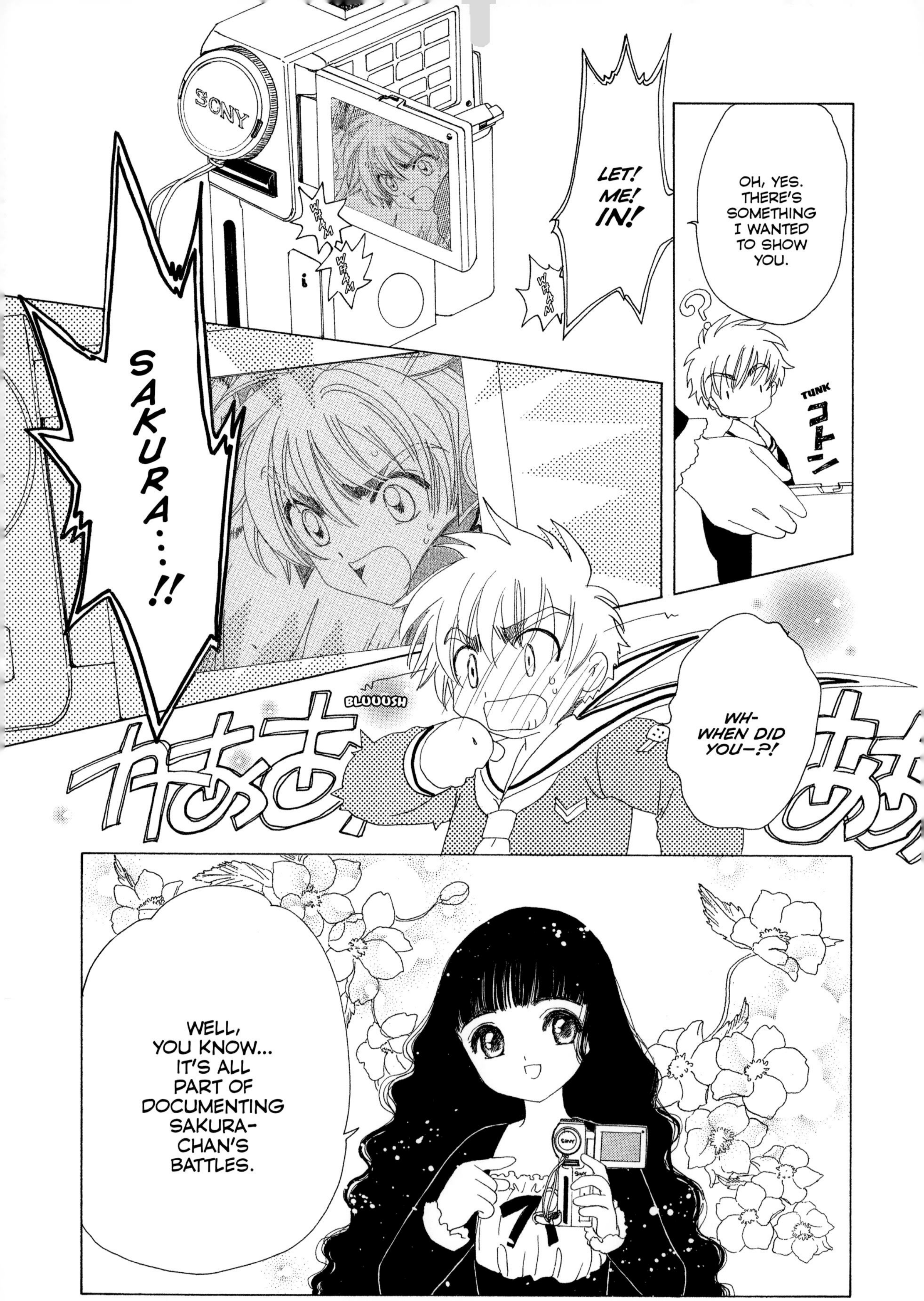
OH, YES. THERE'S SOMETHING I WANTED TO SHOW YOU.
?
TUNK
コトン
LET! ME! IN!
WHAM
WHAM
WHAM
SAKURA...!!
WH-WHEN DID YOU–?!
BLUUUSH
WELL, YOU KNOW... IT'S ALL PART OF DOCUMENTING SAKURA-CHAN'S BATTLES.

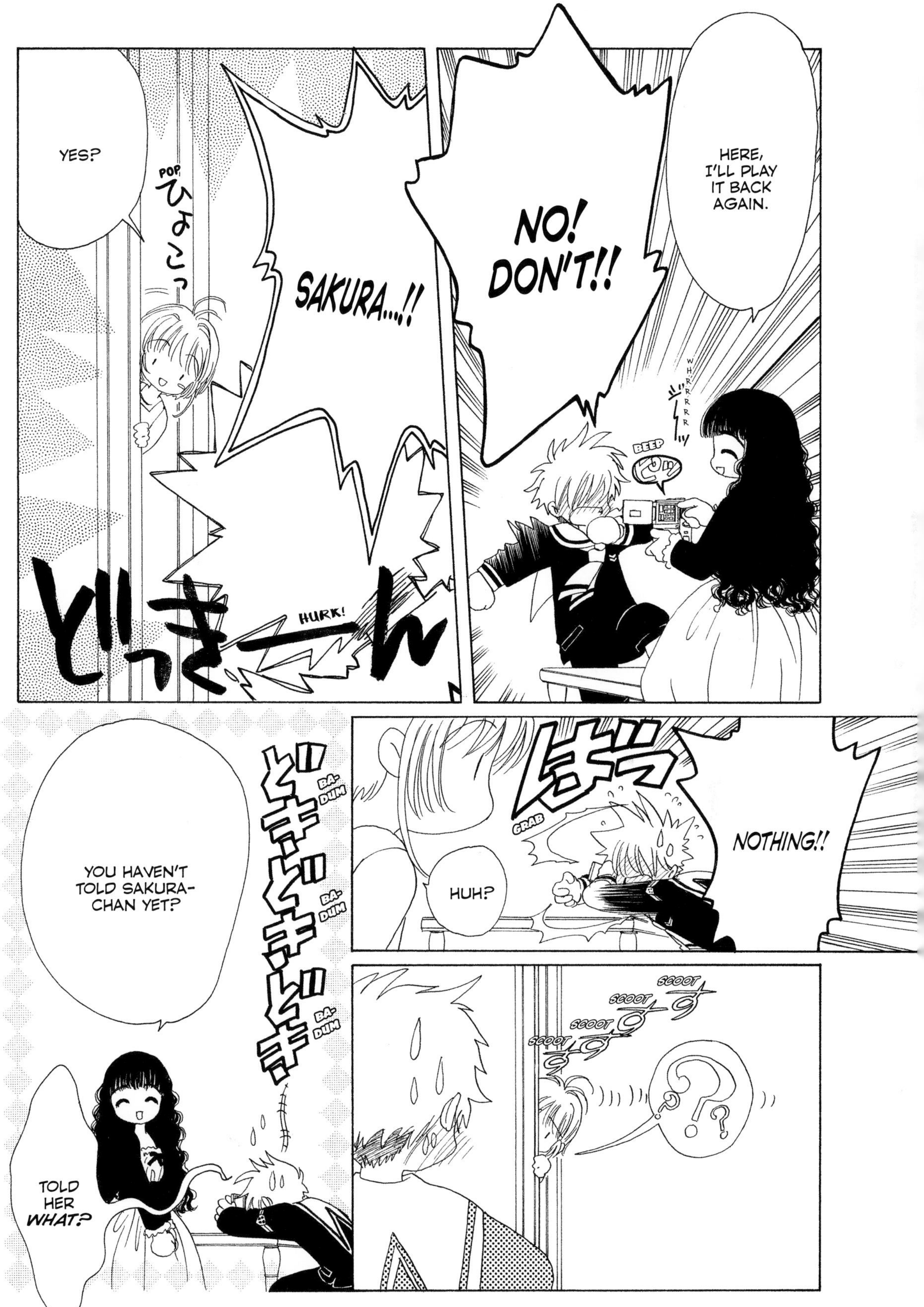
HERE, I'LL PLAY IT BACK AGAIN.
NO! DON'T!!
WHRRRR
BEEP
SAKURA...!!
YES?
POP
HURK!
NOTHING!!
GRAB
HUH?
SCOOT
SCOOT
SCOOT
SCOOT
YOU HAVEN'T TOLD SAKURA-CHAN YET?
BA-DUM
BA-DUM
BA-DUM
TOLD HER WHAT?

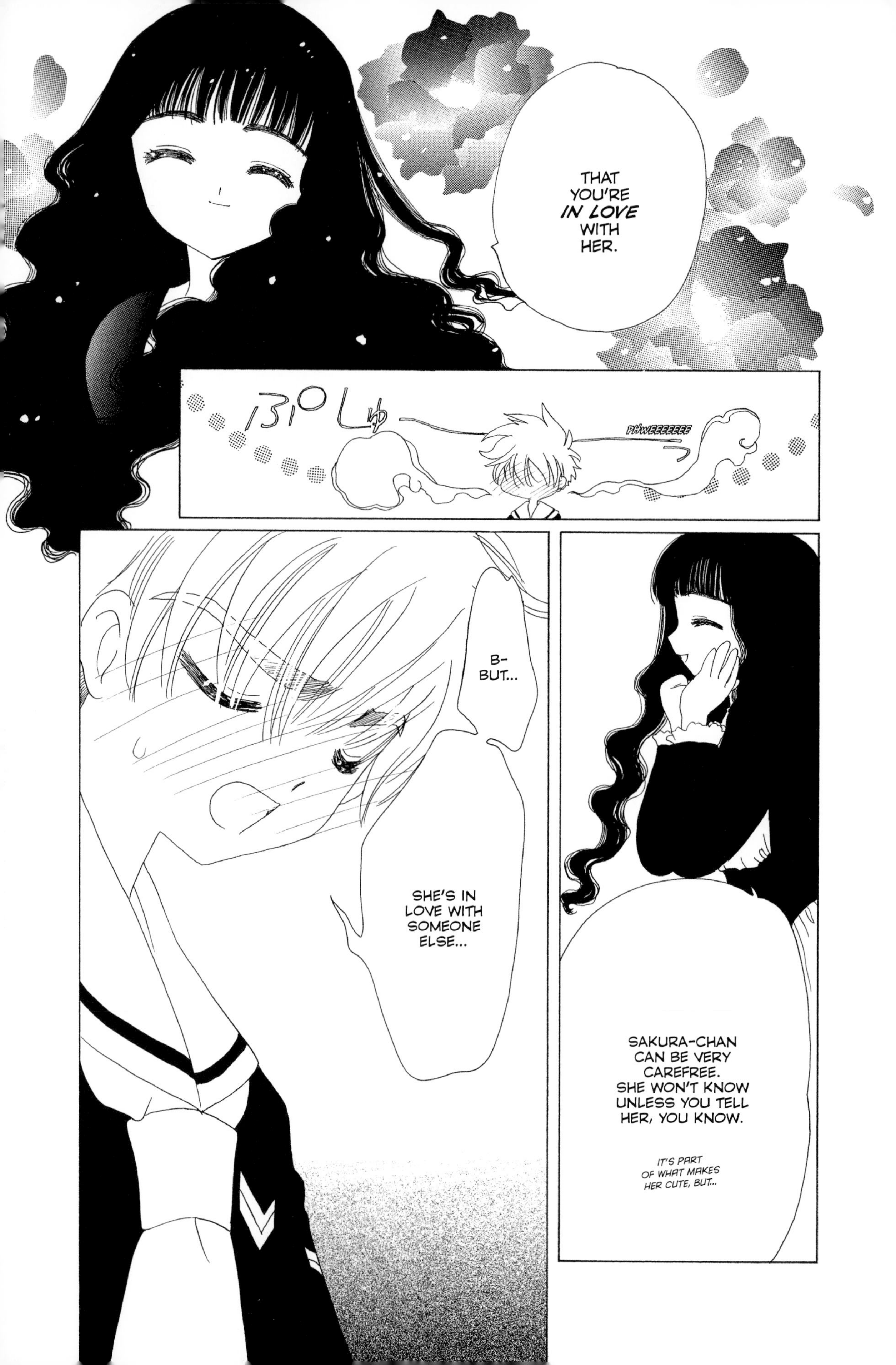
THAT YOU'RE *IN LOVE* WITH HER.
ぷしゅ
PHWEEEEEEEE
SAKURA-CHAN CAN BE VERY CAREFREE. SHE WON'T KNOW UNLESS YOU TELL HER, YOU KNOW.
IT'S PART OF WHAT MAKES HER CUTE, BUT...
B-BUT...
SHE'S IN LOVE WITH SOMEONE ELSE...

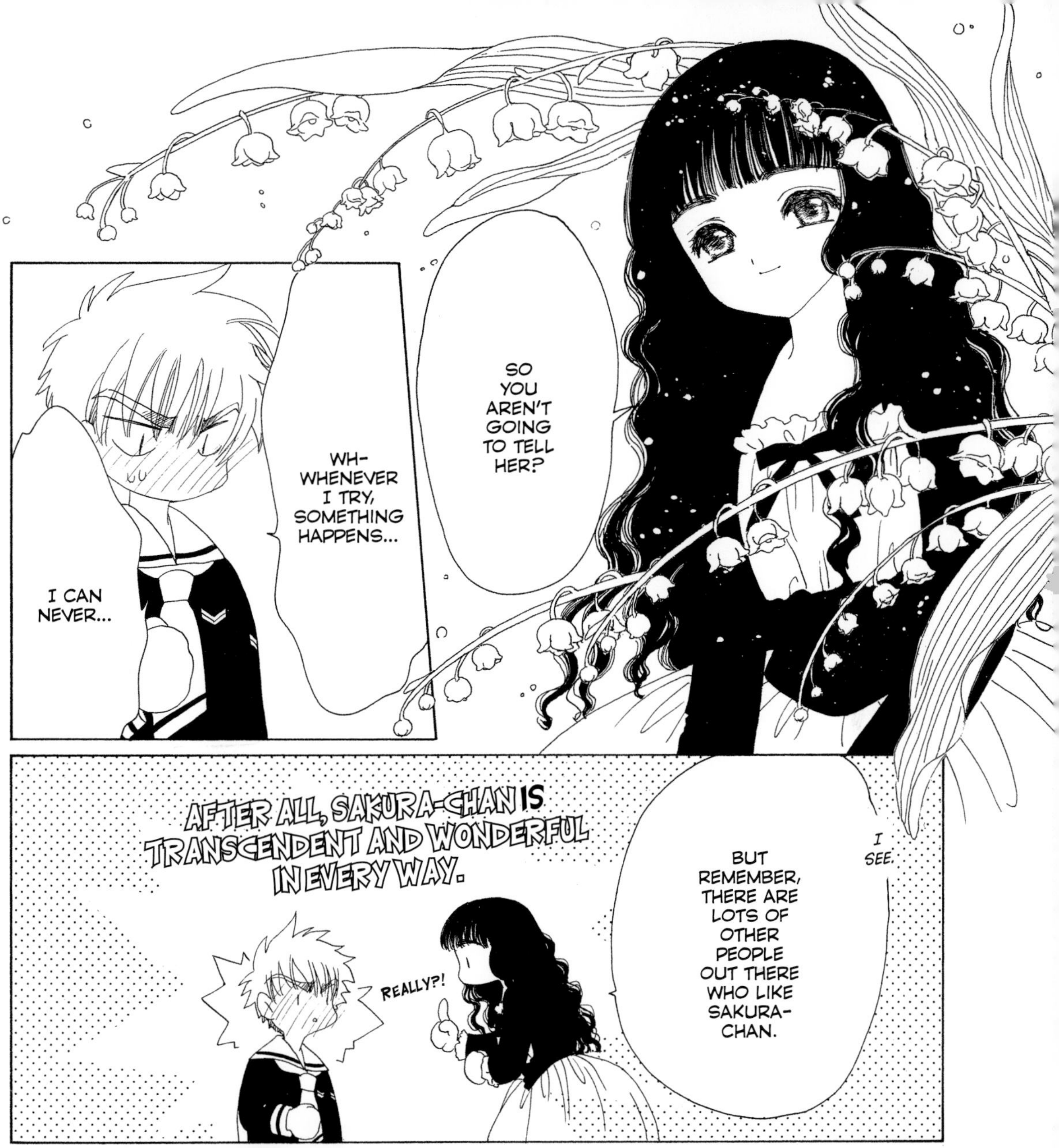
SO YOU AREN'T GOING TO TELL HER?
WH- WHENEVER I TRY, SOMETHING HAPPENS...
I CAN NEVER...
AFTER ALL, SAKURA-CHAN IS TRANSCENDENT AND WONDERFUL IN EVERY WAY.
I SEE.
BUT REMEMBER, THERE ARE LOTS OF OTHER PEOPLE OUT THERE WHO LIKE SAKURA-CHAN.
REALLY?!
MUMBLE
Y... YEAH, THERE ARE...
OH, MY.
...LIKE WHO?
FOR EXAMPLE?

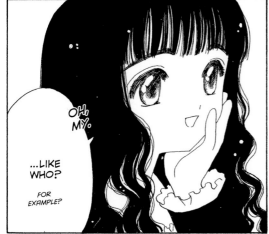

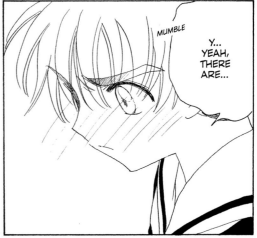

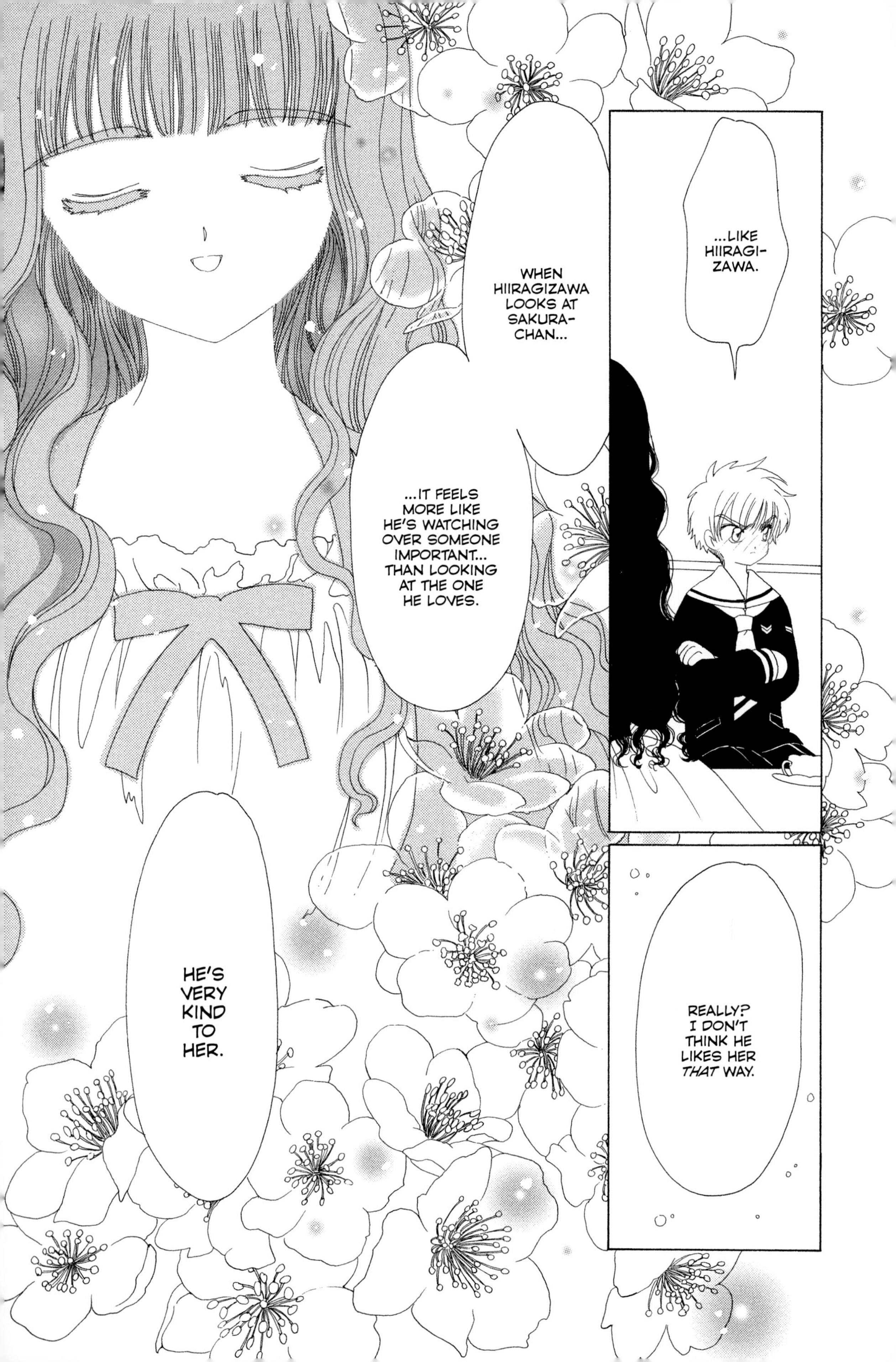
...LIKE HIIRAGI-ZAWA.
REALLY? I DON'T THINK HE LIKES HER *THAT* WAY.
WHEN HIIRAGIZAWA LOOKS AT SAKURA-CHAN...
...IT FEELS MORE LIKE HE'S WATCHING OVER SOMEONE IMPORTANT... THAN LOOKING AT THE ONE HE LOVES.
HE'S VERY KIND TO HER.

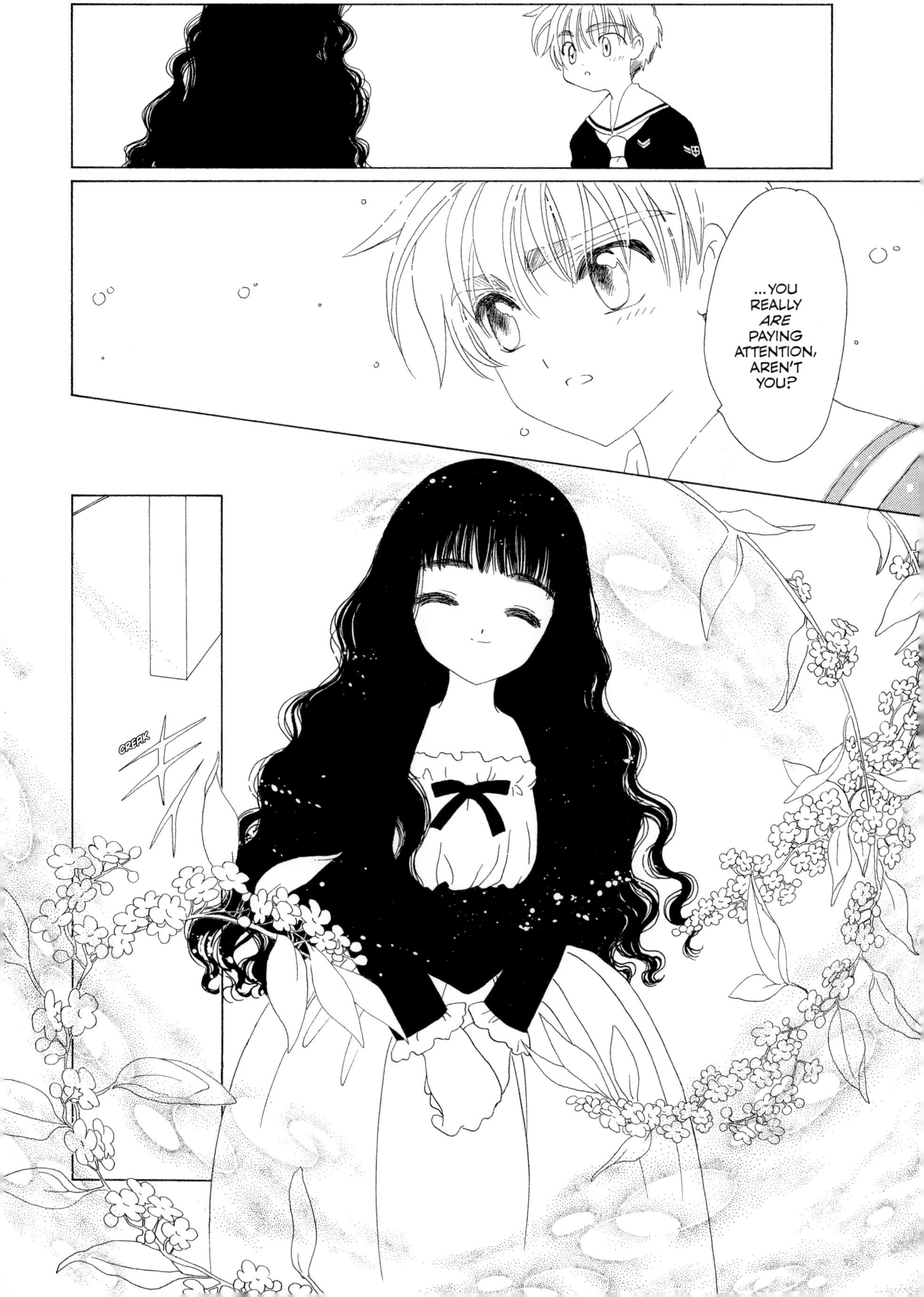
...YOU REALLY ARE PAYING ATTENTION, AREN'T YOU?
CREAK

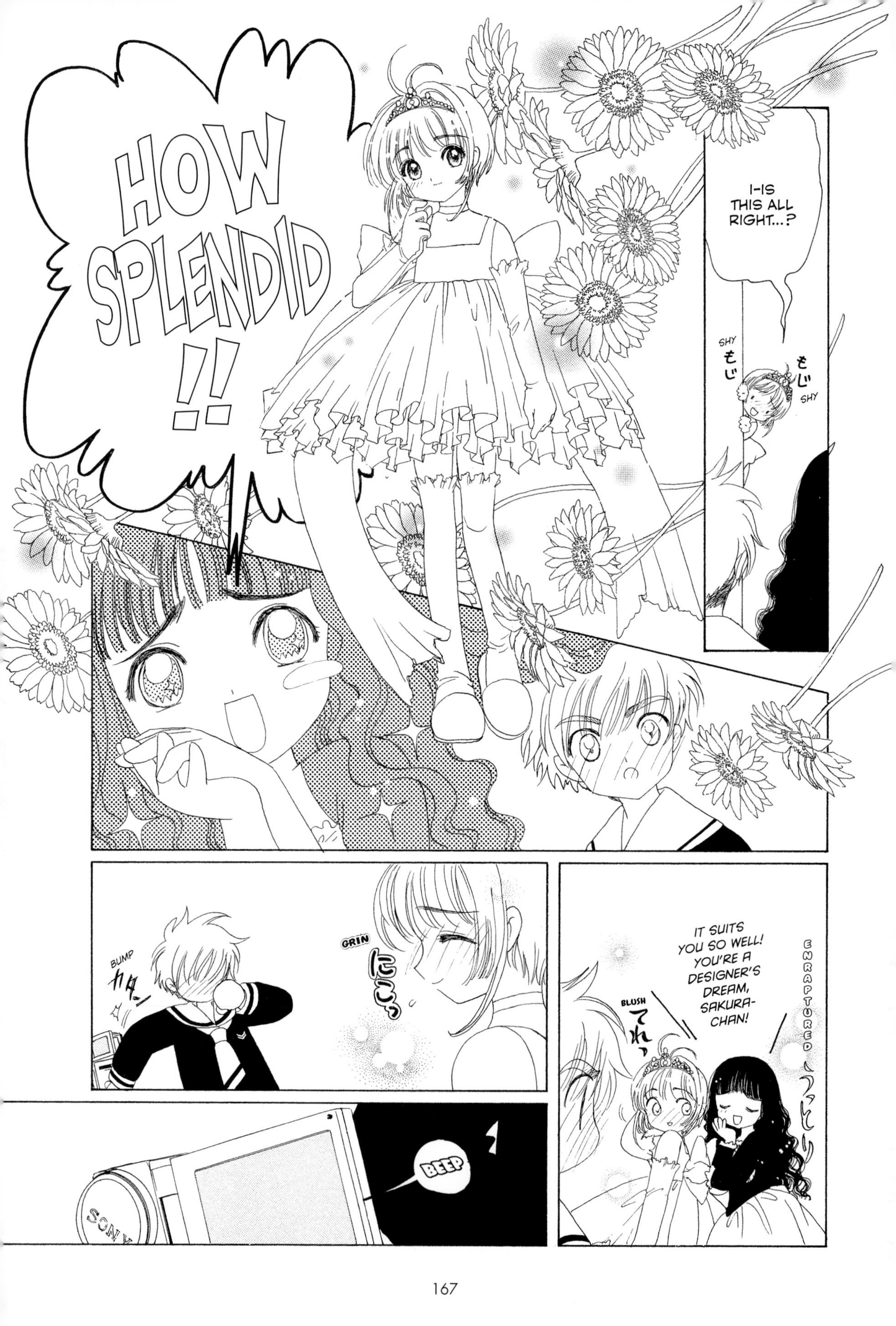

I-IS THIS ALL RIGHT...?
SHY
もじ
もじ
SHY
HOW SPLENDID!!
ENRAPTURED
IT SUITS YOU SO WELL! YOU'RE A DESIGNER'S DREAM, SAKURA-CHAN!
BLUSH
てれ
GRIN
BUMP
BEEP
SONY

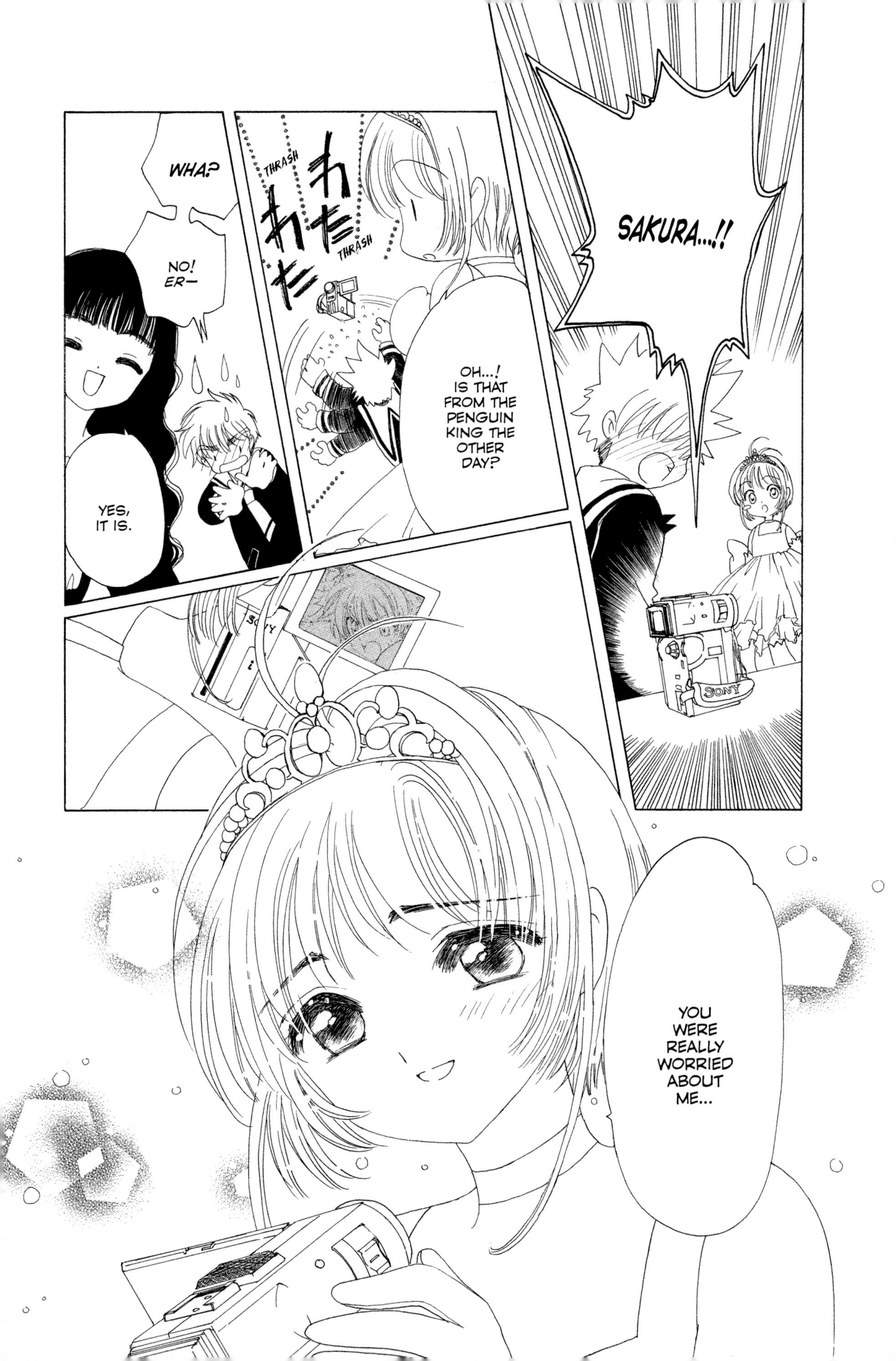

SAKURA...!!
わたわた
THRASH
THRASH
OH...! IS THAT FROM THE PENGUIN KING THE OTHER DAY?
WHA?
NO! ER—
YES, IT IS.
YOU WERE REALLY WORRIED ABOUT ME...

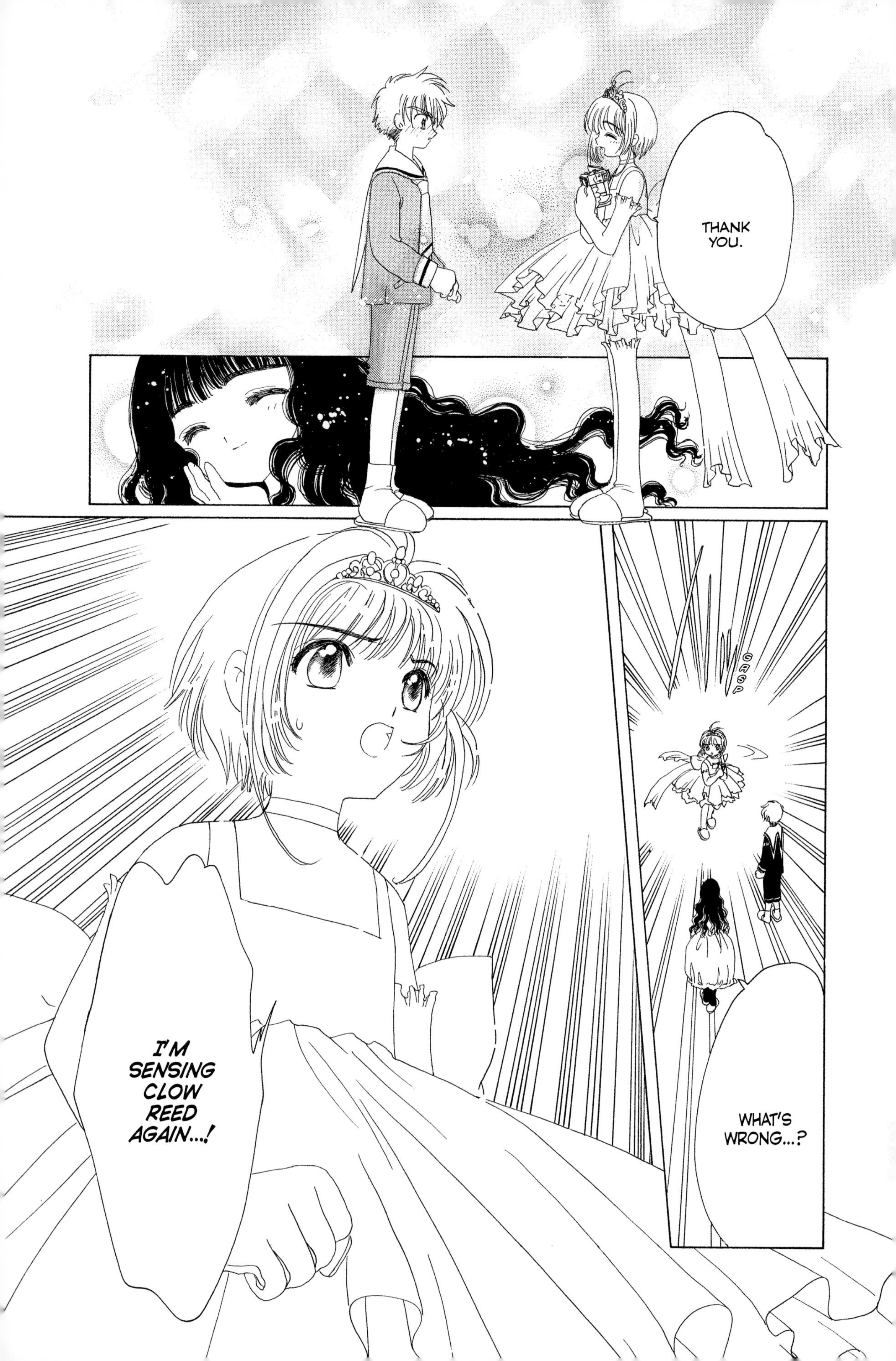
THANK YOU.
GRSP
WHAT'S WRONG...?
I'M SENSING CLOW REED AGAIN...!

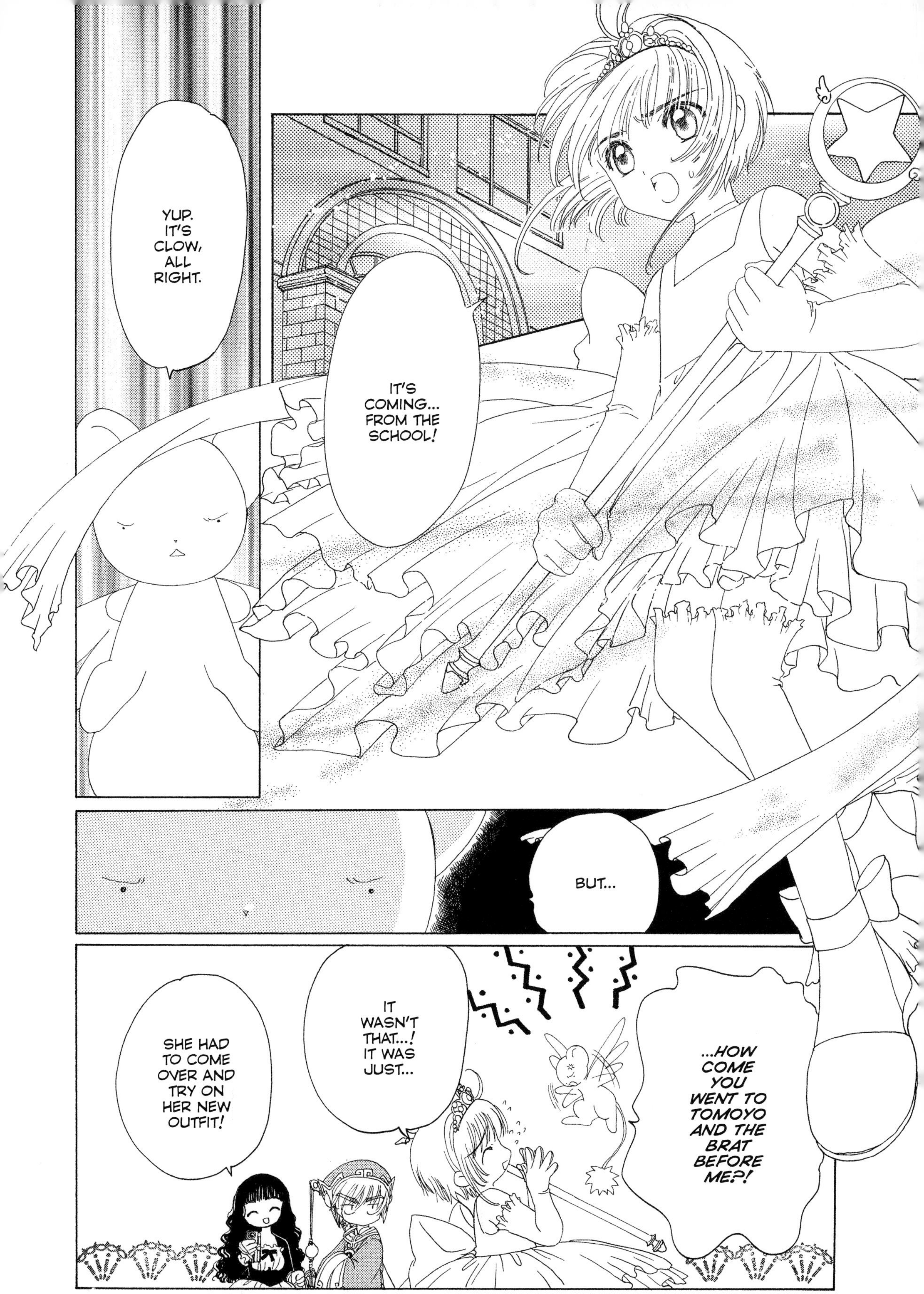
IT'S COMING... FROM THE SCHOOL!
YUP. IT'S CLOW, ALL RIGHT.
BUT...
...HOW COME YOU WENT TO TOMOYO AND THE BRAT BEFORE ME?!
IT WASN'T THAT...! IT WAS JUST...
SHE HAD TO COME OVER AND TRY ON HER NEW OUTFIT!

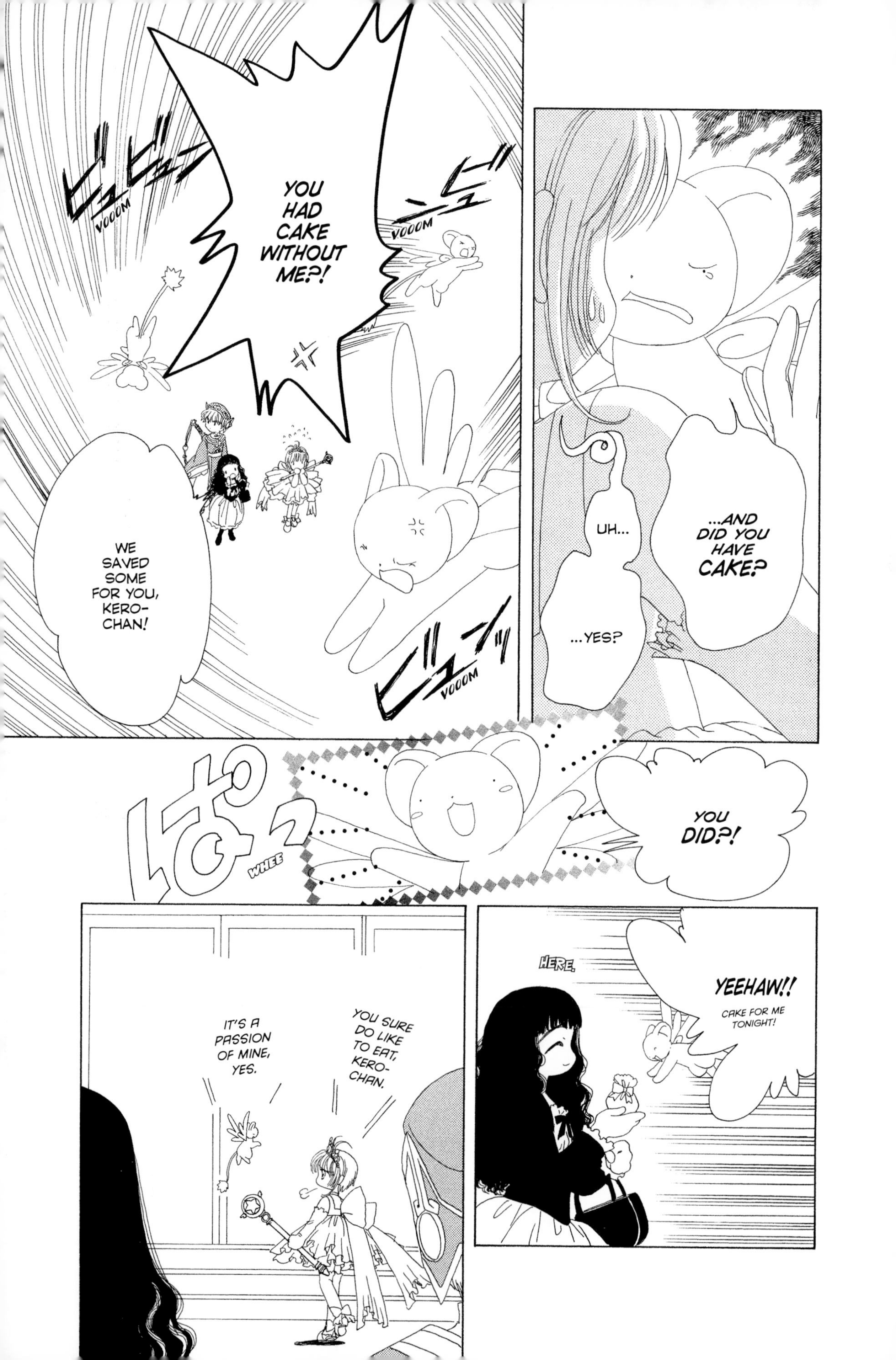
...AND DID YOU HAVE CAKE?
UH...
...YES?
YOU HAD CAKE WITHOUT ME?!
VOOOM
VOOOM
VOOOM
WE SAVED SOME FOR YOU, KERO-CHAN!
YOU DID?!
ぱっ
WHEE
HERE.
YEEHAW!!
CAKE FOR ME TONIGHT!
YOU SURE DO LIKE TO EAT, KERO-CHAN.
IT'S A PASSION OF MINE, YES.

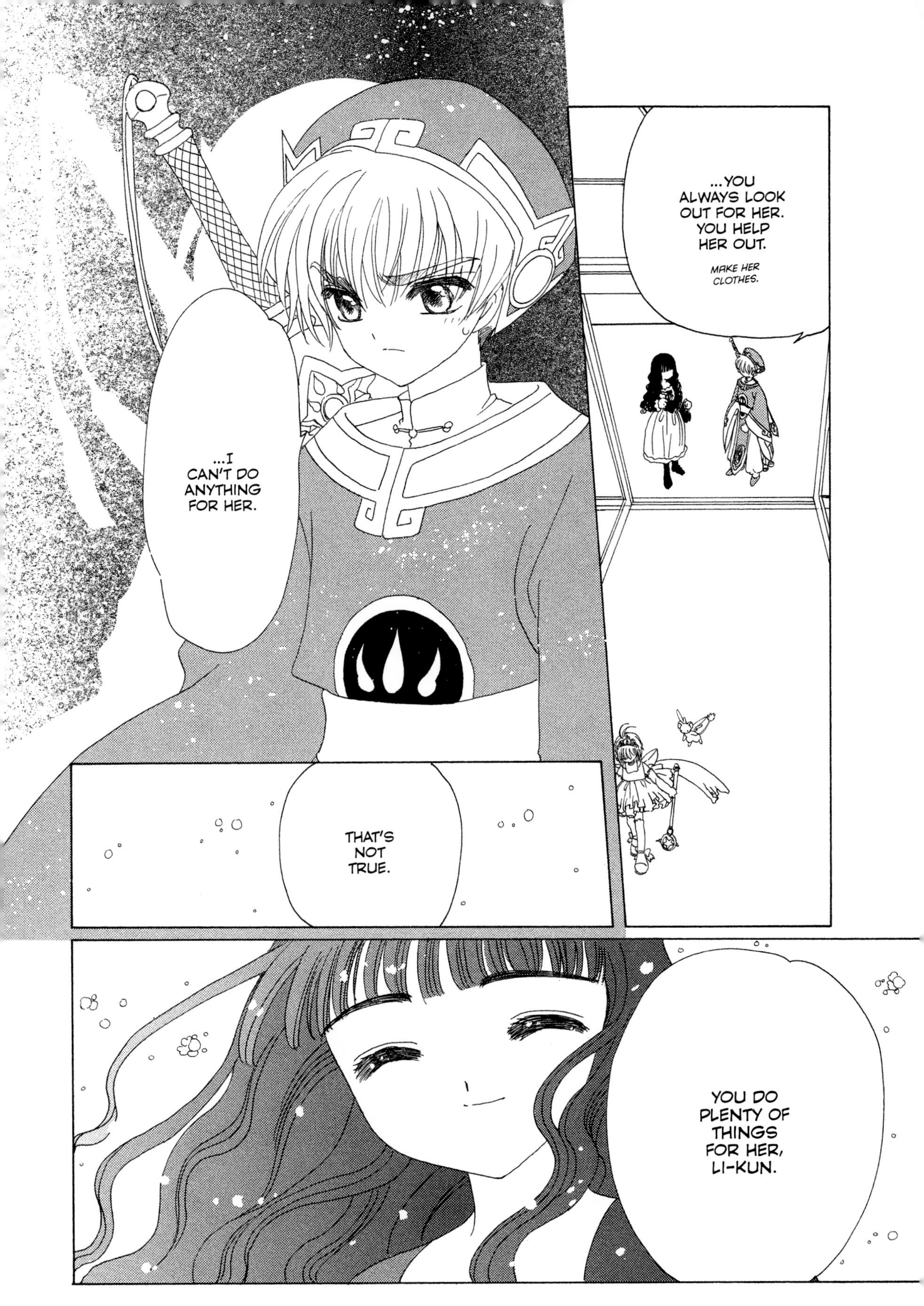
...YOU ALWAYS LOOK OUT FOR HER. YOU HELP HER OUT.
MAKE HER CLOTHES.
...I CAN'T DO ANYTHING FOR HER.
THAT'S NOT TRUE.
YOU DO PLENTY OF THINGS FOR HER, LI-KUN.

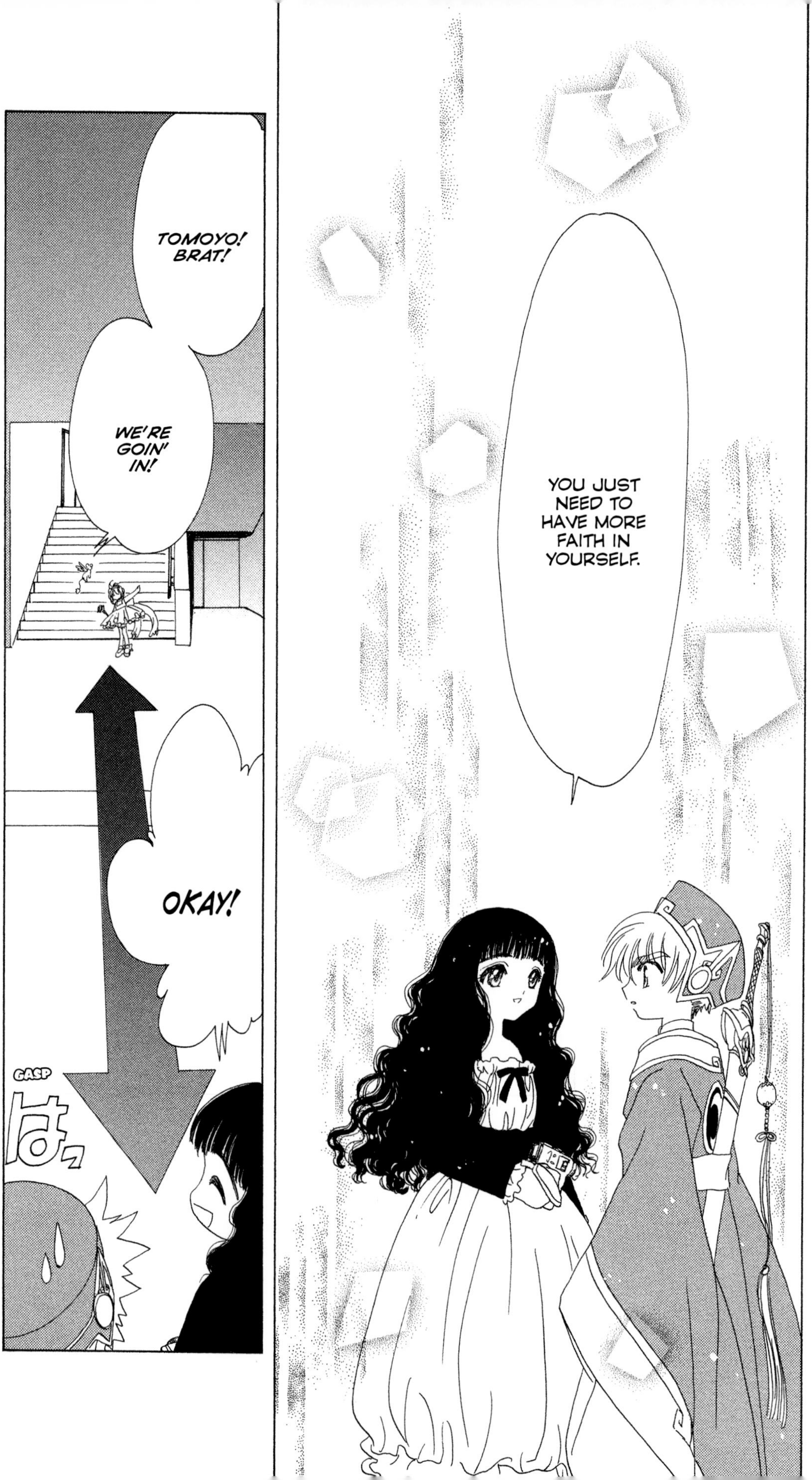
YOU JUST NEED TO HAVE MORE FAITH IN YOURSELF.
TOMOYO! BRAT!
WE'RE GOIN' IN!
OKAY!
GASP
はっ

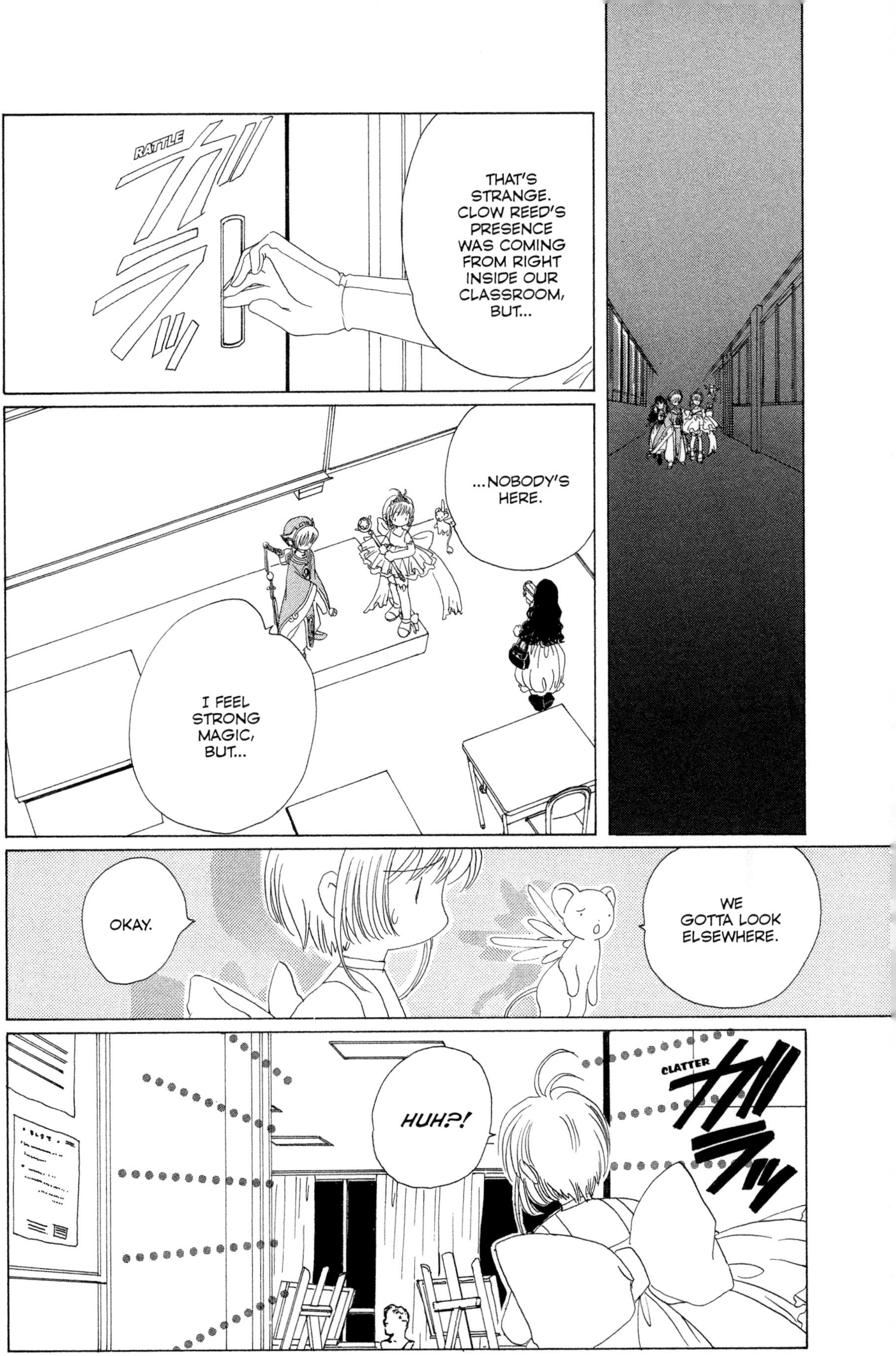
THAT'S STRANGE. CLOW REED'S PRESENCE WAS COMING FROM RIGHT INSIDE OUR CLASSROOM, BUT...
RATTLE
...NOBODY'S HERE.
I FEEL STRONG MAGIC, BUT...
WE GOTTA LOOK ELSEWHERE.
OKAY.
CLATTER
HUH?!

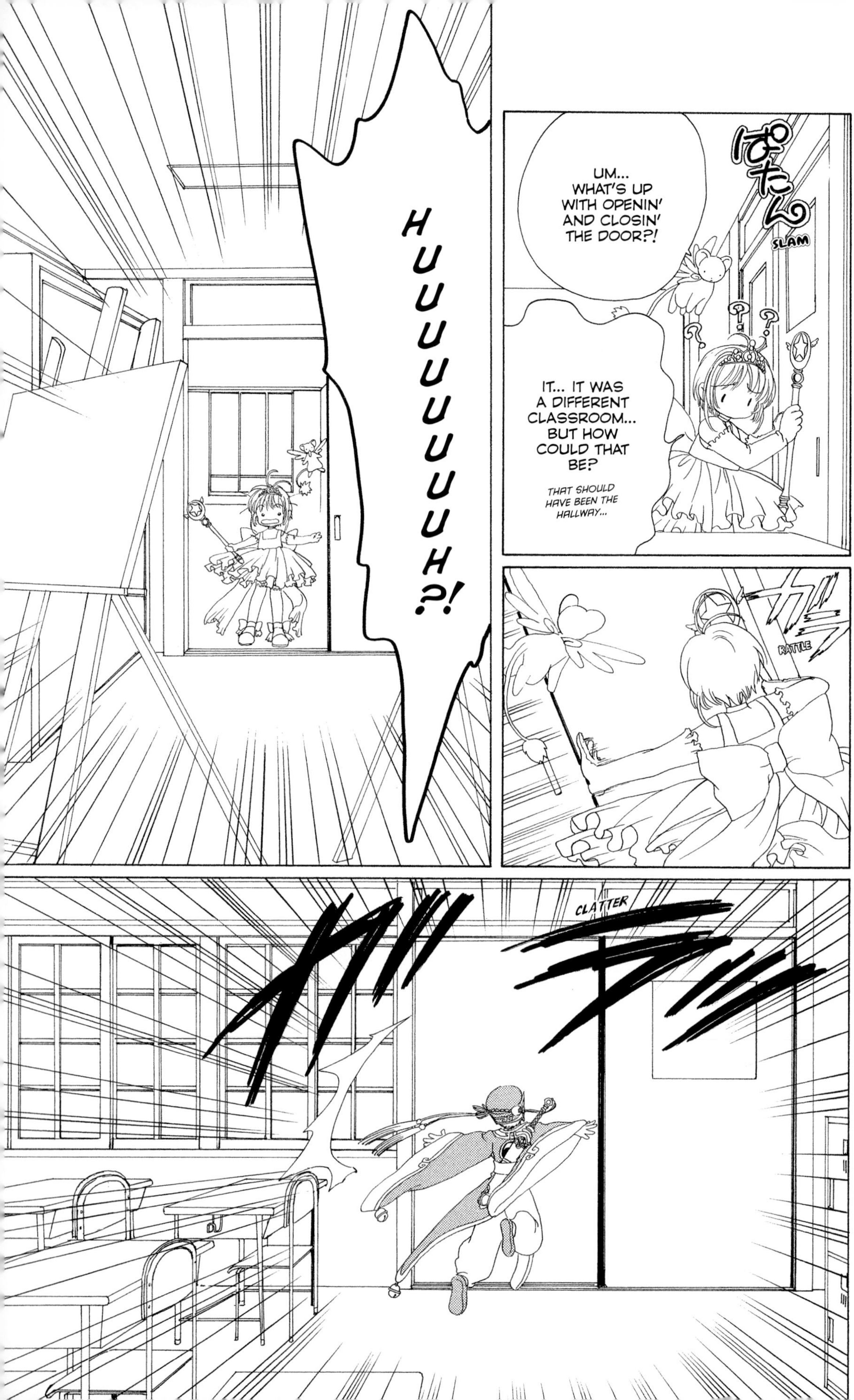
ぱたん
SLAM
UM... WHAT'S UP WITH OPENIN' AND CLOSIN' THE DOOR?!
IT... IT WAS A DIFFERENT CLASSROOM... BUT HOW COULD THAT BE?
THAT SHOULD HAVE BEEN THE HALLWAY...
RATTLE
HUUUUUUUUH?!
CLATTER

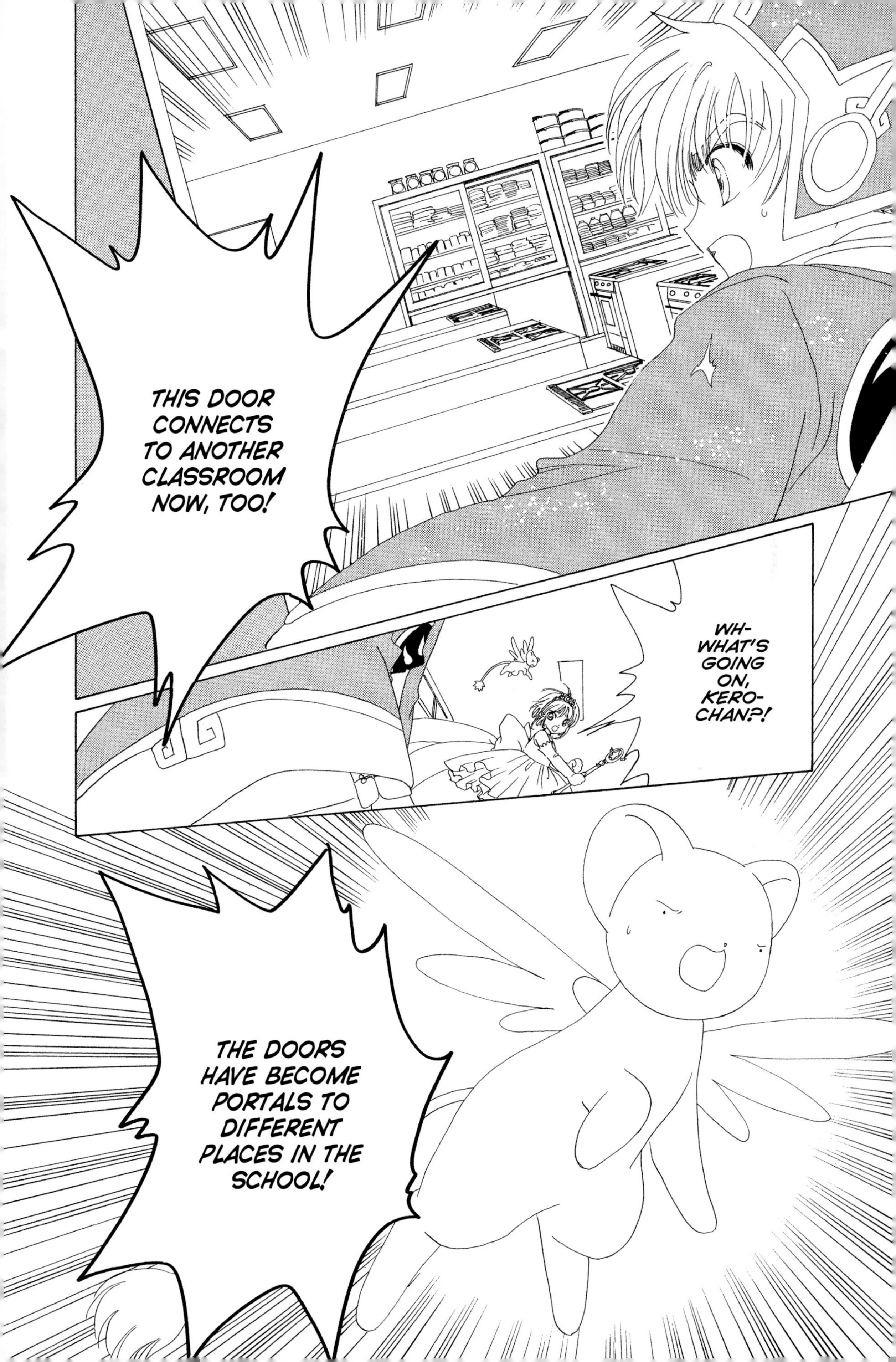
THIS DOOR CONNECTS TO ANOTHER CLASSROOM NOW, TOO!
WH-WHAT'S GOING ON, KERO-CHAN?!
THE DOORS HAVE BECOME PORTALS TO DIFFERENT PLACES IN THE SCHOOL!

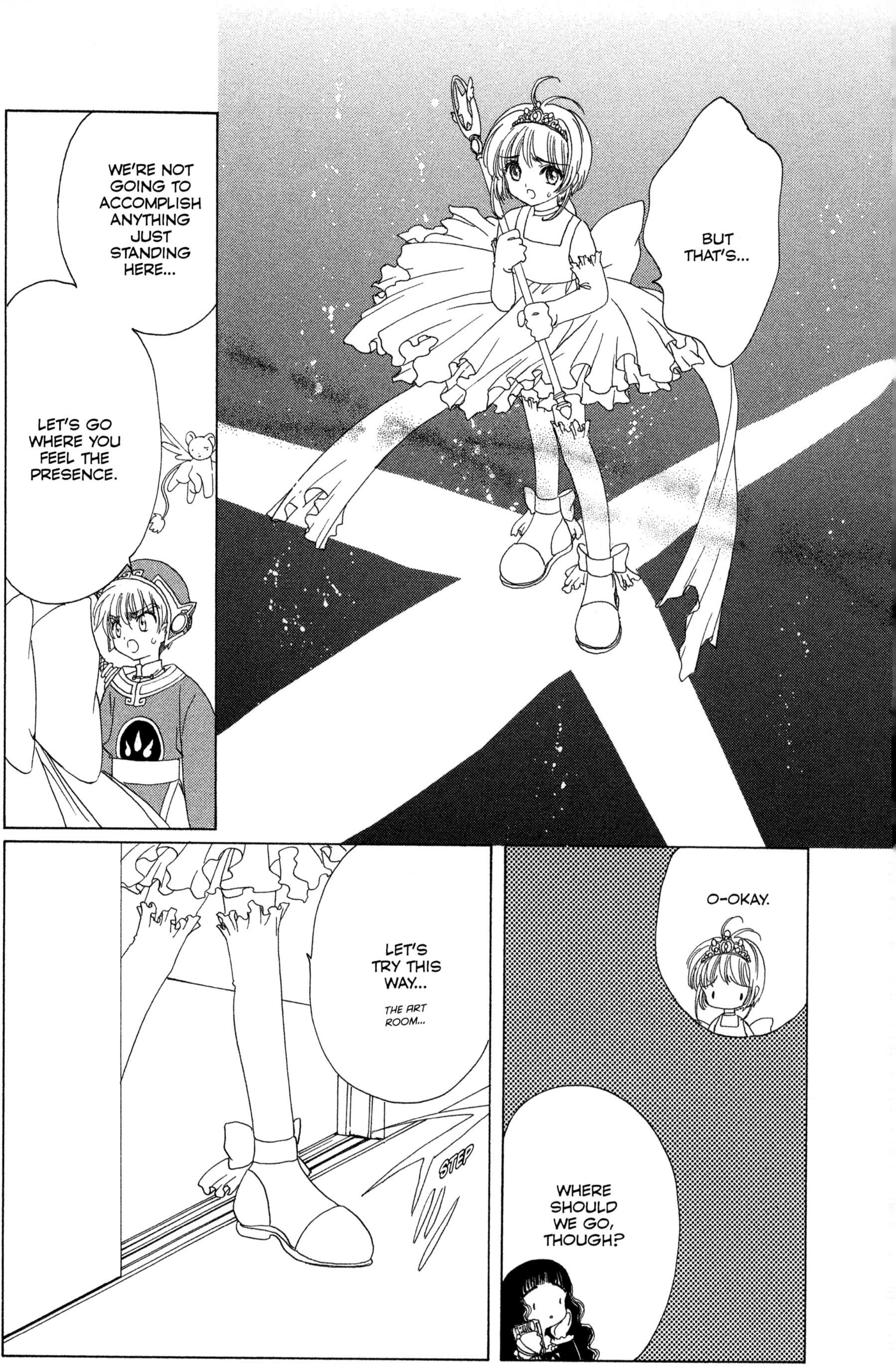
BUT THAT'S...
WE'RE NOT GOING TO ACCOMPLISH ANYTHING JUST STANDING HERE...
LET'S GO WHERE YOU FEEL THE PRESENCE.
O-OKAY.
WHERE SHOULD WE GO, THOUGH?
LET'S TRY THIS WAY...
THE ART ROOM...
STEP

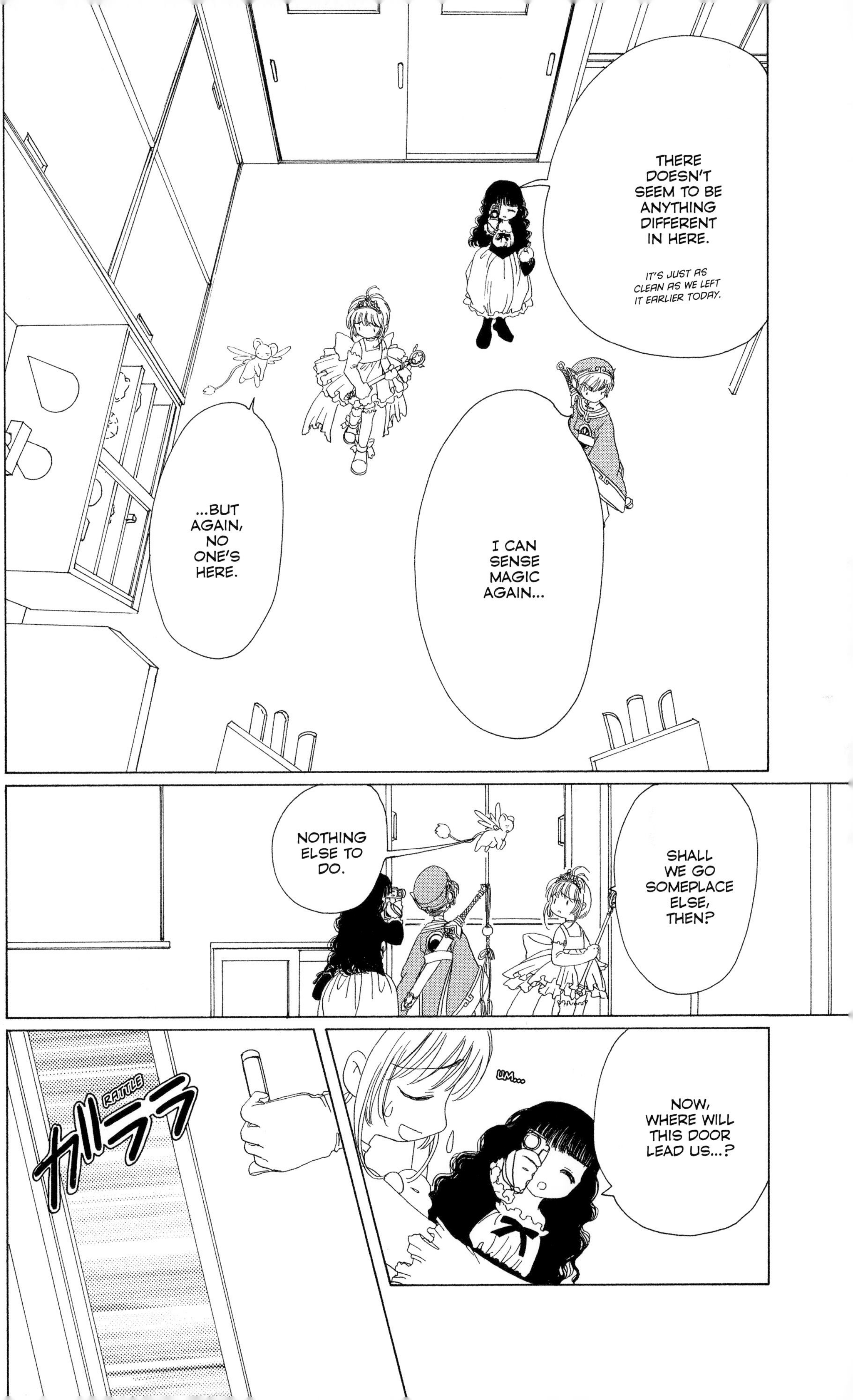
THERE DOESN'T SEEM TO BE ANYTHING DIFFERENT IN HERE.
IT'S JUST AS CLEAN AS WE LEFT IT EARLIER TODAY.
I CAN SENSE MAGIC AGAIN...
...BUT AGAIN, NO ONE'S HERE.
SHALL WE GO SOMEPLACE ELSE, THEN?
NOTHING ELSE TO DO.
NOW, WHERE WILL THIS DOOR LEAD US...?
UM...
カララ
RATTLE

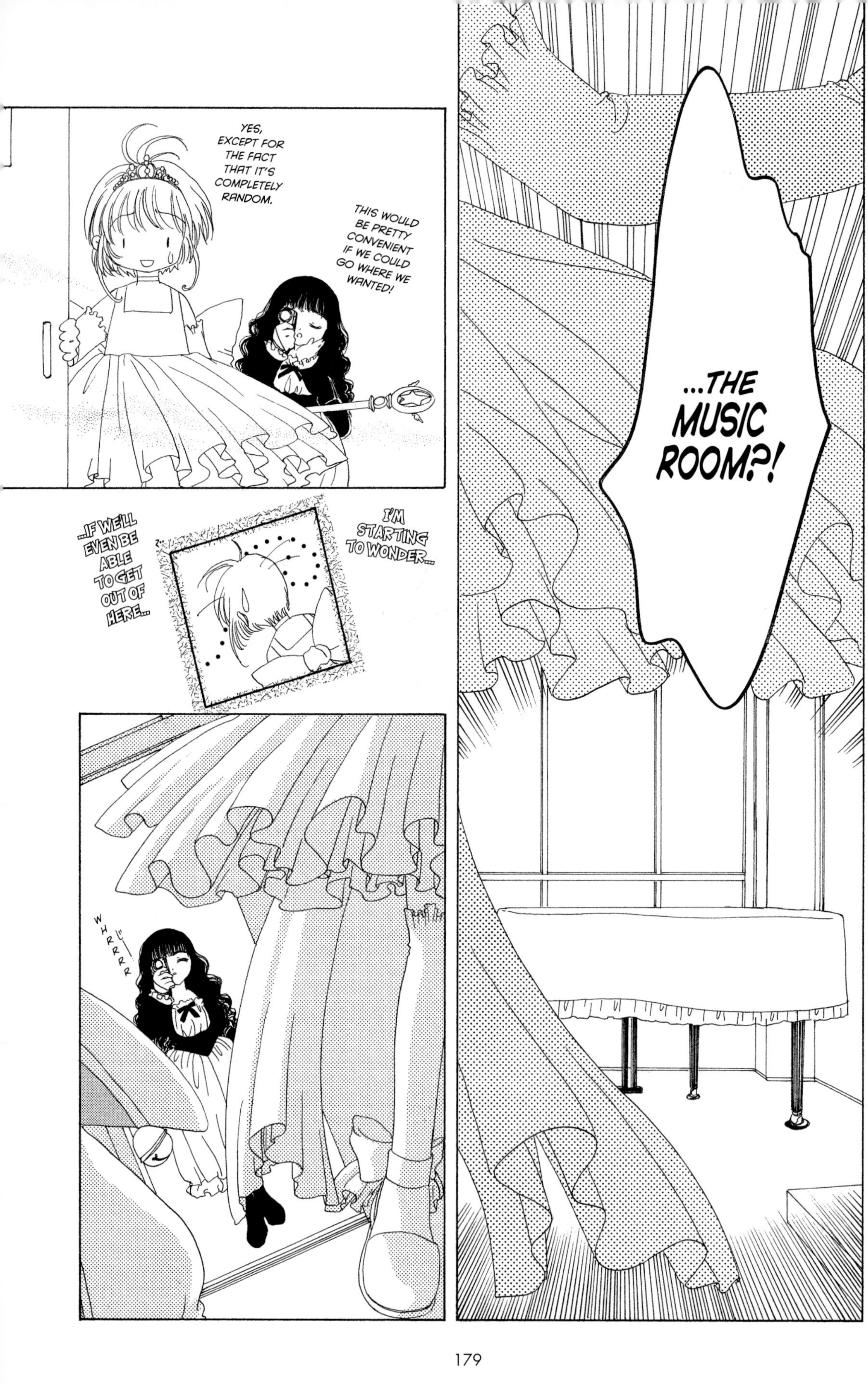
...THE MUSIC ROOM?!
THIS WOULD BE PRETTY CONVENIENT IF WE COULD GO WHERE WE WANTED!
YES, EXCEPT FOR THE FACT THAT IT'S COMPLETELY RANDOM.
I'M STARTING TO WONDER...
...IF WE'LL EVEN BE ABLE TO GET OUT OF HERE...
WHRRRR

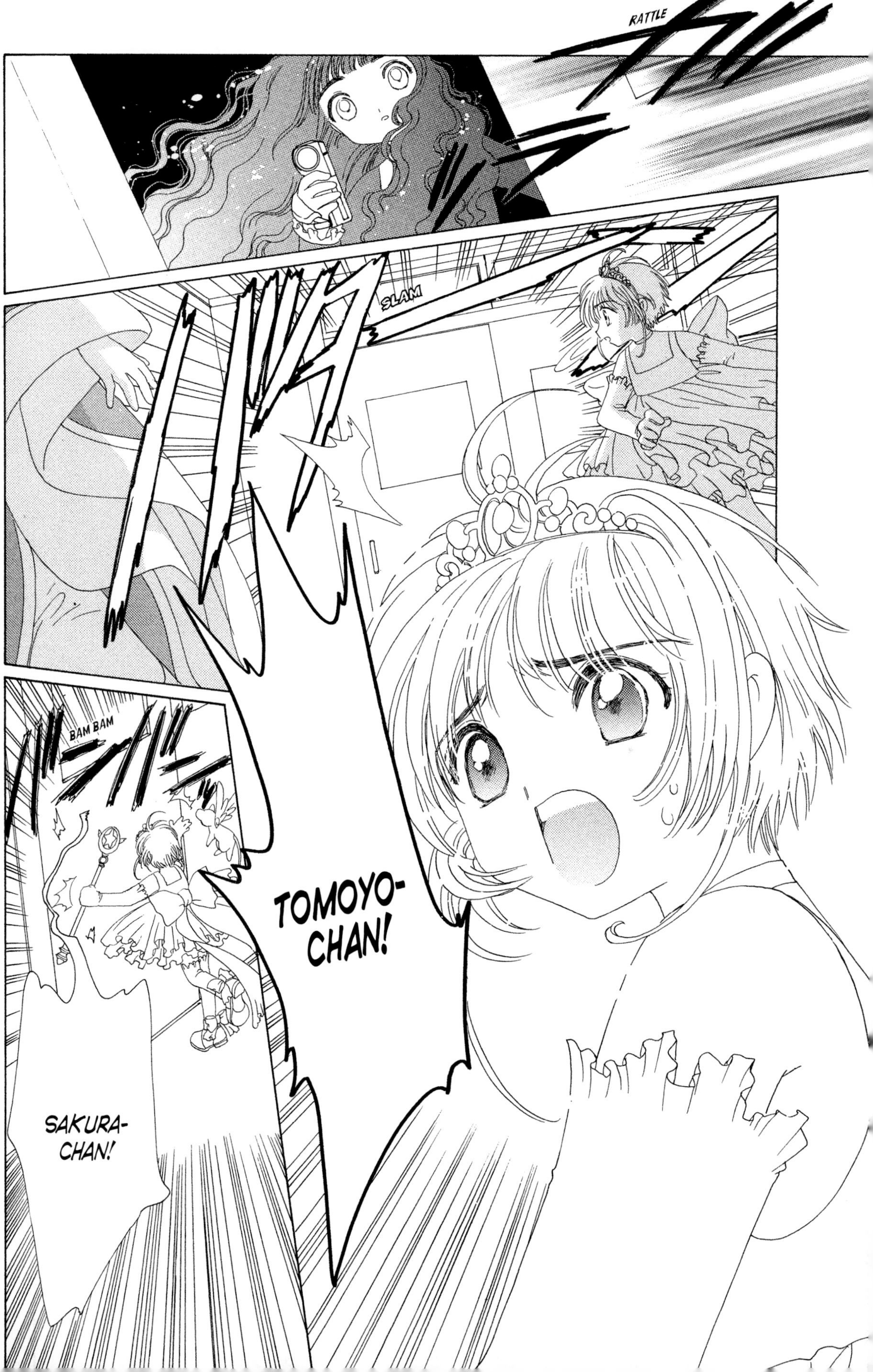
RATTLE
SLAM
TOMOYO-CHAN!
BAM BAM
SAKURA-CHAN!

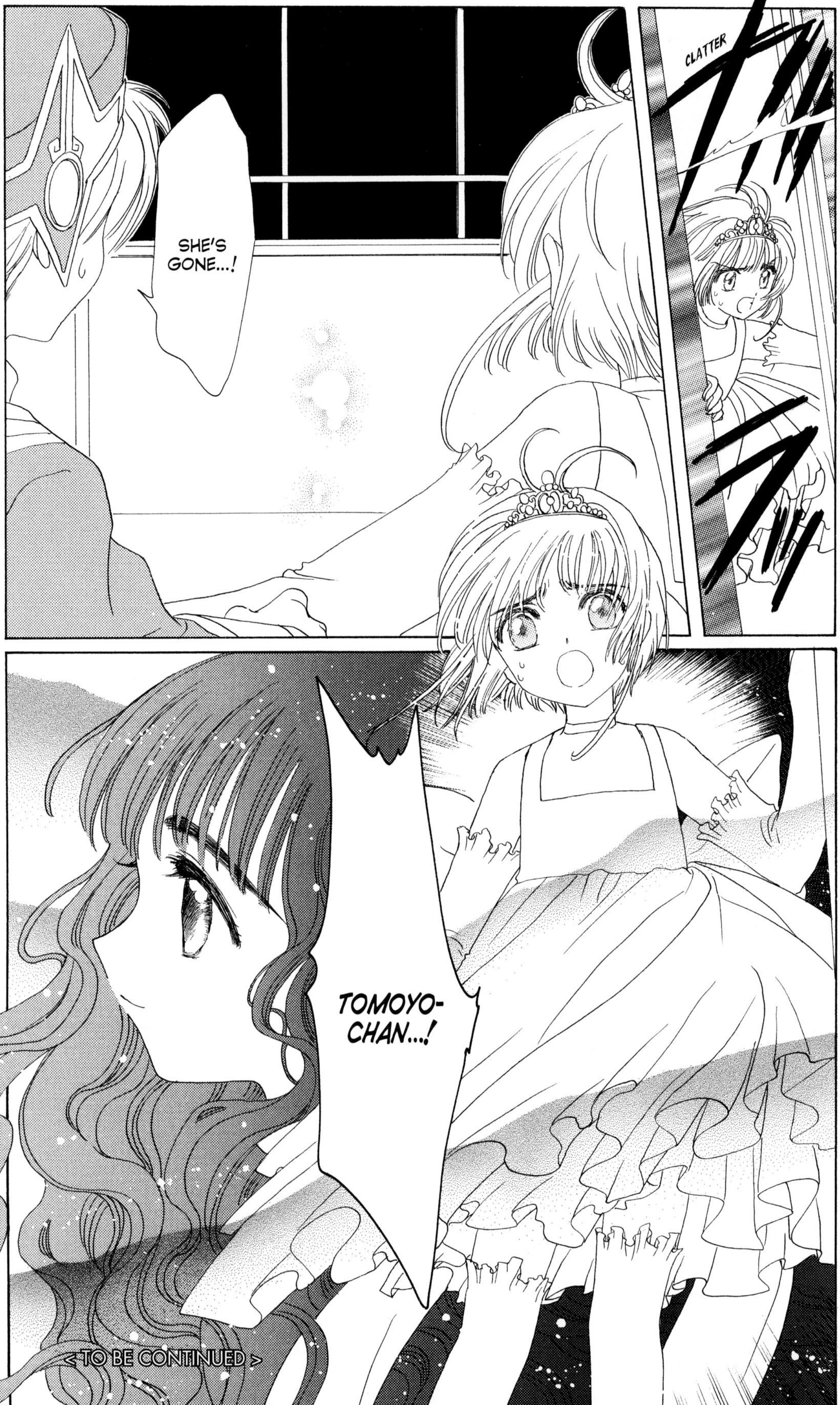
CLATTER
SHE'S GONE...!
TOMOYO-CHAN...!
< TO BE CONTINUED >

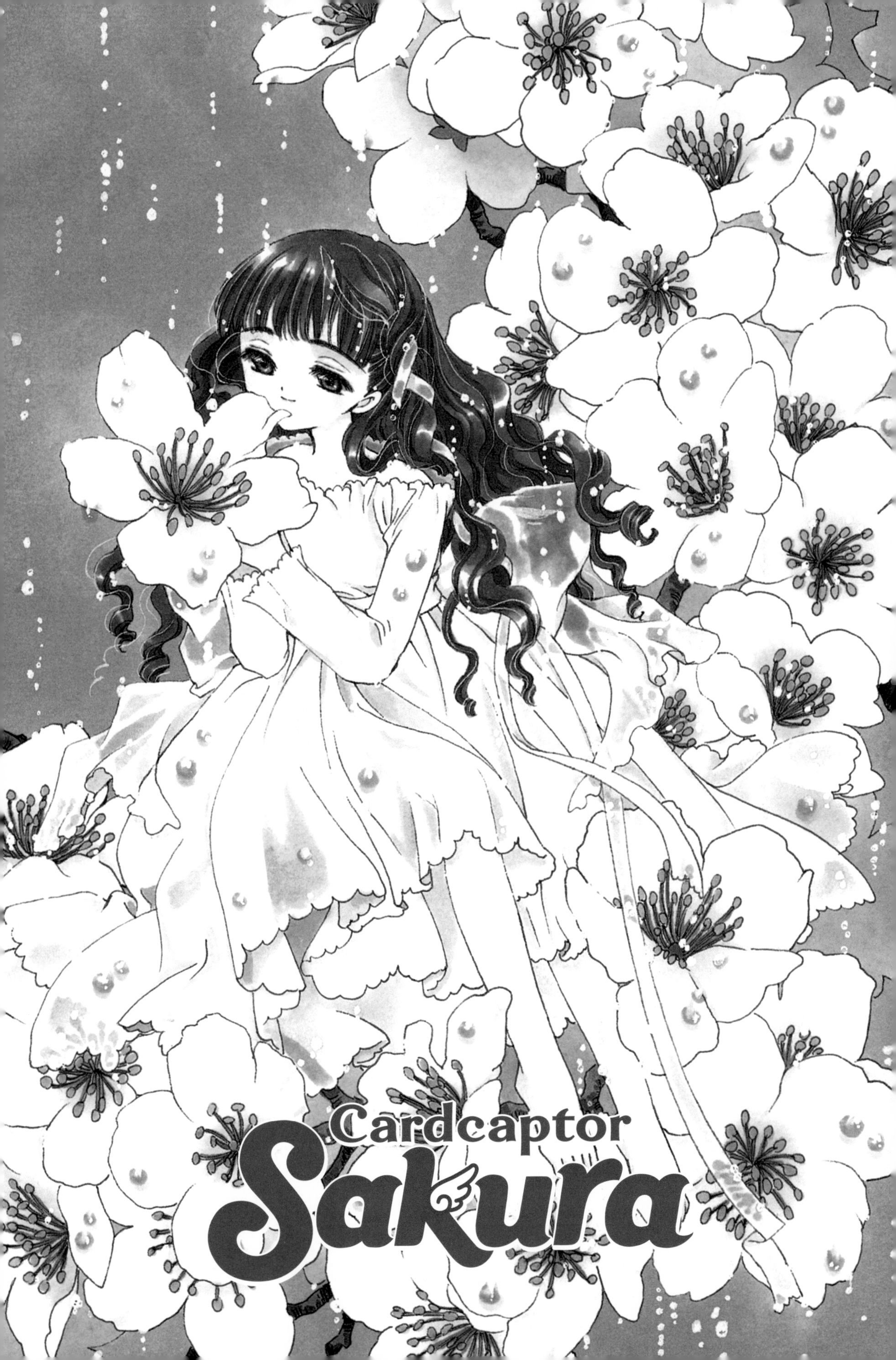
Cardcaptor
Sakura

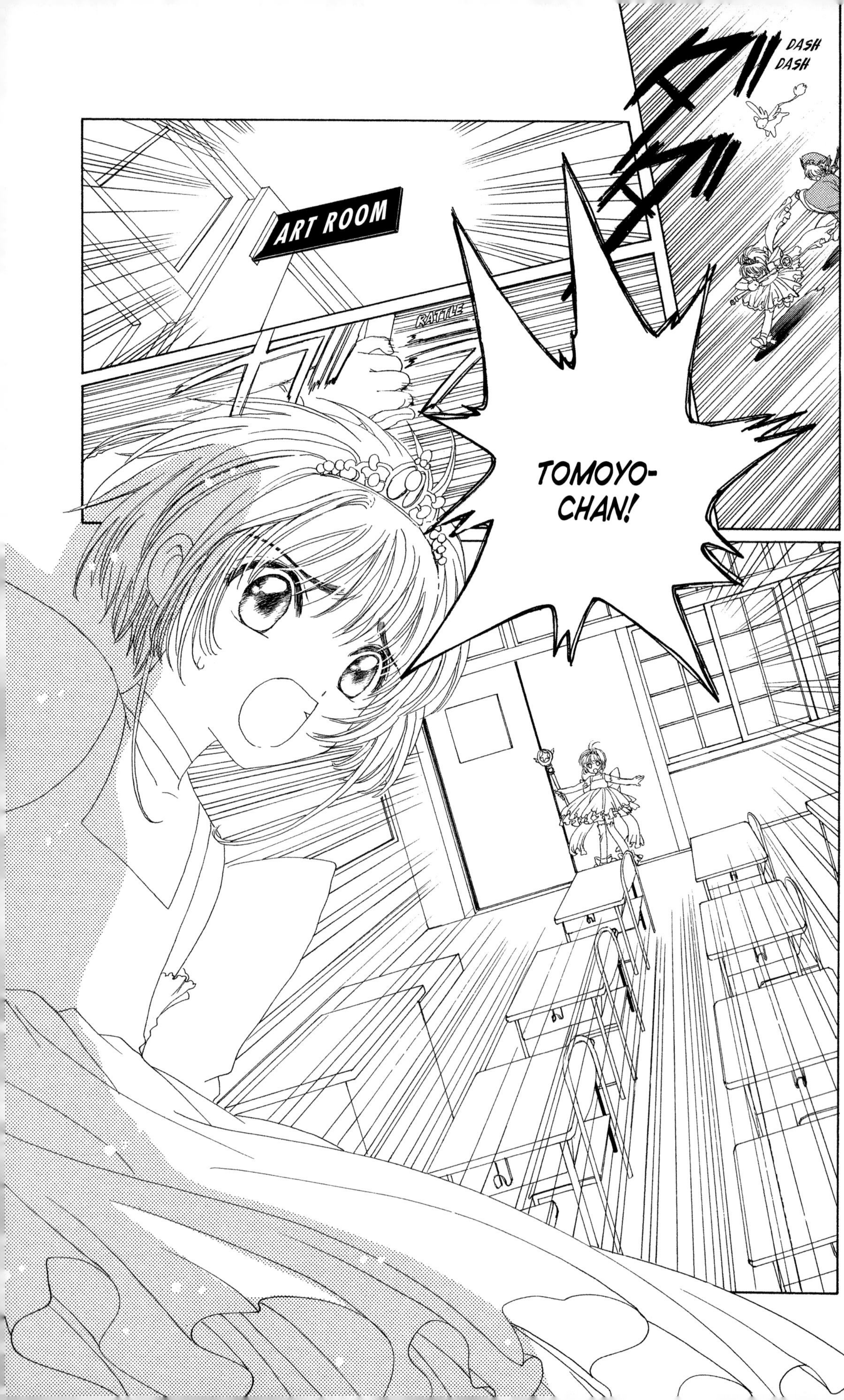
DASH
DASH
ART ROOM
RATTLE
TOMOYO-CHAN!

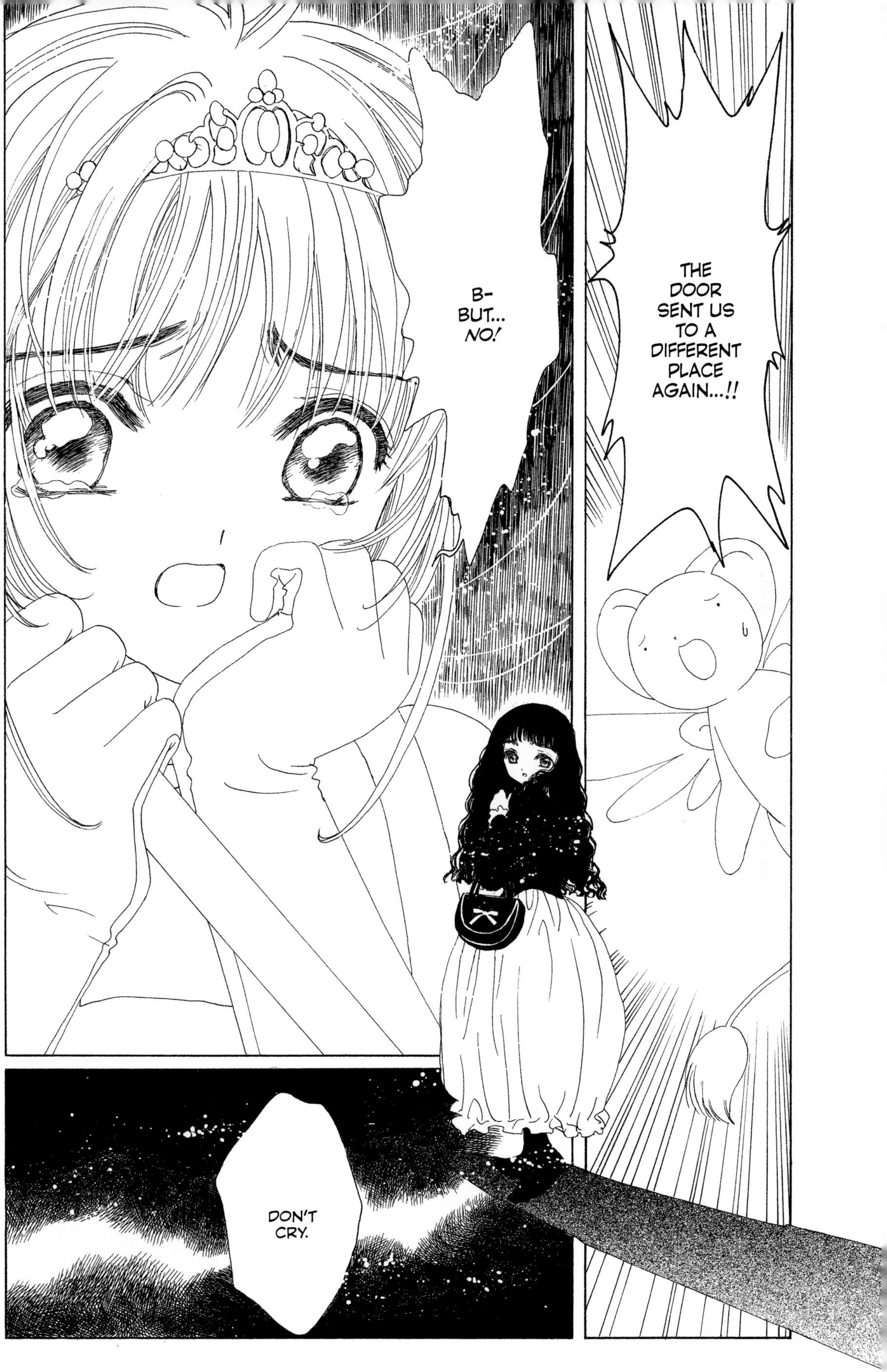
THE DOOR SENT US TO A DIFFERENT PLACE AGAIN...!!
B-BUT... *NO!*
DON'T CRY.

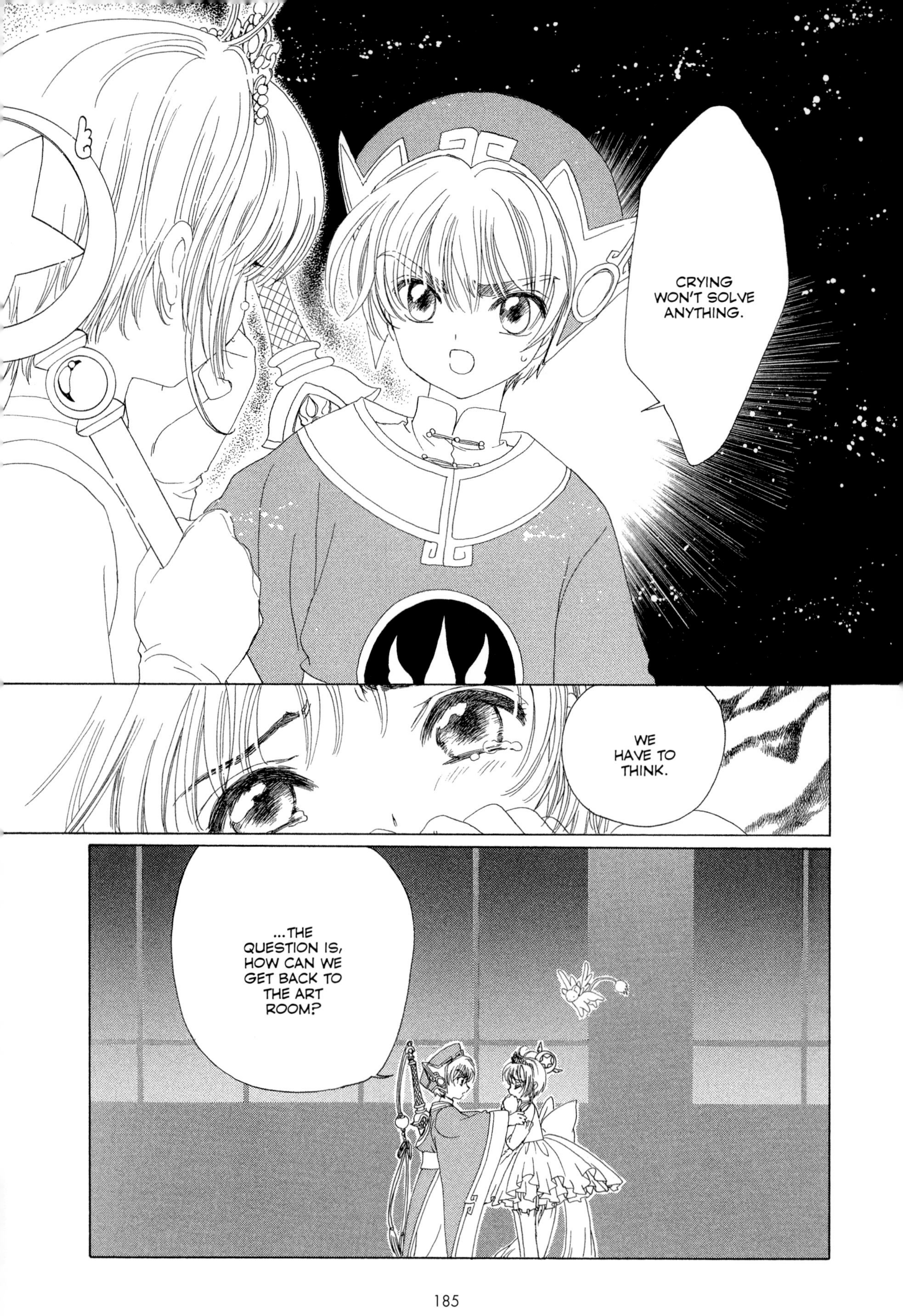
CRYING WON'T SOLVE ANYTHING.
WE HAVE TO THINK.
...THE QUESTION IS, HOW CAN WE GET BACK TO THE ART ROOM?

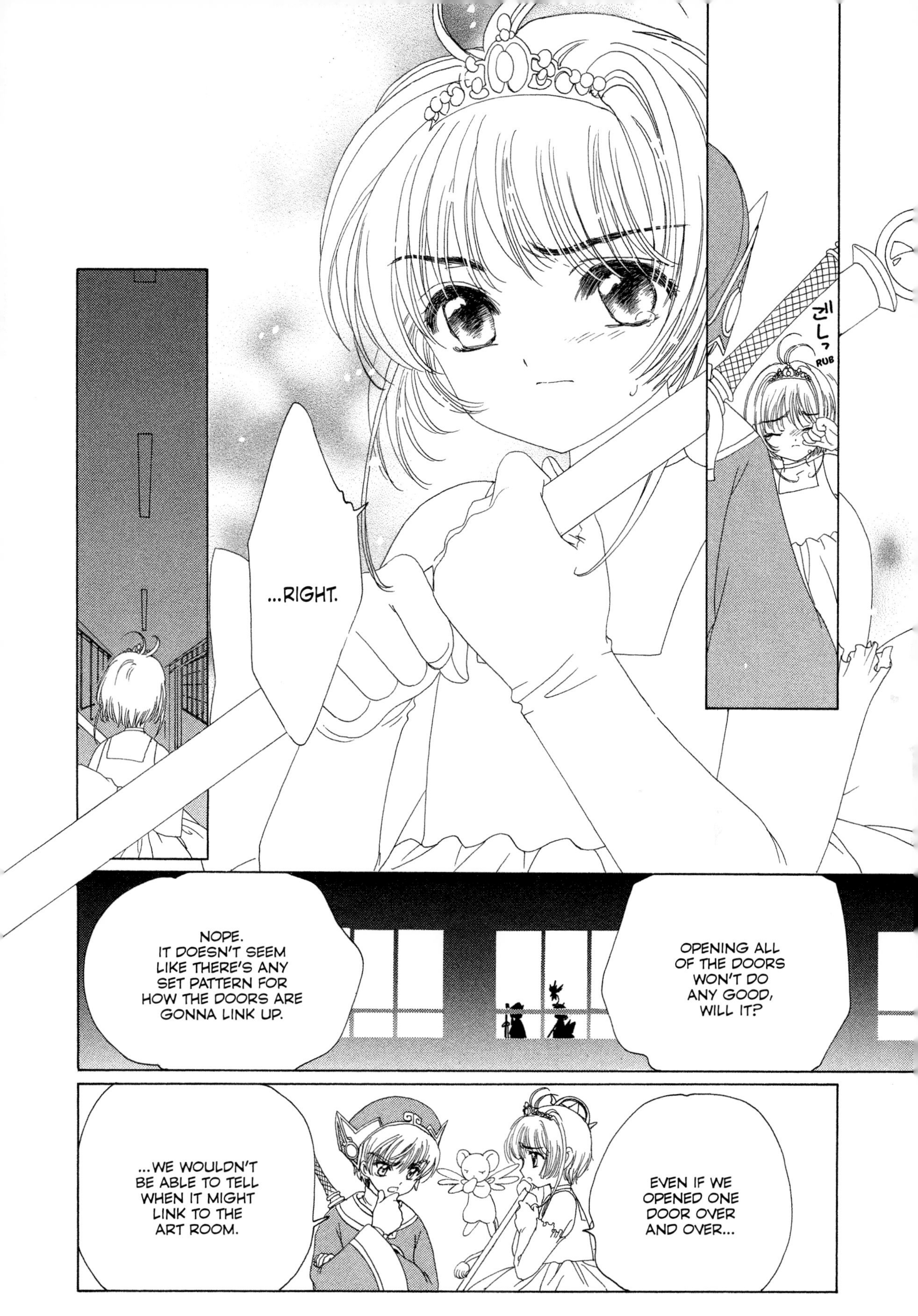
RUB
...RIGHT.
OPENING ALL OF THE DOORS WON'T DO ANY GOOD, WILL IT?
NOPE. IT DOESN'T SEEM LIKE THERE'S ANY SET PATTERN FOR HOW THE DOORS ARE GONNA LINK UP.
EVEN IF WE OPENED ONE DOOR OVER AND OVER...
...WE WOULDN'T BE ABLE TO TELL WHEN IT MIGHT LINK TO THE ART ROOM.

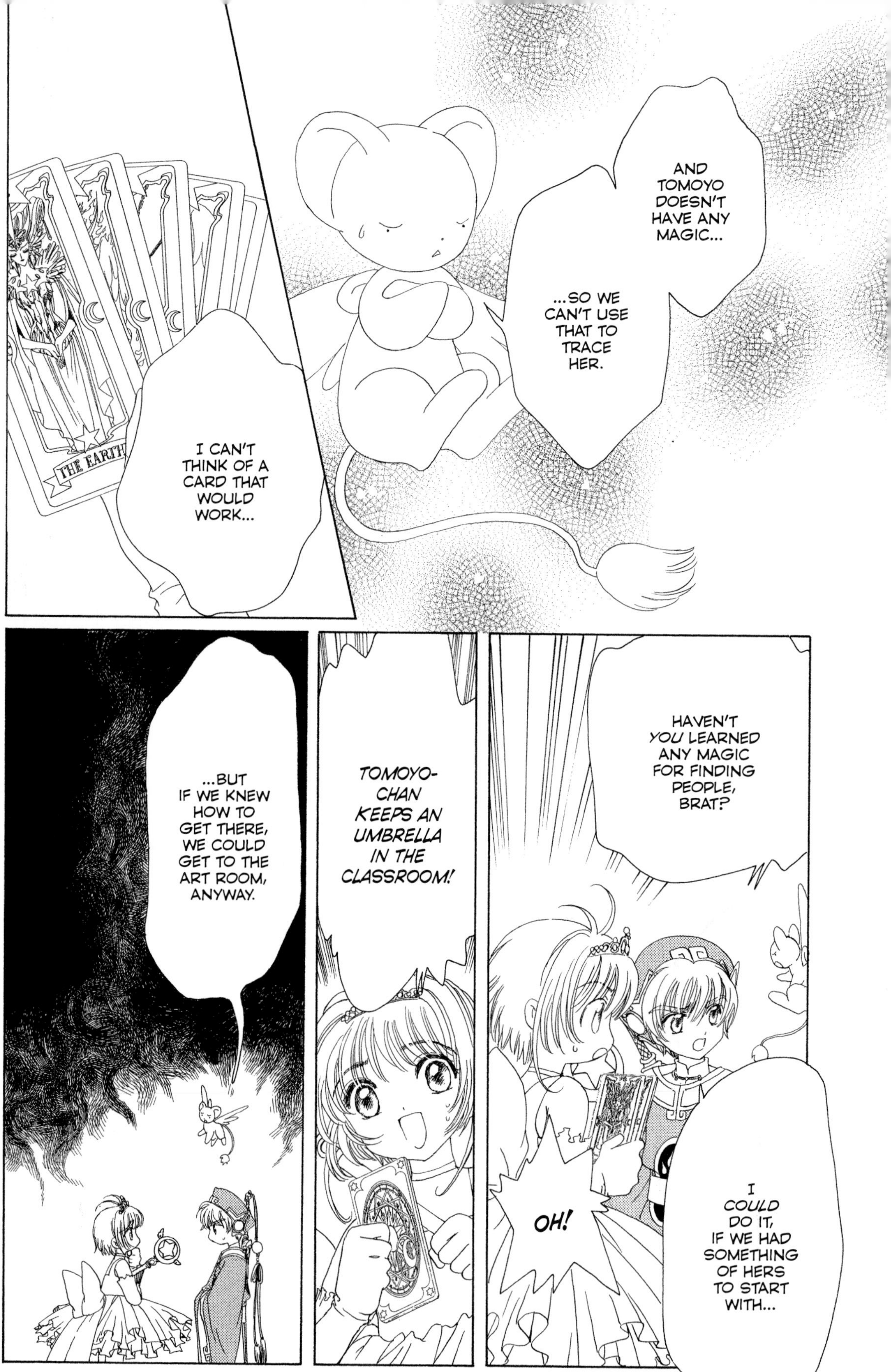
AND TOMOYO DOESN'T HAVE ANY MAGIC...
...SO WE CAN'T USE THAT TO TRACE HER.
THE EARTH
I CAN'T THINK OF A CARD THAT WOULD WORK...
HAVEN'T *YOU* LEARNED ANY MAGIC FOR FINDING PEOPLE, BRAT?
I *COULD* DO IT, IF WE HAD SOMETHING OF HERS TO START WITH...
OH!
TOMOYO-CHAN KEEPS AN UMBRELLA IN THE CLASSROOM!
...BUT IF WE KNEW HOW TO GET THERE, WE COULD GET TO THE ART ROOM, ANYWAY.

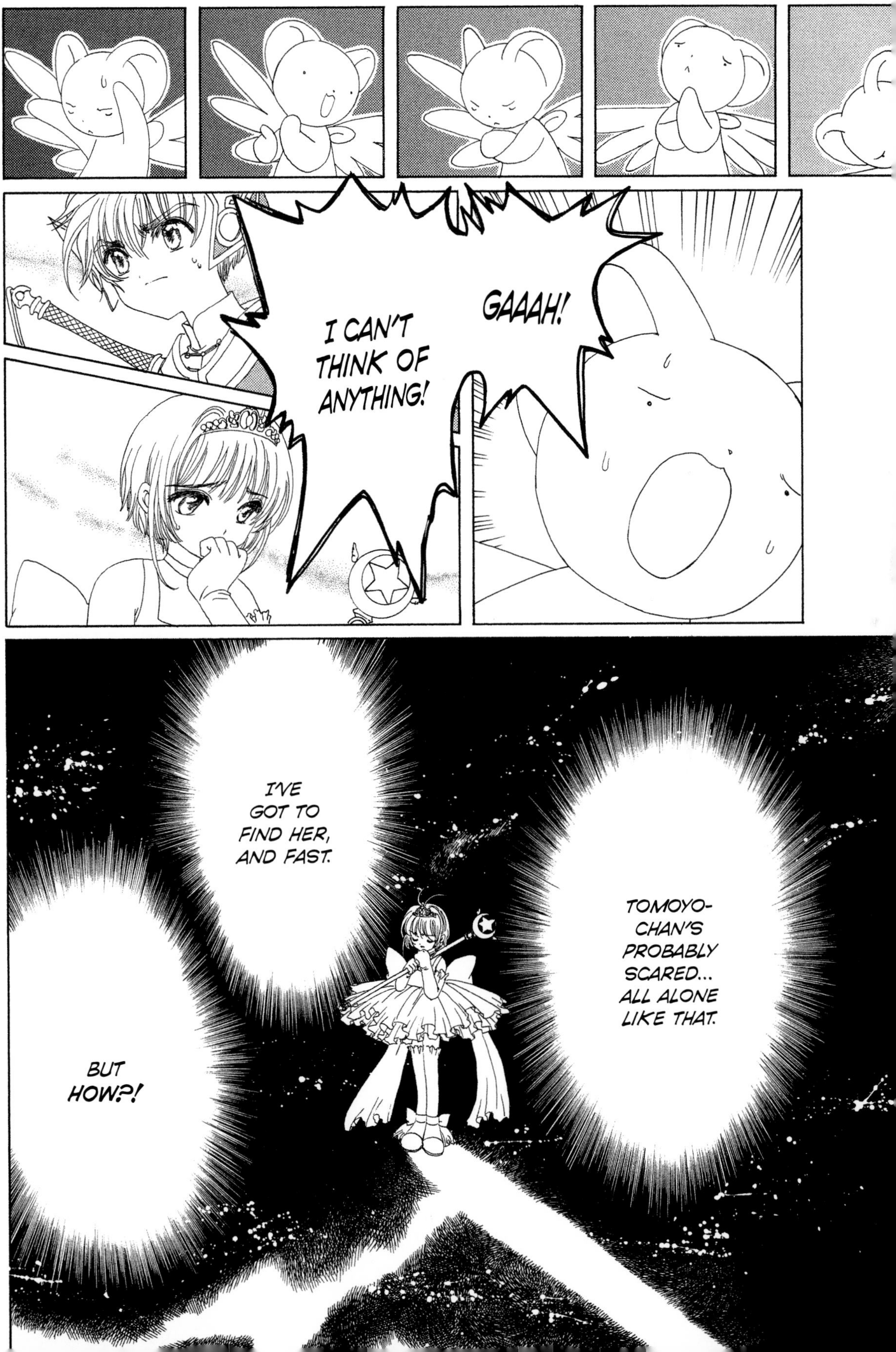
GAAAH!
I CAN'T THINK OF ANYTHING!
TOMOYO-CHAN'S PROBABLY SCARED... ALL ALONE LIKE THAT.
I'VE GOT TO FIND HER, AND FAST.
BUT HOW?!

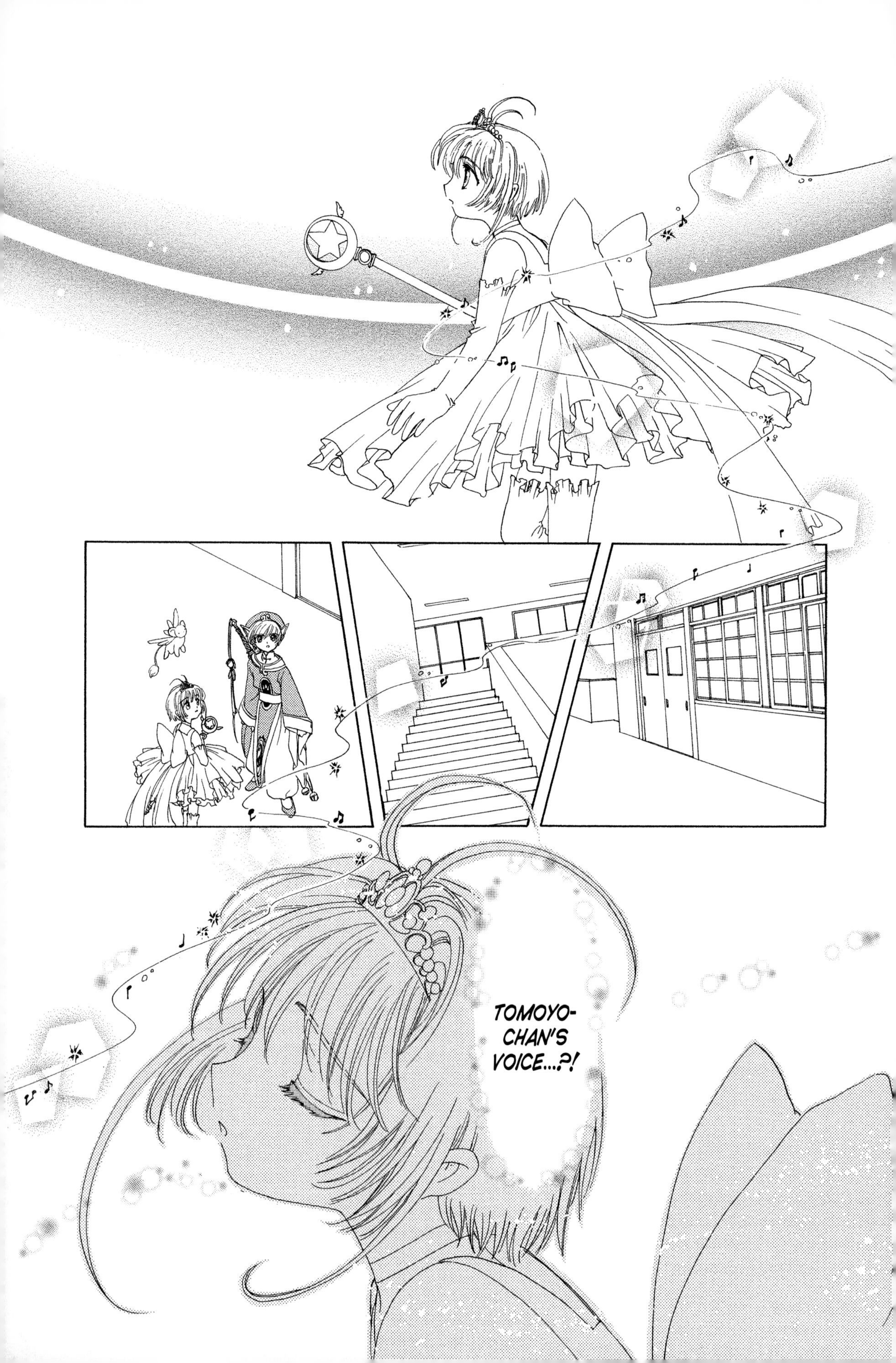
TOMOYO-CHAN'S VOICE...?!

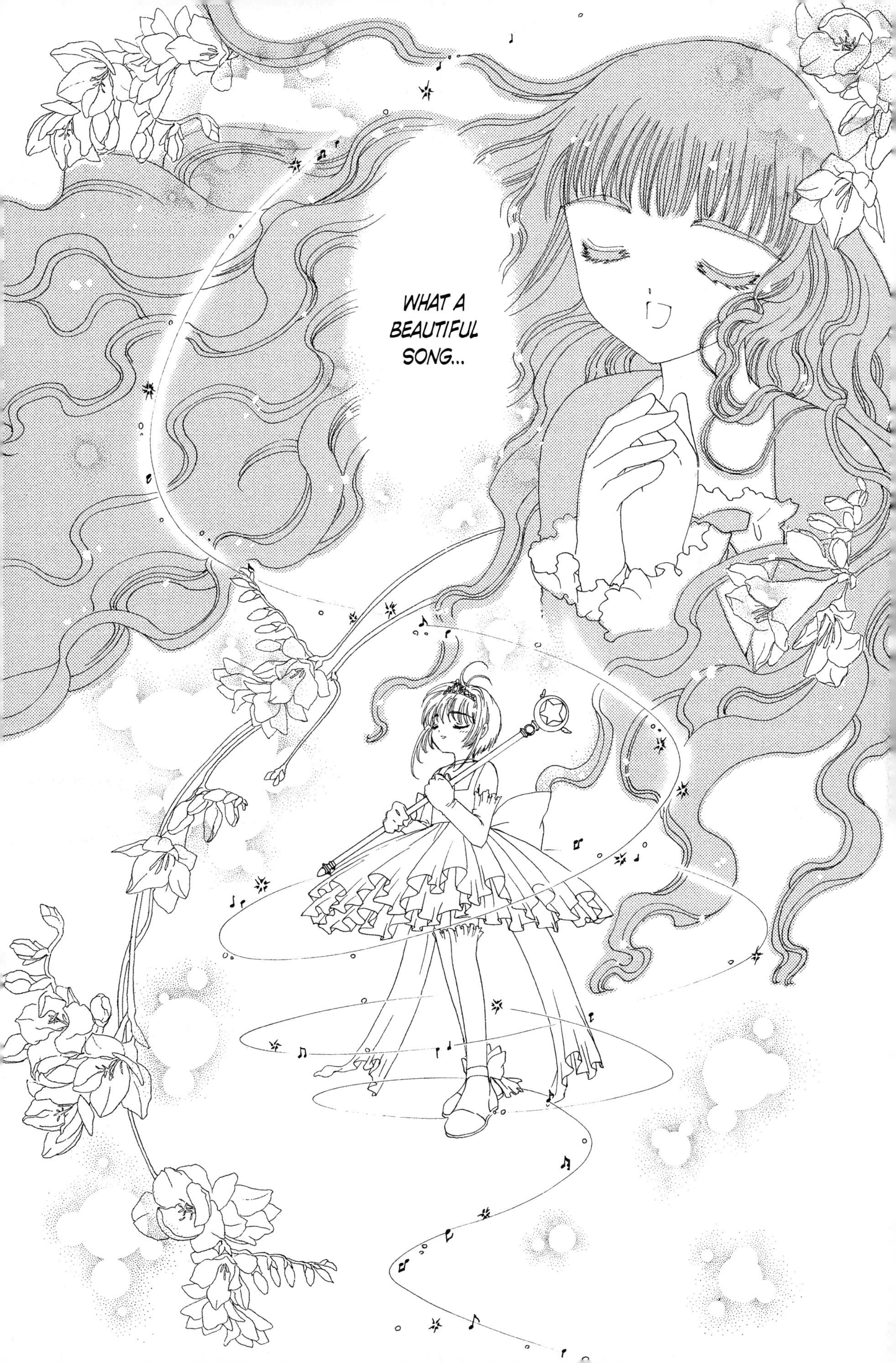
WHAT A BEAUTIFUL SONG...

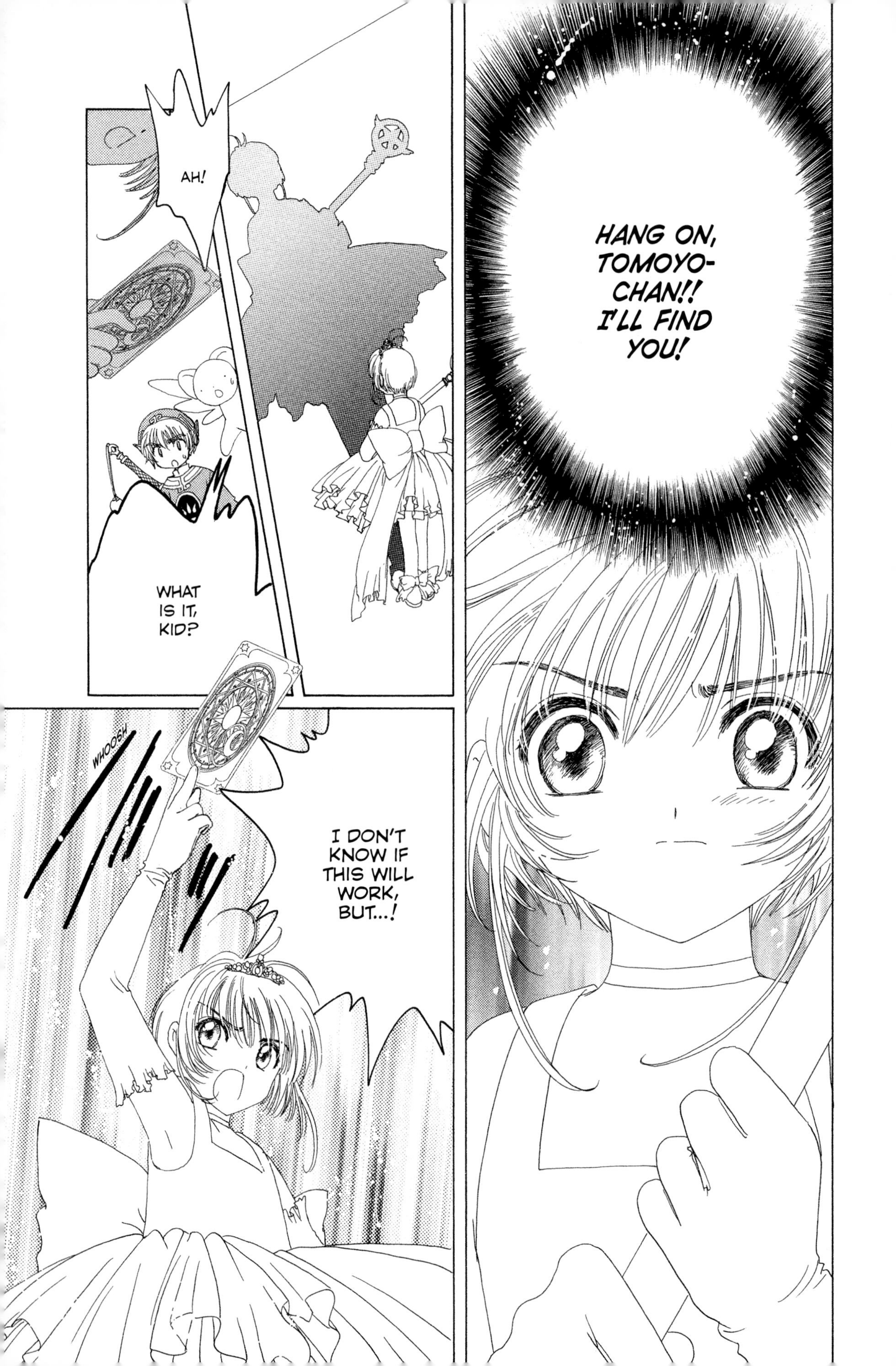
HANG ON, TOMOYO-CHAN!! I'LL FIND YOU!
AH!
WHAT IS IT, KID?
WHOOSH
I DON'T KNOW IF THIS WILL WORK, BUT...!

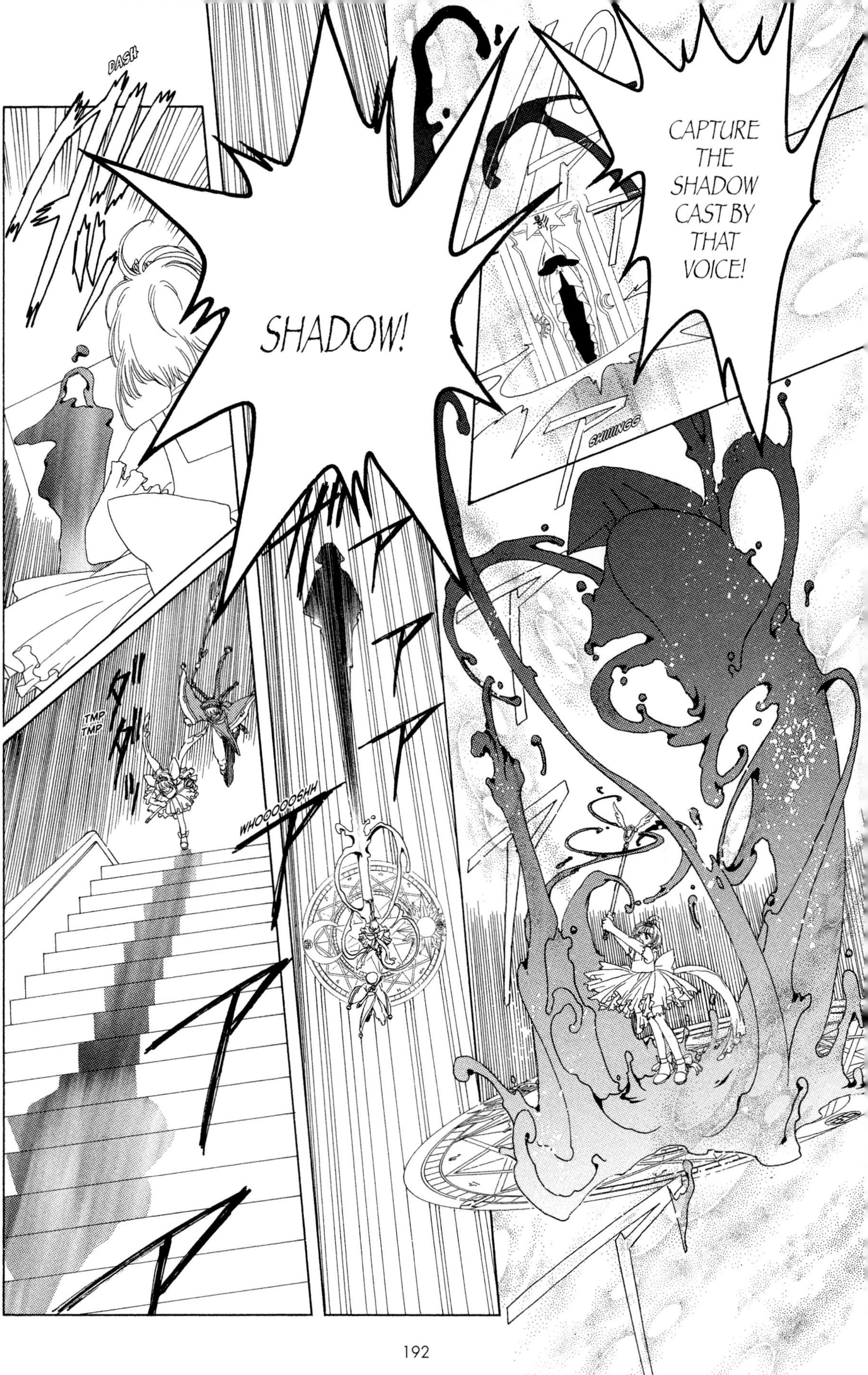
CAPTURE THE SHADOW CAST BY THAT VOICE!
SHADOW!
SHIIIINGG
DASH
WHOOOOOOSHH
TMP TMP

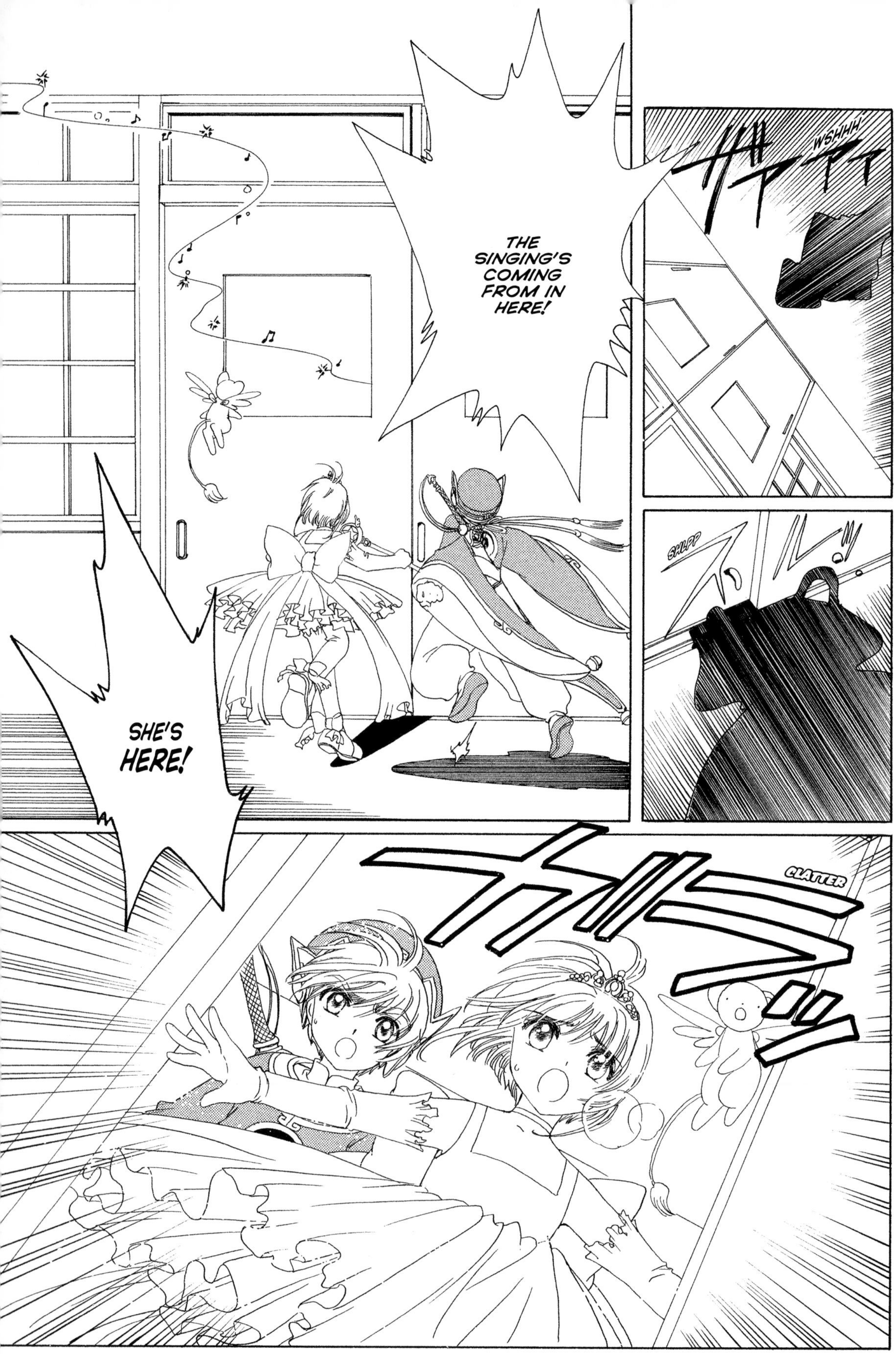
WSHHH
SHPP
THE SINGING'S COMING FROM IN HERE!
SHE'S HERE!
CLATTER

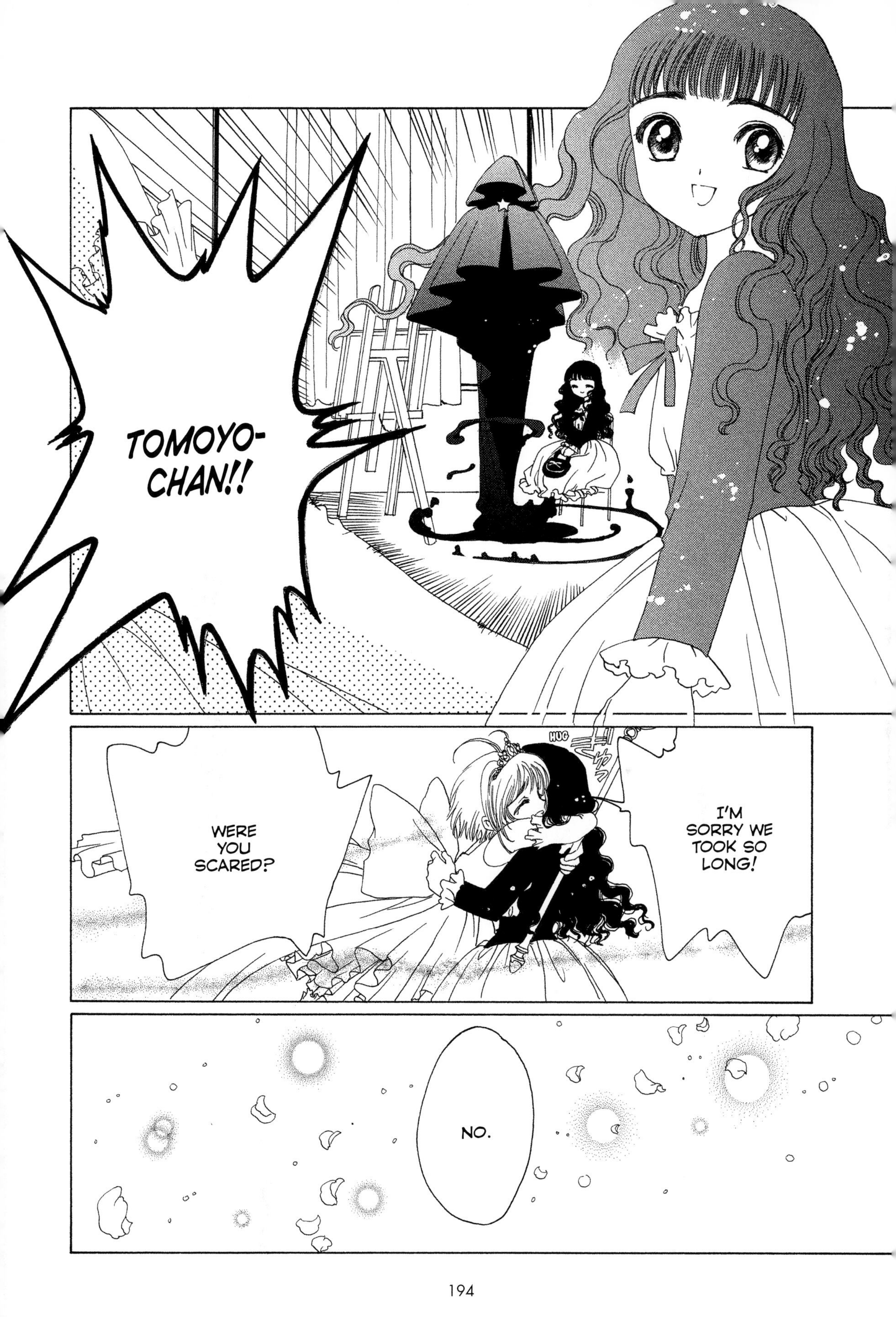
TOMOYO-CHAN!!
I'M SORRY WE TOOK SO LONG!
HUG
WERE YOU SCARED?
NO.

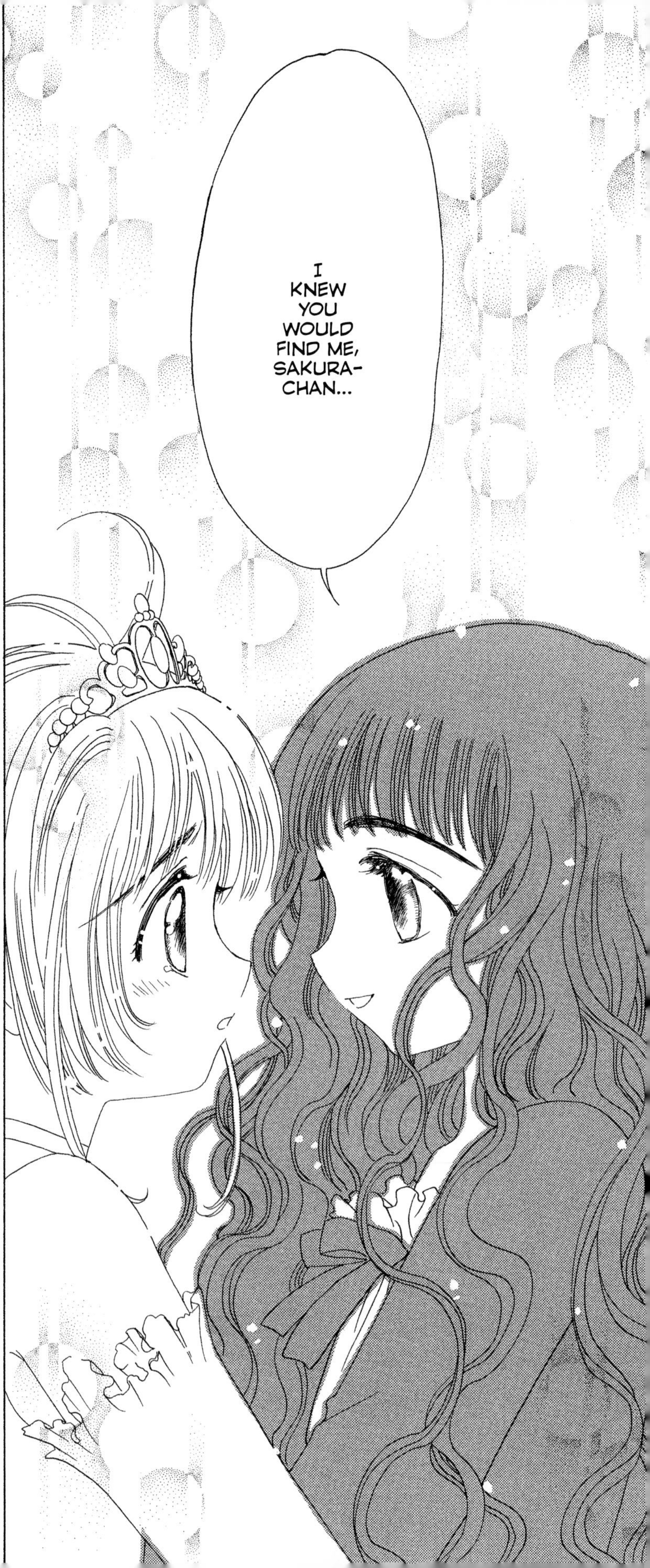
I KNEW YOU WOULD FIND ME, SAKURA-CHAN...

28

TOSHINOBU YAMAMOTO

BIRTHDATE:
APRIL 8

JOB:
ART TEACHER

FAVORITE FOOD:
WILD GREENS

LEAST FAVORITE FOOD:
LEMON

FAVORITE THING:
MORNING WALKS

FAVORITE COLOR:
THE RAINBOW

FAVORITE FLOWER:
CREPE MYRTLE

FAVORITE RECIPE:
RICE POT

WEAK POINT:
ANGER MANAGEMENT

HOBBY:
BROWSING BOOKSTORES

SPECIAL TALENT:
KENDO

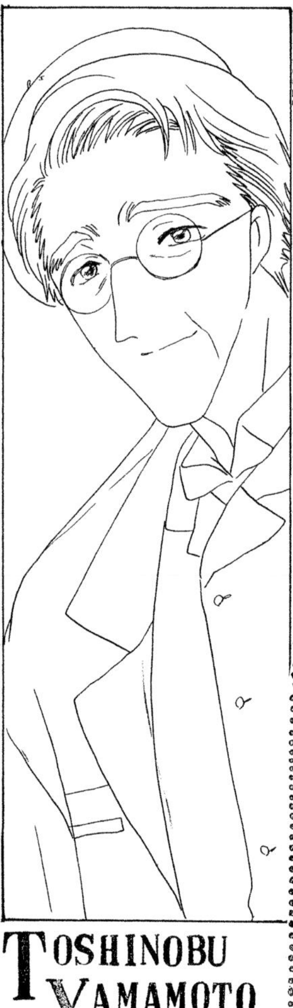

TOSHINOBU YAMAMOTO

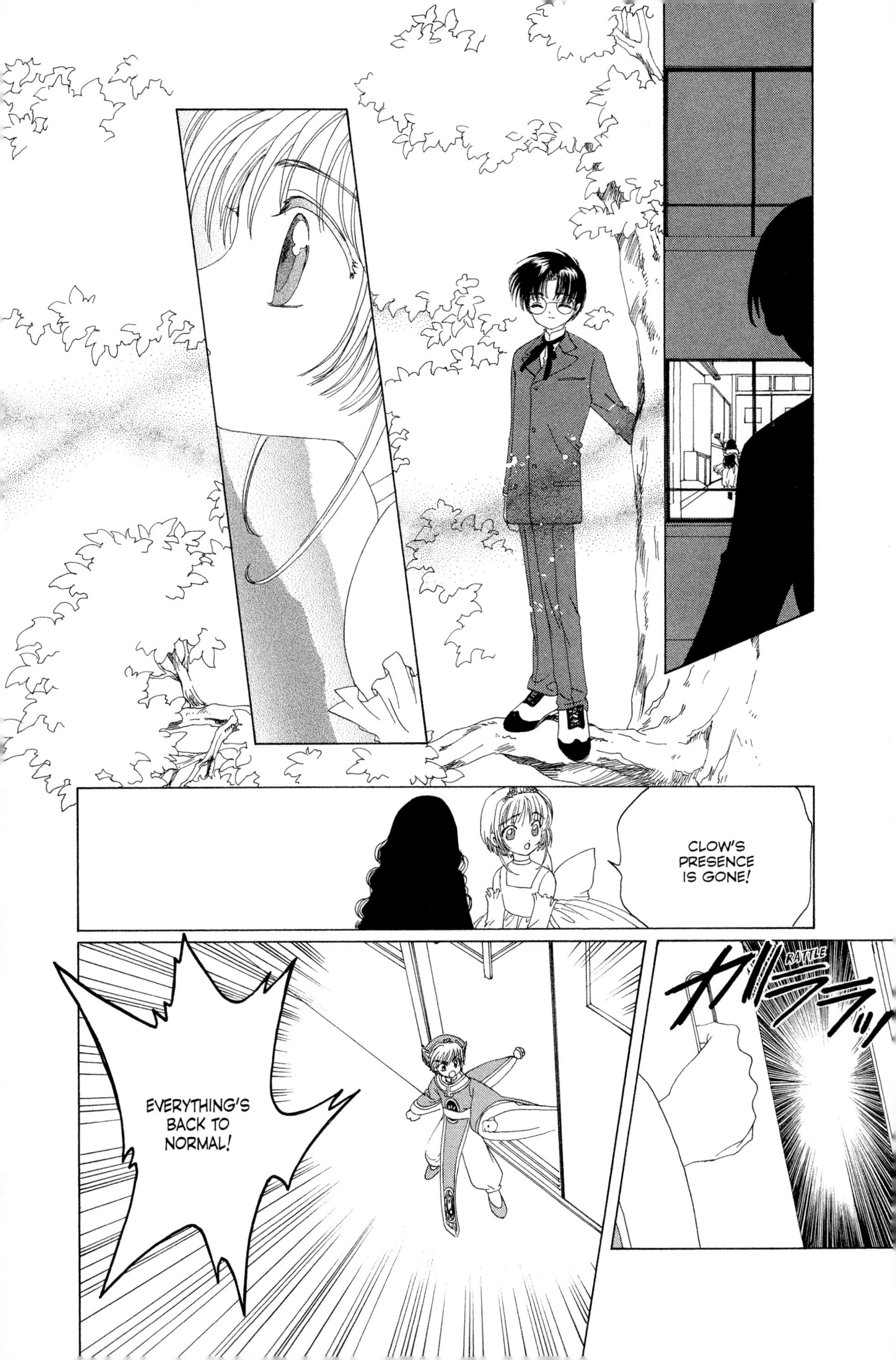
CLOW'S PRESENCE IS GONE!
RATTLE
EVERYTHING'S BACK TO NORMAL!

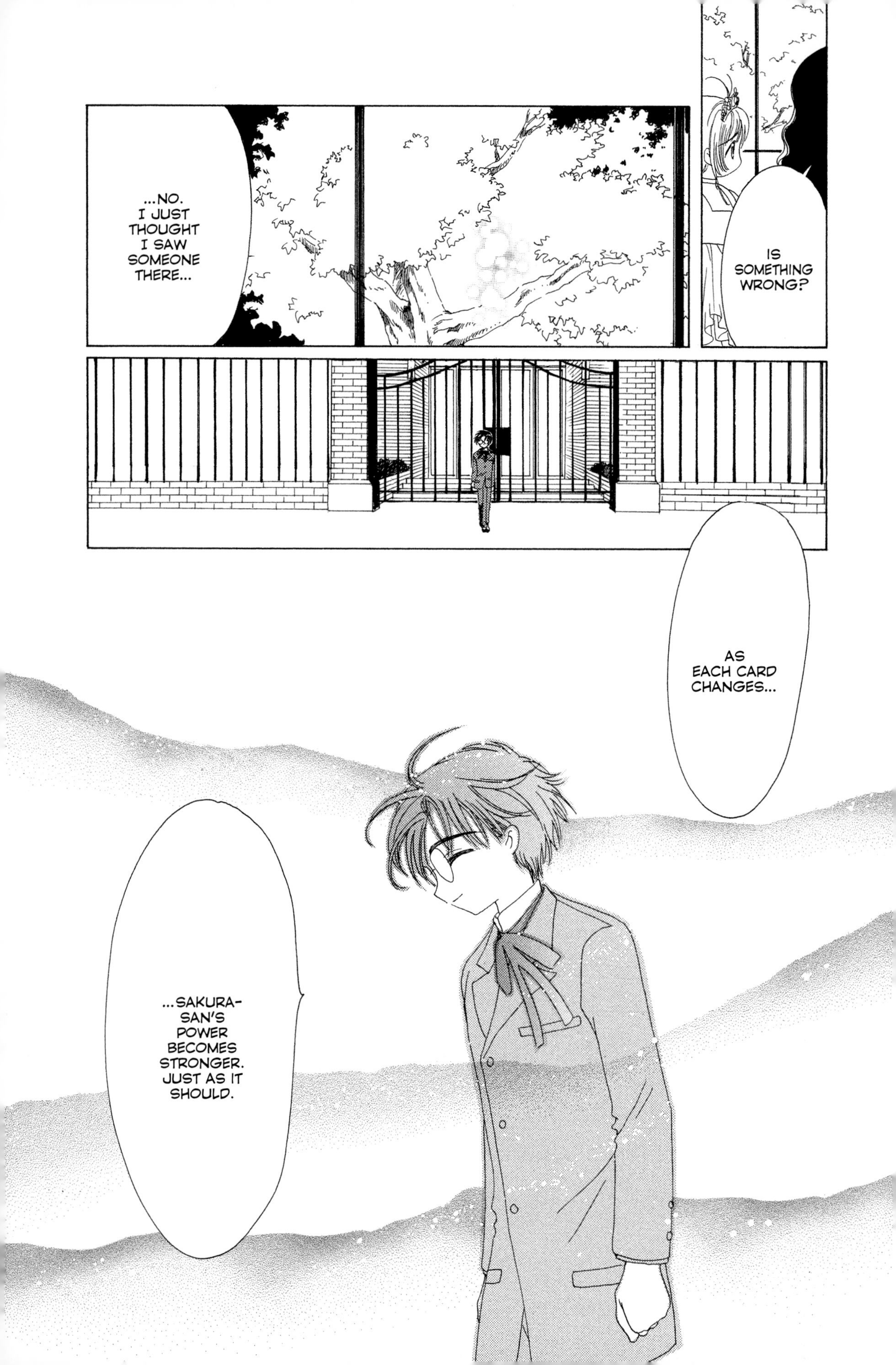
IS SOMETHING WRONG?
...NO. I JUST THOUGHT I SAW SOMEONE THERE...
AS EACH CARD CHANGES...
...SAKURA-SAN'S POWER BECOMES STRONGER. JUST AS IT SHOULD.

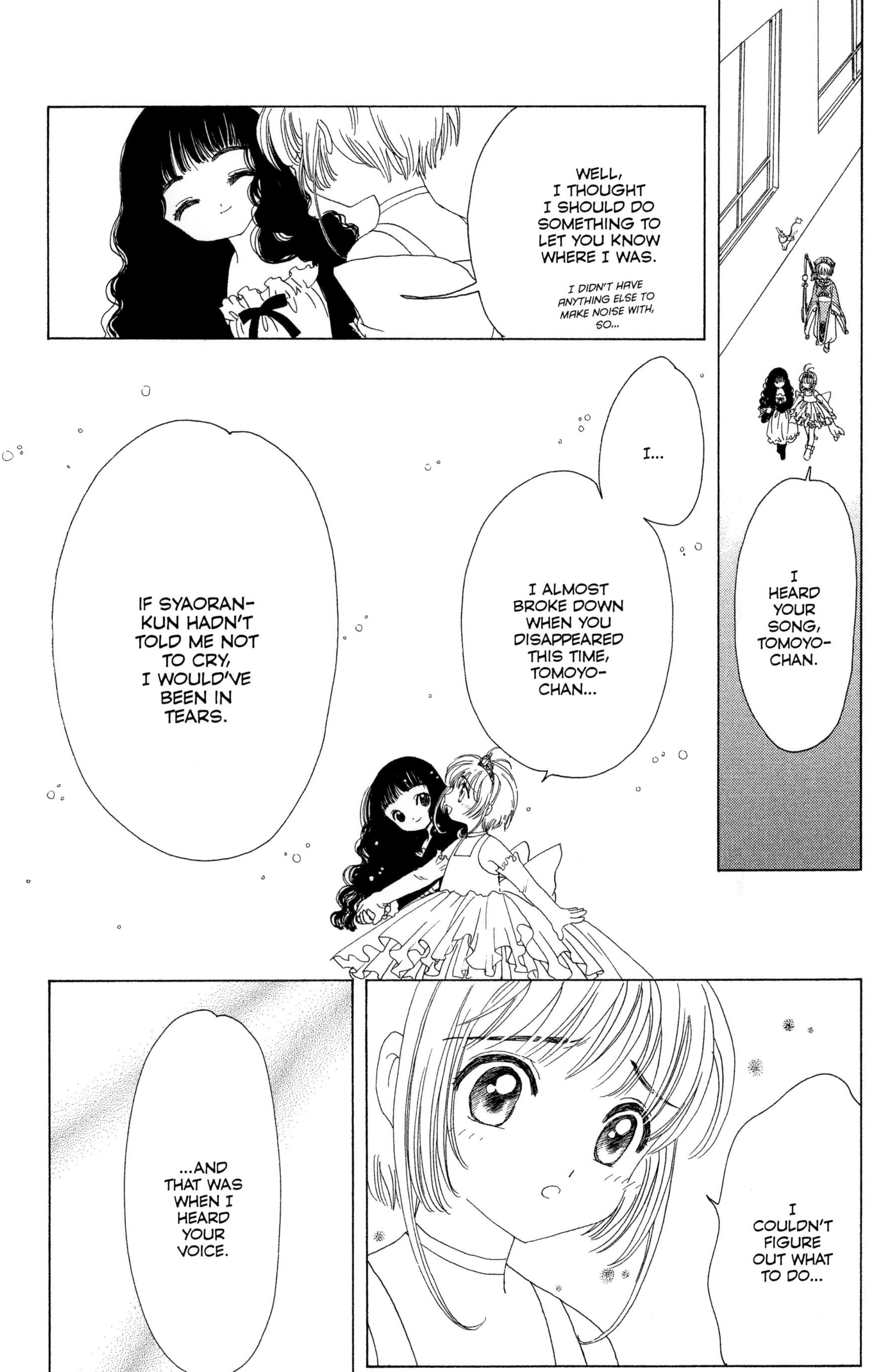
I HEARD YOUR SONG, TOMOYO-CHAN.
WELL, I THOUGHT I SHOULD DO SOMETHING TO LET YOU KNOW WHERE I WAS.
I DIDN'T HAVE ANYTHING ELSE TO MAKE NOISE WITH, SO...
I...
I ALMOST BROKE DOWN WHEN YOU DISAPPEARED THIS TIME, TOMOYO-CHAN...
IF SYAORAN-KUN HADN'T TOLD ME NOT TO CRY, I WOULD'VE BEEN IN TEARS.
I COULDN'T FIGURE OUT WHAT TO DO...
...AND THAT WAS WHEN I HEARD YOUR VOICE.

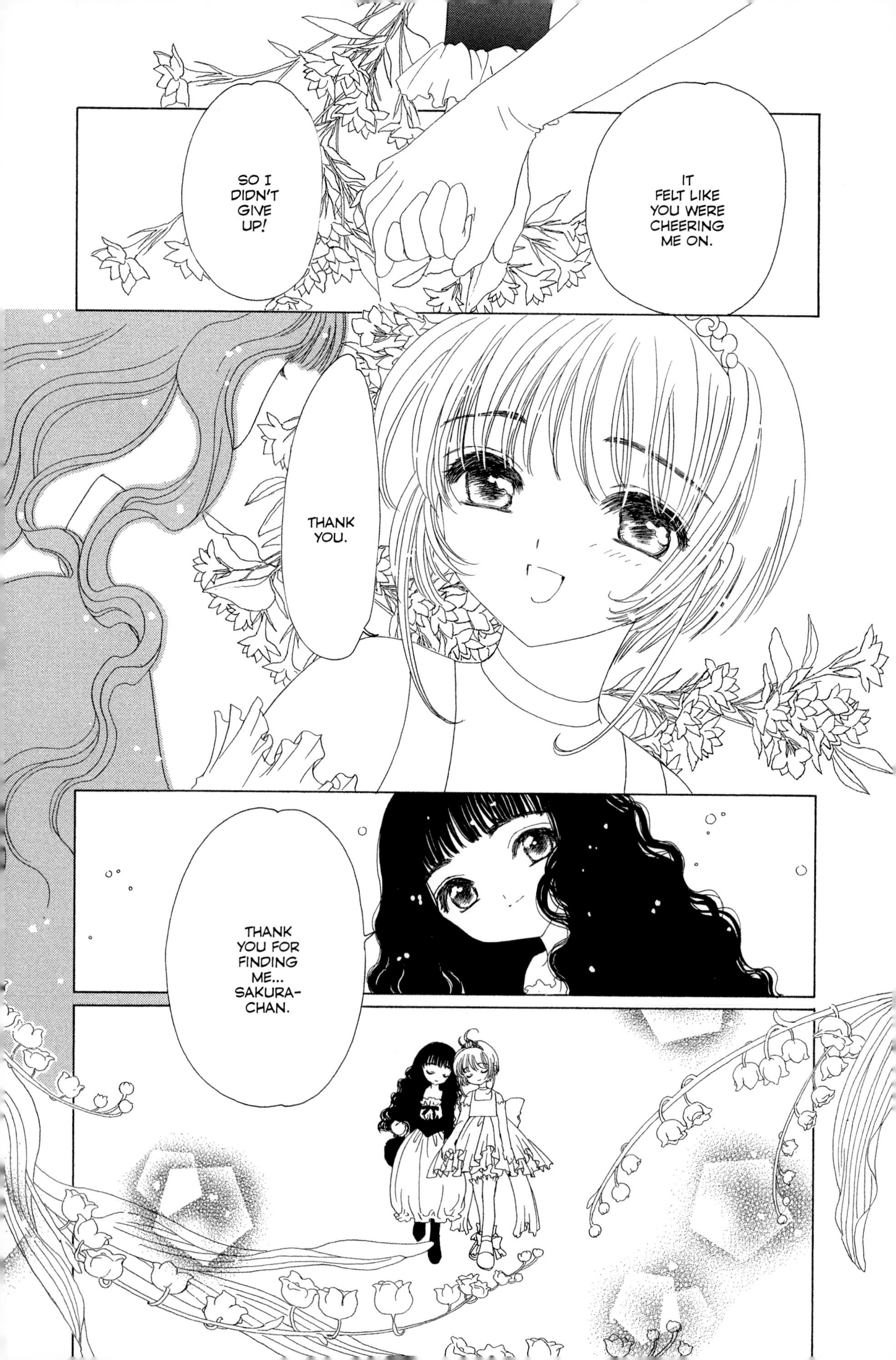
IT FELT LIKE YOU WERE CHEERING ME ON.
SO I DIDN'T GIVE UP!
THANK YOU.
THANK YOU FOR FINDING ME... SAKURA-CHAN.

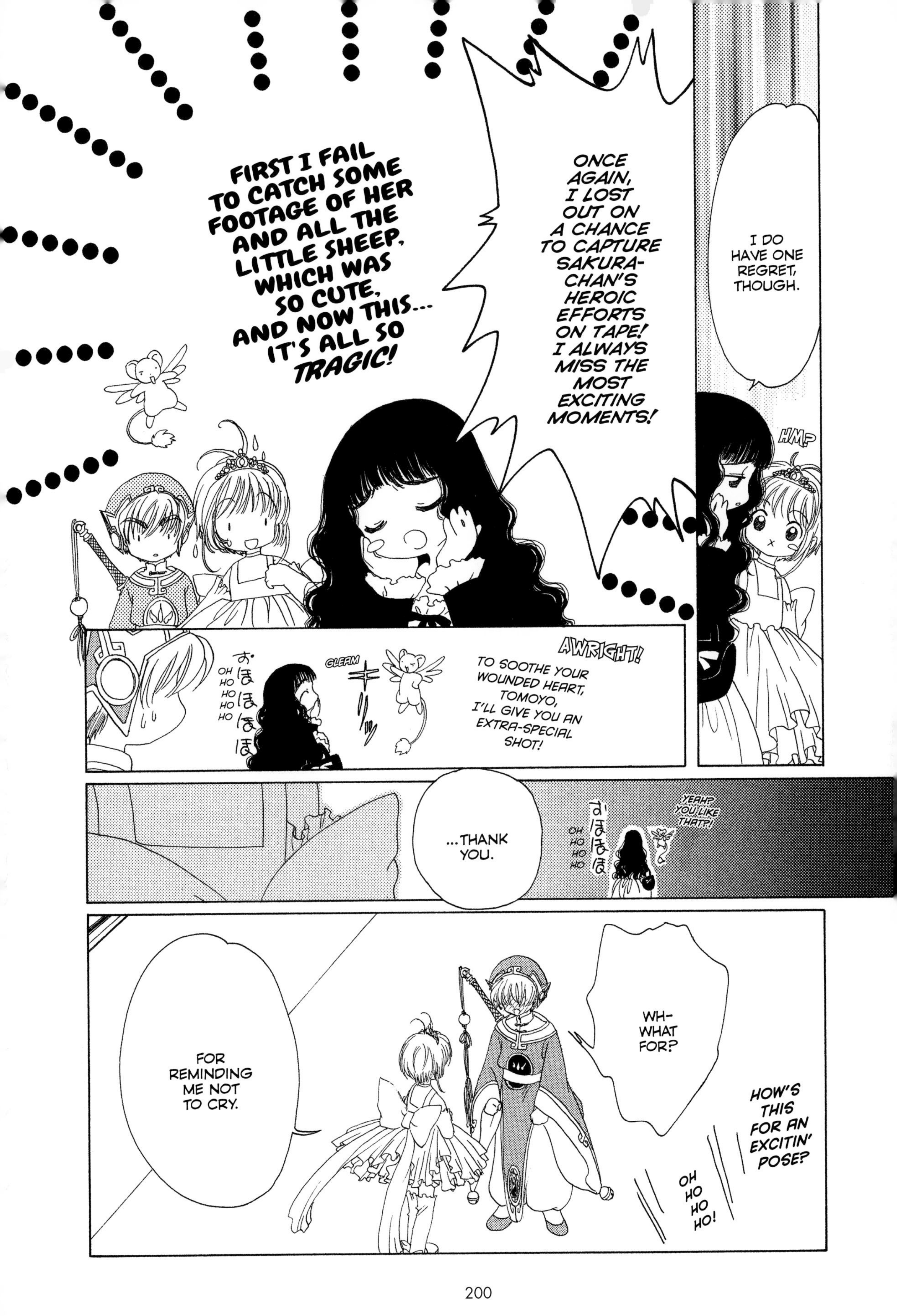
I DO HAVE ONE REGRET, THOUGH.
HM?
ONCE AGAIN, I LOST OUT ON A CHANCE TO CAPTURE SAKURA-CHAN'S HEROIC EFFORTS ON TAPE! I ALWAYS MISS THE MOST EXCITING MOMENTS!
FIRST I FAIL TO CATCH SOME FOOTAGE OF HER AND ALL THE LITTLE SHEEP, WHICH WAS SO CUTE, AND NOW THIS... IT'S ALL SO TRAGIC!
AWRIGHT!
TO SOOTHE YOUR WOUNDED HEART, TOMOYO, I'LL GIVE YOU AN EXTRA-SPECIAL SHOT!
GLEAM
キラッ
おほほほほ
OH HO HO HO HO
YEAH? YOU LIKE THAT?!
おほほほ
OH HO HO HO
...THANK YOU.
HOW'S THIS FOR AN EXCITIN' POSE?
OH HO HO HO!
WH-WHAT FOR?
FOR REMINDING ME NOT TO CRY.

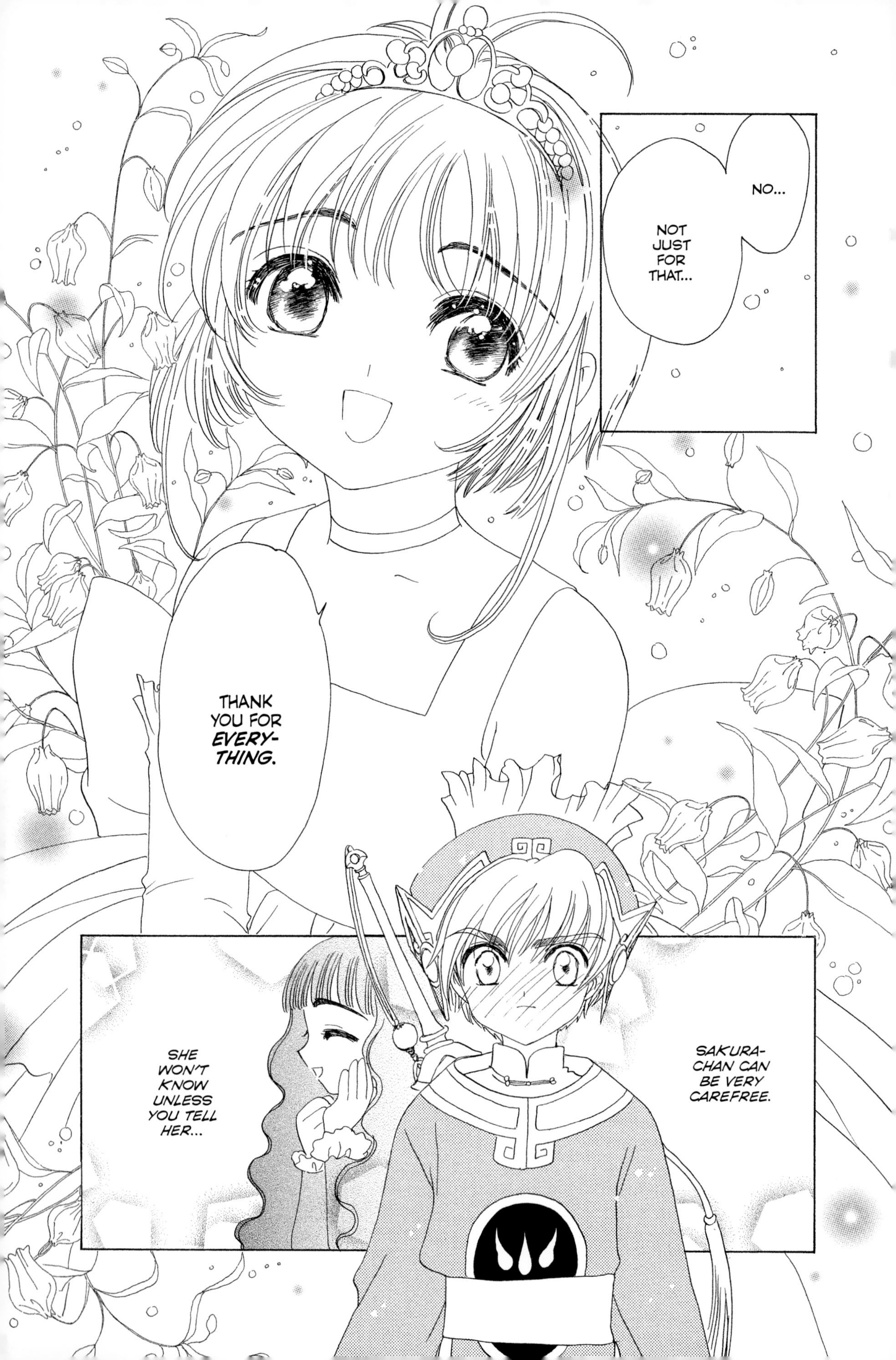
NO...
NOT JUST FOR THAT...
THANK YOU FOR ***EVERY-THING.***
SAKURA-CHAN CAN BE VERY CAREFREE.
SHE WON'T KNOW UNLESS YOU TELL HER...

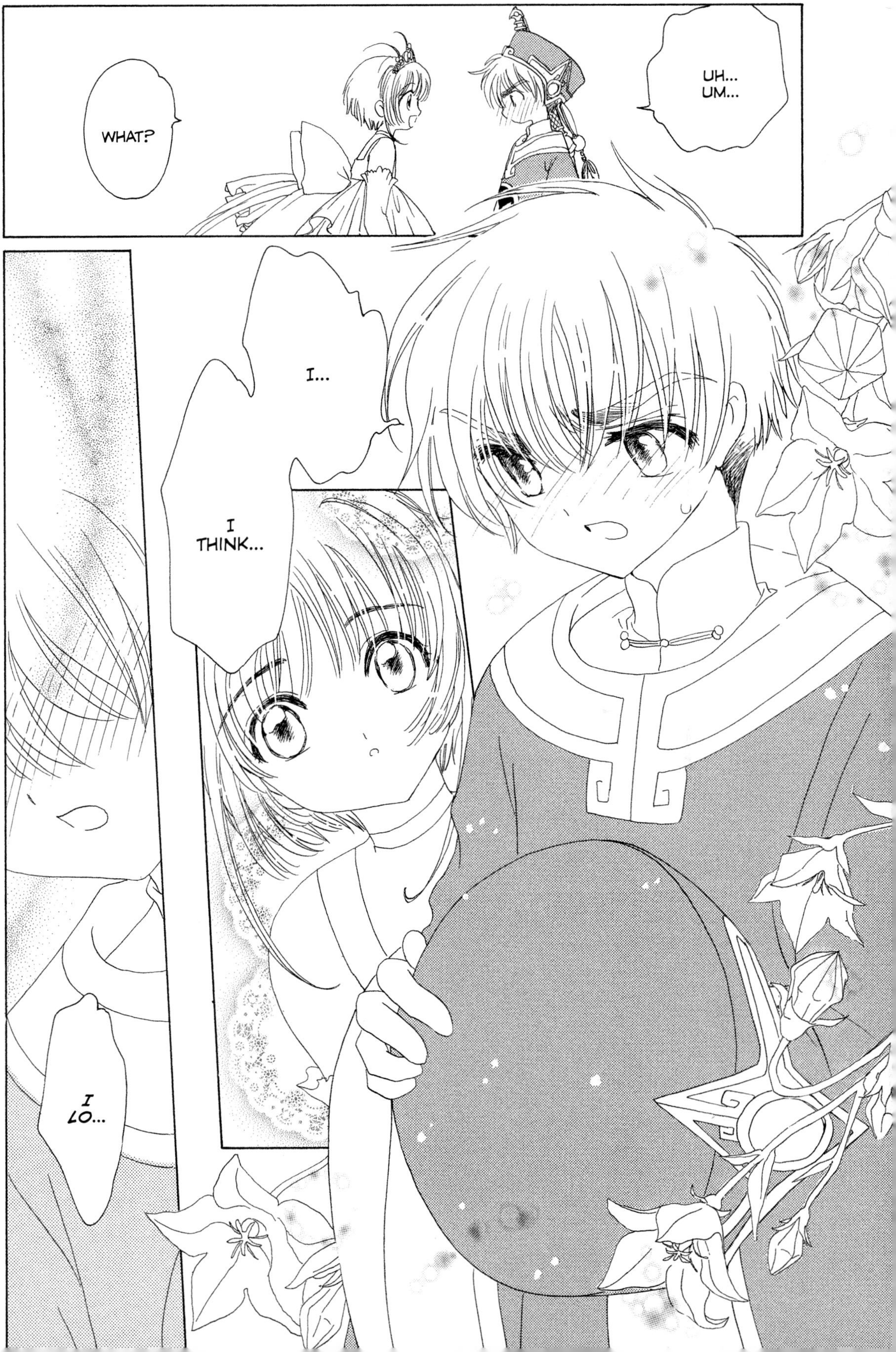
UH... UM...
WHAT?
I...
I THINK...
I LO...

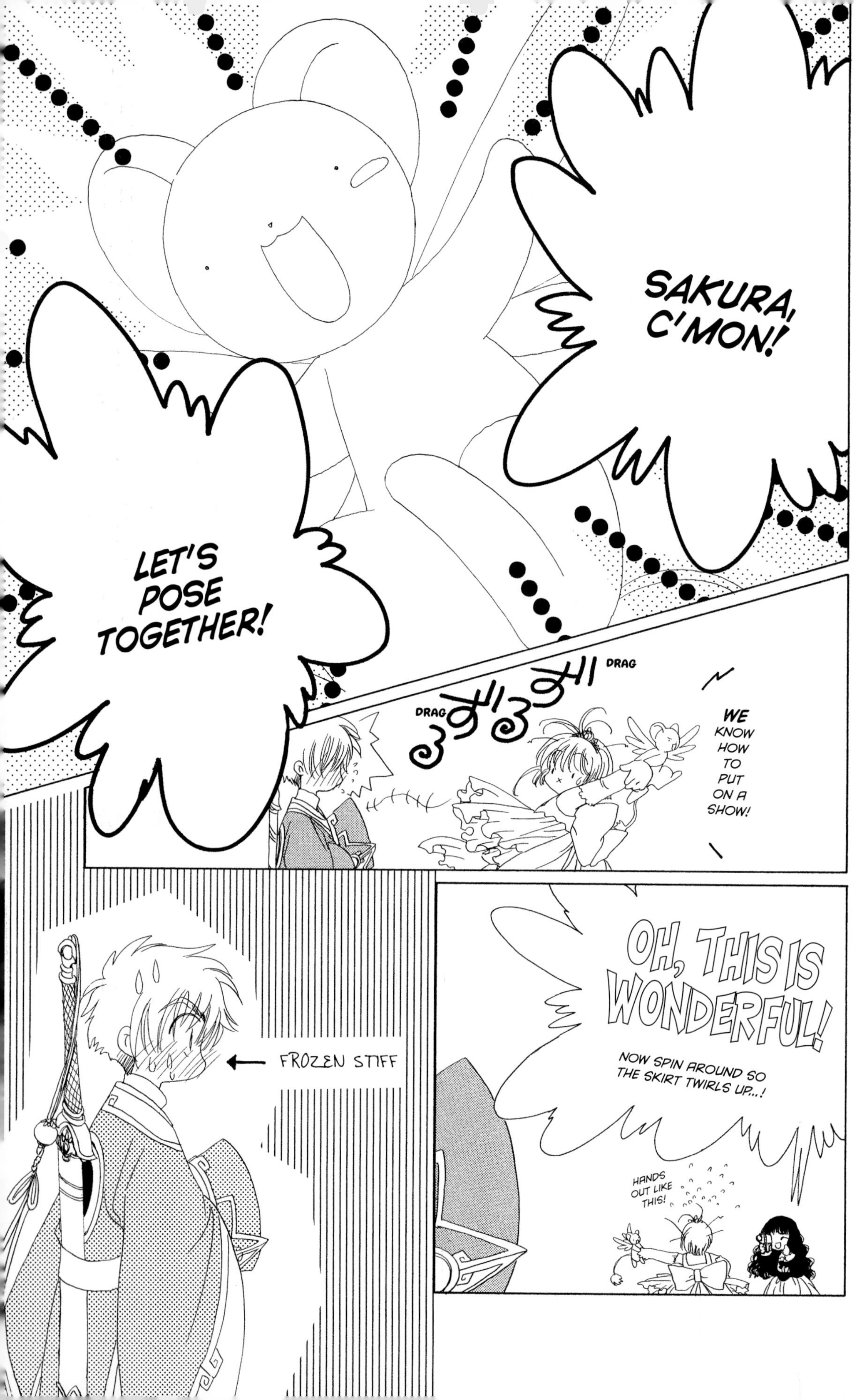
SAKURA, C'MON!
LET'S POSE TOGETHER!
DRAG
DRAG
WE KNOW HOW TO PUT ON A SHOW!
OH, THIS IS WONDERFUL!
NOW SPIN AROUND SO THE SKIRT TWIRLS UP...!
HANDS OUT LIKE THIS!
FROZEN STIFF

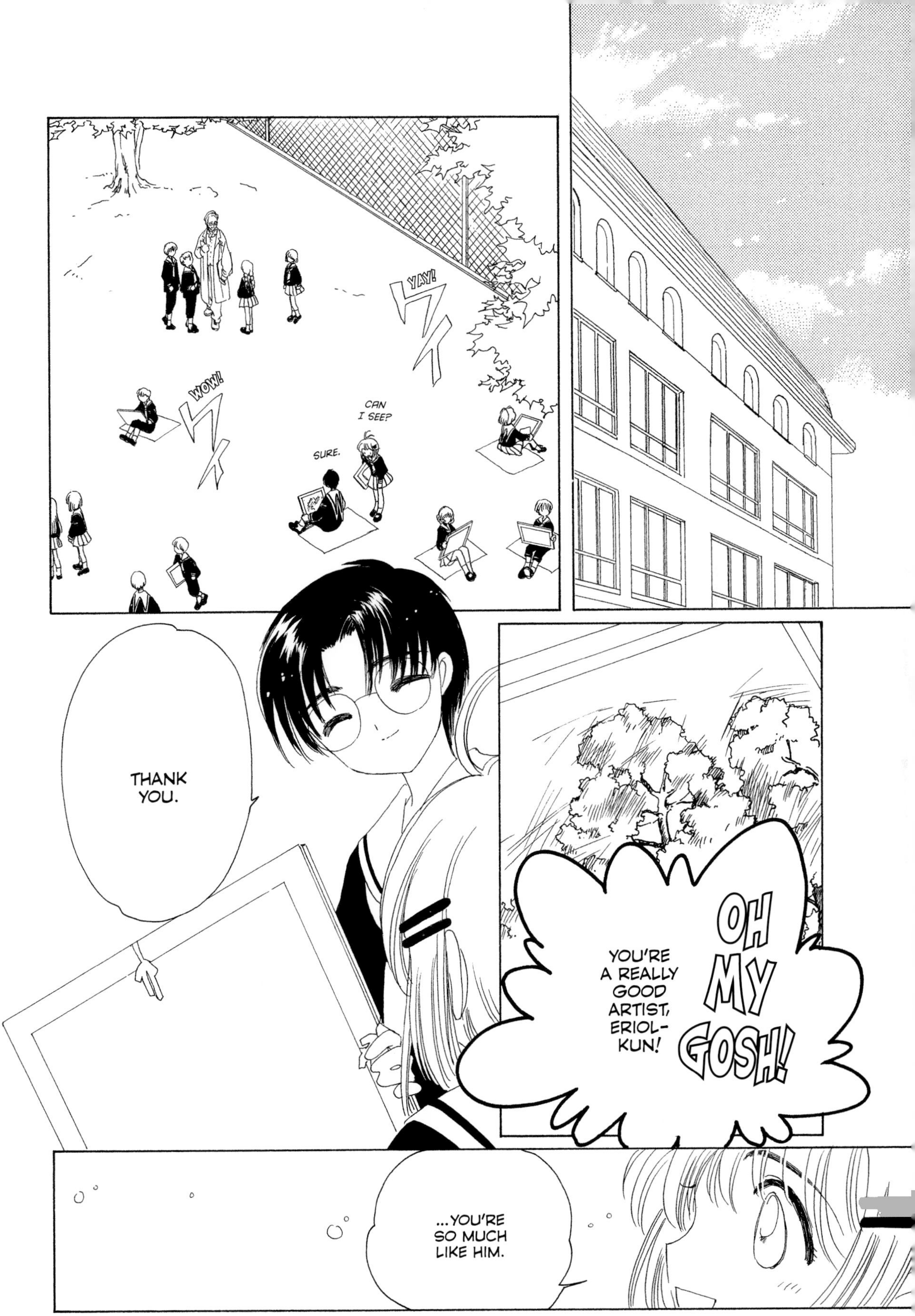
YAY!
WOW!
CAN I SEE?
SURE.
OH MY GOSH!
YOU'RE A REALLY GOOD ARTIST, ERIOL-KUN!
THANK YOU.
...YOU'RE SO MUCH LIKE HIM.

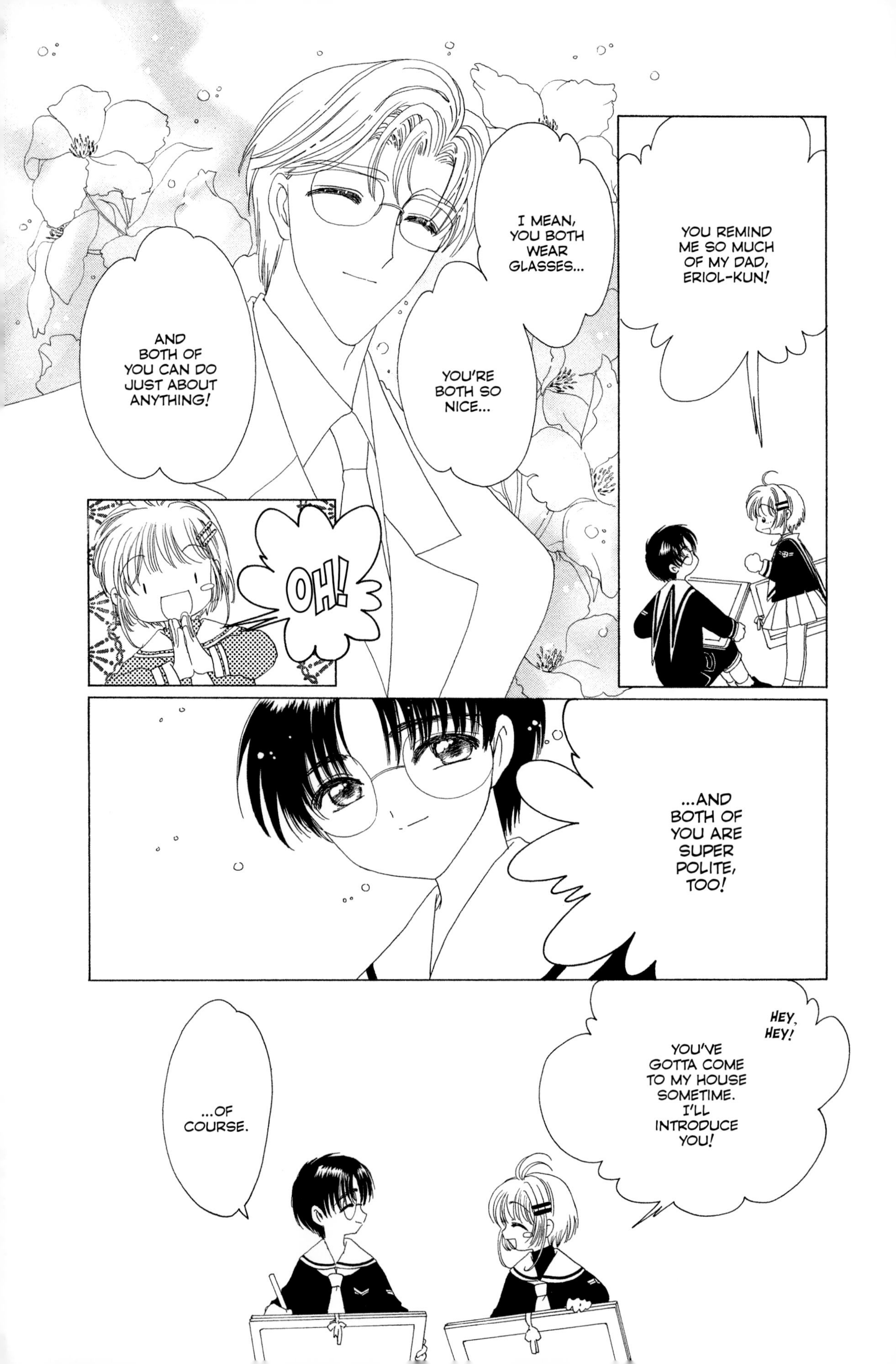
YOU REMIND ME SO MUCH OF MY DAD, ERIOL-KUN!
I MEAN, YOU BOTH WEAR GLASSES...
YOU'RE BOTH SO NICE...
AND BOTH OF YOU CAN DO JUST ABOUT ANYTHING!
OH!
...AND BOTH OF YOU ARE SUPER POLITE, TOO!
HEY, HEY!
YOU'VE GOTTA COME TO MY HOUSE SOMETIME. I'LL INTRODUCE YOU!
...OF COURSE.

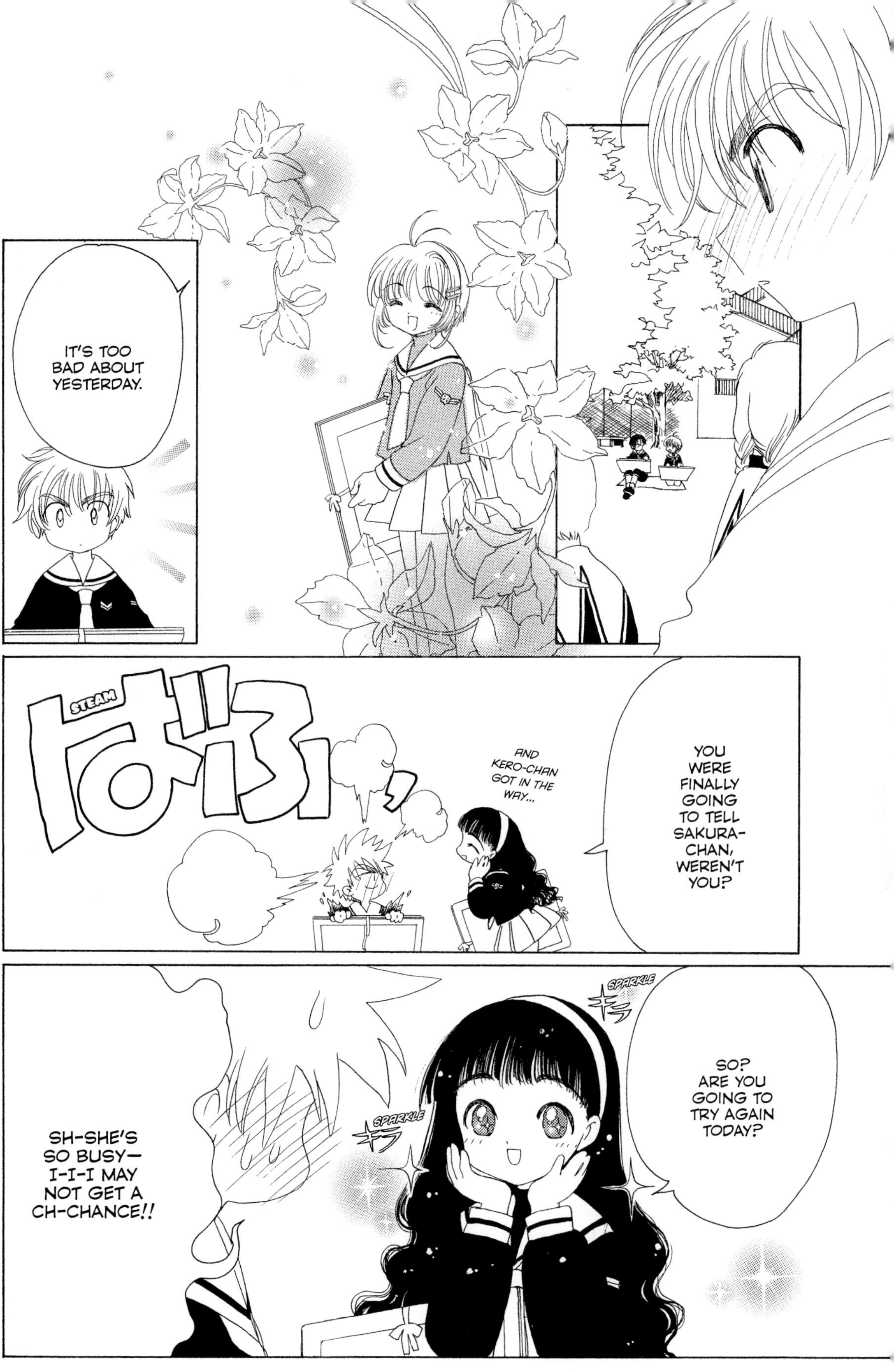
IT'S TOO BAD ABOUT YESTERDAY.
YOU WERE FINALLY GOING TO TELL SAKURA-CHAN, WEREN'T YOU?
AND KERO-CHAN GOT IN THE WAY...
STEAM
SPARKLE
SO? ARE YOU GOING TO TRY AGAIN TODAY?
SPARKLE
SH-SHE'S SO BUSY— I-I-I MAY NOT GET A CH-CHANCE!!

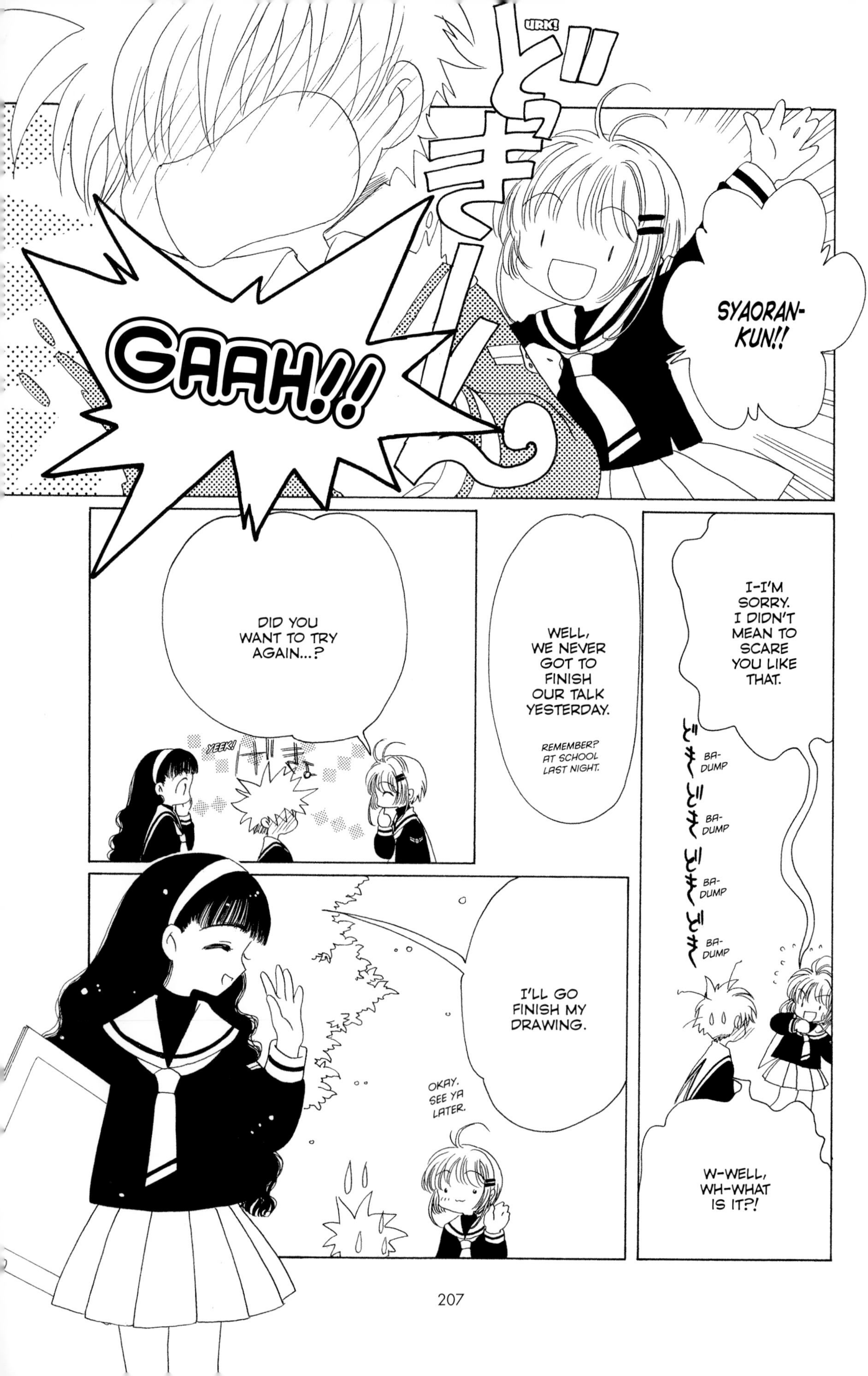
URK!
SYAORAN-KUN!!
GAAH!!
I-I'M SORRY. I DIDN'T MEAN TO SCARE YOU LIKE THAT.
BA-DUMP
BA-DUMP
BA-DUMP
BA-DUMP
W-WELL, WH-WHAT IS IT?!
WELL, WE NEVER GOT TO FINISH OUR TALK YESTERDAY.
REMEMBER? AT SCHOOL LAST NIGHT.
DID YOU WANT TO TRY AGAIN...?
YEEK!
I'LL GO FINISH MY DRAWING.
OKAY. SEE YA LATER.

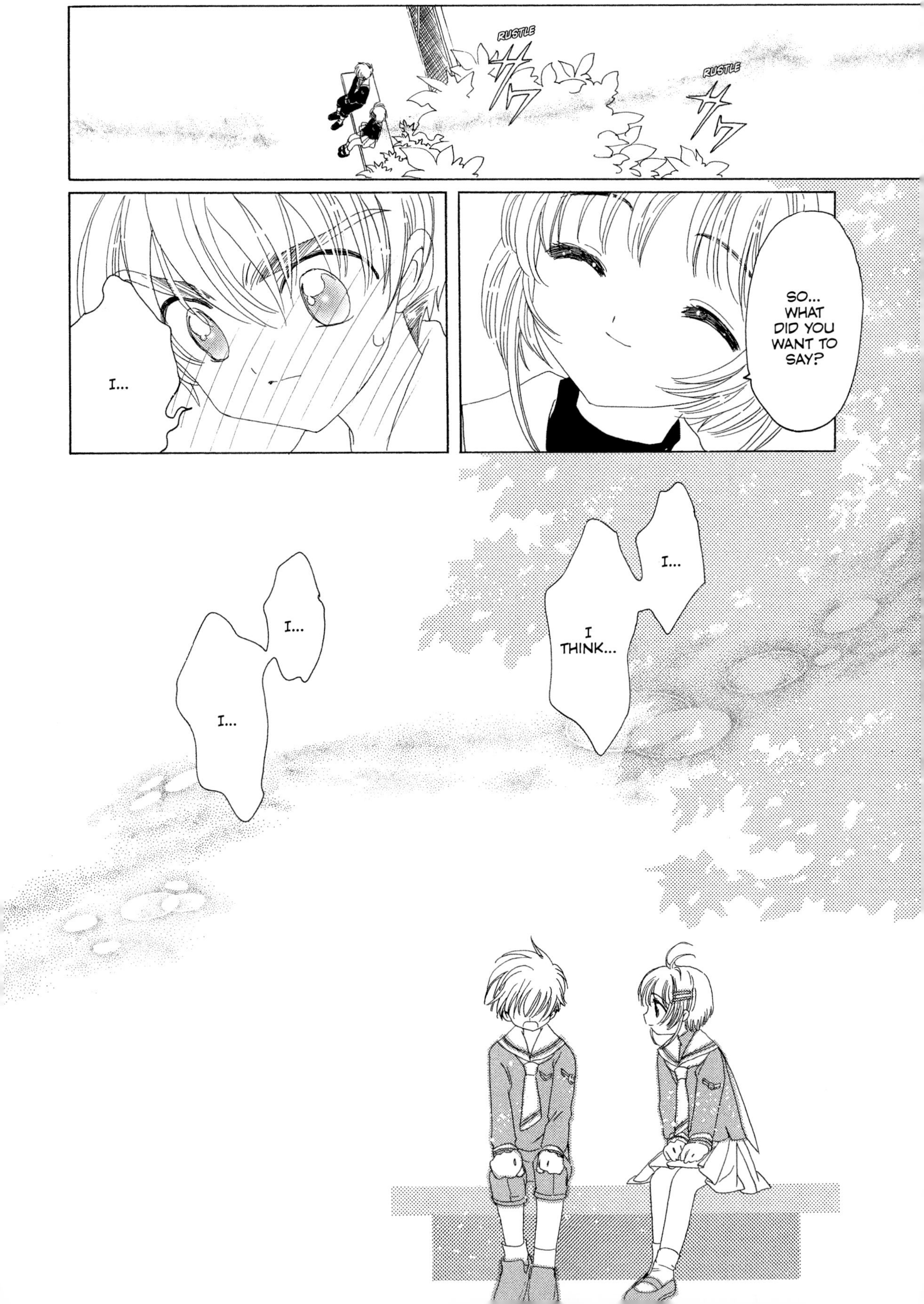
RUSTLE
サク
RUSTLE
サク
SO... WHAT DID YOU WANT TO SAY?
I...
I...
I THINK...
I...
I...

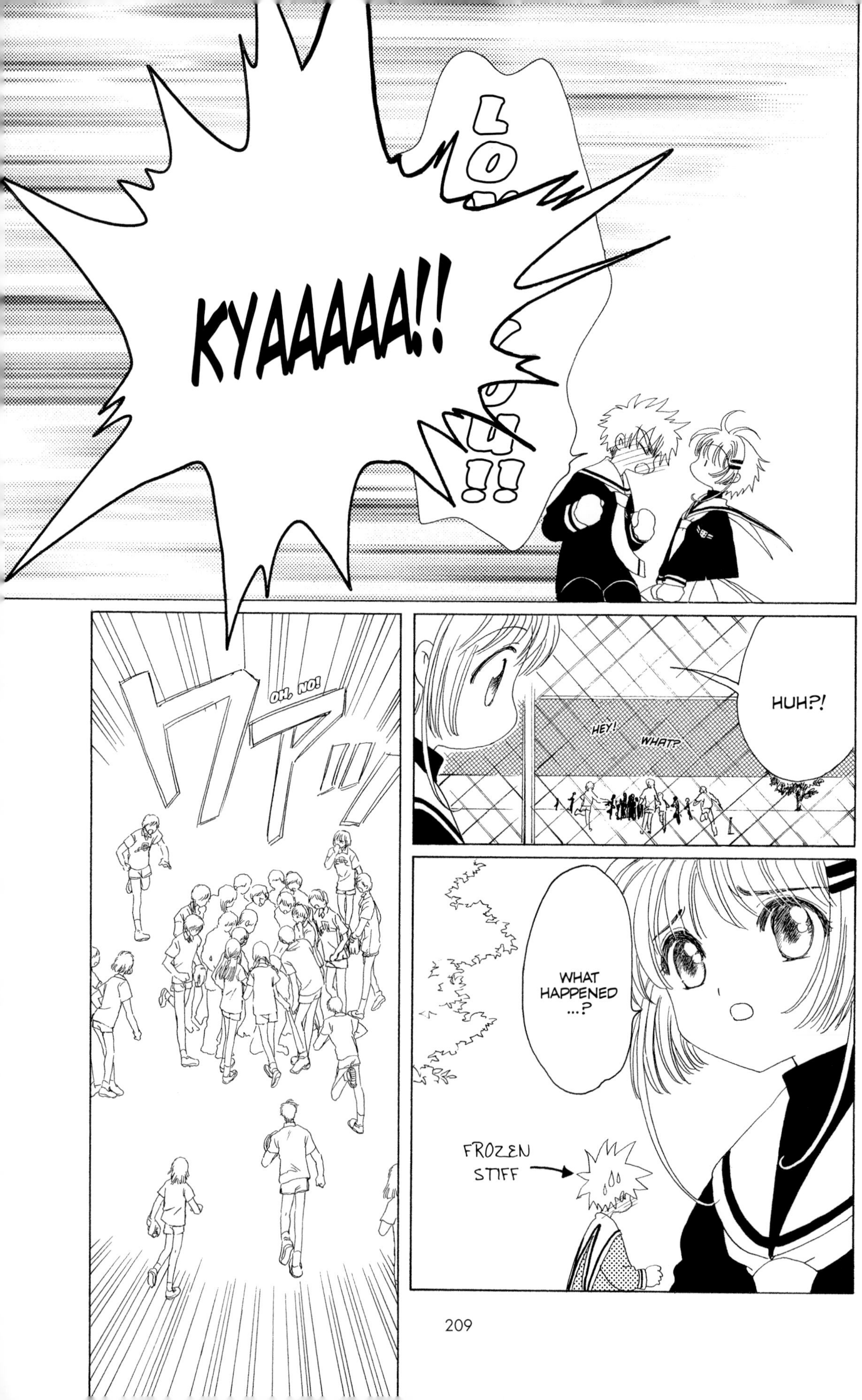
KYAAAAA!!
LO
U!!
HUH?!
HEY!
WHAT?
WHAT HAPPENED ...?
FROZEN STIFF
OH, NO!
ワァッ

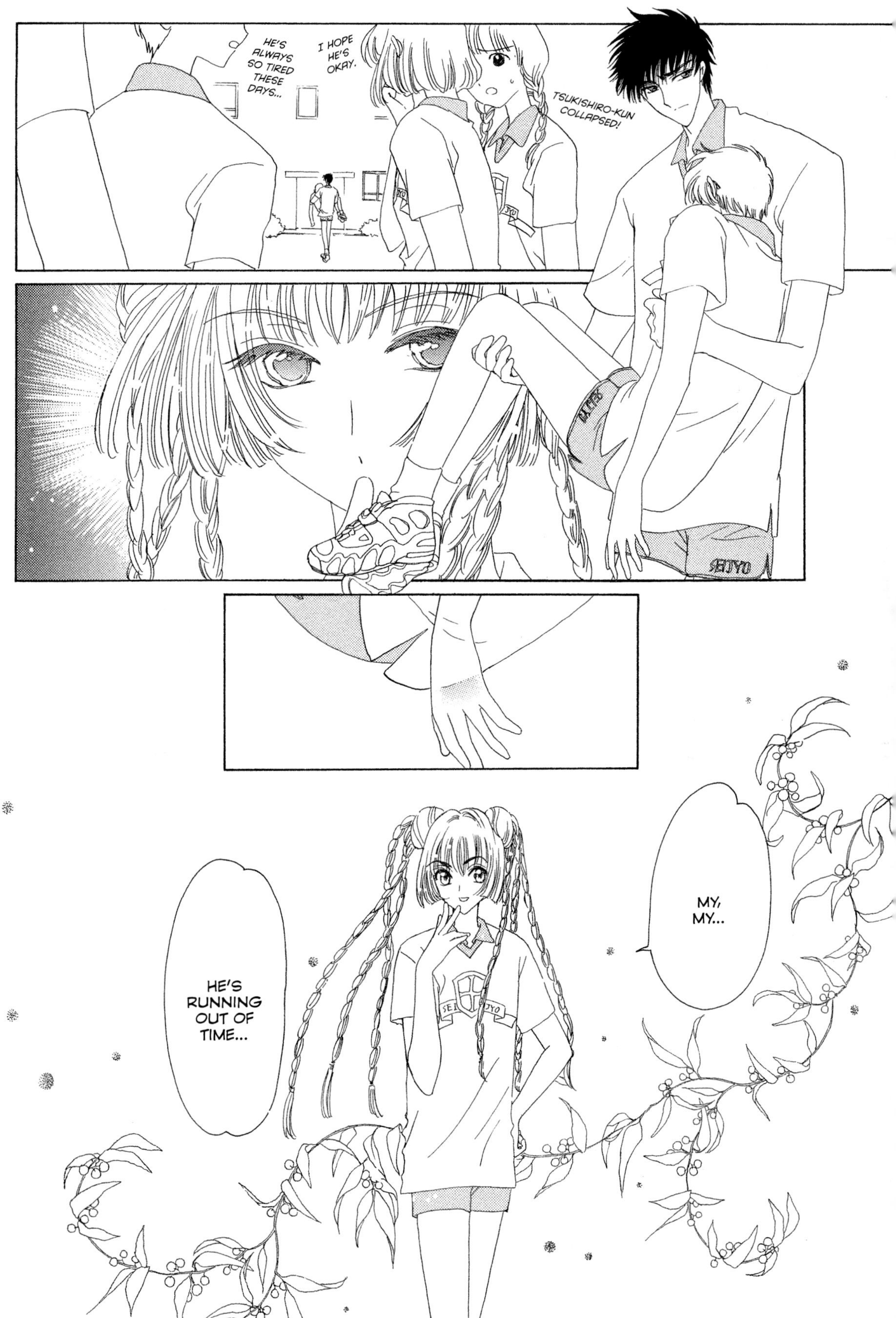
TSUKISHIRO-KUN COLLAPSED!
I HOPE HE'S OKAY.
HE'S ALWAYS SO TIRED THESE DAYS...
MY, MY...
HE'S RUNNING OUT OF TIME...

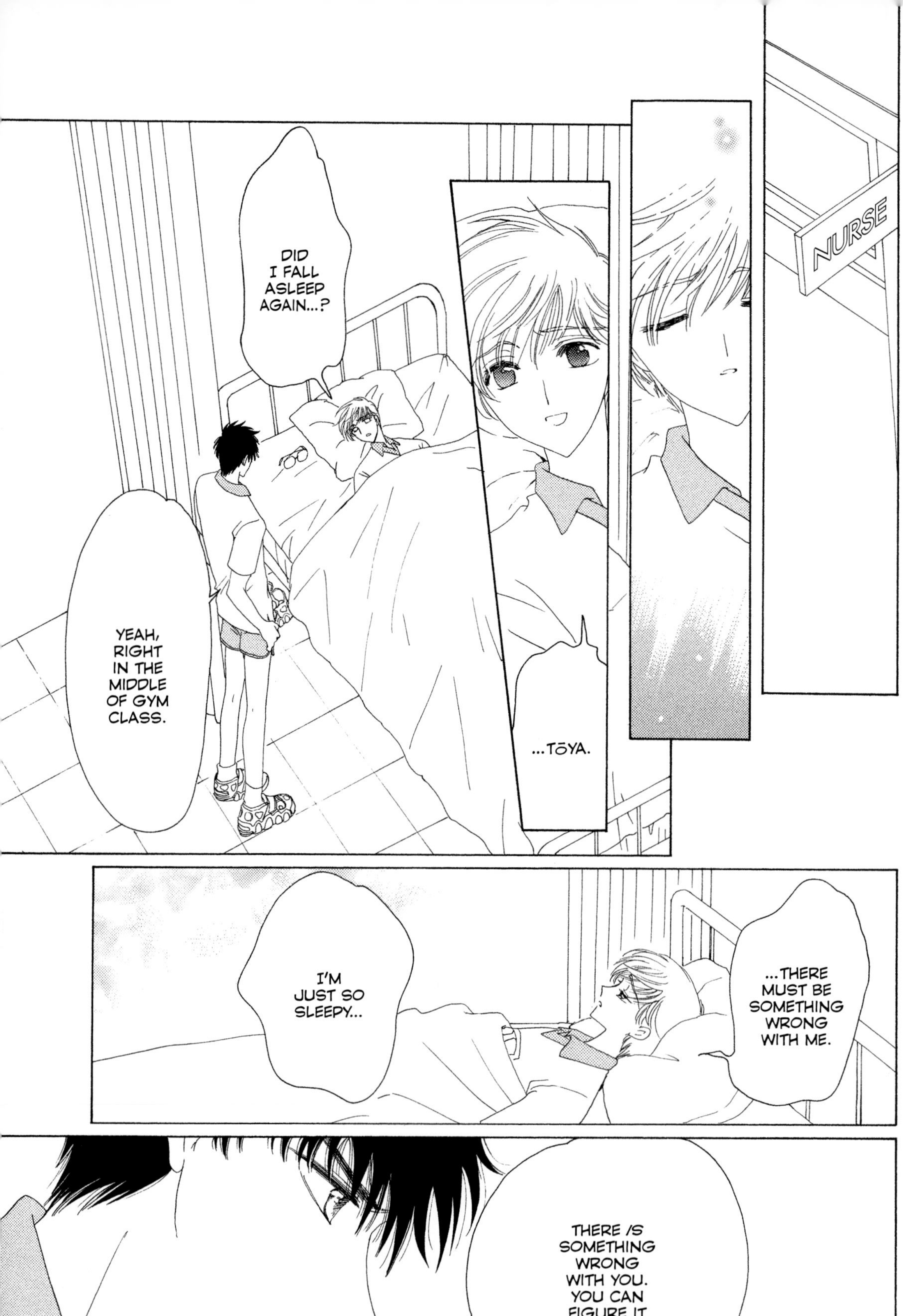
NURSE
...TŌYA.
DID I FALL ASLEEP AGAIN...?
YEAH, RIGHT IN THE MIDDLE OF GYM CLASS.
...THERE MUST BE SOMETHING WRONG WITH ME.
I'M JUST SO SLEEPY...
THERE IS SOMETHING WRONG WITH YOU. YOU CAN FIGURE IT OUT.

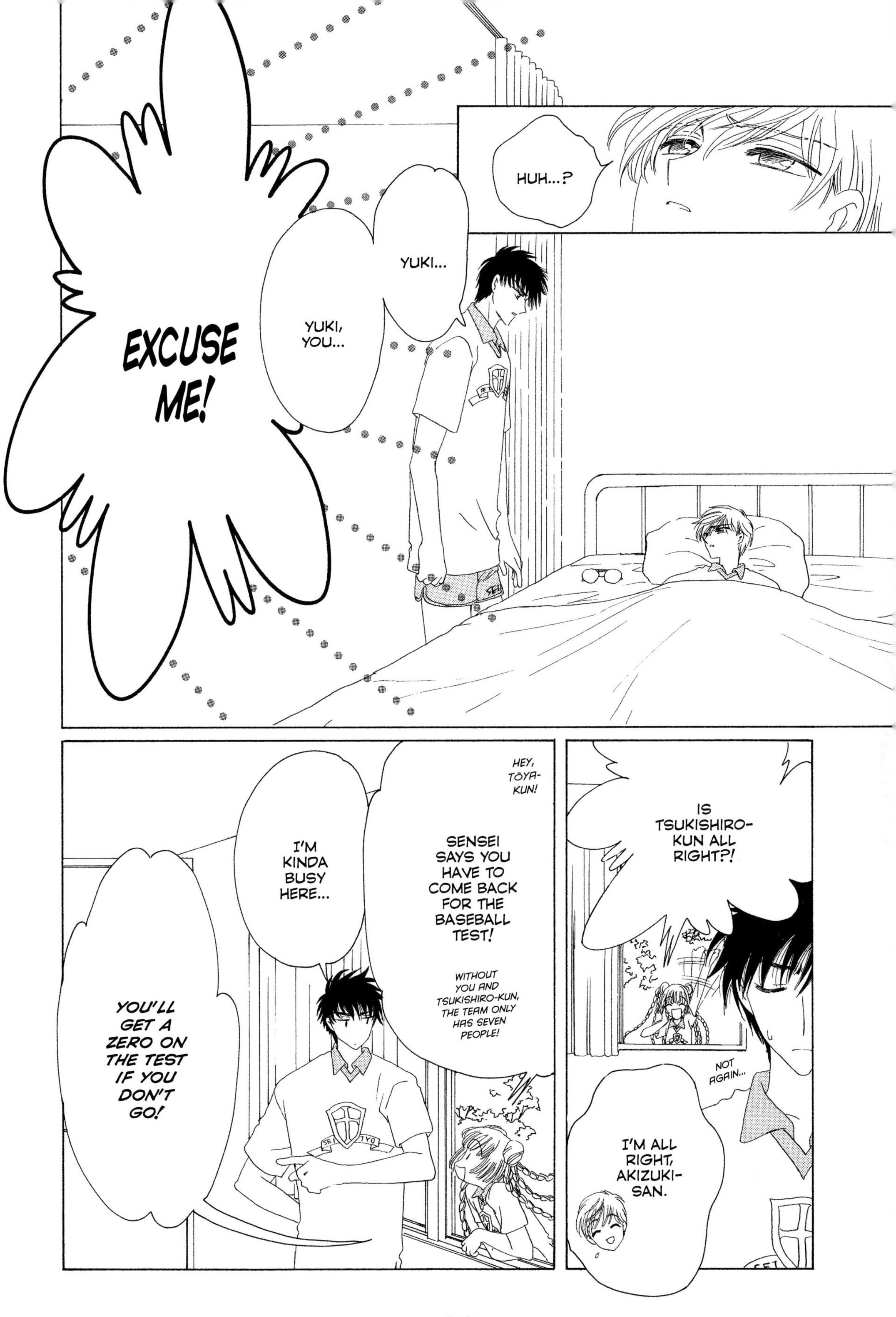
HUH...?
YUKI...
YUKI, YOU...
EXCUSE ME!
IS TSUKISHIRO-KUN ALL RIGHT?!
NOT AGAIN...
I'M ALL RIGHT, AKIZUKI-SAN.
HEY, TŌYA-KUN!
SENSEI SAYS YOU HAVE TO COME BACK FOR THE BASEBALL TEST!
WITHOUT YOU AND TSUKISHIRO-KUN, THE TEAM ONLY HAS SEVEN PEOPLE!
I'M KINDA BUSY HERE...
YOU'LL GET A ZERO ON THE TEST IF YOU DON'T GO!

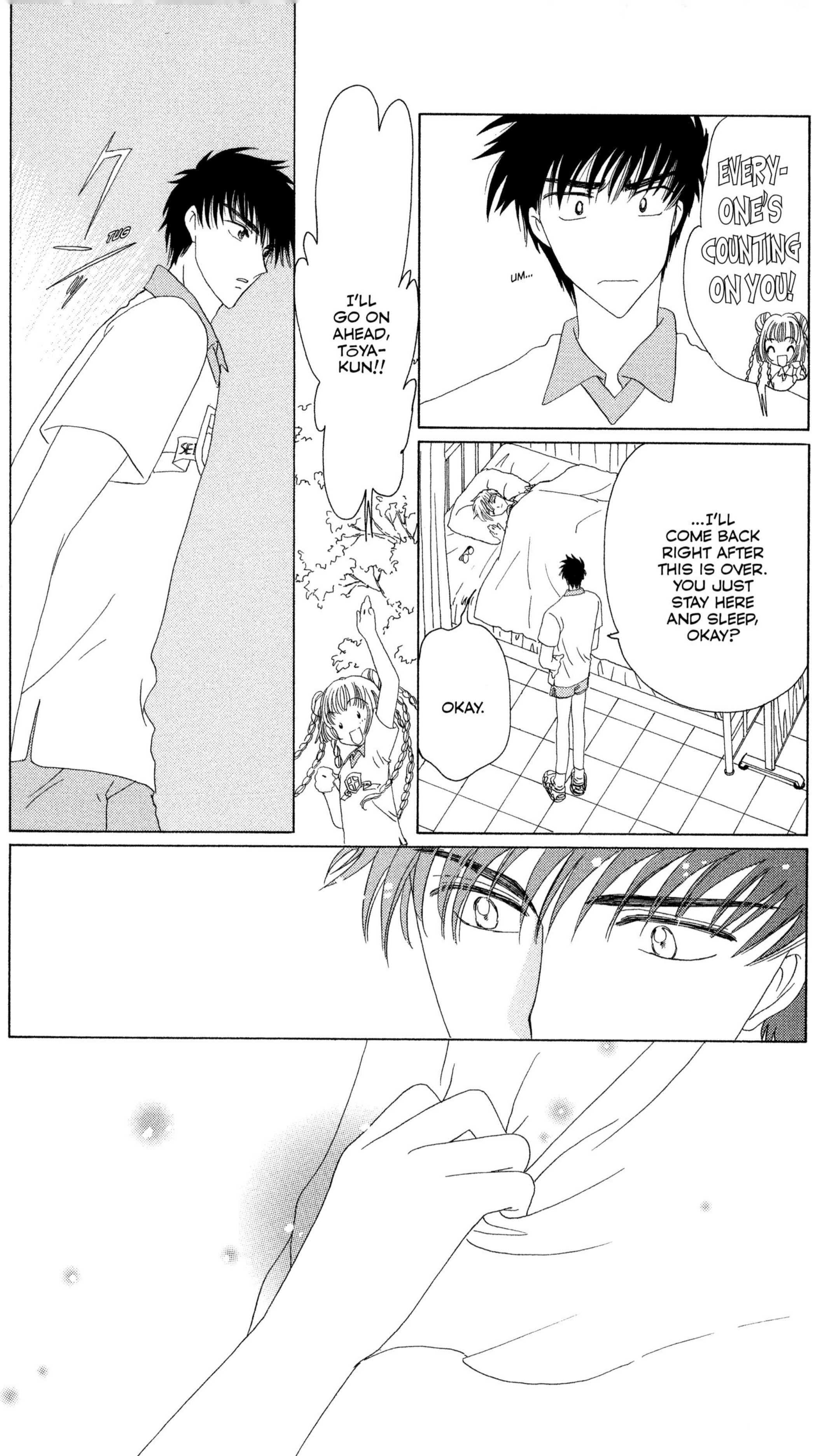
EVERY-ONE'S COUNTING ON YOU!
UM...
...I'LL COME BACK RIGHT AFTER THIS IS OVER. YOU JUST STAY HERE AND SLEEP, OKAY?
OKAY.
I'LL GO ON AHEAD, TŌYA-KUN!!
TUG

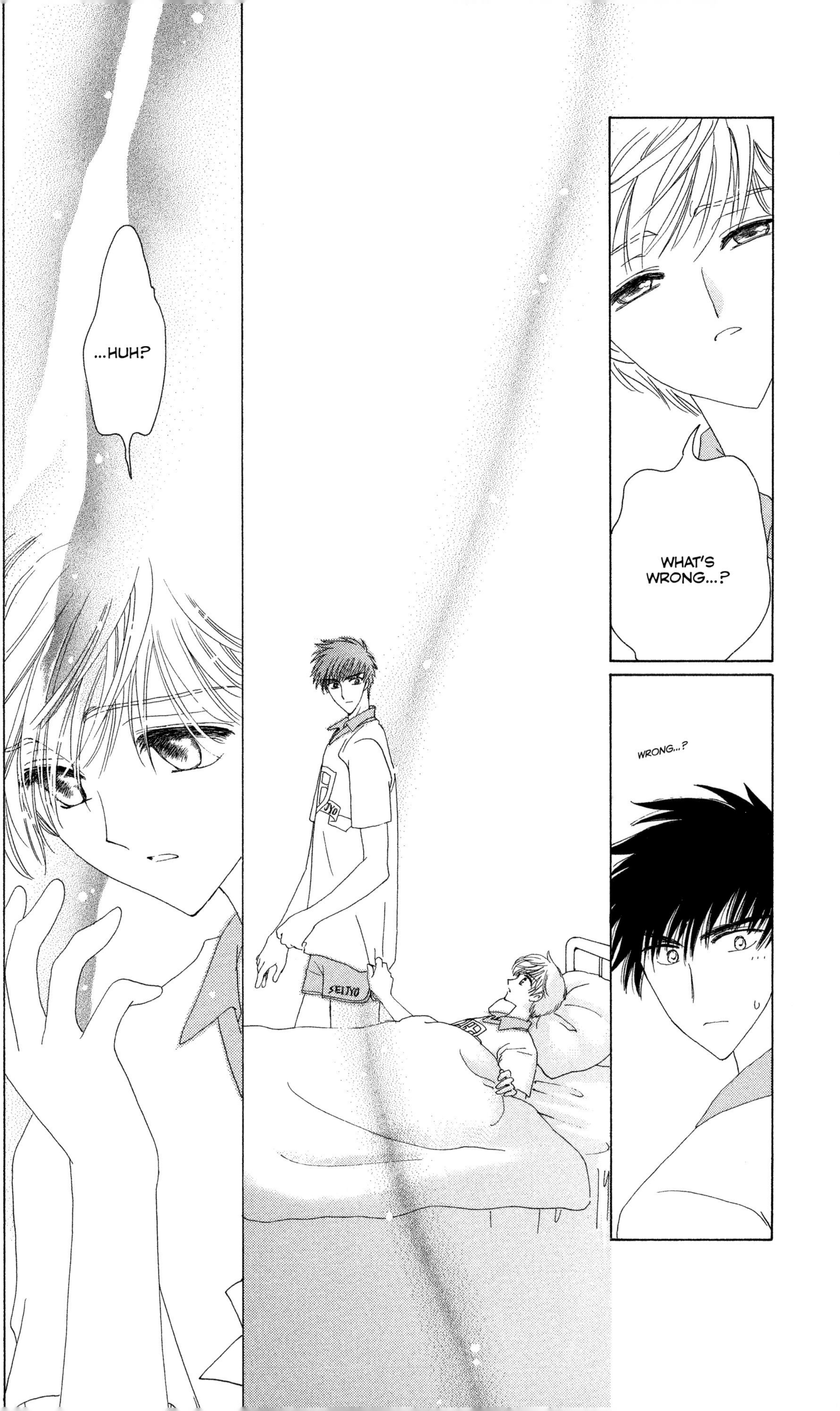
WHAT'S WRONG...?
WRONG...?
...HUH?

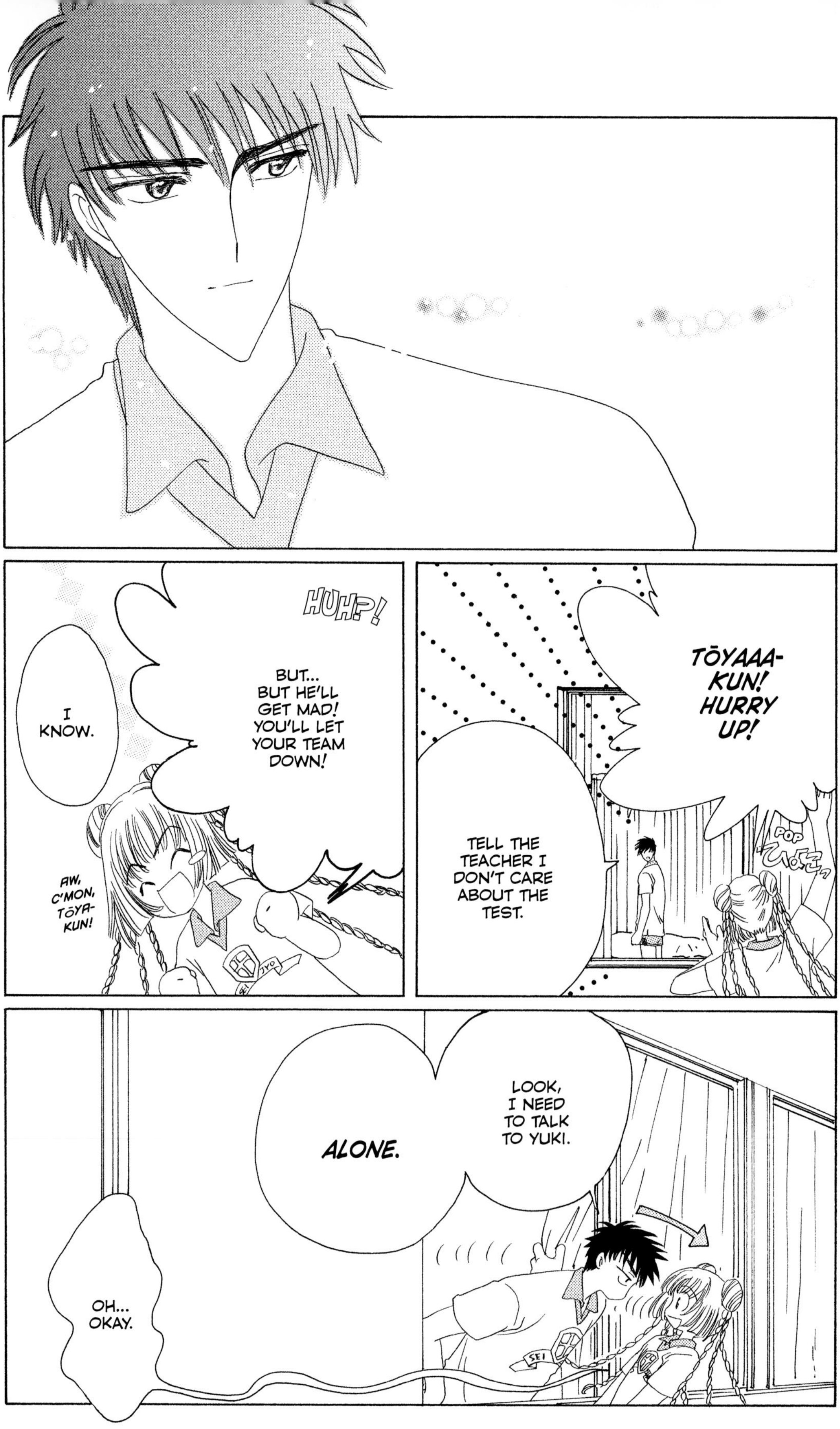

TŌYAAA-KUN! HURRY UP!
POP
TELL THE TEACHER I DON'T CARE ABOUT THE TEST.
HUH?!
BUT... BUT HE'LL GET MAD! YOU'LL LET YOUR TEAM DOWN!
I KNOW.
AW, C'MON, TŌYA-KUN!
LOOK, I NEED TO TALK TO YUKI.
ALONE.
OH... OKAY.

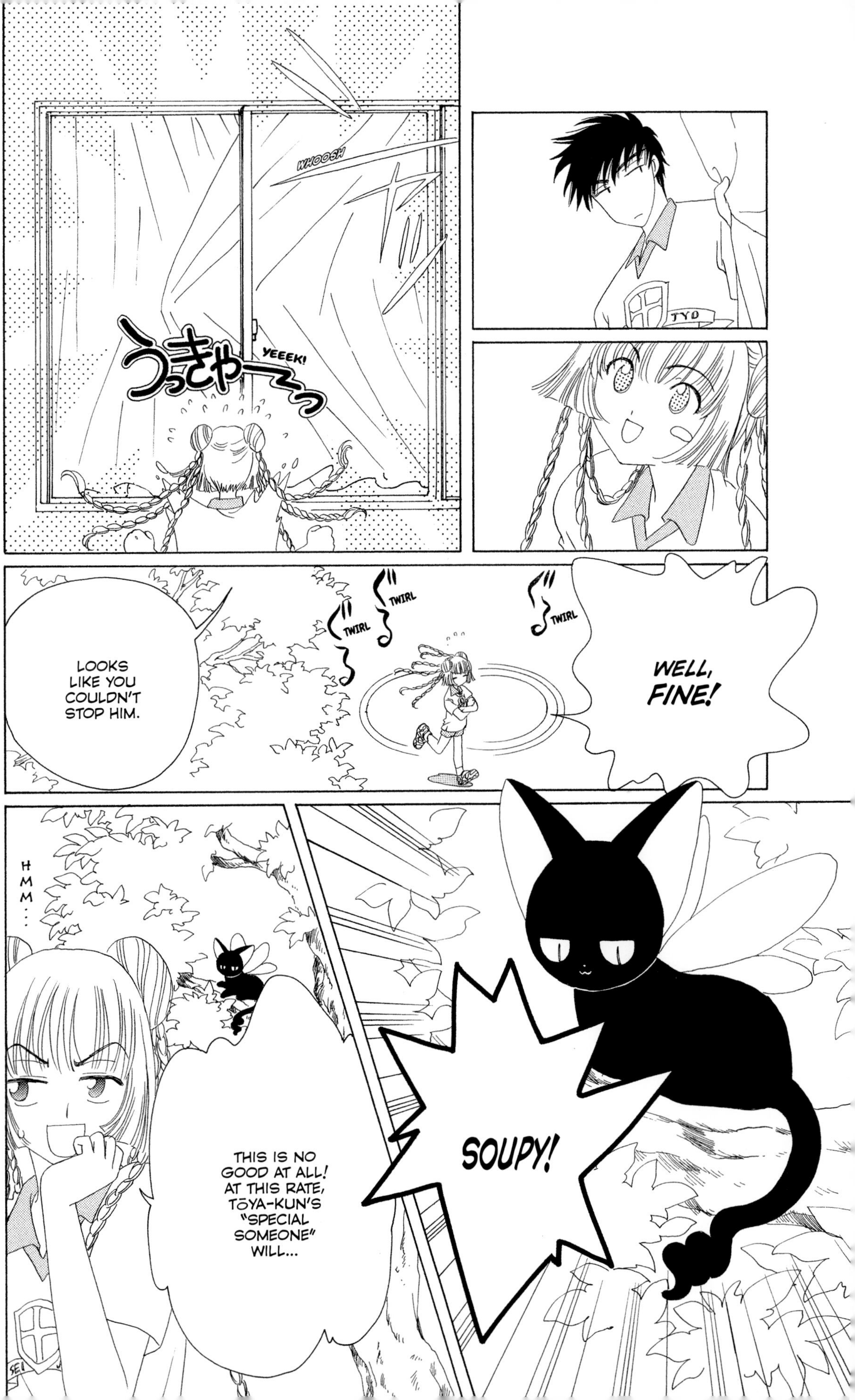
WHOOSH
うっきゃーっっ
YEEEK!
WELL, FINE!
TWIRL
TWIRL
TWIRL
LOOKS LIKE YOU COULDN'T STOP HIM.
SOUPY!
THIS IS NO GOOD AT ALL! AT THIS RATE, TŌYA-KUN'S "SPECIAL SOMEONE" WILL...
HMM...

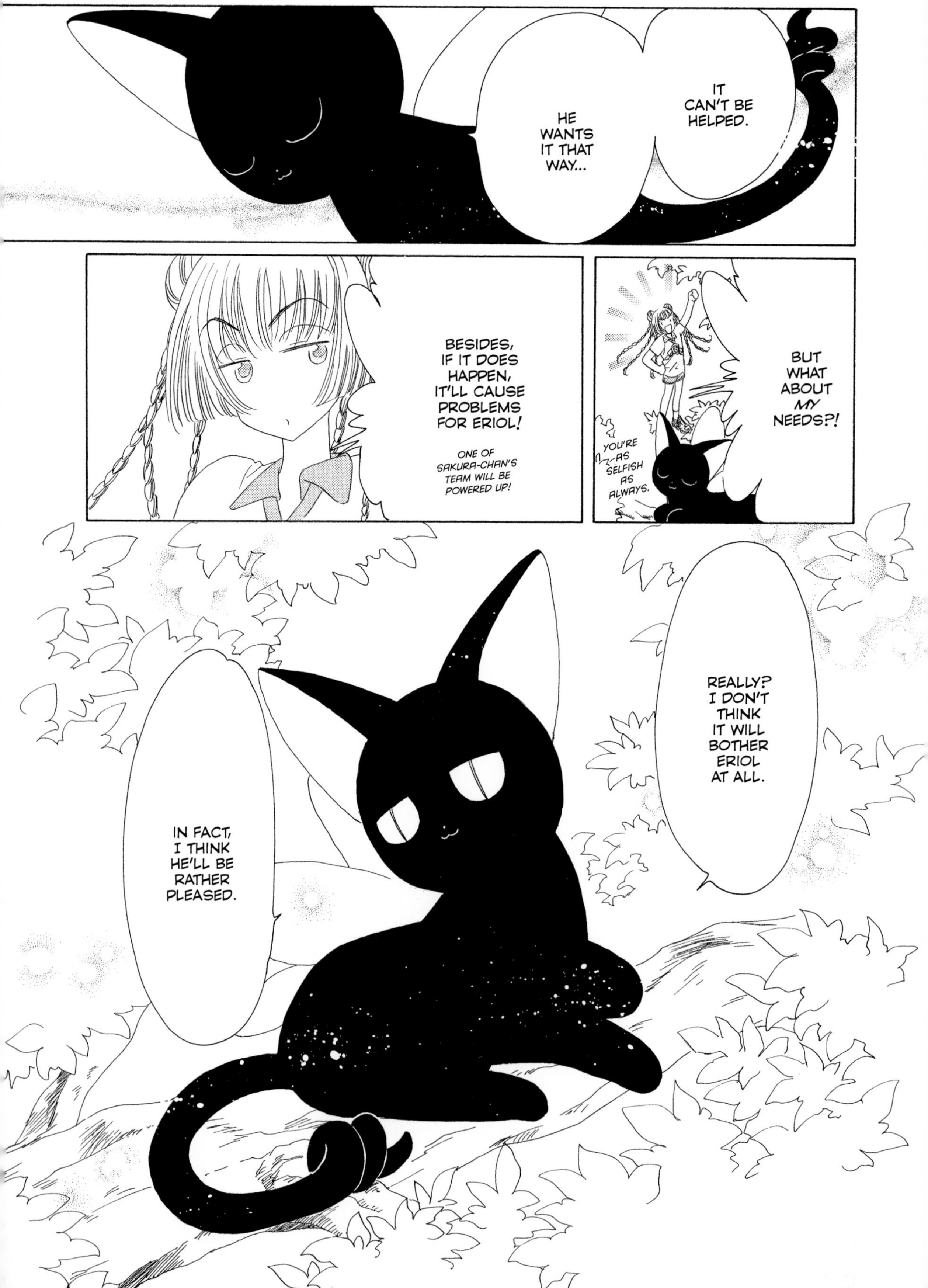
IT CAN'T BE HELPED.
HE WANTS IT THAT WAY...
BUT WHAT ABOUT *MY* NEEDS?!
YOU'RE AS SELFISH AS ALWAYS.
BESIDES, IF IT DOES HAPPEN, IT'LL CAUSE PROBLEMS FOR ERIOL!
ONE OF SAKURA-CHAN'S TEAM WILL BE POWERED UP!
REALLY? I DON'T THINK IT WILL BOTHER ERIOL AT ALL.
IN FACT, I THINK HE'LL BE RATHER PLEASED.

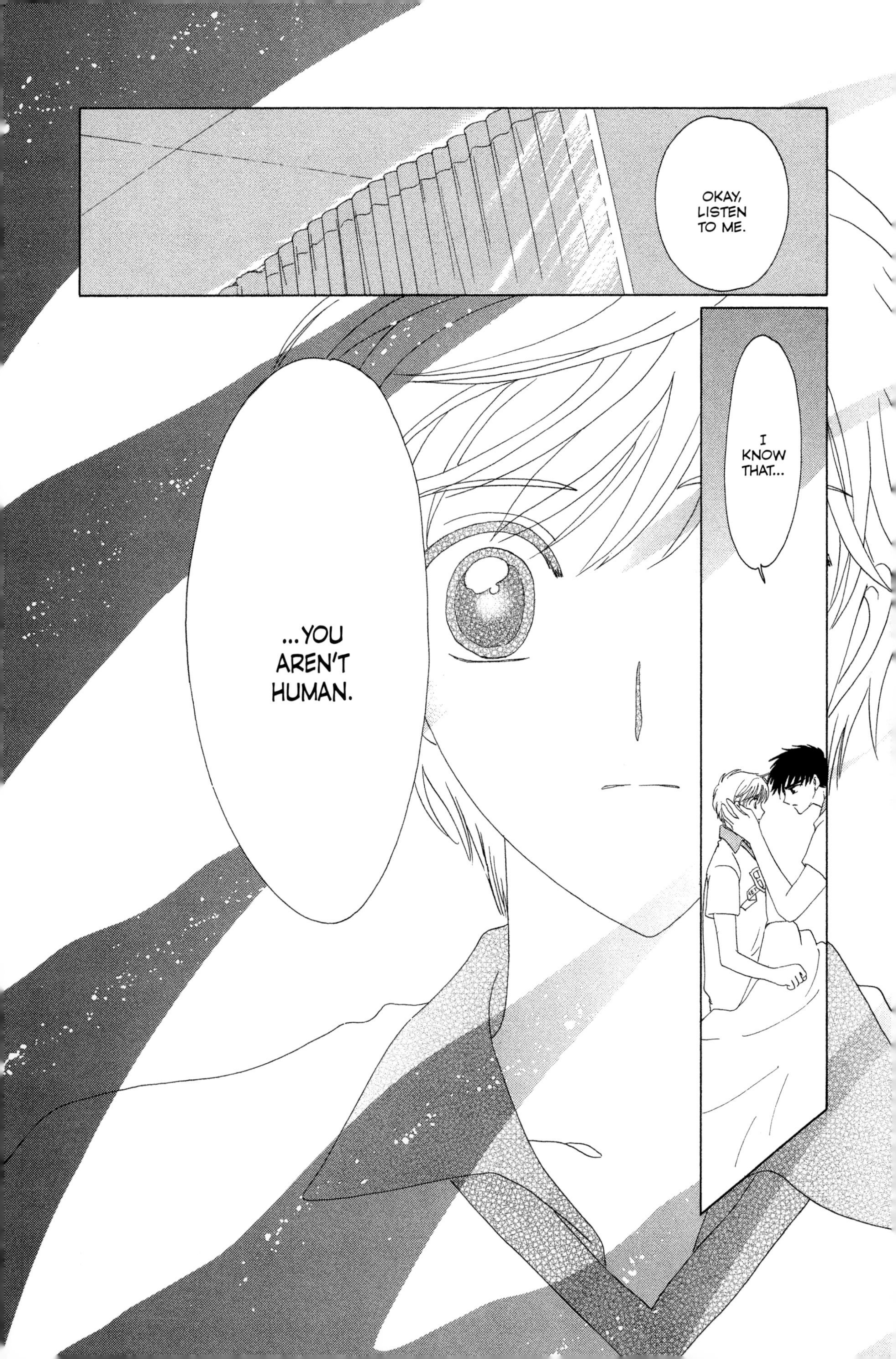
OKAY, LISTEN TO ME.
I KNOW THAT...
...YOU AREN'T HUMAN.

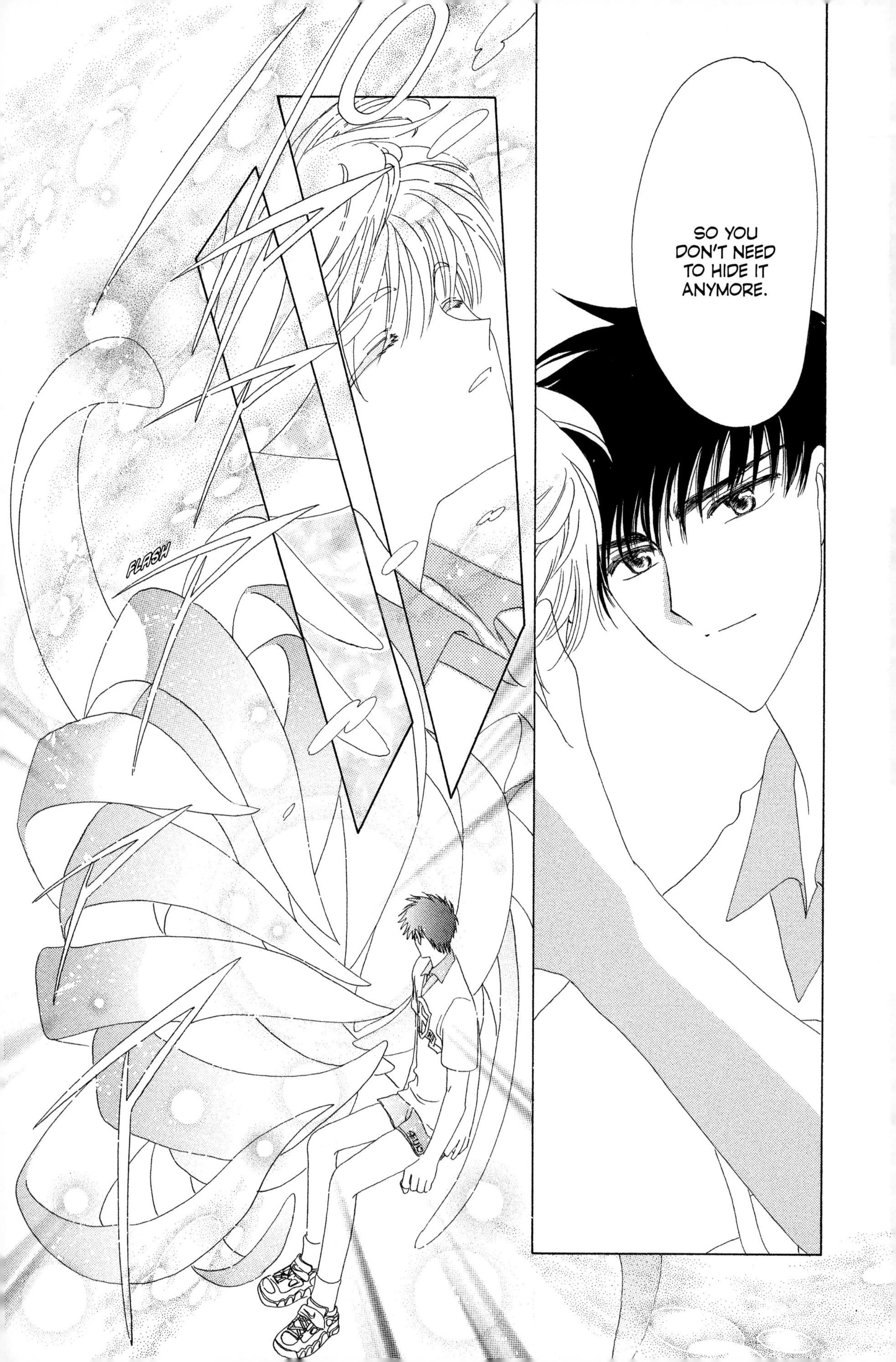
SO YOU DON'T NEED TO HIDE IT ANYMORE.
FLASH

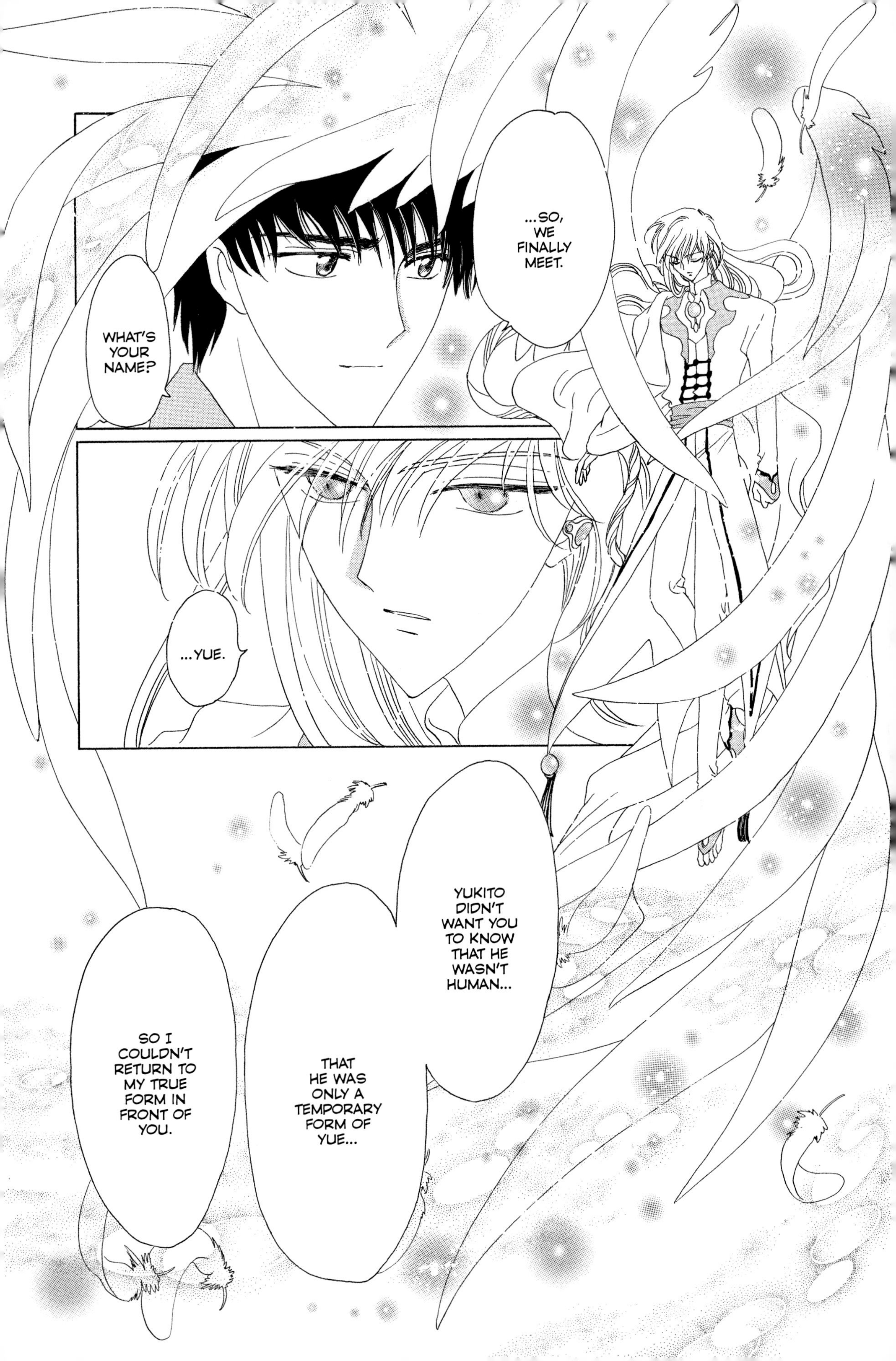
...SO, WE FINALLY MEET.
WHAT'S YOUR NAME?
...YUE.
YUKITO DIDN'T WANT YOU TO KNOW THAT HE WASN'T HUMAN...
THAT HE WAS ONLY A TEMPORARY FORM OF YUE...
SO I COULDN'T RETURN TO MY TRUE FORM IN FRONT OF YOU.

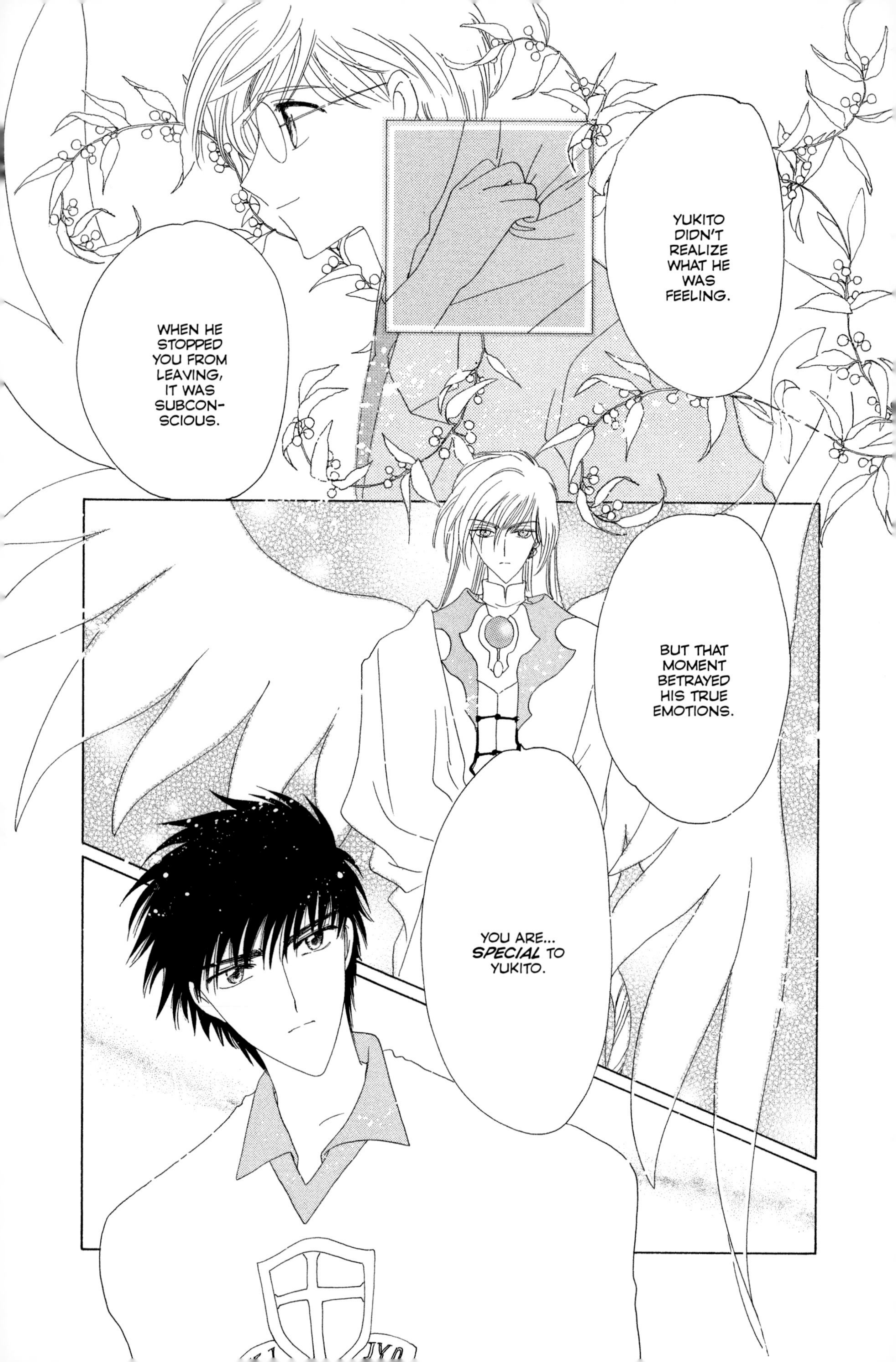
YUKITO DIDN'T REALIZE WHAT HE WAS FEELING.
WHEN HE STOPPED YOU FROM LEAVING, IT WAS SUBCON- SCIOUS.
BUT THAT MOMENT BETRAYED HIS TRUE EMOTIONS.
YOU ARE... *SPECIAL* TO YUKITO.

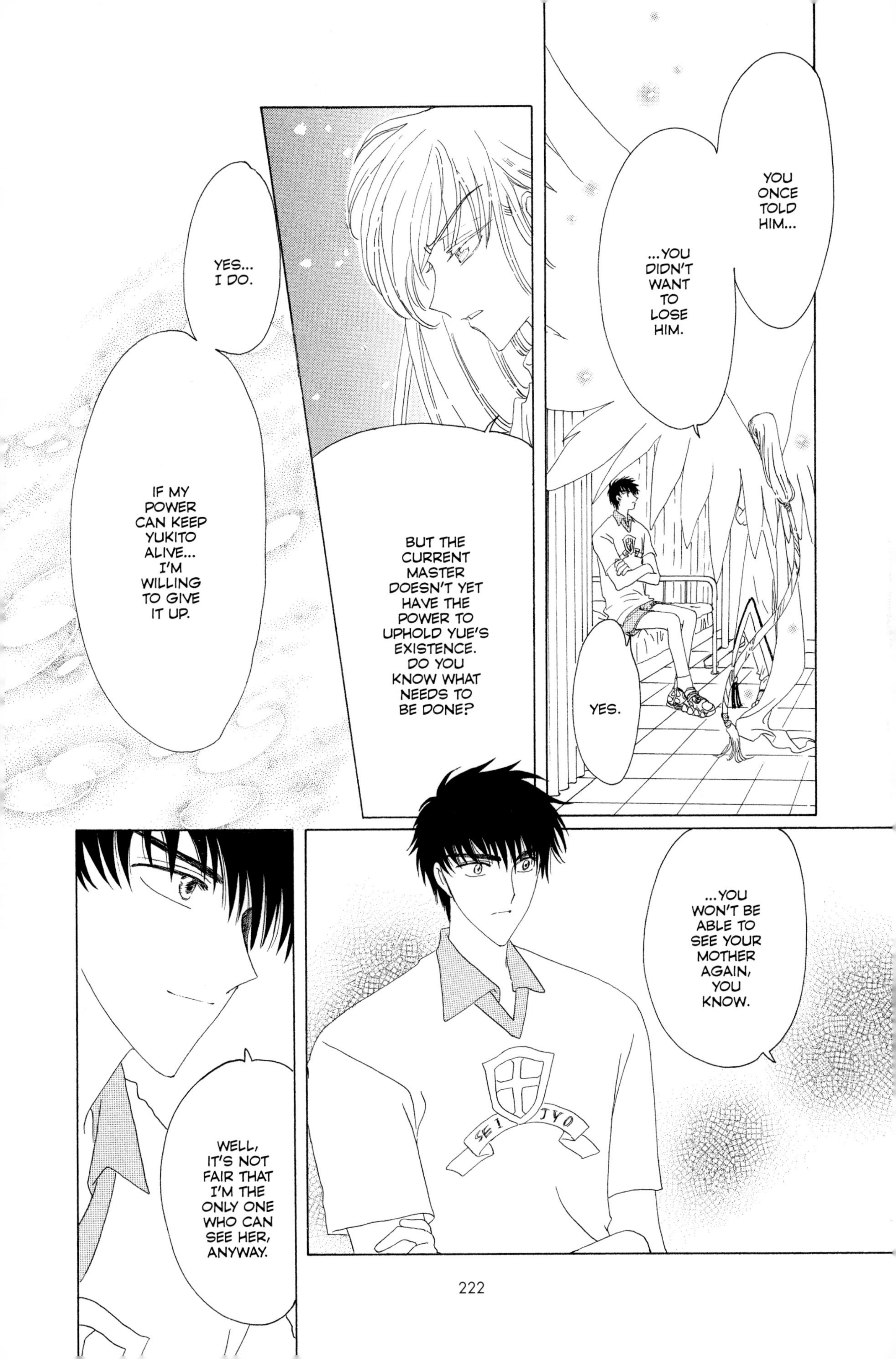
YOU ONCE TOLD HIM...
...YOU DIDN'T WANT TO LOSE HIM.
YES.
BUT THE CURRENT MASTER DOESN'T YET HAVE THE POWER TO UPHOLD YUE'S EXISTENCE. DO YOU KNOW WHAT NEEDS TO BE DONE?
YES... I DO.
IF MY POWER CAN KEEP YUKITO ALIVE... I'M WILLING TO GIVE IT UP.
...YOU WON'T BE ABLE TO SEE YOUR MOTHER AGAIN, YOU KNOW.
WELL, IT'S NOT FAIR THAT I'M THE ONLY ONE WHO CAN SEE HER, ANYWAY.

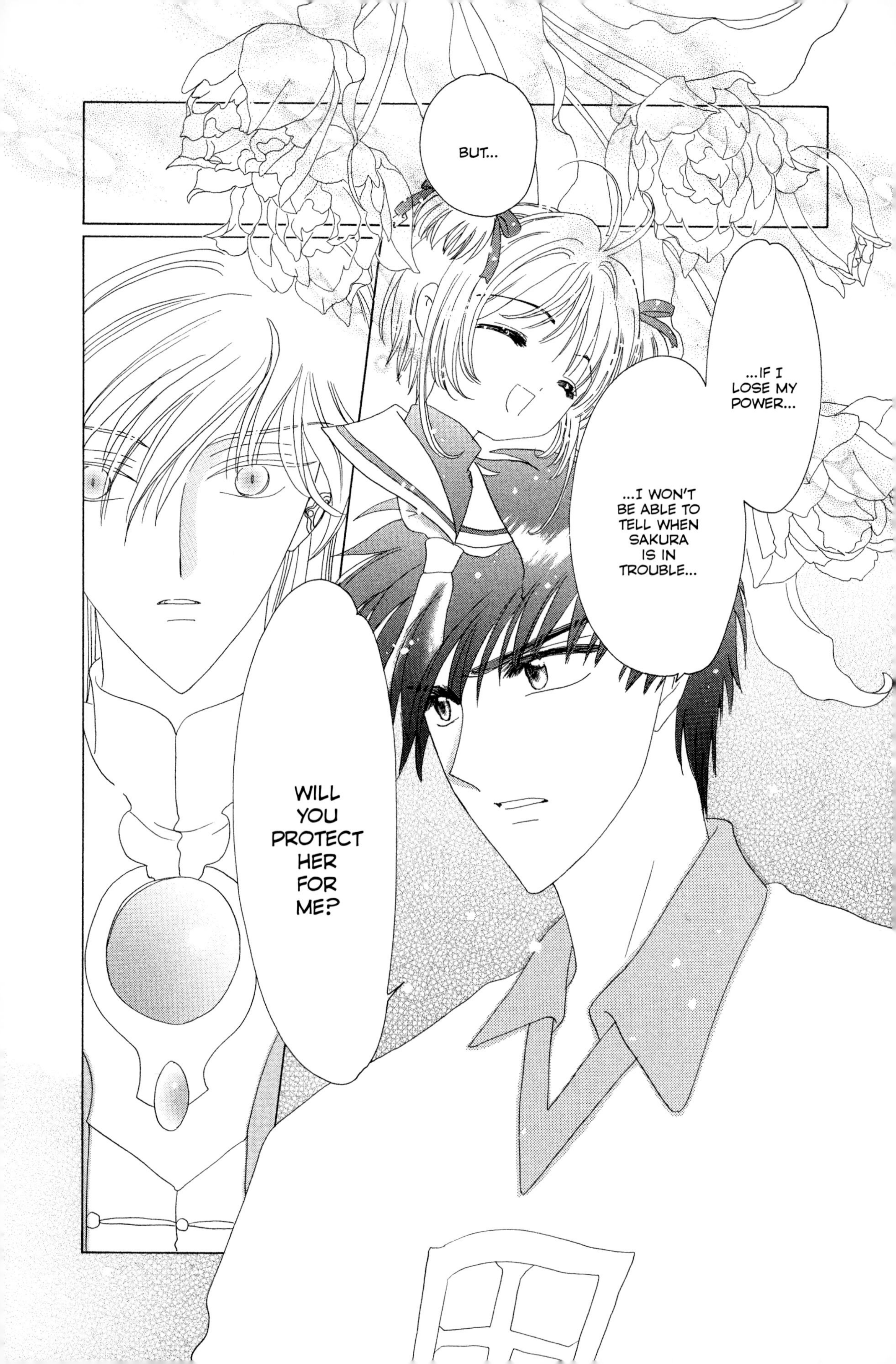
BUT...
...IF I LOSE MY POWER...
...I WON'T BE ABLE TO TELL WHEN SAKURA IS IN TROUBLE...
WILL YOU PROTECT HER FOR ME?

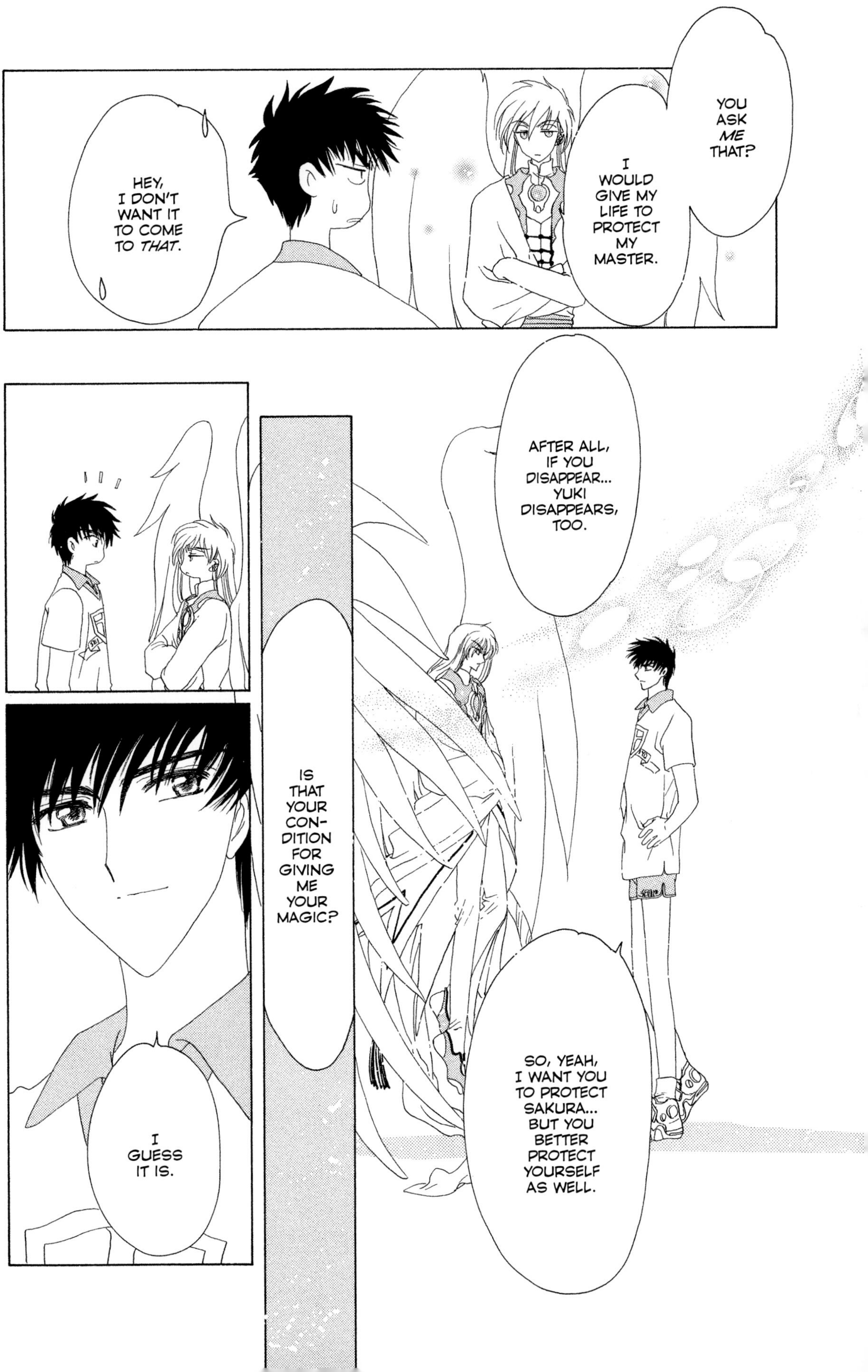
YOU ASK *ME* THAT?
I WOULD GIVE MY LIFE TO PROTECT MY MASTER.
HEY, I DON'T WANT IT TO COME TO *THAT*.
AFTER ALL, IF YOU DISAPPEAR... YUKI DISAPPEARS, TOO.
SO, YEAH, I WANT YOU TO PROTECT SAKURA... BUT YOU BETTER PROTECT YOURSELF AS WELL.
IS THAT YOUR CONDITION FOR GIVING ME YOUR MAGIC?
I GUESS IT IS.

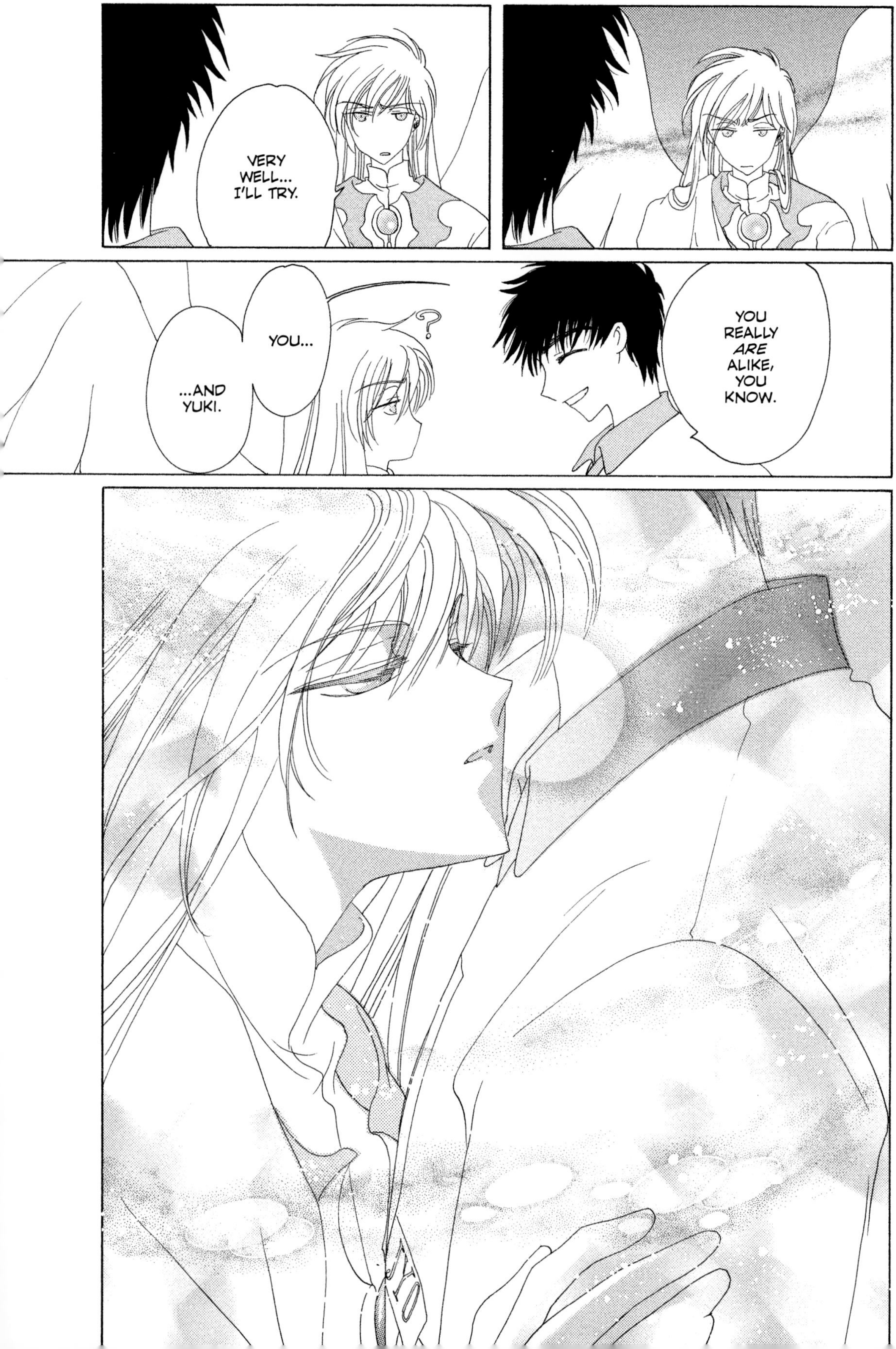
VERY WELL... I'LL TRY.
YOU REALLY *ARE* ALIKE, YOU KNOW.
YOU...
...AND YUKI.

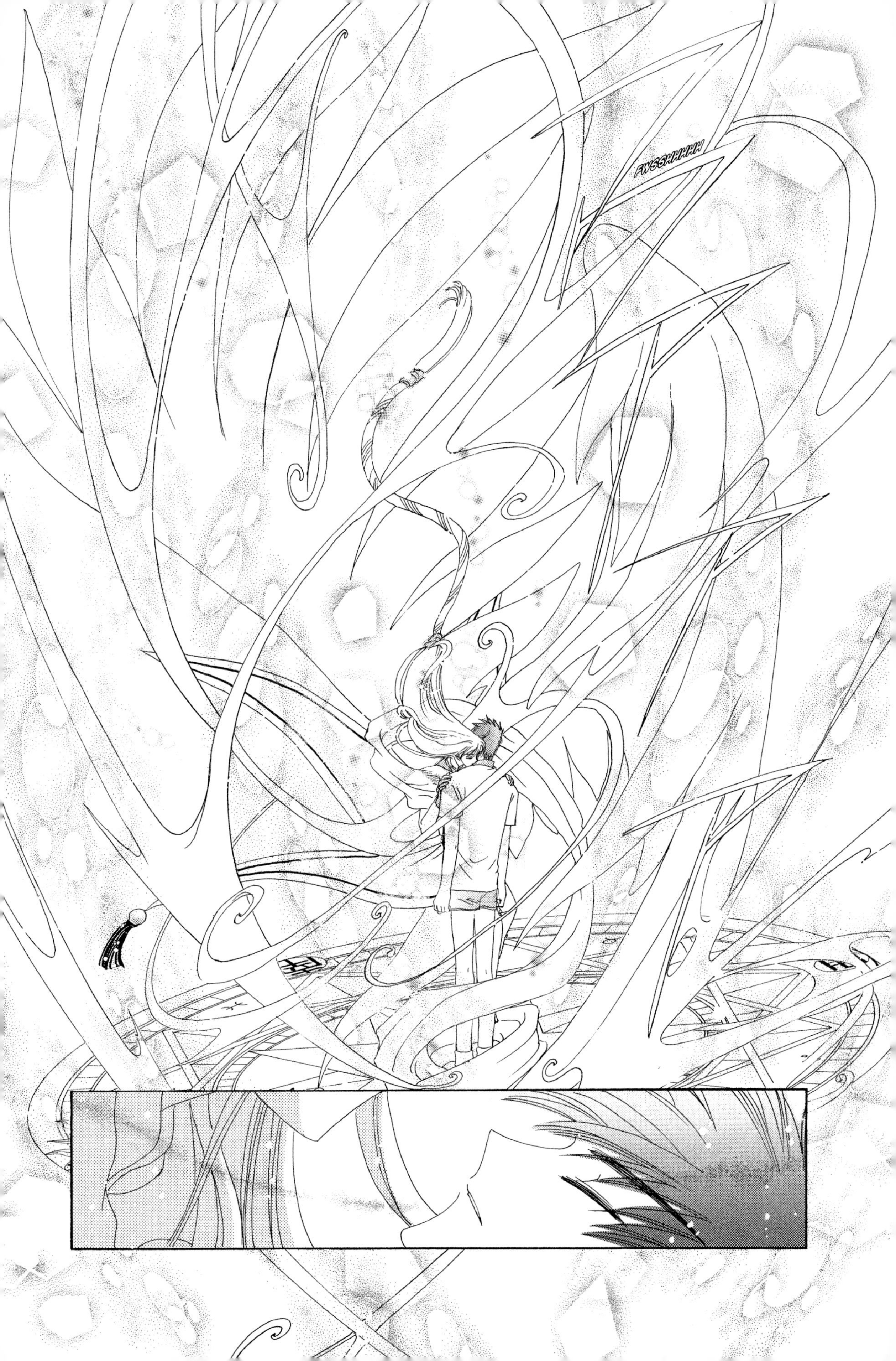
FWSSHHHHH

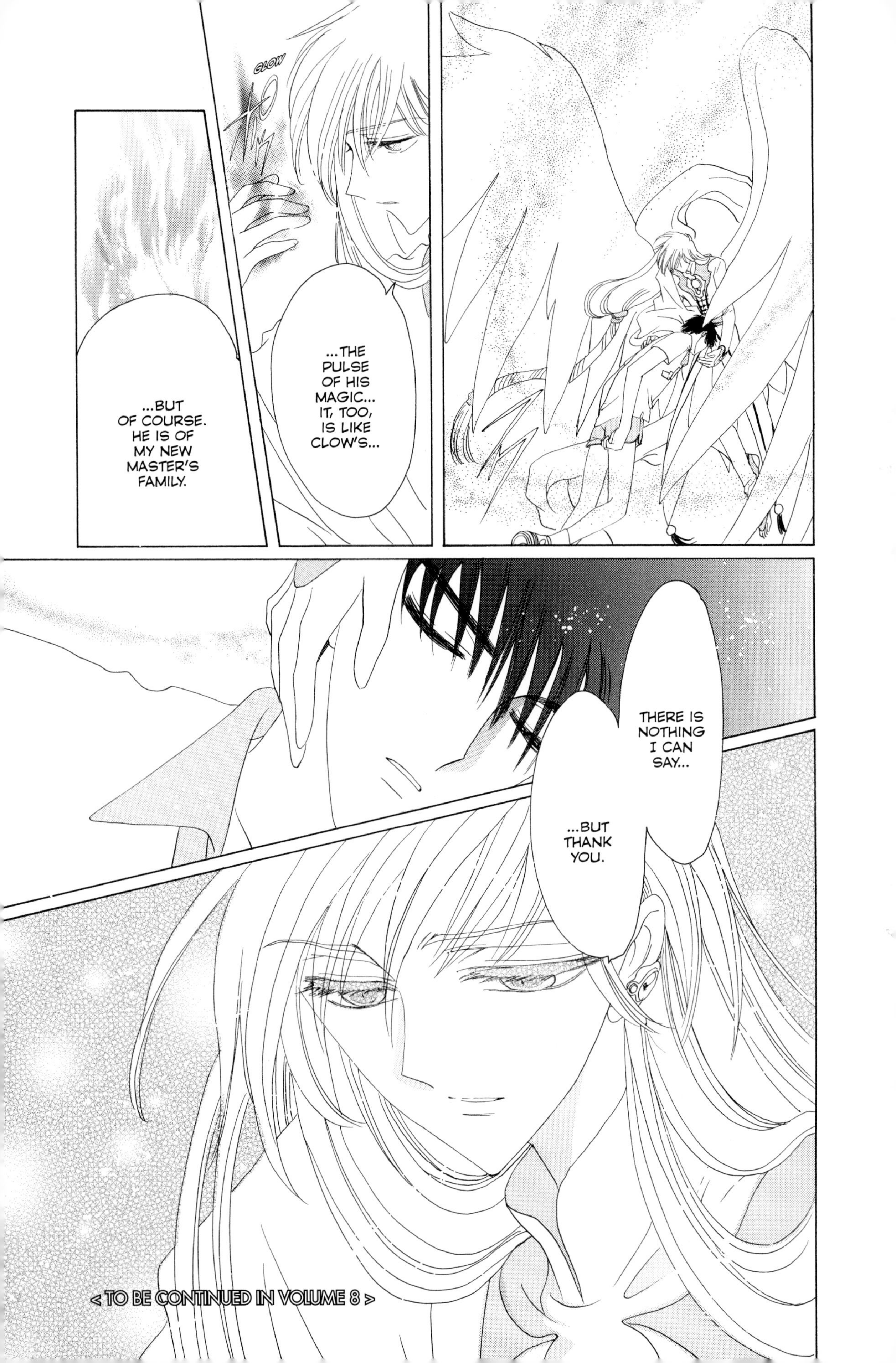
GLOW
...THE PULSE OF HIS MAGIC... IT, TOO, IS LIKE CLOW'S...
...BUT OF COURSE. HE IS OF MY NEW MASTER'S FAMILY.
THERE IS NOTHING I CAN SAY...
...BUT THANK YOU.
< TO BE CONTINUED IN VOLUME 8 >

Translation Notes

Japanese is a tricky language for most Westerners, and translation is often more art than science. For your edification and reading pleasure, here are notes on some of the places where we could have gone in a different direction with our translation of the work, or where a Japanese cultural reference is used.

Nadeshiko blossoms, page 40

Nadeshiko blossoms are a species of *Diantus superbus* (also known as fringed pink) flower native to Japan, and are known for their sweet scent and fringed, pink petals. In Japanese culture, the *yamato nadeshiko* (or *D. superbus longicalycinus*) is often associated with traditional, idealized feminine beauty.

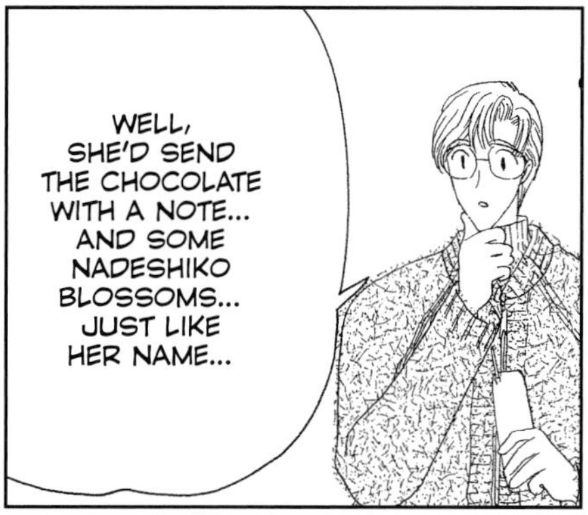
WELL, SHE'D SEND THE CHOCOLATE WITH A NOTE... AND SOME NADESHIKO BLOSSOMS... JUST LIKE HER NAME...

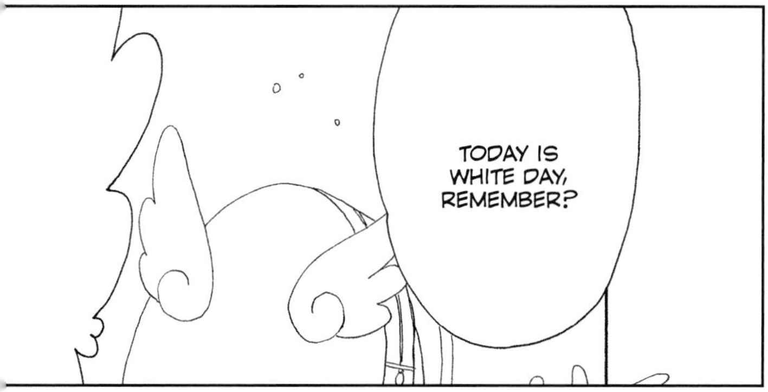
TODAY IS WHITE DAY, REMEMBER?

White Day, page 54

In Japan, White Day is celebrated one month after Valentine's Day, on March 14. While women typically give chocolates to men on Valentine's Day, on White Day men typically return the favor and give chocolates to those who gave them chocolate on Valentine's Day.

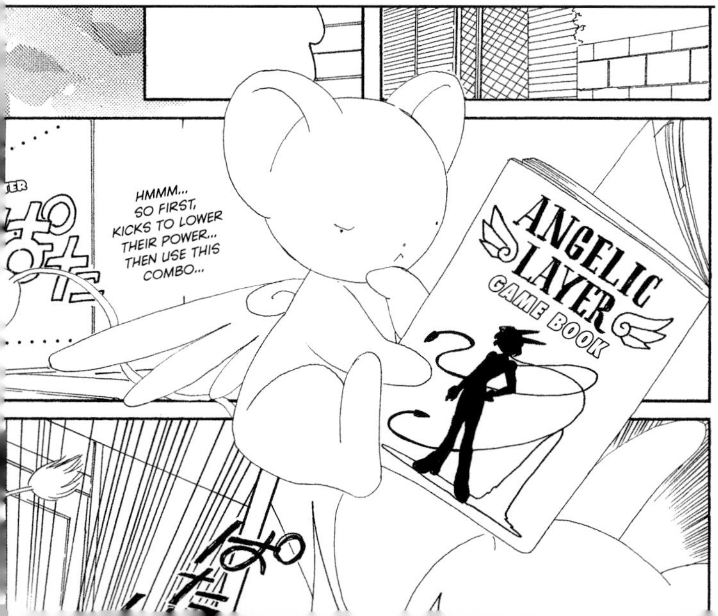
HMMM... SO FIRST, KICKS TO LOWER THEIR POWER... THEN USE THIS COMBO...
ANGELIC LAYER
GAME BOOK

Angelic Layer, page 97

Fans of CLAMP's series *Angelic Layer* may recognize the game book that Kero-chan is reading from the titular manga. In the series, *Angelic Layer* is the name of a popular game in which players buy and custom-design dolls known as Angels, which the player can move and control when the dolls are placed on a special playing field. In the context of *Cardcaptor Sakura*, it appears that Kero-chan is playing a video game adaptation of the *Angelic Layer* franchise.

Cardcaptor Sakura Collector's Edition 7 copyright ©2015 CLAMP • ShigatsuTsuitachi CO.,LTD. / Kodansha Ltd.
English translation copyright ©2020 CLAMP • ShigatsuTsuitachi CO.,LTD. / Kodansha Ltd.

All rights reserved.

Published in the United States by Kodansha Comics, an imprint of Kodansha USA Publishing, LLC, New York.

Publication rights for this English edition arranged through Kodansha Ltd., Tokyo.

First published in Japan in 2015 by Kodansha Ltd., Tokyo as *Nakayoshi 60 Shuunen Kinenban Kaadokyaputaa Sakura*, volume 7.

ISBN 978-1-63236-879-9

Printed in China.

www.kodanshacomics.com

9 8 7 6 5 4 3 2 1
Translation: Mika Onishi & Anita Sengupta
Additional translation: Karen McGillicuddy
Lettering: Aaron Alexovich
Editing: Tiff Ferentini
Kodansha Comics edition cover design by Phil Balsman

Publisher: Kiichiro Sugawara

Director of publishing services: Ben Applegate
Associate director of operations: Stephen Pakula
Publishing services managing editor: Noelle Webster
Assistant production manager: Emi Lotto, Angela Zurlo